AF600587

# ALEXANDER THE GREAT IN THE MIDDLE AGES

## Transcultural Perspectives

EDITED BY MARKUS STOCK

# Alexander the Great in the Middle Ages

## Transcultural Perspectives

UNIVERSITY OF TORONTO PRESS
Toronto Buffalo London

Toronto Buffalo London
www.utppublishing.com

ISBN 978-1-4426-4466-3

**Library and Archives Canada Cataloguing in Publication**

Alexander the Great in the Middle Ages : transcultural perspectives/edited by Markus Stock.

Includes bibliographical references and index.
ISBN 978-1-4426-4466-3 (bound)

1. Alexander, the Great, 356 B.C.–323 B.C. – In literature – Cross-cultural studies. 2. Alexander, the Great, 356 B.C.–323 B.C. – Romances – History and criticism – Cross-cultural studies. 3. Alexander, the Great, 356 B.C.–323 B.C. – Influence – Cross-cultural studies. 4. Literature, Medieval – History and criticism. I. Stock, Markus, editor

PN682.A48A44 2015 809′.93351 C2015-905234-3

University of Toronto Press gratefully acknowledges the financial assistance of the Centre for Medieval Studies, University of Toronto in the publication of this book.

University of Toronto Press acknowledges the financial assistance to its publishing program of the Canada Council for the Arts and the Ontario Arts Council, an agency of the Government of Ontario.

Canada Council for the Arts Conseil des Arts du Canada

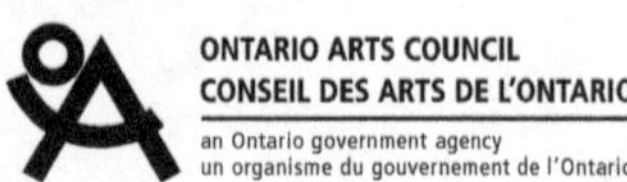


Funded by the Government of Canada Financé par le gouvernement du Canada

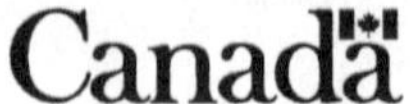

# Contents

# Acknowledgments

This volume would not have seen the light of day had it not been for the support, advice, and encouragement of my colleagues and students. First and foremost, I would like to thank Stefanie Schmitt, who offered her expertise and decisive input during the initial stages of this project. Suzanne Akbari, Lawrin Armstrong, John Magee, Andy Orchard, and David Townsend were very supportive at various stages. I was also very fortunate to have had superb graduate student help: Emily Blakelock, Walker Horsfall, and Christopher Liebtag Miller served as editing assistants and proofreaders; and John Koster contributed translations.

The idea for this book was born during a conference at the University of Toronto, which was sponsored and hosted by the Centre for Medieval Studies, and received generous support from the Social Sciences and Humanities Research Council of Canada (SSHRC), the German Research Foundation (DFG), the Greek Consulate-General at Toronto, the Department of Germanic Languages and Literatures, the Centre for Comparative Literature, and the Centre for Reformation and Renaissance Studies. Publication was generously supported by a subsidy from the Centre for Medieval Studies, for which I am very grateful. I would also like to thank the anonymous external assessors retained by the University of Toronto Press for their thorough reviews of the manuscript and their thoughtful and constructive suggestions, Barbara Porter at the University of Toronto Press, Gillian Scobie, the eagle-eyed copy editor of this book, and, above all, Suzanne Rancourt, senior UTP acquisitions editor, for her wonderful help and guidance, which made all the difference.

# List of Illustrations

**Figures**

# ALEXANDER THE GREAT IN THE MIDDLE AGES

# The Medieval Alexander: Transcultural Ambivalences

MARKUS STOCK

King Alexander III of Macedon was born in Pella in 356 BCE and died in Babylon in 323 BCE. Admired for his deeds and condemned for his pride, he gripped the imaginations of both his contemporaries and of his later biographers for centuries to come. His magnification began during his own lifetime,[1] and by the time the Greek *Alexander Romance* and the writings of Roman historiographers had canonized – starkly contradictory – versions of his *vita* and reputation, there was no doubt that he was indeed "the Great," remarkable not only as a military strategist and ruler, but also magnificent in the character failings ascribed to him.[2] Alexander's continued significance for the European imagination, lasting well into the late Middle Ages, was also based on his perceived role as an eyewitness of the wonders of the East. Reports of the marvels observed by Alexander appear throughout the *Alexander Romance* and its medieval Latin and vernacular rewritings, as well as in the so-called *Letter of Alexander to Aristotle on the Wonders of the East*, often integrated into Alexander narratives, and other sources. The great Alexander was regarded as a witness to geographical, ethnographical, and zoological wonders, such as the ocean at the end of the world, the walls of the Earthly Paradise, dwarfs, giants, and wild men, and many other "marvels" of the eastern parts of the world. In fact, for medieval readers and listeners his conquests and travels formed the experiential basis for a unique ethnography of peoples on the margins of the world, an ethnography that tested the margins of the human itself.[3]

Significantly, it was not only in the European literatures that the life of Alexander was retold and rewritten. Contemporaneous to or slightly following the development and dissemination of European narratives of his life, tales of Alexander spread as far as Persia, India, Mongolia, and Southeast Asia. Largely based on the wide transmission of the much-translated Greek *Alexander Romance*, these rewritings attest to the material's transcultural translatability, a feature that has become a focal point of the scholarship on premodern Alexander literature in recent years, especially in regard to non-European accounts of Alexander the Great from the era coinciding with the European Middle Ages.[4] In many of these "medieval" and "early modern" extra-European cultures (for which these epochal denominators are hardly appropriate), the Alexander traditions are equally notable and Alexander's life and deeds equally invested with significance – and with ambiguities. To be sure, the Alexander legend remains fluid in all its transcultural rewritings, but its different strands also build around nodes recognizable even in the most distant traditions. The reasons for these distant echoes are, of course, manifold, but the similarities can often be traced back to the overwhelming influence of the Greek *Alexander Romance*. Yet it is nevertheless remarkable that the life of Alexander offers points of fascination and challenge capable of attaining similar significance in many different contexts and that such points remain pertinent in multiple cultural, religious, and political circumstances. In very concrete ways, the Alexander material appears at once transculturally relevant and bound to particular local activities of retelling, reappropriating, and transmitting.[5]

The medieval and early modern transmission of Alexander material is thus remarkable in both its spatial and temporal extensions. Its transcultural adaptability and transformativity remains one of the most fascinating phenomena surrounding the multiform postclassical adaptations of this material. The longevity of the ever-changing history of its reception is as striking as its geographical range: unlike virtually any other historical figure from antiquity, Alexander the Great served as a magnet of fascination and an inspiration for cultural production over an exceedingly long temporal stretch. In fact, it is in its postclassical reception that the legendary Alexander *vita* reveals its richest narrative and imaginative potential. This potential was often enhanced by more or less convincing attempts to create genealogical linkages between members of the European aristocracy and Alexander or the Macedonians; and by adding political and religious valence to the figure of Alexander himself by emphasizing his role in the translation of the earthly empire from East to West. His role in the divine plan of *translatio imperii* held potential political significance for any imperial aspirations, of which the German sources especially bear eloquent witness.[6]

This status for the Christian providential historiography is crucial for understanding the significance of Alexander, especially in Middle and Western Europe.[7] Given this adaptability of the material and its function, it is not surprising that the figure of Alexander, as well as iconic scenes and situations of his life, were popular motifs of postclassical visual arts.[8]

With his integration into medieval Christian interpretive models, the ambivalence of the Alexander figure offered medieval European authors both challenges and opportunities. Their new constitutions of meaning were based on old tensions that had accompanied the narratives of Alexander's life from the moment they were first recorded: the questions of the value and meaning of Alexander's conquests, of Alexander's relationship to Greek or to Persian cultural frameworks, and the assessment of the deification or apparent deification of Alexander following his victory over the Persian ruler Darius.[9] It is through these tensions that certain core elements of the narrative, replayed again and again throughout the traditions, attract their particular narrative energy, an energy that in the medieval versions manifests in a variety of ways and that is attested over and over again in the findings collected in this volume.

Such underlying tensions figure not only in the Christian Alexander traditions, in which Alexander, attracting both fascination and criticism, was viewed neither wholly positively nor wholly negatively, and could be tied historically to the present through his functionalization as a part of salvation history.[10] They also play out within Jewish and Muslim traditions, albeit in differing forms, sharing and modifying "symptomatic interests"[11] and common themes. The question of the genealogical foundation of empire, for example, is very much a theme of European, and especially German, Alexander texts,[12] but the outright utopian re-evaluation of concepts of empire also figures prominently in an important text from the Hebrew tradition.[13] Equally, it seems a transcultural trend that the premodern and early modern texts describe Alexander's insatiable hunger to experience the extraordinary, the not-yet-known, and the unknowable: knowledge beyond the knowable is thus another topic that spans both cultures and eras.[14] At the same time, many texts – unsurprisingly, given the subject matter and historical core of Alexander's conquests – also depict struggles over the legitimacy of rule and lay bare the structures as well as the strategies of dominance.

The manifold representations of Alexander's *vita* were not only re-interpretations of what was seen to have been an extraordinary life, but also vehicles for the negotiation of identity and alterity, the discussion of the ethics of power, and the delineation of the world's geo-ethnological boundaries. Alexander served as a catalyst for medieval and early modern concerns of otherness. The legends of Alexander should thus not be read merely as stories of conquest and discovery, but also as documents of migration, translation, cosmopolitanism, and diaspora. At a very basic level, Christian and Muslim literatures of medieval and early modern Europe and Asia share key elements in their narratives about Alexander: almost all the works discussed in this volume are preoccupied with certain nodes of fascination, such as Alexander's transgression of limits, or his ascribed first-hand knowledge of the – terrible and fascinating – wonders to be found in the remote corners of the earth. It is not surprising, therefore, that many texts also explicitly or implicitly thematize the limits of representation in view of the superlatives surrounding Alexander and the spatial, climatic, biological, and human extremes he is said to have experienced. Thus, narratives of Alexander's life, and most prominently among them, the accounts of his travels in the eastern parts of the world, constitute a sphere of connection, the precarious chance of a spatial interconnectedness to every imaginable people and creature, even to the spheres of sky and sea.

Many accounts of Alexander are ambivalent not only in their assessment of the king himself but also in their evaluation of the many struggles for dominance that mark Alexander's advances through the Near and Middle East and into Asia: the almost self-evident, affirmative appeal of Alexander's many victories is checked by many accounts of the resistance offered to the conquering king. This is true for many texts of the European Latin and vernacular traditions in France, Germany, and elsewhere, into which counter-narratives of resistance to Alexander's desire for domination are inscribed, often personified by peoples and rulers such as the Amazons, the Naked Sages, the Persian princess Roxane or the fabulous Merovian queen Candace (in various guises). Comparative and contrastive readings reveal that some of the non-European texts, like those from the Iranian/Persian tradition, formulate resistance by counter-othering Alexander as the intruding force set against local positive figures.[15]

Dominance as a core theme of Alexander texts is often tied in with questions of cosmopolitanism and identity. They are the focus of the first essays of this volume and play an important role throughout the book. Discussing the Alexander *vitae* of Quintus Curtius Rufus, Plutarch, and Arrian, the introductory essay by Thomas Hahn highlights the manner in which the texts produced by Roman historiographers developed symptomatic interests in cosmopolitanism, while at the same time displaying profound ambivalences regarding the eccentric, nomadic life of Alexander and the cultural hybridity and dispersion marking his path to the East. The historians worked to establish Roman "metropolitan" values and "western" identity in reaction to what they perceived as Alexander's path to degeneracy and orientalization. Even in their omissions they remain suspiciously ambivalent, by leaving out many of the confusions and contradictions that govern the multiform reverberations of the Greek *Alexander Romance,* which dwells on the insecurities of Alexander's paternity and identity. Thus, the Roman historians are caught in the ambivalences that infest all Alexander texts: cultural hybridity is inscribed into Alexander's geopolitical path as much as it is into the modelling of his own identity, which eschews any attempt to claim a single, unique identity. Emily Reiner further elucidates this complex by reviewing the "national" designations of Alexander in medieval Latin chronicles, in Walter of Châtillon's *Alexandreis,* and in the Anglo-Norman *Alexander Romance* by Thomas of Kent. She shows that the ambiguities surrounding Alexander also concern his "nationality": geographically, it oscillates between "Greek," "Trojan," and "Macedon," genealogically between his affiliation with the Egyptian sorcerer-pharaoh Nectanabus and Philip of Macedon.

Christine Chism reads the fashioning of the Alexander figure in the Andalusian *Qissat Dhulqarnayn* against the backdrop of the eighteenth sura of the Qur'ān. While Alexander is depicted simply as a world conqueror in the Qur'ān, the *Qissat Dhulqarnayn* adds complexity to the matter by highlighting its potential significance for a central epistemological problem of medieval Islamic culture, for which Alexander's insatiable hunger for conquest and knowledge serves as a telling example. While it is necessary to strive for as much knowledge as possible in order to understand God and his creation, this human endeavour is ultimately bound to fail, as all knowledge rests with God and is thus infinite and incomprehensible. Ruth Nisse discusses the earliest Hebrew *Alexander Romance, Ma'aseh Alexandros,* from the mid-eleventh century, which displays a particular interest in Alexander's conquests in the East among medieval Jewry. Thus, the text stands within a tradition that regards the Jewish diaspora in relation to the phantasma of a politically and culturally autonomous eastern Jewish empire. This empire remains unconquered by Alexander and is conceived as an alternative to the traditional interpretation of Rome as the fourth empire in the

Judeo-Christian concept of the *translatio imperii*, the translation of the empire from East to West.

As both Nisse and Chism show, the mutual influence and discursive alliance of the Alexander material with pre- and early modern scientific discourses and the transmission of medieval scientific discourses in many Alexander texts constitute one of the most important features of the medieval Alexander tradition. This interaction is also at the heart of Shamma Boyarin's essay: his focus is the scientific and historiographical discourses in the Hebrew *Alexander Romance*, which in one of its extant manuscripts names as translator a certain Rabbi Samuel who allegedly also translated the *Guide for the Perplexed* by Maimonides. Though this curious remark is of little help in identifying the real translator of the Hebrew *Alexander Romance*, it points to the context in which this text was situated, namely the reception of Aristotelian concepts in Jewish thinking and theology. Through their connection to the dispute on astrology and Greek philosophy, which was central for Jewish intellectuals in the Middle Ages, the Hebrew Alexander texts display their participation in the Aristotelian paradigms predominant in certain strands of medieval Jewish thought.

Su Fang Ng's inquiry follows the dissemination of the Alexander legend into Southeast Asia following the Islamization of this area between 1400 and 1650. Her essay lays bare the Islamic agenda of the Malay *Alexander Romance* (*Hikayat Iskandar Zulkarnain*). As evidenced by the depiction and evaluation of the Wonders of the East and especially by the central role played by the conversion to Islam, the *Hikayat Iskandar Zulkarnain* seems catered to an audience of recent converts. Thus, for example, Alexander's own conversion to Islam is depicted twice in the text and Alexander's dominance plays out not only through conquest, but also through conversion, since the peoples subdued by him in this text are also turned to Islam.

The next essay investigates the treatment of Alexander in medieval Persian literature. Focusing on a narrative "kernel" of the Greek *Alexander Romance* and its reception in Persian literature, Julia Rubanovich compares versions of the Candace episode in several areas of medieval Persian literature (Alexander romances, historiography, qisas). The figure of Candace, already multi-faceted and complex in the Greek *Alexander Romance*, is rewritten to various degrees in this literature and elicits competing responses and representations by Persian writers and Islamic exegetes, through historical periods and cultures. In addition, an influx of esoteric and mystical elements from Jewish sources seems to be discernible in the Persian texts, which connects this essay with the previous contributions concerning Alexander in Hebrew culture and thought. Instances of transcultural convergence in a non-European Alexander tradition are also at the core of the essay by Faustina Doufikar-Aerts. She presents the miniatures of the Berlin manuscript of the Arabic *Alexander Romance* (*Sīrat al-Malik Iskandar*) and makes a case for a Coptic illuminator as their creator. The essay portrays the intriguing intercultural mixture of Islamic, Christian, and Jewish influences in both the miniatures and the text of the Berlin manuscript.

The following chapters turn to aspects of the Alexander legend in medieval Latin, German, and French literature as well as in medieval and early modern art. Sylvia A. Parsons offers an intertextual reading of two episodes from Walter of Châtillon's *Alexandreis* and its sources. She focuses on the epic self-fashioning of the text, which blends the voice of the protagonist and the narrator into each other, thus highlighting the poetological dimensions of the Alexander figure in Walter's epic. As her analyses show, Walter's vision of Alexander as a self-fashioning epic hero forms the basis of his unique method of epic-making within and across the gaps of the Latin epic tradition. Klaus Grubmüller presents a comprehensive survey of German accounts of Alexander's life from the earliest treatments into the fifteenth century. He is able to distinguish various uses and functions of Alexander in medieval German literature: as God's instrument in the history of salvation, as an example of the vanity of worldly pursuits, and as a model of wise rulership. Maud Pérez-Simon tackles the discursive interplay between the *Alexander Romance* and scientific discourses by presenting a particularly telling example from the French tradition. Her essay is devoted to the interaction of text and image in the Stockholm manuscript of the *French Prose Alexander*, which comprises four scientific insertions from the *Secreta Secretorum* and Brunetto Latini's *Livres dou Tresor*. Both the textual and pictorial insertions shift the *Alexander Romance* closer to scientific and encyclopedic works, once again highlighting the strong bond between Alexander romances and medieval scientific discourses. Thomas Noll presents a survey of Alexander the Great's appearances in medieval and early modern European art. He shows that the medieval and early modern visual representations of Alexander are less concerned with offering illustrations of historical events than with exemplifying an overarching, often moral-didactic theme. Though medieval depictions are dominated by motifs such as Alexander's aerial voyage, the Nine Worthies, and Aristotle as a love slave, the range of topics becomes broader in early modern art, as at the same time Alexander is shown in a more favourable light. In addition, the attempt to represent historical reality becomes more visible in Renaissance works, such as Altdorfer's famous *Alexanderschlacht*, the immense panorama of the Issos battle.

This volume documents the transcultural adaptability of the post-classical Alexander material. More than anything, it attests to the fluidity of the rewritings of Alexander's life in many European and Asian cultures. But the contributions to this volume also show that many of the texts and artefacts are preoccupied with certain nodes of fascination as well as recurrent key elements in the representations of the life of the Macedonian king. At its core, this adaptability is enabled by the ambivalences and competing evaluations surrounding Alexander from the very beginning. At the same time, the fluidity as well as the spatial and temporal spread of the responses inform and multiply the interpretive stances to Alexander's extraordinary life – and thus reinforce those very ambivalences across many cultures and across a remarkable time span.

## NOTES

1 See Paul Cartledge: *Alexander the Great: The Hunt for a New Past* (Woodstock and New York: Overlook, 2004); Pedro Barceló, *Alexander der Große* (Darmstadt: Wissenschaftliche Buchgesellschaft, 2007). Diana Spencer discusses the magnification of Alexander in Roman historiography in her *The Roman Alexander: Reading a Cultural Myth* (Exeter, UK: University of Exeter Press, 2002).

2 *A Companion to Alexander Literature in the Middle Ages*, ed. Z. David Zuwiyya (Leiden and Boston: Brill, 2011); *L'historiographie médiévale d'Alexandre le Grand*, ed. Catherine Gaullier-Bougassas, Alexander redivivus 1 (Turnhout: Brepols, 2011).

3 On the legendary aspects of medieval Alexander *vitae* in Europe and beyond see Richard Stoneman, *Alexander the Great: A Life in Legend* (New Haven and London: Yale University Press, 2008); for the Islamic legends on Alexander, see Z. David Zuwiyya, *Islamic Legends Concerning Alexander the Great* (Binghamton, NY: Global Publications, 2001). For the myriad transmission of Alexander literature in the Middle Ages see *La fascination pour Alexandre le Grand dans les littératures européennes (Xe–XVIe siècle). Réinventions d'un mythe*, 4 vols., ed. Catherine Gaullier-Bougassas,

Alexander redivivus 5 (Turnhout: Brepols, 2014); David J.A. Ross, *Alexander historiatus: A Guide to Medieval Illustrated Alexander Literature*, 2nd ed., Beiträge zur Klassischen Philologie 186 (Frankfurt am Main: Athenäum, 1988); and George Cary, *The Medieval Alexander*, ed. David J.A. Ross (Cambridge: Cambridge University Press, 1956).

4 *The Problematics of Power: Eastern and Western Representations of Alexander the Great*, ed. Margaret Bridges and J. Christoph Bürgel, Schweizer asiatische Studien 22 (Bern and New York: Peter Lang, 1996); *Alexandre le Grand dans les littératures occidentales et proche-orientales. Actes du colloque de Paris 27–29 novembre 1997*, ed. Laurence Harf-Lancner et al. (Paris: Centre des Sciences de la Littérature, 1999); Faustina Doufikar-Aerts, *Alexander Magnus Arabicus. A Survey of the Alexander Tradition through Seven Centuries: from Pseudo-Callisthenes to Ṣūrī*, Mediaevalia Groningana n.s. 13 (Louvain: Peeters, 2010); *The Alexander Romance in Persia and the East*, ed. Richard Stoneman et al., Ancient Narrative Suppl. 15 (Groningen: Barkhuis & Groningen University Library, 2012).

5 On the tension between the transcultural and the local in medieval Alexander literature, see *Alexanderdichtungen im Mittelalter. Kulturelle Selbstbestimmung im Kontext literarischer Beziehungen*, ed. Jan Cölln et al., Literatur und Kulturräume im Mittelalter 1 (Göttingen: Wallstein, 2000); *Herrschaft, Ideologie und Geschichtskonzeption in Alexanderdichtungen des Mittelalters*, ed. Ulrich Mölk, Literatur und Kulturräume 2 (Göttingen: Wallstein, 2002); on the question of "nationality" and genealogical relevance of Alexander see Emily Reiner in this volume, 30–50.

6 See Klaus Grubmüller in this volume, 200–16; see also Ralf Schlechtweg-Jahn, *Macht und Gewalt im deutschsprachigen Alexanderroman*, Literatur, Imagination, Realität 37 (Trier: Wissenschaftlicher Verlag, 2006); Mölk, Herrschaft (see note 5); Elisabeth Lienert, *Deutsche Anitkenromane des Mittelalters*, Grundlagen der Germanistik 39 (Berlin: Erich Schmidt, 2001), 26–71; Cölln et al., *Alexanderdichtungen* (see note 5).

7 See Emily Reiner's account of the *longue durée* of the concept of *translation imperii*, starting with Orosius, and its connection to Alexander the Great, in this volume, 30–50.

8 On the *mise en image* of the Medieval Alexander see *Alexander the Great in European Art*, ed. Nicos Hadjinicolaou (Athens: Pergamos, 1997); Thomas Noll, *Alexander der Große in der nachantiken bildenden Kunst* (Mainz: Philipp von Zabern, 2005); Maud Pérez-Simon, *Mise en roman et mise en image. Les manuscrits du* Roman d'Alexandre en prose (Paris: Champion, 2013); and the essays by Noll, Pérez-Simon, and Faustina Doufikar-Aerts in this volume, 153–76, 217–43, 244–63.

9 See Cartledge, *Alexander the Great* (see note 1), and Barceló, *Alexander der Große* (see note 1).

10 The Alexander texts' hybrid character between historiography and romance has often been noted, for example and very prominently for the French tradition; see: Catherine Gaullier-Bougassas, *Les Romans d'Alexandre. Aux frontières de l'épique et du romanesque* (Paris: Champion, 1998); and Gaullier-Bougassas, *L'historiographie* (see note 2); the intertextual tensions within one of the most artistically sophisticated medieval Alexander texts, Walter of Châtillon's *Alexandreis*, is brought to the fore in the reading by Sylvia Parsons in this volume, 177–99.

11 See the essay by Thomas Hahn in this volume, 13–29.

12 See the essay by Klaus Grubmüller in this volume, 200–16.

13 See the essay by Ruth Nisse in this volume, 76–87.

14 See especially the essays by Christine Chism, Shamma Boyarin, Su Fang Ng, and Maud Pérez-Simon in this volume, 51–75, 88–103, 104–22, 217–43.

15 See Stoneman, Erickson, and Nisson, *The Alexander Romance* (see note 4); Marina Gaillard, *Alexandre le Grand en Iran. Le Dārāb Nāmeh d'Abou Tāher Tarsusi* (Paris: De Boccard, 2005); and the essay by Julia Rubanovich in this volume, 123–52.

# East and West, Cosmopolitan and Imperial in the Roman Alexander

THOMAS HAHN

The Alexander preserved in the accounts of the Roman historians Quintus Curtius, Plutarch, and Arrian may well be the most authentic Alexander we possess. The authority of the Greek Alexander – based on the witness of the generals and naval officials, diarists and chroniclers, memoir and letter writers, including perhaps Alexander himself – survives mainly as shards excavated from the texts of later writers and then reorganized as a *mélange* of testimonials, providing an icon of the king that appears fact-based but that is frequently incoherent or openly contradictory.[1] The very nature of the evidence within these Roman historians – subtly embedded and carefully groomed as it is – signals to us that these narratives took shape through a set of historiographical principles and cultural assumptions that reflect the time and place of their origins. That all three appeared in the course of a single century or so (approximately 40–140 CE), and that they answered the gap noted by Arrian – "no prose history, no epic poem had been written about him" (67) – further suggest that they are driven by motives distinctive to the Roman Empire.[2] My aim in the present essay is to highlight and characterize some of these symptomatic interests, and in passing to contrast these with the traits (already in circulation at this time, but largely suppressed by these Roman writers) that characterize the Alexander of the Hellenistic *Romance*, and, even more distantly, of the medieval Latin *Historia de preliis* based on a version of the *Romance*.

In his foundational history of the Republic and early Empire, Livy (59 BCE–17 CE) delineates an image of Alexander that insistently colours the writings of the Roman historians. Writing almost two generations earlier than Quintus Curtius, he figures Alexander not as world conqueror but as an eccentric, impulsive, and lucky opportunist, on tour in Asia with a crew of drunkards; far from the Great King of Persia, in Livy's retelling his main opponent was a shadow king, "dragging after him a train of women and eunuchs."[3] In what he pointedly calls a digression from the actual history of Rome, Livy sketches out a death-match with the Macedonian, which comes down to an assertion that "my Roman *patria* can beat your Greek *polis* – or *cosmopolis*." Livy claims that any number of perfectly competent Roman generals, working under an efficient, well-oiled military and state apparatus, might have defeated the great Macedonian. An encounter with Rome, Livy says, would have made Alexander "often ... tempted to wish that the Persians and Indians and effeminate Asiatics were his foes"; recycling a taunt that Alexander heard during his own conquests of the East, he claims that soon enough the king "would have confessed that his former wars had been waged against women."

Although clearly fixed upon Alexander as a central subject and not a digression from the history of Rome, Curtius, Plutarch, and Arrian all structure their narratives around this Livian conceit, which associates the East with effeminacy, deviancy, and excess, and then associates Alexander with the East. In an almost calculable way, each of these historians calibrates Alexander's path to degeneracy by the distance he moves from the *West* – that is, from a Rome projected back into Alexander's epoch, which embodies the familiar metropolitan values of the first and second centuries. The farther Alexander proceeds geographically and geopolitically, the more he dissipates through the adoption of "Asiatic" dress, the practice of oriental customs, and contact with exotic people. These encounters often implicate Alexander in a failure of purity, a cultural promiscuity, a contamination of proper values, as these are embodied in the metropolitan *probitas* of the Eternal City, the stable centre to which all roads lead.

These metropolitan assumptions, as I'll call them, emanate from writers whose lives, strangely – or perhaps not so strangely – took place far from the metropolis. Curtius's origins (?1–70 CE) were sufficiently obscure that Tacitus cattily labels him "ex se natus," a self-made man, his own ancestor without a proper pedigree.[4] He served as *praetor* of Africa under Tiberius; after a time out of public service (when he may have written his life of Alexander), he returned to Africa, and died there after serving for ten years as proconsul. Plutarch (?50–120 CE) was born at Chaeronea, near Thebes (which Alexander notoriously obliterated), and studied at the Academy in Athens. Through connections he achieved Roman citizenship; though he visited the city at least twice, he seems not to have spent extended periods there.[5] He became one of the two permanent priests of the Oracle at Delphi, and eventually returned to Chaeronea, though the Emperor Trajan graced him with the honours of consul.

Arrian (?86–150 CE) was born to Roman parents of high standing at Nicomedia (modern Izmit, in northwestern Turkey), in the province of Bythinia.[6] He took an active role in Greek religious rites, studied Greek philosophy with Epictetus (with the future emperor Hadrian as his fellow student), and was the first "easterner" to take command of a legion, campaigning north of the Danube (where Alexander fought his first battles) and elsewhere. He entered political office at the earliest possible age; Hadrian appointed him praetor and proconsul of Andalusia, and he may have crossed the straits and visited Africa with the emperor in 128. He became consul at Rome about 130, then governor of Cappadocia (extending from modern eastern Turkey to the Euphrates), and led two legions in a smashing defeat of the invading Alans. Arrian left public life around 137, and settled in Athens, where he held both civic and religious office, and became an honorary citizen. As a Roman military commander, Arrian certainly spoke, and probably wrote Latin, and he produced one book – on the teachings of Epictetus – in the *koine* Greek commonly spoken in his own Bythinia, Greece, and throughout the Hellenistic world. His other surviving works, however, reproduce classical Attic, which had become the written standard of elite intellectuals. The one exception to this Atticizing standard is his book on India, a tour de force composed for effect in the Ionic dialect, suggesting the depth of artifice entailed in compositions deploying any of these fossilized book languages. The tensions and contradictions that mark Arrian's identity and writing are epitomized in the common opinion that he is the first author to articulate the phrase "We Romans" in Greek.[7]

These Roman historians, then, are all outliers, beginning and ending their lives at the peripheries of the Empire, in Africa, Asia, and the Peloponnese. What I wish to suggest is that their marginal status plays out, paradoxically but inevitably, in their attempts to understand, or to reclaim, an eccentric, nomadic, and ultimately cosmopolitan Alexander for the centralizing values of the metropolis. In their accounts, the difference and deviancy projected onto the East work to define the standards of Rome as proper, invariant, universal, and timeless. Curtius makes the depravity and dangers of Asia clear from the outset: Darius and his royal guard dress like women, more interested in ornament and extravagance than in arms, and they lead "a herd of eunuchs (who are not at all held in contempt by these peoples)," along with three-hundred-and-sixty concubines.[8] Babylon is a place of "unparalleled" corruption and "unbridled passions," where parents pimp their own children (Book 5.1, 29–38). In these circumstances, Alexander suffers a complete collapse into "the depraved customs of foreigners and conquered nations," preferring such ways to those of his own country, and through such behaviour alienating true-born Macedonians faithful to proto-European mores (6.2, 1–5). Alexander's affair with Bagoas, who had been a sexual partner of Darius, constitutes a traffic in eunuchs that clearly weds him to the Persians (6.5, 22–3). Alexander surrenders to his appetites, bringing hundreds of concubines and "hordes of eunuchs practiced in playing the woman's part" into the royal quarters (6.6, 8). This emblem of degeneracy is refigured in Curtius's paradox that, by wearing Asian dress – and, even worse, "with the clothes adopting Persian habits" – Alexander had turned victory into defeat; his adoption of *proskynesis* forces Europeans to "lie prostrate on the ground to venerate him," making his manly soldiers in turn play the woman's part as if they too were caitiffs (6.6, 3; 6.6, 9–10; 8.7, 11–15). Alexander's appropriation of Darius's signet ring to seal decrees to Asia, and simultaneous use of his own ring for those sent back to Europe, likewise forms a cultural schizophrenia that appears the counterpart of polymorphous sexuality: in trying to unite these geopolitical antitheses, the increasingly degenerate king demonstrates that "one man's mind could not cope with the fortunes of two" (6.6, 4–8). Alexander's political opponents and victims – such as Clitus, Callisthenes, and Hermolaus – speak through the text with a moral fervour that seems unmistakably to articulate Curtius's own views: Clitus, in a line that Livy steals, tells the king that he has conquered nothing but women in the East (8.1, 33–7). Callisthenes claims that Alexander should resist "degenerating into outlandish and foreign customs" ("ne in peregrinos ritus externosque degenerare"); he is himself content with the ways of his own country, and his speech wins approval from the Europeans "who were offended by the substitution of foreign customs for their established traditions" (8.5, 14 and 20). Hermolaus, the leader of the Pages' Conspiracy, asserts that Alexander has delivered his own men to the barbarians by revelling in Persian clothes and Persian ways, and that their cabal thus intended to assassinate a Persian, not a Macedonian king (8.7, 1–15).

Plutarch's Alexander is considerably more deliberative and intellectual than either Curtius's or Arrian's: when not strategizing or conquering, he frequently consults his favourite authors or engages in philosophical exchange. Moreover, Alexander often spontaneously erupts in direct quotations of Homeric or tragic verse, using these to contextualize or dramatize particular encounters. In Plutarch, the common soldiers are more susceptible to "Persian wealth, women, and barbaric luxury" (24.2), and when his own companions grow "luxurious and extravagant in their way of living ... he reproved them in gentle and reasonable terms," explaining from the Persians' example that "it was the most abject and slavish condition to be voluptuous" (40.2).[9] He puts on "barbaric dress" not through depravity, but through some combination of ennui and a belief that "community of race and custom" might make "the work of civilizing them the easier" (45.1); "he adapted his own style of life still more to the natives' way of living, and tried to bring them also as near as he could to Macedonian customs, thinking that intermixing and common practice" will produce mutual regard (*eunoias*) and eventually bring Hellenistic hegemony. With the same goals in mind, Alexander recruits thirty thousand youths, and orders that they first be taught Greek, and then drilled in Macedonian military discipline (47.3). The priority assigned by Alexander to language as a tool for cultural conformity reproduces Plutarch's own estimation of literacy as a disciplinary principle: early on in his *Life*, he mentions the king's devotion to Homer's *Iliad*, which he keeps under his pillow, in Aristotle's critical edition. The king regards this "casket copy" as "the most excellent treasury of all military virtue and knowledge" (8.1–2), and when he is presented with the single most precious and stunning artefact from Darius's possessions – a Persian casket – he uses it to encase his *Iliad*. As both informational resource and symbolic icon, the authentic text of Homer represents the ultimate repository of Greco-Roman values, and Plutarch seems clearly to assume the uncontaminated purity and stability of the poem: wherever it is carried, under whatever circumstances it is read, the work remains identical to itself, an unmediated channel to the metropolitan values championed by Plutarch and the other Roman historians. It would, however, be possible to regard the casket not simply as a glorious casing for this unchanging kernel of meaning, but as the marker of the changing material environment in which the text is received: on this view, we might speculate just what any of the thirty thousand foreign recruits, doubtless trained in *koine* rather than literary Attic Greek, might make of the *Iliad*, or of the Persian treasure that held it. Even to consider the two items together pushes us to rethink Alexander's multifaceted policies of intermixing and integration, recognizing that "to bring [Asians] ...

as near as he could to Macedonian customs" effects not unilateral but mutual change. Even if we chose to believe that an authentic original of the *Iliad* once existed, in its immaculate reception in later times, a Persian-encased Homer is no longer Aristotle's unspoiled text, but an icon of the fusion and the cosmopolitan values that Alexander so insistently pursued in the last five years or more of his life.

At this point, before turning to Arrian, I'd like to spend a few moments addressing what I mean by "cosmopolitan values." The word *kosmopolites*, citizen of the world, may well have been known to Alexander, since Diogenes the Cynic – with whom the king allegedly exchanged barbs – used it as a crucial term in his philosophy.[10] It implied a rejection of local ties, in particular to the *polis*, and arose at the same moment that Philip of Macedon, as *hegemon* of the League of Corinth, "rendered obsolete" the traditional ties of the *polis*.[11] Rather than tracing out these early philosophical or historical developments, I'd like to take the term *cosmopolis* as suggesting the polity as a world unto itself, and set this in contrast to a *metropolis* – with Rome as the obvious ancient example.[12] In this model, a metropolis sits at the hub of a hierarchy of communities, through military power dominating the political, economic, and cultural life of those lesser entities, and engaging in asymmetrical reciprocity with cities, towns, countryside, and all other settlements through frontier outposts. The centre organizes the geopolitical and cultural space around it, and influence radiates outward. Metropolitan practices and artefacts are in many respects homogenized, sharing formal, thematic, content-driven elements: the projects of Curtius, Plutarch, and Arrian, carried out at different times and in very different places, are recognizably Roman in character. Even in the most remote locales, prestige, recognition, and success rest on Roman standards of excellence. Metropolitan values are unique and non-replicable, pure, unchanging, and normative.[13]

My contention, then, is that we can best understand Alexander, or at least some of the distinctive elements in his multiple histories, by turning to a model of cosmopolitanism, defined as dispersed and decentred, syncretistic and impure, multiform and continuously replicable. To illustrate this notion, I'd like to look at Alexander's reputation as a founder of cities: Plutarch in the *Moralia* contends that Alexander established "more than seventy cities among savage tribes," whereas the Hellenistic *Romance* credits him with twelve, all of them (with the exception of a handful of *Alexandropoleis*) called Alexandria. Some of these – Kandahar (Alexandria in Arachosia), al-Iskandariyah on the

Euphrates thirty-five miles south of Baghdad, Alexandria (Eskendereyya) in Egypt – still preserve the remnants of his name. We have detailed accounts of the urban planning and architectural design that preceded the building of Alexandria, and it seems that in his later sites he followed a uniform plan in layout and construction, and in the inclusion of administrative, religious, and civic edifices.[14] Rather than viewing this building- and naming-policy as rampant megalomania (or as nothing more than this), I'd like to propose that Alexander was experimenting with the replicability of civilization: each of these foundations takes shape as a *cosmopolis*, a world unto itself, linked to other *cosmopoleis* by *koine* Greek as a *lingua franca*, and by other shared regional, commercial, and cultural interests. Together they constitute a decentred, reciprocal network, rather than a series of satellites answerable to a metropolis like Rome. As the ancient historians make clear, many of these cities were created by brutal top-down imposition, through depopulation and resettlement. Modern historians have sometimes claimed they functioned through a kind of cultural apartheid, in which governmental ghettos remained closed off from local populations.[15] Yet despite rigid stratification and hierarchies, massive intermingling must have taken place. The proliferation of neologisms like *mixobarbaros* and *mixellenes* articulate the reality of cultural interpenetration.[16] The extent of systematic relations and daily face-to-face contact emerges much more vividly in the materialization (attested in all the historians) of thirty thousand Afghan, Arab, and Iranian troops, all Greek-speaking, Macedonian-trained, and battle-ready for European-style warfare.[17] Within the five years or so before they reported to Susa (in present-day Iraq) in 324, Alexander must have put in place an infrastructure, cosmopolitan in its design and effects, that could process this massive and dispersed population, no doubt speaking a vast array of local dialects, and bring them to a point where they could communicate unambiguously and cooperate in intricate manoeuvres upon which not just victory but life itself depended. Their willingness to leave not just their birth-tongues but their birth places behind and become an integral part of Alexander's army – his *epigone* or successors – illustrates a syncretistic, replicable, multiform cosmopolitanism at the level of both motive and action, and of institutional and cultural practice.[18]

To return to Arrian, I'd like to argue that it is precisely these elements of cosmopolitanism in the life – or lives – of Alexander that both draws him in and puts him off, and that this attraction–revulsion response has much to do with his status – and that of Curtius and Plutarch – as both insiders and outsiders in Rome. Though he is less moralistic and sensational than Curtius, Arrian offers similar critiques of Alexander's indulgence in "Eastern extravagance and splendor, and the fashion of barbaric kings of treating their subjects as inferiors" (4.7, 4). Rather than survey or sample these views throughout the *Anabasis*, I will focus on the seventh and last book, which presents several crucial encounters that occur during the last year of Alexander's life. The first events take place at Susa, and begin with the massive wedding ceremony Alexander arranged for himself (he married women descended from the two branches of the Persian royal family) and for his Companions and officers, in which eighty to ninety unions were publicly and simultaneously solemnized. The records indicate that all of these were mixed marriages – Macedonian men and Asian women – command performances celebrated in the "Persian style" (7.4, 4). The king had clearly determined to make the bonds between Europeans and easterners official and permanent; he had induced all the most important men in his command to commit to this mingling of peoples, and had chosen the Persian style to convey to the assembled Macedonian, mercenary, and Asian troops the legitimacy of such rites. Part of Alexander's plan seems to have been to emphasize a sense of parity and mutuality between himself and the Macedonian elite, who had clearly expressed resentment over his distance from them – though, ironically, he did this by inducting them into the very customs some found so obnoxious. Alexander affirms that part of his plan is to "be uncle to Hephaestion's children" (7.4, 5), and later, that he had married as his men had married, "and many of you will have children related by blood to my own" (7.10, 3). Beyond the individual bloodlines, however, lies the prospect of creating a broader kinship among the offspring of Asians and Europeans. The marriages also inaugurated an affinity between Macedonian men and the male relatives of the brides, and this, like the relations between the husbands and wives, created hierarchical rather than lateral or symmetrical connections. Alexander also provided dowries for the notables. Finally, he sought out all the common soldiers who had married Asian women – who numbered ten thousand – and gave them wedding gifts as well, a further gesture of both comradeship and kinship, conferring legitimacy on what may otherwise have been casual liaisons without any thought or prospect of permanency (7.4, 8).

Alexander next received the officials from his newly built cities (*poleon ton neoktiston*), and these cosmopolitan overseers collectively delivered the thirty thousand trained youths who had been groomed over the last five years (7.6, 1). Alexander immediately designated these his *Epigoni* – his successors; predictably his veteran troops felt displaced, and to this Arrian adds a further list of simmering dissatisfactions: Alexander's Median dress, the Persian weddings, Peucestas's adoption of Persian dress and language, and Alexander's approval or encouragement of his going native (*to barbarismo autou echairen Alexandros*) (7.6, 2–6). They objected too to the introduction of foreign troops into the elite cavalry – not just the Persian Euacae, but a whole series of other Asians whom Arrian lists by name: Bactrian, Sogdianian, Arachotian, Zarangian, Areian, and Parthyaean (7.6, 3). Alexander next announced a new cavalry regiment, with a significant proportion of non-Macedonians, the enrolment of a group of high-ranking Asians in the elite guard, and the issue to these of Macedonian weapons. Arrian makes clear that the arrival of a vast number of fresh troops, the shake-up of the battalions, and the reorganization of the command conveyed to the veterans that Alexander no longer wished to depend on professional soldiers whose loyalty arose mainly from ethnic, territorial, or local political ties. At the same time, it seems plain that all of these fighters (beyond the *Epigoni*) who were at this moment integrated into Alexander's elite corps must have proven their skill and loyalty over time, fighting not inside the army proper, but alongside it; what the Macedonians resented then was not the presence of foreign fighters – who had long formed part of Alexander's military organization – but what appeared to them as a new level of military and administrative blending, for this cosmopolitanism revealed that "Alexander was going utterly barbarian at heart" (*hos pante de barbarizontos te gnome*; 7.6, 5).[19]

Within a month Alexander moved his base to Opis (in or near modern Baghdad), where his first action was to confirm the veterans' fears, and dismiss from the army all those he deemed unfit. At this juncture, his soldiers again murmured about his Persian dress, the new Asian troops, the foreign officers in the cavalry, and his claims to be the son of god – that is, all those features that signal Alexander's adoption of a mixed, non-Macedonian identity. Alexander responded by haranguing the men as ingrates, charging that his father Philip had found them skin-clad herders wandering the hillsides, and that "he made you city dwellers" (*poleon te oikētoras*), and in this way established good laws and customs (7.9, 1 ff.). He then assigned all the household duties to his Persian guard, designating these men alone his "kinsmen," with exclusive access to his person and presence. Finally, he further reorganized the crack units, bestowing on Persians the hallowed names of

Macedonian fighting units (*agema, pezhetairoi* (foot companions), *asthe-teroi*, and silver shields (*arguraspidoi*; 7.11, 1–3). All this provoked the Macedonians to plead with him for nothing more than equal access with the Persians, including the right to the ceremonial kiss, and to the formal status of "kinsmen." Alexander responded, with astonishing disingenuousness or ruthless manipulation: "But I regard all of you as my kinsmen, and from this time forth I shall give you that name" (7.11, 7). In a single stroke, Alexander has used the crisis – and the years of tension, infighting, and creeping innovation that preceded it – to redefine the fundamental notion of kinship, detaching it from its link to bloodlines, ethnicity, marriage, and *polis* within tribal societies and city states, and making it a matter of affiliation and personal choice. In this new deterritorialized model of social relations, a person – whether Bactrian, Persian, or Indian, Greek, Macedonian, or *barbaros* – may *elect* kinship with the Great King without necessarily losing competing or complementary features of ethnic or natal identity. In effect, Alexander has forced upon the Europeans a new regime of overlapping private and political bonds, mediating local and global cultures through a system that depends upon networks of shared interests, individual qualities, established offices, the king's word, and the policies and infrastructures that lie behind these.

In order to mark this reconciliation – or radical renovation – Alexander, who was celebrated for the lavishness of his table, arranged what is perhaps the grandest (and certainly the last) public banquet of his reign. He seated himself at the centre, arranging the Macedonians, Persians, and other foreign dignitaries around him, and had his guests drink from the same bowl and pour the same libations – partaking in this way in a communion of sorts (7.11, 8). Arrian reports that the king, in an effort at syncretism, brought in both Greek prophets and eastern Magi, and that nine thousand joined in the rites and added their voices to the victory cry. The particular prayer that Alexander utters – for *homonoia*, that is, unity, concord, that those present should be of one mind – potentially makes this the signature event of cosmopolitanism in the histories of Alexander, though the meaning of the prayer, and the banquet at large, has aroused some of the sharpest debate in modern Alexander scholarship. The possibility that Alexander intended a fusion of peoples or races, or that this public ceremony (like the weddings at Susa) might signal the legitimation of a fundamental shift in political and social relations, has been widely (and scornfully) dismissed in mainstream classical scholarship.[20] Yet, like the weddings, the banquet simultaneously, and effectively, enforces parity and hierarchy, establishing palpable structures for a deliberate, dynamic yet bounded and asymmetric mixing of peoples, based upon a shared medium of communication, the replication of civic space, and continuously transforming institutions.

In this view, cosmopolitanism is not a sentimental, idealistic, or anachronistic imposition based upon principles of the unity of all peoples or the brotherhood of mankind, or a proto–United Nations advocating universal equality and human rights.[21] What the Roman historians provide is evidence of a largely pragmatic, frequently violent, deeply resented course of action that began with profound impact upon military and administrative organization, and that achieved lasting effects, in the Hellenistic world and the Empire, on educational, political, economic, social experiences of peoples throughout the Mediterranean and the Near East.[22] We might indeed contend that the very work of these diasporic Roman historians is one after-effect of Alexandrian cosmopolitanism. Much of this was fostered by a single medium of communication – *koine* Greek as *lingua franca* – and a proliferating network of Alexandrias containing mixed populations. In dramatizing Alexander's public response to the Pages' Conspiracy, Curtius has Alexander spell out his motives and goals for cosmopolitanism: "the Persians whom we have defeated are held in high regard by me! ... I did not come into Asia to wipe out its races [gentes] or to transform half the world into a desert. Rather it was to make the people I conquered in warfare feel no regret at my victory. As a consequence, you have men fighting alongside you and shedding blood for your empire [pro imperio vestro] ... If we wish to hold Asia and not merely pass through it ... It is their loyalty which will make our empire stable and enduring [stabile et aeternum faciet imperium] .... I am foisting Persian habits on to the Macedonians. True, for I see in many races things we should not blush to imitate, and the only way this great empire can be satisfactorily governed is by our transmitting some things to the natives and learning others from them ourselves" (8.8, 10–13). Curtius repeatedly uses the charged word *imperium* in this speech, and it may well be that his Roman sensibility was no less offended or incredulous than that of Alexander's Macedonians at the notion of an empire that might be syncretic, dispersed, and continuously reinventing itself through the founding of new *cosmopoleis*.

Several of the other events that Arrian assigns to Alexander's last months underscore his systematic reproduction of mixed institutions.

The reconciliation banquet at Opis ironically allowed the king to demobilize and separate from his standing army ten thousand Macedonians, whom he declared unfit for service, and ready for repatriation to Europe; their place would be more than filled by the thirty thousand freshly trained troops, whose vim and prowess aroused deep resentment. Moreover, Alexander simultaneously intervened to hold back all children these men had produced with Asian wives, guaranteeing that these mixed offspring would be raised by him – presumably through the new infrastructure supported by the burgeoning Alexandrias – in European (read: mixed) ways (7.12, 2–3). These children are clearly the successors to the Successors, the thirty thousand *Epigoni* who had appeared a month before in Susa; these children literally embody the cosmopolitanism associated with Alexander, since their homogeneity depends on their hybridity – not Asian, not European – and their upbringing will prepare them for a world where such commingled identities are normative. Soon after he moved on to Babylon, Peucestas – whose seamless assimilation of Persian language, dress, and customs had so alienated the Macedonians – arrives with an additional twenty thousand troops, mainly Persians, with smaller units, perhaps contributed by Alexandrias in other provinces. In addition, other local commanders deliver contingents from Lydia, Caria, and elsewhere (7.23, 1–2). Arrian, who wrote a book on military organization and tactics, goes on to specify just how Alexander reorganized the fundamental units of his new battalion: each company consisted of twelve foreign soldiers (who were not issued European weaponry) and four Macedonians. The level of detail makes clear that while Alexander (like western field commanders in twenty-first-century Iraq) may have felt reservations about equipping non-Europeans with the latest weaponry, he nonetheless regarded the present changes as permanent and as models for further revamping, as the mixed character of the army, and the Alexandrias that supported it, proliferated.

Had he lived another ten years, and founded another dozen or seventy Alexandrias, the Roman historians might have been able to provide us with even fuller evidence of what this brand of cosmopolitanism means. But no matter how long Alexander's career, how powerful his charisma, or how brutal his policies, his achievements matter mainly in how they mobilize and make use of cultural and historical forces that far exceeded his plans and actions. Alexander is a flashpoint for the version of cosmopolitanism I wish to define here, and in this way a useful lens for speculation and analysis. At the same time, I hope it's clear that to use "cosmopolitanism" in the way I'm suggesting is not to celebrate or endorse it, but rather to deploy it as a tool towards a fuller understanding of the events and texts that confront us. Moreover, it's worth emphasizing that cosmopolitanism is not simply practice and policy on the ground, as it affects the lives of communities, but also something that imperial readers and listeners a half millennium after Alexander's time would have recognized and responded to as a cultural phenomenon, an avid interest, an alarming concern. The Roman historians' open hostility and profound ambivalence mark their reaction to hybridity, dispersion, and replication, which helps explain not only the evidence they chose to include and how they presented it, but also the events and stories they chose to omit – namely, just the material that makes up the heart of the Hellenistic *Romance*. The *Romance*, in installing a welter of confusions, possibilities, and contradictions concerning Alexander's paternity and identity – he is Macedonian, Greek, Egyptian, Persian, perhaps Ethiopian, divinely sired, monstrously conceived, entirely human – clearly eschews the pursuit of origins or the claim of a single, unique identity, and puts in its place a kind of cosmopolitan multitudinousness. In order to read such elements symptomatically and sympathetically, we need to abandon customary genetic / genealogical assumptions, which patently propel the Roman historians' pursuit of the "real" Alexander, and their consequent disregard of the *Romance* as evidence. We need a model of transmission that – unlike Plutarch's vision of Homer's text, uncontaminated and unchanging no matter what its surroundings – highlights the dynamic, dispersed, mixed conditions of textual reception, whose problems and potentialities are so vividly illustrated by the Hellenistic *Alexander Romance* and its many offspring. An anecdote from Aelian may help expand our consciousness of possibilities: he reports that "Ptolemy Philopator [221–204 BCE] built a temple to Homer [in Alexandria]. He set up a fine statue of the poet, and around it, in a circle, all the cities that claim Homer as theirs. The painter Galaton [then] depicted Homer being sick, with the other poets drawing in his vomit."[23] The passage suggests a remarkable model of transmission and reception, literalizing the regurgitation and absorption of random, predigested nuggets of meaning, as would-be writers and readers greedily swallow whole whatever comes down to them from the classical canon. This image of uncontrolled circulation and dispersed, undifferentiated, wholesale ingestion stands in stark contrast to "the repristinization" of Attic Greek and the immaculate reception of authentic texts produced by the careful search for the *lectio difficilior*.[24] Yet it also reminds us of the way in which such methods sometimes mask the messy business of making meaning, with Curtius, Plutarch, and Arrian screening out, or smoothing out, lumps of matter that are not to their taste. And the description offers a shocking and salutary alternative to our usual assumptions about authority, originality, and authenticity, suggesting how materials regarded as sensationally inauthentic or genetically unrelated to the story of Alexander survived and flourished in the cosmopolitan Hellenistic *Alexander Romance*.

NOTES

1 The fragments appear in English translation in Charles Alexander Robinson, Jr., *The History of Alexander the Great* (Providence, RI: Brown University Press, 1953), based upon Felix Jacoby, *Die Fragmente der griechischen Historiker*, volumes IIB and IID (Berlin: Weidmann, 1927, 1930).

2 For a sketch of Alexander's preeminent and multivalent status among Imperial writers – standard or antitype of *Romanitas*, counterpart of the "orientalized" Antony, "Greek savior" bringing culture to the "barbarians" in a world of "Greek chic" – see Diana Spencer, *The Roman Alexander: Reading a Cultural Myth* (Exeter, UK: University of Exeter Press, 2002), 1–38, especially 25, 31–8.

3 Titus Livius, *Ab urbe condita*, Book 9, sections 17–19; *The History of Rome*, ed. and trans. Benjamin Oliver Foster, Vol. 4, Loeb Classical Library (hereafter LCL) (Cambridge, MA: Harvard University Press, 1926). Though I have consulted Foster's translation, the rendition offered here is my own.

4 Elizabeth Baynham, *Alexander the Great: The Unique History of Quintus Curtius* (Ann Arbor: University of Michigan Press, 1998) offers a full account of the African *praetor*'s biography, though she seems ultimately to prefer a more obscure *rhetor* as the author of Alexander's life.

5 For a brief account of Plutarch's life, see James R. Hamilton, *Plutarch, Alexander: A Commentary* (Oxford: Clarendon, 1969), xiii–xxiii, who points out that despite his Roman citizenship, Plutarch "never mastered the finer points of [literary] Latin" (xv).

6 Albert B. Bosworth discusses Arrian's writings in "Arrian and his Historical Production," in *From Arrian to Alexander: Studies in Historical Interpretation* (Oxford: Clarendon, 1988), 16–37.

7 Arrian uses the phrase *'Ρωμαίοις ... 'εξελοῦμ* in his *Circumnavigation of the Black Sea*; this has been widely noted, though Simon Swain, *Hellenism and Empire: Language, Classicism, and Power in the Greek World, AD 50–250*

(Oxford: Clarendon, 1996) cautions that "too much should not be made of the first person plural verb" (244, n11), by which I understand he suggests that this is not exceptional but commonplace.

8 Quintus Curtius Rufus, *Historiarum Alexandri Magni Macedonis Libri*, Book 3, sections 17, 23; *History of Alexander*, ed. and trans. John C. Rolfe, 2 vols., LCL (Cambridge, MA: Harvard University Press, 1946). Though I have consulted Rolfe's translation, together with that by John Yardley, *The History of Alexander* (London: Penguin, 1984), the rendition offered here is my own.

9 *Plutarch's Lives*, ed. and trans. Bernadotte Perrin, Vol. 7, LCL (Cambridge, MA: Harvard University Press, 1919). I have also consulted the Dryden translation, revised by Arthur Hugh Clough (New York: Modern Library, 1932). In general I have followed the latter, though I have altered or modernized (based on the Greek text) at several points.

10 On Cosmopolitanism as a distinctive feature of the Hellenistic world, see Peter Green's chapter, "Zeno, Diogenes, Epicurus, and Political Disenchantment," in *Alexander to Actium: The Historical Evolution of the Hellenistic Age* (Berkeley and Los Angeles: University of California Press, 1990), 52–64. John Moles discusses philosophical cosmopolitanism in "Le Cosmopolitisme cynique," in *Le Cynisme ancient et ses prolognements*, ed. Marie-Odile Goulet-Cazé and Richard Goulet (Paris: Presses Universitaires de France, 1993), 259–80, and on the ideals and practice of the first century in Rome, see Gerard B. Lavery, "Never seen in Public: Seneca and the Limits of Cosmopolitanism," *Latomus* 56 (1997), 1–13.

11 Green, *Alexander to Actium* (see n. 10), 52.

12 Steven Vertovec and Robin Cohen provide an overview and general discussion of competing models in "Introduction: Conceiving Cosmopolitanism," in their collection *Conceiving Cosmopolitanism: Theory, Context, and Practice* (Oxford: Oxford University Press, 2002), 1–22; Robert Fine and Cohen address differential histories in "Four Cosmopolitan Moments," ibid., 137–62.

13 This argument attempts to draw as well on historical studies of margins and centres; the essays collected in *Centre and Periphery in the Hellenistic World*, ed. Per Bilde et al., Studies in Hellenistic Civilization 4 (Aarhus: Aarhus University Press, 1993) provide several helpful models; see especially Susan E. Alcock, "Surveying the Peripheries of the Hellenistic World" (ibid., 162–75), and Inge Nielson, "From Periphery to Centre: Italic Palaces" (ibid., 210–70), which considers Italy before Rome was a metropolitan power.

14 Peter M. Fraser, *Cities of Alexander the Great* (Oxford: Clarendon, 1996) presents a thorough but guarded account. See also Green, *Alexander to*

*Actium* (see note 10), on city planning (and the cities' "mass-production") as a crucial element of Hellenism: "The New Urban Culture: Alexandria, Antioch, Pergamon," 155–70.

15 Green, *Alexander to Actium* (see note 10), several times emphasizes the separation of cultures and races, though he also provides some of the social and linguistic evidence for syncretism mentioned in the next sentences; see for example his comments on assimilation and colonialism, 312 ff., and his skeptical remarks about "universal brotherhood" at 394.

16 See Green, *Alexander to Actium* (see note 10), 319, and Henry George Liddell and Robert Scott, *Greek-English Lexicon* (New York: Harper, 1872), s.v. *μιξέλληνες*, and *μιξοβάρβαρος* with citations.

17 Plutarch 71; Arrian, *Anabasis* 7.6; *Arrian*, ed. and trans. Peter A. Brunt, 2 vols., LCL (Cambridge, MA: Harvard University Press, 1983), Vol. 2, 217 ff. I have also consulted *Arrian: The Campaigns of Alexander*, trans. Aubrey de Sélincourt, rev. ed. (London: Penguin, 1971), and frequently follow the phrasing of this version. There is a lacuna in Curtius's history at this point, though the arrival of the troops is implied in the continuing narrative.

18 In the light of this episode, Alexander's decision to keep with him in Asia the thousands of children born to Greek men and non-European women hardly seems an impulsive or generous gesture, but an extension of his policy to augment the mixed populations with which he surrounded himself. This policy likewise reflects the existence of an educational and institutional infrastructure that could accommodate these cosmopolitan youths, just as it had already produced the thirty thousand *epigoni* within five years; the likelihood is that such training depended not upon one massive military academy, but on a host of centres replicated within the cities Alexander had founded.

19 For a careful review of just what the sources report about the shake-up of Alexander's army, and of the motives and effects of these changes, see Albert B. Bosworth, "Alexander and the Iranians," *Journal of Hellenic Studies* 100 (1980), 1–21, along with Brunt's, Arrian, *Anabasis* (see note 17) notes in his edition, and his Appendix XIX ("Military Questions"), 483–90.

20 W.W. Tarn's contention that Alexander consciously believed in the unity of mankind, and set about implementing a policy of fusion among all peoples, was opposed with such force by Ernst Badian, "Alexander the Great and the Unity of Mankind," *Historia* 7 (1958), 425–44, that later scholars have in general refrained from even considering the issues surrounding the toast (Bosworth, "Alexander and the Iranians," [see note 19], reinforces Badian's line). Some recent work points towards a rethinking of the episode's meaning: Paul Cartledge, *Alexander the Great: The Hunt for a*

*New Past* (Woodstock and New York: The Overlook Press, 2004), alludes to Alexander's exceptional willingness "to extend Greek-oriental collaboration, on a permanent and relatively egalitarian basis, to the home and even the bedroom" (338–9). Simon Swain, *Hellenism* (see note 7) provides evidence that Plato, Plutarch, Dio of Prusa (a city in Bithynia, Arrian's place of origin) deploy the word and concept *homonoia* in their political writings and speeches, and that *poleis* sometimes made it policy by inscribing it on coins (178–82, 219–20, 294–5).

21 Badian's dismissal of *homonoia* as merely mawkish and anachronistically modern has excluded the examination of precedents and contexts, of the distinctively innovative features of Alexander's actions or policies, and of the implications of ancient cosmopolitanism, whether in the Hellenistic world for which Alexander laid the foundations, or in the contested discourses that enveloped the Roman historians and their audiences.

22 Curtius, Plutarch, and Arrian were sensible to these effects, for the contaminations for which Alexander had opened the way had long since become a living reality of the world they inhabited. Greg Woolf discusses the sometimes defensive response of Imperial writers to the Greek world in "Rome and Greece," *Cambridge Illustrated History of the Roman World*, ed. Greg Woolf (Cambridge: Cambridge University Press, 2003), 90–105; likewise, in "Roman Law AD 200–400: From Cosmopolis to Rechtstaat?" *Approaching Late Antiquity: The Transformation from Early to Late Empire*, ed. Simon Swain and Mark Edwards (Oxford: Oxford University Press, 2004, 109–32), Tony Honoré demonstrates how Alexander's "going native" provides a precedent for a vision of Roman law that reflects "the cosmopolitan outlook of the period," whereby peoples throughout the Empire adapt the law, rather than having it be the possession of an elite group in the metropolis.

23 Aelian, *Varia Historia*, ed. and trans. Nigel G. Wilson, LCL (Cambridge, MA: Harvard University Press, 1997), 13.22. I cite Wilson's translation.

24 Swain, *Hellenism* (see note 7) underscores the artifice and effort required by Hellenistic elites to reproduce a long dead Attic Standard, or to recover or reconstruct their precariously surviving texts; the phrase quoted here occurs at 34.

# Meanings of Nationality in the Medieval Alexander Tradition

EMILY REINER

The ambiguity of Alexander in medieval texts is well-known: he has long been noted for his ability to be excessive, proud, and cruel, while also being well-educated, generous, and chivalrous. Another facet of Alexander's ambiguity is his changeable nationality. In medieval texts, Alexander can be described, in varying degrees, as a Greek, as a Macedonian, or as both. As the son of an Egyptian necromancer in some works, he is also linked with Egyptians. In one chronicle, he is even a member of the Trojan lineage. In the following pages, I trace how Alexander's nationality differs through several medieval chronicles, epics, and romances, and suggest how certain specific nationalities are connected with particular collections of attributes and connotations. The nationalities of Alexander, and the ways they influence his depiction, do not fall into neat categories, but they do point to some ways of understanding Alexander based on what being Greek, Macedonian, Egyptian, or even Trojan meant to medieval readers.

The construction of national identity has recently been a topic of much discussion, in modern contexts as well as medieval. Anthony D. Smith and Alan Hastings have made significant contributions to the study of both modern and premodern nationality; both investigate the role of religion in the self-definition of a nation.[1] In medieval literature, national identity, especially the role of the hero in defining the nation, has been examined by such critics as Diane Speed, Thorlac Turville-Petre, Alan Ambrisco, Geraldine Heng, and Suzanne Conklin Akbari.[2] Though these critics provide insights largely into later medieval English nationhood, their works are nevertheless useful to a study of medieval nationality in general, and the national identity of Alexander in particular. In her examination of nationhood in Chaucer's works, Akbari notes that national identity in the fourteenth and fifteenth centuries is based largely on a shared language; earlier, as evidenced by the encyclopedic works of Isidore of Seville, Vincent of Beauvais, and Bartholomaeus Anglicus, both language and geography can be seen to feature in the definition of a nation.[3] A "nation," to these medieval authors, is a group of people who inhabit a geographical area, whose language defines them, and who can have a scheme of characteristics proper to themselves.

In my inquiry into what the particular nationalities of Alexander could mean to medieval authors, my definition of "nation" is comparable to those used by the medieval encyclopedists mentioned above. Rather than those meanings of "nation" based on religion or heroism often used by scholars of modern or medieval nationality,[4] I take *natio*, in its stricter Latin definition, to refer to the group and location into which Alexander was born, and the linguistic group of which he was a part. This definition is closer to Thorlac Turville-Petre's discussion of the "ethnic basis of the English nation,"[5] and is appropriate to Alexander texts especially because of the concern of many medieval authors with the parentage of Alexander. Nationality, in this sense, is at once both genealogical descent and geographical location; it encompasses the double sense of "birth, whether the territory in which one is born or one's parentage."[6]

To be sure, the question of Alexander's nationality can be understood simply by historical facts: he was born in Macedon as the son of Philip, the king of Macedon, so Alexander can be called a Macedonian. Macedon was one of the many kingdoms of Greece, Alexander spoke Greek, controlled much of Greece, and led Greek forces on his conquests; hence he can also be called a Greek. The nationalities ascribed to Alexander in medieval texts do not end here, however, and the epithets "Greek" or "Macedonian," "Trojan" or "Egyptian," and the connotations and meanings of these nationalities for medieval authors and readers, can point to Alexander's place in providential history, his role in the history of Europe, and a generally positive or negative portrayal of his character.

I take as a starting point the work of Martin Gosman, who has pointed out the difficulty in differentiating between the terms "Macedonian" and "Greek" in Old-French Alexander texts. Gosman notes this confusion of Alexander's nationality and states that it is not clear what the difference might be between the terms Greek and Macedonian.[7] Two texts in which he has found this ambiguity, the *Roman d'Alexandre* and the *Roman de toute chevalerie*, are like many medieval works on Alexander in that they do not make a real distinction between Greeks and Macedonians. From time to time both works distinguish Greeks from Macedonians, but at other points the groups are lumped together. In these works, Alexander is called both "king of Macedon" and "ruler of Greece"; he addresses his soldiers collectively as Greeks, then Macedonians, and sometimes it seems that the two groups are actually separate. It is not only medieval works such as these that seem to use these terms interchangeably; in a recent article, Laurence Harf-Lancner refers to Alexander as "the Macedonian," then calls Alexander and his forces "the Greeks."[8] Using the descriptors like this could be a way of avoiding repetition by providing variation; however, it seems that the attribution of Alexander's nationality in medieval works, at least, is more than a stylistic choice.

I will begin, and end, my examination of Alexander's nationality with one of the texts that Gosman uses to point out Alexander's ambiguous heritage, the *Roman de toute chevalerie*, a romance written in Anglo-Norman between 1175 and 1185 by Thomas of Kent, probably at the court of Henry II. In it, Alexander is an exemplar of chivalry, as the title of the work suggests: he is courteous, extremely well-educated, a valiant knight, and a superior military strategist. Alexander is described by Thomas of Kent as both a Greek and a Macedonian. Early on, before he inherits the kingship of Macedon from his father, Philip, Alexander self-identifies as a Greek: when Darius, the king of Persia, demands tribute from King Philip, Alexander says to Darius's messenger that "Gregois ne deivent servir par hontage / Ne jeo ensurketut ne hom de mon parage / A prince ne a roy de terre sauvage" (No Greek, and certainly not me nor any part of my family, should have to suffer the dishonour of serving a prince or king of a foreign land, *Roman de toute chevalerie*, lines 948–50).[9] He again claims to be a Greek when he tells the Persian messenger that "Roy greu ne deit unc sur li aver hontage" (A Greek king should never be shamed, line 952). Calling Alexander "Greek" according to the definition of *natio* that includes language would be appropriate, as Thomas also notes that Alexander writes various letters to Darius in Greek (line 1463).

Conversely, Philip is said to hold the empire of Macedon ("Mort est li rois qui tint de Macedoigne l'empire," line 1040), but the newly crowned Alexander is shortly thereafter called the king of Greece ("roys est de Grece," line 1045). Of the 15,000 men who reinforce Alexander's army after his accession, 700 are named as being born in Greece (lines

1065–6). At some points, Alexander refers to himself and his troops as Macedonians, and he seems to think of Macedon as his homeland, a nationality based on where he was born, the stricter sense of *natio* mentioned above. Alexander's troops are collectively sometimes referred to as Macedonians (line 1259), sometimes as Greeks (line 1355); they sometimes seem to be two different groups within Alexander's larger army, made up of "cil de Macedoigne, Egypcien e Greu" (those of Macedon, Egyptians and Greeks, line 2191), as well as soldiers from other lands that Alexander has conquered. Sometimes these groups are conflated, sometimes they are distinguished from one another; sometimes Alexander is one, then the other, though it seems that Alexander refers to himself more often as a Greek than as a Macedonian in the *Roman de toute chevalerie*.

What could these different nationalities mean? Are there differences between them? What would a medieval reader have thought when encountering Alexander as a Greek, or Alexander as a Macedonian? Are there things that one must be if one is a Greek, or a Macedonian, or even a Trojan or Egyptian? To answer these questions, several medieval texts that shed light on the associations readers and authors might have made when they encountered the various nationalities of Alexander will repay examination. It is useful to begin with the world chronicle of Paulus Orosius, the *Seven Books of History Against the Pagans*, a text that was well-known throughout the Middle Ages. Written at the behest of St Augustine, it features Alexander in a crucial role. Orosius's aim was to give a history of the world from Adam to Rome in order to counteract popular opinion and prove that the sack of Rome and the misery of the fifth century were not the result of the abandonment of the old gods in favour of the Christian God; rather, God had foreordained the rise and fall of empires.

The main feature of the *Seven Books of History* that concerns Alexander is this concept of *translatio imperii*, the movement of imperial domination from East to West. Orosius lists the succession of empires as beginning in the great kingdom of Babylon, travelling to the brief empires of Macedon and Carthage, before settling finally in Rome, the permanent home of *imperium*, the right to rule.[10] The Macedonian empire described by Orosius is, of course, that of Alexander; he and his armies are called Macedonians. Orosius is concerned not with "nation," but with "empire," a unit that necessarily comprises various "nations"; however, Orosius's schema can still further an understanding of the connotations of a particular "nation." The Macedonian empire to which Orosius refers is named after the land and the people who govern that land. Orosius notes that Alexander is the son of Philip, the "Macedonian king" (Macedoniae regem, Orosius, *Seven Books of History*, I. 154, 3.12.14) and is born in Macedon; he is named the ruler of Macedon and forges an empire that bears the name of his homeland. At the centre and beginning of the Macedonian "empire," made up of disparate peoples and places (and "nations"), there is a Macedonian "nation," a people who share location, language, and ancestry.

Alexander the Macedonian is described by Orosius in quite unflattering terms; he is bloodthirsty and his methods are brutal. For instance, Orosius claims that Alexander killed all of his relatives before setting off for Persia ("Inde profecturus ad Persicum bellum omnes cognatos ac proximos suos interfecit," I.164, 3.16.3). He is "a bloody lord" (cruentumque ... dominum, I.173, 3.20.8) who held much of the world in fear. Orosius says that "Alexander, insatiable for human blood, whether of enemies or even allies, was always thirsting for fresh bloodshed" (Alexander, humani sanguinis inexsaturabilis siue hostium, siue etiam sociorum, recentem tamen semper sitiebat cruorem, I.170, 3.18.10).

Despite being depicted like this, Alexander is still part of providential history, and plays a crucial role in Orosius's conception of *translatio imperii*. In Orosius's quadripartite schema, Alexander is the custodian of imperial authority as it moves in succession from Babylon in the East, to Macedon in the North, to Carthage in the South, and finally to Rome in the West. Alexander is the caretaker of empire for a brief, intense period, providing a model for world dominion to Augustus and to Rome, which in its Christianity will be the fulfillment of all empires. In this context, as Akbari notes, Alexander is "a fitting counterpart to the Roman emperor who achieved universal peace and concord, preparing the way for the establishment of Christianity on the foundations of the Empire."[11] The three earlier empires, Babylon, Macedon, and Carthage, are part of God's plan for the world: they ended at their appointed times after they had played their historic roles; they were full of warfare and bloodshed, and led up to the Roman Empire, which was the setting into which Christ was born and saved the world. Alexander is called a Macedonian in Orosius's framework and is an actor in God's plan for the salvation of the world. Although his depiction as a bloodthirsty tyrant was not always included in medieval texts that used Orosius as a source, he remained an agent by which the Christian empire could finally be born.

Alexander's national identity is inconsistent but unsurprising: while the *Roman de toute chevalerie* describes him sometimes as a Greek and sometimes as a Macedonian, he is only called a Macedonian in Orosius's history. Medieval authors did not limit themselves to the nationalities supported by historical sources, however. Alexander appears in a new guise in the seventh-century chronicle of Frankish Gaul by the author known as Fredegar, who was the first to transpose the soon-to-be popular story of the Trojan foundation myth, found most influentially in Vergil's *Aeneid*, to northern Europe.[12] In the story of the Trojan dispersal found in the *Aeneid*, Aeneas flees the Greek destruction of Troy, lands eventually in Italy, and founds the Roman people. Vergil's motive for writing of Aeneas's deeds was to give the Roman emperor Augustus, his patron, imperial legitimacy and a place in the Trojan genealogy. This Trojan lineage was used in a similar way by the authors of many nations of Europe who claimed, embellished, and expanded Vergil's account of Aeneas in their own chronicles.[13]

The Trojan foundation myth became so popular because it supported the idea that both Rome and other European nations derive their right to rule from the mighty city of Troy – it allowed other nations of Europe to be practically coeval with Rome. These other nations became less like children of Rome, and more like brothers. According to Fredegar, concerned with the history and lineage of the Franks, Aeneas and other Trojans flee the sack of Troy by the Greeks and find themselves in Europe, where they split into two different groups: some Trojans stay in the Eastern regions, while some venture to the West, where they found the nation of the Franks, named after their leader, Francio.

The other group of Trojans, staying in the East, finds itself in Macedon, a region that is oppressed by neighbouring peoples. So that they can help the Macedonians against their neighbours, the Trojans are invited to stay in Macedon.[14] The Trojans settle there and intermarry with the inhabitants, and the Macedonians subsequently become fierce fighters because of their Trojan blood. From this newly rejuvenated nation springs the lineage of King Philip and his son, Alexander the Great:

> Per quos postea cum subiuncti in plurima procreatione crevissent, ex ipso genere Macedonis fortissimi pugnatores effecti sunt; quod in postremum in diebus Phyliphy regis et Alexandri fili sui fama confirmat, illorum fortitudine qualis fuit.
>
> [Later, when they (the Trojans) had joined with them and they increased by intensive procreation, from that stock the Macedonians were made

into the strongest of warriors. Tradition confirmed this in the days of King Philip and his son Alexander: how great was their strength! *Fredegarii et aliorum chronica*, 2.6, 45–6]

Thus the Trojans not only found the Frankish people in Europe, but also begin the line that ends with Alexander. Fredegar's Alexander is certainly Macedonian, but from Trojan stock: Fredegar defines Alexander's nationality by claiming that this group of Trojans "were called Macedonians after the people by whom they were received and after the region of Macedon" (vocati sunt Macedonis secundum populum, a quem recepti sunt, et regionem Macedoniae, 2.6, 45–6). Not only does Fredegar's notion of "nationality" fit with those of his contemporary chroniclers, but this additional Trojan nationality means that the European audiences of this chronicle could feel a sense of pride that they were in some way related to Alexander, who had controlled much of the known world. But being part Trojan also places Alexander at a more comfortable distance from his own history.

In Fredegar's telling, Alexander's Trojan origins link him to the heritage of Europe, and also distance him from the Greeks, whom the Trojans were fleeing. This runs counter to nearly all ancient reports of Alexander: those of Arrian and Plutarch, and also the medieval *Alexandreis* of Walter of Châtillon, which I discuss below, claim that he is a proud descendant of the Greeks who sacked Troy. The Greeks at Troy are characterized in a negative way in medieval works, as deceitful, treacherous, and cruel.[15] Seeing Alexander as this type of Greek was not necessarily desirable in the Middle Ages, and most medieval accounts of Alexander are unwilling to present him as being allied to the Greeks at Troy. According to Terence Spencer, "medieval sentiment was generally favourable to the Trojans and hostile to the Greeks. This bias was due … to the legendary descent of many of the nations of Europe from Trojan exiles."[16] The myth that Trojans founded European nations would have been a reason not to depict Alexander as a Greek. Fredegar's chronicle increases the multiplicity and ambiguity of Alexander's nationality. Alexander is here a Trojan Macedonian, a hero and conqueror, brother to the Franks and distanced from the Greeks at Troy, to whom, in reality, he felt a close kinship.

In my survey of the various nationalities ascribed to Alexander, I turn next to the famous twelfth-century chronicler Otto of Freising. His chronicle, *The Two Cities*, picks up Orosius's succession of empires, but his description of Alexander's nationality is not quite as clear-cut.

Where Orosius had stated that the right to rule moved from Babylon to Macedon to Carthage to Rome, according to Otto, *imperium* moved from Babylon, to Persia, to Greece, and finally to Rome. Where Orosius had called Alexander and his empire "Macedonian," Otto instead calls the empire "Greek." But he is inconsistent in his description of Alexander: sometimes Otto calls Alexander a Macedonian, sometimes he calls Alexander a Greek. The fact that Otto uses Orosius's schema but adds another nationality for Alexander may at first seem like a fine distinction, but Otto's chronicle repays further examination.

Because he believes that Rome is the final holder of *imperium* and will last until the end of the world, Otto felt the need to explain the sack of Rome and the rise of other European nations. The right to rule, says Otto, continuing where Orosius ended, moved from Rome, to the Greeks, to the Franks, who as "Roman Emperors" had every justification to empire. By "Greeks," Otto here actually means the Byzantine Greeks, who after the fall of Rome held the sole claim to empire. *Imperium* moved, in Otto's conception, through the (Hellenistic) Greeks and came back to the (Byzantine) Greeks again. Like Alexander, a pre-Roman Greek, the "Roman Greeks," the Byzantines, play the role of mediators in the passage of empire to the West. Otto claims that the Byzantine Greeks held the right to rule *solo nomine*, "in name only": like Alexander, they are only placeholders, and hold imperial rule for a finite period of time before it is transferred to its rightful place.[17] Otto uses the term "Greek" for both Alexander's empire and the Byzantines, and thereby connects them, both by name and by the transitional mode in which they are depicted.

The different peoples and characteristics connected with the term "Greek" begin to expand. Medieval readers might think of the Greeks at Troy, who were not seen in a positive light in the Middle Ages because Western Europeans identified themselves with the enemies of the Greeks, the Trojans. The Byzantine Greeks were similarly suspect, especially in the period when Otto was writing this work, between the First and Second Crusades. The Byzantine Greeks were regarded with suspicion by the West after the schism between the Orthodox and Catholic churches in 1054, and because the Byzantines did not aid the western crusaders as they were expected to.[18] Otto calls yet another people "Greek" besides the Byzantines and Alexander: the Greeks who were conquered and subsumed by Rome. In his explanation of Aeneas's lineage in Italy, Otto explains how Aeneas's grandson, Aeneas Silvius, was the fourth Latin king. Otto then makes a striking statement:

> Exhinc Greci et Latini quasi in uno semine coalescentes quandam et morum et linguae affinitatem habere ceperunt aliasque gentes tamquam rationis acumine et oris venustate minus utentes barbaros vocare consueverunt.
>
> [From this time on the Greeks and the Latins, uniting as into one seed, so to say, began to have a certain kinship of customs and language, and they were wont to call other races barbarians on the ground that they lacked keenness of intellect and elegance of language. *Ottonis episcopi frisingensis Chronica* I.27, 62]

Otto conflates Greeks with Latins, presumably to incorporate the philosophy and knowledge of the Greeks into the fabric of Roman society. Otto's chronicle complicates Alexander's nationality by calling him both a Macedonian, as Orosius did, and a Greek. By using the term "Greek" in other contexts, a term he originally used for Alexander, Otto links Alexander to both the Byzantines and the Greeks conquered by the Romans. In a way, by seeing him as a "Greek," Otto changes Alexander's function in history, from Orosius's bloodthirsty tyrant in a divinely sanctioned succession of empires, to a predecessor of empire for Rome, who as a Greek is linked to the enemies of the West, some of whom had been conquered and subsumed, and some of whom the West wished to conquer. The different groups that Otto of Freising calls "Greeks" – Macedonians, the Byzantine Greeks, and the Greeks subsumed by the Romans – inhabit a transitional space and allow the movement of *imperium* and learning, and are made less threatening by being designated as "Greeks."

While most medieval authors shied away from linking Alexander to the Greeks at Troy, one notable exception is Walter of Châtillon's popular Latin epic, the *Alexandreis*, written between 1176 and 1181. Walter calls Alexander "the Macedonian" and calls his army Macedonian and Greek.[19] He uses the first-century CE work of Quintus Curtius Rufus, the *Historia Alexandri*, as his main source, and expands on the narrative of Curtius when he describes Alexander's trip to Troy, the first place he visits in Asia. Curtius's text was missing several of its books; these were supplemented in the Middle Ages and available to Walter.[20] The medieval interpolated text of Curtius notes that Alexander sacrificed at the tombs of the heroes at Troy ("Ylion ergo pertransiens, ad tumulos eorum qui Troiano bello ceciderant, paterntauit" 332–3).[21] Walter, however, is more specific: he explains that Alexander reveres the Greek hero of the Trojan War, Achilles. Alexander pours wine on the tomb of Achilles and burns incense: "sterilem mulso saciauit harenam, / Et suffire locum sumpta properauit acerra" (and on the barren sands he poured pure wine, / hastening to perfume the place with incense, I. 476–7).[22] Alexander claims that Achilles's highest honour is that he is immortalized by Homer: "summum tamen illud honoris / Arbitror augmentum, quod tantum tantus habere / Post obitum meruit preconem laudis Homerum" (yet this is the highest increase in his honour – / or so I judge – that such a man in death / should merit such a herald of his praise / as Homer, I. 480–3). Most interestingly, Walter compares Alexander's warlike youth to that of Neoptolemus, Achilles's son: "tunc indomitum tunc tanta uideres / Velle Neoptolemum que uix expleret Achilles" (One might then have seen Neoptolemus unsubdued, / desiring things even his sire Achilles / might scare accomplish, I. 198–9).

Similar to the connections many early authors drew, Walter comes very close to identifying Alexander with the Greeks who sacked Troy.[23] In the *Alexandreis*, Alexander is both historical Macedonian conqueror and more closely tied to the Greeks at Troy than in other medieval texts. The combination of these nationalities and their connotations can make Alexander seem like a hybrid creature. "Macedonian" can mean both historical conqueror, and within an Orosian framework, part of divine providence working in history. Being a "Greek" places Alexander at a distance from a medieval reader because of the myth of the Trojan origins of Europe and associates him with both the Greeks subsumed by Rome and with the Byzantines, as Otto of Freising did, but also links him with the philosophical and scientific texts newly available to Europe in the twelfth century, as I treat later in my discussion of Alexander's "Greek" education.

There are multiple nationalities ascribed to Alexander, just as there are multiple paternities. Here we move from the macrocosm to the microcosm, from Alexander's national identity to his specific parentage: his *natio* with regard to his own father, especially as it relates to the *Roman de toute chevalerie*, the text with which I will end my discussion. In any exploration of the nationalities of Alexander, one has to account for the fact that some medieval texts are freighted with the possibility that Alexander is not really very Greek, or Macedonian, or Trojan at all, but the son of an Egyptian magician, Nectanabus.[24] This parentage is first found in the Greek account of Alexander's life by Pseudo-Callisthenes, translated into Latin in the fourth century CE by Julius Valerius and called the *Res gestae Alexandri Macedonis*, which was available in the Middle Ages only through an abbreviation, the so-called *Zacher Epitome* (named after its nineteenth-century editor), written no later than the ninth century.[25] In the account of Julius Valerius, Alexander's father is not Philip, but rather Nectanabus, the Egyptian sorcerer who, having disguised himself as the god Ammon, deceives the Macedonian queen Olympias and fathers Alexander. Having a powerful magician, or a god, as Nectanabus appears, as a father could be beneficial to Alexander: he could be revered as a god himself, or inherit some of his father's magical powers. However, Alexander can also be considered, as Akbari has put it, a "half-breed bastard" who has a lesser claim to legitimacy and inheritance.[26]

This fanciful idea of Alexander's heritage and nationality can be found, in slightly different versions, in several medieval Alexander texts, including Pfaffe Lamprecht's *Alexander*, the Middle English *Romance of Alisaunder* and the *Roman de toute chevalerie*. As Shamma Boyarin notes in his essay in this volume, the medieval Hebrew *Alexander Romance* tradition also emphasizes Alexander's Egyptian paternity, naming Nectanabus as Alexander's father. According to Saskia Dönitz, the type 3 Hebrew *Alexander Romance* "differs widely from the Greek source" as it places Alexander's homeland and place of birth in Egypt.[27] Not only is Alexander born in Egypt to Philip, King of Egypt, in this tradition, but he is illegitimate as well: his mother is seduced by an Egyptian wizard, Bildad.[28]

Though Alexander is not usually portrayed in medieval texts as having been born in Egypt, the fact that he is sometimes depicted as the half-Egyptian son of a magician complicates Alexander's already multifold nationalities by bringing up the spectre of illegitimacy and dubious powers. Twelfth-century Alexander texts, such as the first *Roman d'Alexandre* of Albéric de Pisançon, the decasyllabic *Roman d'Alexandre*, and the *Roman d'Alexandre* of Alexandre de Paris, are troubled by and reject this notion of Alexander's illegitimacy. In the opinion of Catherine Gaullier-Bougassas and Laurence Harf-Lancner, "Ils la rejettent comme une calomnie qu'auraient inventée de son vivant des adversaires politiques du roi, pour briser sa carrière. … une souillure irrémédiable, qui rend le héros indigne de l'exercise du pouvoir royal" (They reject it [Alexander's parentage] as a smear that the king's political enemies invented during his lifetime to harm his career. … an indelible stain that renders the hero unworthy of wielding royal power).[29] The *Roman de toute chevalerie*, however, is forthright about Alexander's complicated parentage. Gaullier-Bougassas and Harf-Lancner note that Thomas of Kent is extremely concerned about being faithful in his translation of his source, the *Pseudo-Callisthenes* and its Latin derivatives noted above, which include Nectanabus's seduction of

Alexander's mother, Olympias. Gaullier-Bougassas and Harf-Lancner point to Thomas of Kent's desire to add romance adventures to his subject matter by adding the seduction of a queen, the magic practised by Nectanabus, and less of an emphasis in his work on Alexander being a "mirror of princes," but rather a flawed but great ruler.[30]

After having seen some of Alexander's nationalities and the characteristics with which they are associated, it is useful to end the discussion of the nationalities of Alexander with the *Roman de toute chevalerie*, where Alexander is described as Macedonian and Greek, and is the son of Nectanabus. The associations of the terms used to describe Alexander expand. An author or reader in the late twelfth century could readily have connected the term "Macedonian" with the Orosian notion of *translatio imperii*. "Greek" meant, if one had Otto of Freising in mind, not only Alexander's empire, but the Byzantine Greeks and the Greeks conquered by the Romans. These different conceptions of Alexander's nationality affected how the *Roman de toute chevalerie* was read. For instance, Alexander's role as world conqueror in the *Roman de toute chevalerie* can be made clearer if we view him as "the Macedonian" fulfilling his necessary role in providential history. This particular nationality can signal that he plays a crucial role in God's plan for the world, as he is a Macedonian in Orosius's well-known scheme of *translatio imperii*. In Otto of Freising's *translatio imperii*, the Greek Alexander also plays the part of a temporary place-holder of empire, but is linked by nationality to other groups of Greeks whom Otto does not view entirely favourably.

We can also understand Alexander's character and remarkable education better through the lens of both his Greek and Egyptian identities, as Alexander is educated by both the Greek philsopher Aristotle and by his natural father, the Egyptian Nectanabus, in the *Roman de toute chevalerie*.[31] Western medieval readers and writers typically associated Egypt and Egyptians with the magic, astrology, and esoteric knowledge connected with Hermes Trismegistus. In fact, as Brian Copenhaver states, in the twelfth century, "a revival of the Platonic tradition also reawakened curiosity about the Hermetic writings."[32] The *Roman de toute chevalerie*, written in this time period, in particular emphasizes Alexander's education: not only that provided by Aristotle, as I will treat below, but also by Nectanabus.[33]

Nectanabus teaches Alexander astronomy and astrology, and Thomas of Kent seems to be concerned with the scientific knowledge that Alexander acquires on his journeys.[34] When Alexander is not learning the seven liberal arts from Aristotle and his other masters, he is taught by

Nectanabus every night, "De soleil e de lune e de meinte esteille / Les engins e les sortz e de charmes la merveille" (The magic power and the destinies and the wonder of spells of the sun and the moon and the many stars, *Roman de toute chevalerie*, lines 480–1). Calling Nectanabus a "fals truant" ("deceptive scoundrel," line 357), Thomas of Kent rejects the notion that Nectanabus is actually the Egyptian god Ammon, in whose guise he seduces Olympias, but notes the benefits his Egyptian father brings to Alexander: the circumstances of his illegitimacy "contribuaient encore à sa gloire. L'astrologue et magicien Nectanabus constitue en effet toujours une ascendance prestigieuse, bien qu'humaine, parce que son savoir occulte et ses pouvoirs extraordinaires lui permettent de dépasser certaines limites de la condition humaine" (contribute to his glory. Nectanabus the astrologer and magician constitutes a prestigious and human parentage because his occult knowledge and his extraordinary powers permit him to surpass certain limits of the human condition).[35] Nectanabus may not be a "sulphurous magician" for Thomas of Kent; rather, he is "un personnage qui, pour lui, incarne la science et la croyance aux pouvoirs infinis de la raison humaine" (a personage who, for him, embodies science and the knowledge of the infinite powers of human reason).[36]

The connection to the knowledge of Egypt through Nectanabus is integral to the Alexander of the *Roman de toute chevalerie*, as is his connection of Greeks to philosophy and learning. As we have seen, being "Greek" takes numerous forms. In the *Roman de toute chevalerie*, Alexander as a Greek can be seen as part of the culture and philosophy that made Rome great. In the *Two Cities*, Otto of Freising speaks of the language and knowledge of the Greeks, and of how the Latins integrated these into their culture. Here, as in the medieval Hebrew Alexander romances studied by Shamma Boyarin in this volume, Alexander's education and link to Greek philosophy are strong: he is renowned for his learning, and Aristotle is his chief teacher. Aristotle's writings had been newly rediscovered, studied, and revered in the West of the twelfth century. Especially popular was the pseudo-Aristotelian *Secretum secretorum*, a manual of science and princely conduct supposedly written by Aristotle for Alexander. The work is supposed to have been first compiled in Syriac in the eighth century, translated into Arabic in the ninth century, into Latin around 1125, and then into numerous vernacular languages.[37] In an offhand remark, Thomas of Kent asserts that Aristotle "fu le plus sage, ceo sievent clerc e prestre, / Qe unqes fut el siecle for Jesu le celestre" (was, as clerks and priests know, the wisest man who lived before Christ, *Roman de toute chevalerie*, lines 456–7). Alexander's education is stressed in many medieval texts, and his connection to Aristotle, and Greek philosophy, would have been a positive association.

Alexander's nationality, this time implicit, can also play a role in understanding one of his most interesting incarnations in the *Roman de toute chevalerie*. As several critics have noted, Thomas of Kent goes to the unusual length in the *Roman de toute chevalerie* of making Alexander seem like a crusader.[38] His main enemy, Darius the Persian, is clearly meant to be seen as a Saracen; Darius' army is described as consisting of Saracens from around the world:

La est Dayres assis e cent mil Sarazin –
Il n'i ad cely qui ne croit en Apolin –
Toz de Inde majur desqu'al mont Taurin
E d'Aufrique la grant tote la gent Darin.
Ne remist Turc n'Escler, Caldeu ne Barbarin
Ne vienge a cest bosoing, si trop nen est frarin.

[Darius is seated there with one hundred thousand Saracens – there was no one there who did not believe in Apolin – they came from Greater India up to the Taurus mountains and from immense Africa, and all were the vassals of Darius. Turks, Slavs, Chaldeans and Berbers, all came to him because he needed them, except those who did not have the strength, *Roman de toute chevalerie*, lines 1604–9.]

Darius himself claims to be part of the Saracen "pantheon," the trinity of Apolin, Muhammad, and Tervagent, typical to *chansons de geste* and romances: "roy des roys e cosin Tervagant, / Parent Mercurie e Apolin le vaillant" (the king of kings and cousin of Tervagant, relative of Mercury and the brave Apollin, lines 1391–2).[39]

Alexander, as the enemy of this Saracen king, can thus be viewed as a crusader. He is even depicted as having a sword that Thomas of Kent compares to Durendal, the sword of the Christian hero Roland in the *Chanson de Roland* (*Roman de toute chevalerie*, line 4150). In his opposition to the Saracen Darius and through his association with Roland, Alexander is the prefiguration of a Christian crusader. This association is even clearer when we consider that the *Roman de toute chevalerie* includes an episode where Alexander worships the God of the Jews in Jerusalem, an episode taken from Flavius Josephus's *Jewish Antiquities*.[40] In these passages, Alexander's nationality is not mentioned, but the description of Darius as a Saracen and the association of Alexander with a famous "crusader's" sword can point to him being from one of the nations of Western Europe, whence crusaders came. Alexander as "crusader," like Alexander as "Trojan," would have made him seem appealingly familiar and similar to the audience of *Roman de toute chevalerie*.

While Alexander can be seen as a crusader in a twelfth-century romance, there are other Greeks in the twelfth century who are involved in the Crusades. If a reader with Otto of Freising in mind associates Alexander with the Byzantine Greeks, seeing Alexander as a crusader is more complicated. In the later twelfth century the Byzantines were held in suspicion because of what was seen as their treachery against western crusaders. The *Roman de toute chevalerie* was written after the disastrous Second Crusade, and the alleged perfidy of the Byzantines had been duly noted by chroniclers such as Odo of Deuil in his *De profectione Ludovici VII in Orientem*.[41] If Alexander is associated with the treacherous Byzantines when he is called "Greek," his status as proto-Christian crusader is problematized. He is a spectacularly successful crusader-before-the-fact, fighting a Saracen Darius and visiting Jerusalem, but he can also be associated with the Byzantines, the antithesis of good crusaders. Alternately, Alexander may have been seen as a prefiguration of a crusader, and as a model for a Greek who has gotten crusading right. As a Greek who was bold and eschewed the treachery commonly associated with the Byzantines,[42] he could have been a "fantasy Greek" in the eyes of a western audience.

Through many years and by many authors, Alexander has been labelled as "Greek," "Macedonian," "Trojan," and even "Egyptian." As a Macedonian, he is part of providential history, as he fits into the Orosian concept of *translatio imperii*, where he is the temporary holder of world dominion and plays a divinely sanctioned role, though he himself is sometimes an odious character. As a Trojan, Alexander is a brother to Europeans, coming from the same Trojan stock that founded the Romans, the Franks, and other nations. As the son of an Egyptian magician, Alexander gains the knowledge of Egyptian magic and astrology, but is also problematically illegitimate and linked to the god Ammon, in whose guise Nectanabus seduced Olympias. Even more complicated, though, is seeing Alexander as a Greek. He can be linked to Aristotle and admirable Greek philosophy and learning. He can be seen as a "good" Greek crusader, unlike the Byzantine Greeks, who were often viewed as treacherous in the West. But he is also connected to the Greeks at Troy, in direct opposition to his appearance as a Trojan. Alexander is ambiguous: his nationalities have meant numerous, even contradictory things, and colour how a writer, or reader, would approach and use a hero who could be divinely inspired conqueror, enemy, brother, educated statesman, or bloody overlord.

NOTES

1 Anthony D. Smith, *The Nation in History: Historiographical Debates about Ethnicity and Nationalism* (Cambridge: Polity Press, 2000); Adrian Hastings, *The Construction of Nationhood: Ethnicity, Religion, and Nationalism* (Cambridge: Cambridge University Press, 1997).
2 Diane Speed, "The Construction of the Nation in Medieval English Romance," in *Readings in Medieval English Romance*, ed. Carol M. Meale (Cambridge: D.S. Brewer, 1994), 135–57; Thorlac Turville-Petre, *England the Nation: Language, Literature, and National Identity, 1290–1340* (Oxford: Clarendon Press, 1996), esp. 1–26; Alan S. Ambrisco, "Cannibalism and Cultural Encounters in *Richard Coeur de Lion*," *Journal of Medieval and Early Modern Studies* 29 (1999), 499–528; Geraldine Heng, "The Romance of England: *Richard Coer de Lyon*, Saracens, Jews, and the Politics of Race and Nation," in *The Postcolonial Middle Ages*, ed. Jeffrey Jerome Cohen (New York: St Martin's, 2000), 135–71; Suzanne Conklin Akbari, "The Hunger for Identity in *Richard Coer de Lion*," in *Reading Medieval Culture: Essays in Honor of Robert W. Hanning*, ed. Robert M. Stein and Sandra Pierson Prior (Notre Dame, IN: University of Notre Dame Press, 2005), 198–227; *Imagining a Medieval English Nation*, ed. Kathy Lavezzo (Minneapolis and London: University of Minnesota Press, 2004).
3 Suzanne Conklin Akbari, "Orientation and Nation in Chaucer's *Canterbury Tales*," in *Chaucer's Cultural Geography*, ed. Kathryn L. Lynch (New York and London: Routledge, 2002), 102–34, 114.
4 The hero's foundational role in the English nation in such medieval English romances as *Havelok the Dane* and the *Romaunce of Richard Coer de Lion* has been well studied. As Diane Speed explains, "The nation is defined and asserted essentially as a response to the unknown": the hero ventures outside of his homeland to face challenges and tests, he learns and matures, then returns; his homecoming "marks a return to order for himself and his society" (Speed, "The Construction of the Nation,"[see note 2], 146). In her summary of the work of Speed and Geraldine Heng, Suzanne Conklin Akbari has noted that there is a tendancy in medieval romance "to identify the hero with the nation he leads, so that his origin and destiny come to stand for that of the people as a whole" (Akbari, "The Hunger for National Identity," [see note 2], 198–9). Unlike King Richard, Alexander does acquire knowledge but

does not come back to his homeland; unlike Havelok, Alexander's reign does not secure a long period of peace and stability for his nation (or empire).

5 Thorlac Turville-Petre, "*Havelok* and the History of the Nation," in *Readings in Medieval English Romance*, ed. Carol M. Meale (Cambridge: D.S. Brewer, 1994), 121–34, 128.

6 Suzanne Conklin Akbari, "From Due East to True North: Orientalism and Orientation," in *The Postcolonial Middle Ages*, ed. Jeffrey Jerome Cohen (New York: St Martin's Press, 2000), 19–34, 24.

7 Martin Gosman, *La Légende d'Alexandre dans la littérature française du 12e siècle: Une réécriture permanente*, Faux titre 133 (Amsterdam and Atlanta, GA: Rodopi, 1997), 7n15.

8 Laurence Harf-Lancner, "Medieval French Alexander Romances," in *A Companion to Alexander Literature in the Middle Ages*, ed. Z. David Zuwiyya (Leiden and Boston: Brill, 2011), 201–29, 202 and 203.

9 All references in my text to Thomas of Kent's *Roman de toute chevalerie* refer to *The Anglo Norman Alexander (Le Roman de toute chevalerie) by Thomas of Kent*, ed. Brian Foster and Ian Short, 2 vols., Anglo-Norman Text Society 29–33 (London: Anglo-Norman Text Society, 1976–7). Unless otherwise noted, all translations are my own.

10 "Praeterea intercessise dixeram inter Babylonium regnum, quod ab oriente fuerat, et Romanum, quod ab occidente consurgens hereditati orientis enutriebatur, Macedonicum Africanumque regnum, hoc est quasi a meridie ac septentrione breuibus uicibus partes tutoris curatorisque tenuisse" (Furthermore, I had said that between the Babylonian Empire which arose in the West and was nourished by the heritage of the East, there intervened the Macedonian and African Empires, that is, that in the North and the South in brief intervals they played the roles of protector and guardian, III.17–18, 7.2.4). Paulus Orosius, *Historiae adversum paganos*, in *Orose: Histoires (Contre les Païens)*, ed. and trans. Marie-Pierre Arnaud-Lindet, 3 vols. (Paris: Les Belles Lettres, 1990). Numbers refer to book and page number of edition, and book, chapter and section of work. Translation taken from Paulus Orosius, *The Seven Books of History Against the Pagans*, trans. Roy J. Deferrari (Washington, DC: Catholic University of America Press, 1964).

11 Suzanne Conklin Akbari, "Alexander in the Orient: Bodies and Boundaries in the *Roman de toute chevalerie*" in *Postcolonial Approaches to the European Middle Ages: Translating Cultures*, ed. Ananya Jahanara Kabir and Deanne Williams (Cambridge: Cambridge University Press, 2005), 105–26, 110.

12 For a discussion of Fredegar's and other medieval authors' uses of the Trojan foundation myth, see Richard Waswo, "Our Ancestors, the Trojans: Inventing Cultural Identity in the Middle Ages," *Exemplaria* 7.2 (1995), 269–90. Waswo notes that Fredegar's chronicle "survives in thirty-four

manuscripts, making it ... if not the age's equivalent of a best-seller, at least a moderate success" (271–2).

13 On the Trojan foundation myth, see especially Andrew Erskine, *Troy Between Greece and Rome: Local Tradition and Imperial Power* (Oxford: Oxford University Press, 2001); Heather James, *Shakespeare's Troy: Drama, Politics, and the Translation of Empire* (Cambridge: Cambridge University Press, 1997); Sylvia Federico, *New Troy: Fantasies of Empire in the Late Middle Ages* (Minnesota and London: University of Minnesota Press, 2003); Terence Spencer, "Turks and Trojans in the Renaissance," *Modern Language Review* 47 (1952), 330–3; Margaret Meserve, "Medieval Sources for Renaissance Theories on the Origins of the Ottoman Turks" in *Europa und die Türken in der Renaissance*, ed. Bodo Guthmüller and Wilhelm Kühlmann (Tübingen: Max Niemeyer Verlag, 2000), 409–36.

14 "Exinde origo Francorum fuit. Priamo primo regi habuerunt; postea per historiarum libris scriptum est, qualiter habuerunt regi Friga. Postea partiti sunt in duabus partibus. Una pars perrexit in Macedoniam, vocati sunt Macedonis secundum populum, a quem recepti sunt, et regionem Macedoniae, qui oppremebatur a gentes vicinas, invitati ab ipsis fuerunt, ut eis praberent auxilium" (After that was the origin of the Franks. They had Priam as their first king; it is written in the history books how they then had Friga for a king. Afterwards, they were divided into two groups. One group ventured into Macedon, and they were called Macedonians after the people by whom they were received and after the region of Macedon. The people were being oppressed by neighbouring races and the Trojans were invited to give them aid, 2.6, 45–6). *Fredegarii et aliorum chronica*, ed. Bruno Krusch, Monumenta Germaniae Historica, Scriptores rerum Merovingicarum II (Hanover: Hahn, 1888).

15 In particular, medieval works on the Trojan War, such as the *Roman de Troie* of Benoît de Sainte-Maure and the *Historia destructionis Troiae* of Guido delle Colonne, highlight these characteristics. For a discussion of the medieval depictions of ancient Greeks, see Emily L. Reiner, "The Ambiguous Greek in Old French and Middle English Literature." PhD diss., University of Toronto, 2008.

16 Spencer, "Turks and Trojans in the Renaissance" (see note 14), 330.

17 "Constantinus, ut dixi, sedem regni Bizancium transtulit. . . . Ex hoc regnum Romanorum ad Grecos translatum invenitur mansitque propter antiquam Urbis dignitatem solo nomine ibi" (As I have said, Constantine transferred the seat of empire to Byzantium. . . . Since that time the rule of the Romans is known to be transferred to the Greeks and remains there in name only on account of the ancient dignity of the City, 4.5, 191). Otto of Freising, *Ottonis episcopi frisingensis Chronica; sive, Historia de duabus civitatibus, Editio*

*altera*, ed. Adolfus Hofmeister, Scriptores rerum germanicarum in usum scholarum ex Monumentis Germaniae historicis separatim editi (Hanover: Impensis Bibliopolii Hahniani, 1912). Translation from Otto, Bishop of Freising, *The Two Cities: A Chronicle of Universal History to the Year 1146 A.D.*, trans. Charles Christopher Mierow, ed. Austin P. Evans and Charles Knapp (New York: Columbia University Press, 1928).

18 Odo of Deuil, Louis VII's chaplain, blamed the failure of the Second Crusade on the treachery of the Byzantines; he writes his chronicle, he says, "ut sciant posteri Graecorum dolosa facinora" (so that posterity may know about the Greeks' treacherous actions, Bk. 5, 99). Odo of Deuil, *De profectione Ludovici VII in Orientem: The Journey of Louis VII to the East*, ed. and trans. Virginia Gingerick Berry (New York: Columbia University Press, 1948).

19 Maura Lafferty argues that "for Walter, Alexander is a Greek" (186). "Walter of Châtillon's *Alexandreis*," in *A Companion to Alexander Literature in the Middle Ages*, ed. Z. David Zuwiyya (Leiden and Boston: Brill, 2011), 177–99.

20 For an edition of the missing books of Curtius that were supplemented in the Middle Ages, see Edmé Smits, "A Medieval Supplement to the Beginning of Curtius Rufus's *Historia Alexandri*: An Edition with Introduction" in *Viator* 18 (1987): 89–124.

21 Ibid., 114.

22 Walter of Châtillon, *Alexandreis*, ed. Marvin L. Colker (Padua: Editrice Antenore, 1978). Translation from Walter of Châtillon, *The Alexandreis: A Twelfth-Century Epic*, trans. David Townsend (Peterborough, ON: Broadview, 2007).

23 See Alexander's visit to Troy in Plutarch's *Alexander*, Section 15, Part 4. *Plutarch's Lives*, trans. Bernadotte Perrin (Cambridge, MA: Harvard UP and London: William Heinemann, 1919).

24 For a discussion of Nectanabus and Alexander, see B.E. Perry, "The Egyptian Legend of Nectanabus," in *Transactions and Proceedings of the American Philological Association*, 97 (1966), 327–33; Catherine Gaullier-Bougassas, *Les Romans d'Alexandre. Aux frontières de l'épique et du romanesque* (Paris: Champion, 1998), 348–79; Gaullier-Bougassas, "Nectanabus et la singularité d'Alexandre dans les *Romans d'Alexandre* français" in *Alexandre le Grand dans les littératures occidentales et proche-orientales: Actes du colloque de Paris, 27–29 novembre 1997*, ed. Laurence Harf-Lancner et al. (Nanterre: Université de Paris X-Nanterre, 1999); Gaullier-Bougassas, "Les mystifications de l'enchanteur Nectanabus et les 'origines' des *Romans d'Alexandre* du Pseudo-Callisthène et de Thomas de Kent" in *Deceptio. Mystifications, tromperies, illusions de l'Antiquité au XVIIe siècle*, Vol. 2 (Montpellier: Publications de l'Universtié Paul-Valéry Montpellier-III, 2000), 339–66.

25 For an explanation of the Pseudo-Callisthenes tradition, see George Cary, *The Medieval Alexander*, ed. D.J.A. Ross (Cambridge: Cambridge University Press, 1956), 9–12. See also *L'historiographie médiévale d'Alexandre le Grand*, ed. Catherine Gaullier-Bougassas, Alexander redivivus 1 (Turnhout: Brepols, 2011) for its essays on the medieval Pseudo-Callisthenes tradition. For the addition of Nectanabus into Alexander texts, especially those written in French, see Catherine Gaullier-Bougassas, *Les Romans d'Alexandre* (see note 24), 345–79.

26 Suzanne Conklin Akbari, *Idols in the East: European Representations of Islam and the Orient, 1100–1450* (Ithaca and London: Cornell University Press, 2009), 67–111.

27 Saskia Dönitz, "Alexander the Great in Medieval Hebrew Traditions," *A Companion to Alexander Literature in the Middle Ages*, ed. Z. David Zuwiyya (Leiden and Boston: Brill, 2011), 21–39, 35.

28 This romance dates from the fourteenth century and is included in the *Book of Memories*, compiled by the Rhinelander Eleazer ben Asher ha-Levi. The Jewish Alexander tradition is not consistent in its portrayal of Alexander: the First Book of Maccabees portrays Alexander in a "clearly negative" light, as the Book of Daniel does, as he is linked to the wicked king Antiochus, whose rule is "clearly seen as hostile to the Jews" (ibid., 22). The Jewish historian, Flavius Josephus, however, has a more positive view of Alexander in his *Antiquitates*, where he describes Alexander visiting Jerusalem and prostrating himself before the high priest of the Jews.

29 Thomas de Kent, *Le Roman d'Alexandre, or Le roman de toute chevalerie*, ed. Brian Foster and Ian Short, trans. Catherine Gaullier-Bougassas and Laurence Harf-Lancner (Paris: Champion, 2003), xvii–xviii.

30 Ibid., xviii.

31 For a discussion of the influence of both Nectanabus and Aristotle on Alexander, see Catherine Gaullier-Bougassas and Hélène Bellon-Méguelle, "Rêves de connaissance et d'exotisme: l'Alexandre aventurier en langue français," in *La fascination pour Alexandre le Grand dans les littératures européennes (Xe-XVIe siècles). Réinventions d'un mythe*, ed. Gauillier-Bougassas, 4 vols., Alexander redivivus 5 (Turnhout: Brepols, 2014), Vol. 3, 1331–1488.

32 Brian P. Copenhaver, *Hermetica: The Greek* Corpus Hermeticum *and the Latin* Asclepius. *New English translation, with notes and introduction* (Cambridge: Cambridge University Press, 1992), xlv.

33 Gaullier-Bougassas, *Les Romans d'Alexandre* (see note 24), 304.

34 Thomas de Kent, *Le Roman d'Alexandre, or Le roman de toute chevalerie* (see note 29), xxv–xxvi and Catherine Gaullier-Bougassas, *Les Romans d'Alexandre* (see note 24), 302–8.

35 Catherine Gaullier-Bougassas, *Les Romans d'Alexandre* (see note 24), 349.

36 Thomas de Kent, *Le Roman d'Alexandre, or Le roman de toute chevalerie* (see note 29), 9 n1.

37 See the Introduction in *Secretum Secretorum: Nine English Versions*, ed. Mahmoud A. Manzalaoui, 2 vols., EETS 276 (Oxford: Oxford University Press, 1977), 1: ix–l; and the recent volume *Trajectoires européennes du 'Secretum secretorum' du Pseudo-Aristote (XIIIe-XVIe siècle)*, ed. Catherine Gaullier-Bougassas et al., Alexander redivivus 6 (Turnhout: Brepols 2015).

38 Suzanne Conklin Akbari, "Alexander in the Orient" (see note 11), 114; Donald Maddox and Sara Sturm-Maddox, "Introduction: Alexander the Great in the French Middle Ages," in *The Medieval French Alexander*, ed. Donald Maddox and Sara Sturm-Maddox (Albany: State University of New York, 2002), 1–16, 3; Thomas of Kent, *The Anglo Norman Alexander (Le Roman de toute chevalerie) by Thomas of Kent* (see note 9), 2: 66.

39 On the "gods" of the Saracens in the *chansons de geste*, see John V. Tolan, *Saracens: Islam in the Medieval European Imagination* (New York: Columbia University Press, 2002), esp. chap. 5, "Saracens as Pagans," 105–34; Suzanne Conklin Akbari, "Imagining Islam: The Role of Images in Medieval Depictions of Muslims," *Scripta Mediterranea* 19–20 (1998–9), 9–27; C. Pellat and Y. Pellat, "L'Ideé de Dieu chez les Sarrasins des chansons de geste," *Studia Islamica* 22 (1965), 5–42; and Suzanne Conklin Akbari, *Idols in the East* (see note 26).

40 The *Jewish Antiquities* was known to the Middle Ages through the Latin version attributed to Rufinus of Aquileia. It was included in the $I^2$ recension of the *Historia de preliis* and gained an even wider audience by being included in the popular *Historia scholastica* of Petrus Comestor, ca. 1170. The episode is not included in one of the most popular French Alexander texts, the twelfth-century Old French *Roman d'Alexandre* of Alexandre de Paris. See also René Bloch, "Alexandre le Grand et le judaïsme: la double stratégie d'auteurs juifs de l'Antiquité et du Moyen Âge," in *Les voyages d'Alexandre au paradis: Orient et Occident, regards croisés*, ed. Catherine Gaullier-Bougassas and Margaret Bridges, Alexander redivivus 3 (Turnhout: Brepols, 2013), 147–64.

41 See note 18.

42 Alexander's attitude towards treachery can best be understood by an examination of three exemplary scenes from the *Roman de toute chevalerie*. In these episodes, he pardons a Persian soldier who disguises himself as a Greek and tries to kill Alexander by stabbing him in the back (vv. 3141–296). Alexander also punishes the betrayal of one of his men by another (vv. 2789–848). While Alexander will not suffer treason in his ranks, he punishes treachery that benefits him: he executes the treacherous murderers of his enemy, King Darius (vv. 3654–769).

# Facing the Land of Darkness: Alexander, Islam, and the Quest for the Secrets of God

CHRISTINE CHISM

As a late medieval work that amalgamates both Islamic and non-Islamic traditions of writing about Alexander, the medieval Andalusian *Qissat Dhulqarnayn* is a good starting place for examining how Muslim writers appropriate the classical pagan figure of Alexander and use him to negotiate a deep-running epistemological problem in Islamic culture. Diverging from classical Islamic literary traditions that exclude the pagan figure of Alexander as a suitable topic for Islamic literature, the *Qissat Dhulqarnayn* adapts peregrinated forms of the Greek *Alexander Romance*, while drawing from the Muslim literary genre of the *Qiṣaṣ al-anbiyāʾ* or *Tales of the Prophets*. In several *qisas* collections, the figure of Alexander the Great, renamed Dhu'l-qarnayn ("the two-horned one"), becomes a minor prophet in the long line of pre-Islamic sages.[1] However, the *Qissat Dhulqarnayn* diverges from the *qisas* collections, which are often as historically oriented or popular as they are religious, and imbues its narrative with the ultimate Islamic authority by situating itself within an explicitly Qurʾānic frame. At its beginning, the *Qissat Dhulqarnayn* references the Qurʾānic Sura of the Cave (Sura 18), which is where the enigmatic figure of Dhu'l-qarnayn, identified by most medieval commentators as Alexander the Great, enters Islamic traditions. However, the Qurʾān makes Dhu'l-qarnayn an exemplar not of world conquest and mortality, but of the breadth of divine knowledge and the depth of human ignorance. This chapter argues that the *Qissat Dhulqarnayn* offers a sophisticated response to an explicitly Qurʾānic Dhu'l-qarnayn, shifting the central questions surrounding Alexander from the passing glories of world conquest to the wonders and dangers of a world imbued with God's hidden secrets. In so doing it negotiates an essential epistemological conflict that profoundly shapes medieval

Islamic culture: the conflict between the intellectual need to investigate, explore, and acquire as much knowledge as possible in order to better know both God and his creation, on the one hand; and, on the other, the Qur'ānic admonition that all knowledge is ultimately God's and human investigation of what God has hidden is both futile and presumptuous.

The chapter's first section reads the Qur'ānic Sura of the Cave to show how the story of Dhu'l-qarnayn is used to emphasize the troubling but needful mysteriousness of God's intentions for his creation, and castigate those who try to penetrate his secrets. The second section examines the *Qissat Dhulqarnayn*'s treatment of this theme in the episode where Alexander disregards the advice of his guiding angel and chooses to penetrate into the Land of Darkness in which lies hidden the spring of immortality.

## I The Problem of Knowledge in Islamic Cultures and the Sura of the Cave

The Alexander figure of the *Qissat Dhulqarnayn* begins his career not as a conqueror but as a pre-eminent student (the narrative actually opens with what amounts to his qualifying exam from Aristotle). He is a seeker whose deepest need is the need to know. This makes him an apt hero for Muslim audiences. The search for knowledge in Islam is actually given a name, "Talab al 'ilm" and it is a duty for all Muslims.[2] There is a proverb still circulating in the Arab world: *'utlubu l-'ilm wa lau fi s-Sin*: "Seek knowledge even in China." The quest for knowledge is crucial to Islam as a religion because Islam makes each individual solely responsible for his own faith, religious practice, and moral judgment; and knowledge implicates the human power to recognize God through his revelations and his creations, to choose right, and to keep from error.[3] However, the search for knowledge in Islam leads in many, many directions, none of which are mandated. For instance, there is no single, institutionally acknowledged means for becoming a religious leader or person of learning, one of the *'ulama* – which literally means "those who know." Entry into the *'ulama*, to an enormous extent, is a matter of individual initiative, persistence, and, sometimes, luck. Historically, one could seek entrance into different madrasas (or religious schools) all over the Muslim world: the two most ancient, continuously functioning universities in the world are the Muslim universities of al-Azhar in Cairo and al-Karaouine in Fez, which was founded by a woman, Fatima al-Fihri, in 859 and can boast Maimonides as its most famous non-Muslim alumnus. The present-day Taliban's fundamentalist rigour derives from a Kandahar madrasa, and, though most adherents are Pashtun and non-Arab, their name derives from the Arabic word for "student." But one need not become an *'alim* ("knower," scholar) by going to a university. One can find an individual teacher or shaykh, or enter a small Islamic seminary, led by a *shaykh*, of recent or ancient provenance; the transmission of teaching between *shaykh* and student works very differently in Sunni, Shi'a, Sufi, and Isma'ili traditions. The Ayatollah Khomeini, one of the few *'ulama* ever to become a head of state, was the product of one such scholarly seminary.

Furthermore, one can become an *'alim* through an intuitive revelation from God, either directly or transmitted from teacher to teacher (this is a very strong tradition in Sufism). Or one can pursue stringent training in intellectual reasoning and precedence in one of the four medieval Sunni traditions of jurisprudence. The extent to which the very language of religious learning might determine or compromise its character was and is a topic of hot debate; many Muslims refuse to translate the Qur'ān, even if they speak no Arabic. Classical Arabic and its correct recitation have become part of the armament of knowledge. Holy men all over the Muslim world have been and are now praised and respected for such feats as the memorization of the whole Qur'ān and entire traditions of *hadith* (the sayings of the Prophet as witnessed and passed down through his Companions). Paul E. Walker emphasizes that the hadith promote "the value of knowledge, its reward and the duty to seek it, to gather and preserve it, to journey abroad in search of it."[4] It is in pursuit of these injunctions that the Muslim translators of the eighth and ninth centuries sought out, translated, preserved, and augmented a legacy of classical learning that would reshape western intellectual history from the tenth century on.

Closer to the purposes of this chapter, one could also seek knowledge by travelling to other lands, such as China and India in medieval times, or the West now. Two very different examples of this are Ibn Battuta, the early fourteenth-century traveller from the Maghrib whose perambulations of the medieval Muslim world took him on a journey three times the length of Marco Polo's and occupied the whole of his mature life; or the twentieth-century theorist of the Muslim Brotherhood movement, Sayyid Qutb, whose difficult experience of post-graduate work in the United States galvanized his critique of the West and his reinvention of what he considered the essential Muslim values.

Yet in the midst of all this epistemological urgency, the Qur'ān itself, the single most authoritative religious document for every Muslim across the board, sounds a warning note. In sura after sura, the Qur'ān admonishes that only God's knowledge counts: it is infinite and imponderable. All humanity can do is try to recognize it: *'arifa*; they cannot hope to actually *know* it with certainty: *'alama*. God is kind to his children, encoding his creation with signs of truth and offering them to humanity to make use of. However, looking for the signs God has left in the wonders of his creation becomes an experience of the fear of God, not a celebration of human capacity.

> It is he who made the sun a shining radiance and the moon a light, determining phases for it so that you might know the number of years and how to calculate time. God did not create all these without a true purpose; He explains his signs to those who understand. In the succession of night and day, and in what God created in the heavens and earth, there are truly signs for those who are aware of Him. Those who do not expect to meet Us and are pleased with the life of this world, contenting themselves with it and paying no heed to Our signs, shall have the Fire for their home because of what they used to do. (*Quran*, 10: 5–8)[5]

Here, the Qur'ān stresses the infinity of God's knowledge to the point that all human cognition dwindles virtually to futility, an "understanding" whose etiology remains in God's hands. The reading of God's signs becomes a matter less of cognizance but of a willed openness to recognition and worship.[6] Similar admonitions are found throughout the Qur'ān but loom with greatest urgency in Sura 18: the Sura of the Cave. This is also the sura, in which, by no accident, the enigmatic figure of Dhu'l-qarnayn – usually identified with Alexander the Great by medieval scholars – enters Islamic tradition at its most authoritative and enigmatic source.

## II The Sura of the Cave as Epistemological Warning

The Sura of the Cave transmits one of the most uncomfortable of all Muhammad's revelations.[7] The story of how it came to be written (its *asbab al-nuzul*, "reasons/circumstances for the revelation") reinforces the lesson of the sura itself. Ibn Ishaq's story of its background packs a double punch for those who think they have some control over knowledge, reminding them both of the immensity of God's knowledge and the puniness of human cognition. It originates in a hostile test of Muhammad's prophetic knowledge by his contemporaries and ends with one of God's harshest epistemological lessons to his beloved prophet.[8] The same story is carefully retold at the beginning of the *Qissat Dhulqarnayn*. The narrator of the Islamic Alexander romance evidently wants the reader to be thinking of what the prophet suffered to obtain the revelation of the Cave, as she reads about the campaigns of Dhu'l-qarnayn in his quest for the secrets of God.

Ibn Ishaq tells that the Sura of the Cave was revealed to Muhammad near the beginning of Muhammad's prophetic career, when he was still gradually receiving revelations from the angel Gabriel (Jibra'il) in Mecca and teaching them there, before his Night Journey, heavenly investiture, and emigration to Yathrib, later renamed Medina, to establish the first Muslim community. Muhammad was the orphaned son of one of the minor clans of the powerful Quraysh tribe and under the protection of his uncle, Abi Talib, but with little clan authority or influence himself. Thus his growing ministry and the numbers of converts to his new monotheism did not sit well with the shaykhs and elders of the Quraysh who ruled the city and region. Yet the more they attempted to nullify his influence, the more it spread, penetrating even the upper echelons of clan authority, and earning Muhammad more powerful protectors, until the Quraysh were bitterly divided among themselves. So the Quraysh called an assembly and those who spoke against Muhammad decided to send two envoys to Yathrib to ask the learned Jewish rabbis there to concoct a test of Muhammad's prophetic authority. They thus moved their challenge of Muhammad from the dangerous realm of intra-tribal politics to the more figuratively devastating one of epistemology. The Quraysh instructed their envoys: "Ask [the Rabbis] about Muhammad; describe him to them and tell them what he says, for they are the first people of the scriptures and have knowledge which we do not possess about the prophets."[9] In response, the rabbis devised their test – three big questions about abiding mysteries. If Muhammad could answer them, he would prove his prophethood, and if not, he would be discredited. The first question was about a young man who disappeared in ancient times (a reference to the story of the Sleepers of the Cave), and the third was about the soul. It is the second question that preoccupies this chapter. "Ask him about the mighty traveler who reached the confines of both East and West" (*Life of Muchammad*, 136). Who could this traveller be?

When the leaders of the Quraysh presented Muhammad with their questions, he sent them away, promising that he would have the answers on the following day. That night he waited for Gabriel and the angel did not come. The next day was also devoid of revelation, and the day after that – with increasing desperation, Muhammad temporized, while a full fifteen days passed. During this time "the people of Mecca began to spread evil reports, saying, 'Muhammad promised us an answer on the morrow, and today is the fifteenth day we have remained without an answer'" (*Life of Muchammad*, 136–7). When Gabriel finally turned up with the revelation on the fifteenth day, Muhammad reproached him: "You have shut yourself off from me, Gabriel, so that I have become apprehensive." The angel was unperturbed, "We descend only by God's command, whose is what lies before us, behind us, and what lies between, and thy Lord does not forget" (*Life of Muchammad*, 137). The angel also brought a scolding for the abashed prophet. "Say not of anything 'Verily I shall do that tomorrow," except if thou sayst, 'if God wills'" (*Life of Muchammad*, 137). (This incident and others like it are behind a phrase that to this day is endemic to all the Arab cultures, whatever their religion, *"in sha' allah."*) Only after Muhammad has been forced to realize his own helplessness to either put God on a schedule or know anything without guidance, can he glimpse the extent of God's infinite knowledge. Satisfied, Gabriel conveyed God's help, informing Muhammad of the revelations that are expressed in the Sura of the Cave.

This story, which underscores Muhammad's distress, draws attention to the dark, helpless, unenlightened space between question and answer, challenge and revelation; and more broadly between the richly overwritten pre-Islamic palimpsest of religious cultures and the slowly coalescing new religion. The difficult space of Islam's halting emergence becomes palpable in the extended discomfort of Muhammad himself.

To extend the discomfort further, the revelations brought by Gabriel in the Sura of the Cave are not so much answers, I will argue, as a further enforced realization of ignorance. They succeed in placing readers in the same uncomfortable gap between mystery and knowledge that Muhammad had to negotiate during those long weeks, waiting for the tardy angel. The revelation is as frustratingly enigmatic as it is revealing, and as we read the sura, we also are forced to realize our helplessness truly to know, unless God wills it.

In the Sura of the Cave, God assumes a storyteller's role, not to convey information but to dramatize his power to hide it. It consists of three stories (which answer the three questions) and two exempla, which reinforce the central lesson. The first story tells about the Sleepers of the Cave, as an example of human inability to encompass God's power even when it is personally experienced. Several youthful men of faith and a dog seek refuge in a cave from their sinful society. When they enter the cave, God "seals up their ears" (*fa darubna 'ala adhanihim*), putting them to sleep so that they retain no consciousness of the passing of time. As the centuries roll by, the sun rises and sets, playing eerily over their slowly turning bodies. When they wake, no one among them knows how long they have been there. When they send a representative out to the city to find out when they are, revealing their story to the wondering inhabitants, no one in the city knows who they are, or can agree on how to commemorate them. As time passes, even their number, which the sura does not specify, is forgotten and people dispute about it, making different counts – three, five, and seven – but always with the careful addition of the dog – a wonderful detail that shows how happily pedantry can bob afloat on a tide of complete ignorance.

The second story also underscores the enigmas of its telling. It recounts the tale of Musa and his servant, who are looking for the place where two seas meet. They lose their fish there (I know this sounds strange, but I'm trying to illustrate how allusive the story is), and on retracing their steps, encounter an unidentified "servant of God," who demonstrates to them how incapable Musa is of interpreting the "servant's" inexplicable actions, which nonetheless are seen to reflect God's will once they are explained.

The last story treats Dhu'l-qarnayn himself, a mysterious figure to whom God has "given the means to achieve all things" (*Qur'ān*, 18:84). He journeys to the uttermost West and East, working God's will, and builds the barrier between two mountains that will hem in Gog and Magog and preserve the local inhabitants from their depredations. This barrier will stand until God chooses to level it and unleash Judgment day upon the world.

In my reading, these three stories compose a potted history of human ignorance, spanning past, present, and future. The ancient story of the cave persists as an enigma – even at the time, the sleepers themselves had no idea what they were undergoing, and subsequent speculation as to what occurred has only intensified the historical mystery. The second story of Musa and the "servant of god" shows how God's plan for the world is invisible in the present: the inexplicable actions of "God's servant" rely for their rationale on privileged knowledge to which we, as well as Musa, have no access. Finally, in the third story we are shown that we cannot tell how God's judgment will be enacted in the future. Dhu'l-qarnayn is God's deputy but he only presages God's final judgments, working within a providential plan whose ultimate ends neither he nor any of us can predict or guess.

The sura's stories allude to the ancient, classical, legendary Arabic, Christian, and Jewish traditions with which the Jewish rabbis of Ibn Ishaq's tale were familiar (interestingly, in the *Qissat Dhulqarnayn*'s retelling, it is Christians who ask the questions). Their mysteries might be illuminated by reference to, for instance, Gilgamesh's search for Utnapishtim who lives at the source of two rivers, has the gift of eternal life himself, and knows about the plant of life with which Gilgamesh can save his beloved friend, Engkidu; or the Christian story of the seven sleepers of Ephesus; or the traditional Arabic figure of al-Khidr, which means "The Green Man," who comes to figure esoteric knowledge and the keeping of secrets in Arabic traditions;[10] or a story from the Jewish Midrash about the journey of Rabbi Joshua and Elijah, where Joshua's patience is tested by Elijah; as well as Greek, Syriac Christian, and Ethiopic versions of the Alexander romance itself – especially the story of Alexander and his cook Andreas and the spring of the waters of life. For as the sura weaves these tales together into its three central legendary exempla, it changes or erases names, amalgamates its sources in a deliberately obscure and allusive way, and omits vital bits of information even as it turns the stories to its own ends. By conveying these stories only partially, the sura forces readers to enact the ignorance that is its object lesson.

Essentially, in keeping its versions of the three stories enigmatic, the Sura of the Cave redoubles its performative power. On the one hand, the sura's tantalizing omissions tempt readers to seek illumination from other pre-existing legendary traditions, while, on the other, the sura intimates that the reader's curiosity to fill those gaps is already a transgression of the central lesson – not to probe beyond what God chooses to reveal. By resorting to sources and analogues for the Qur'ān, are we not indulging in exactly the kind of ignorant pedantry illustrated in the story of the Sleepers of the Cave, fussing about how many sleepers, (to say nothing of the dog!), questing beyond revealed knowledge, and indulging in unwarranted speculation? The sura, spoken by God in the first person, thus effectively enacts God's appropriative power over human narration, as it entices us to perform our own inability to understand even historical events, let alone God's signs and mysteries. The sura almost taunts the reader at one point: "That was one of God's signs. He whom God guides is rightly guided but he whom He confounds shall find no friend to guide him" (*Qur'ān*, 18:17).

However, this Qur'ānic warning to wait upon God's guidance was an impossible one for the emergent Islamic writers to heed, either for this sura or many others. Early Muslim commentators and the isra'iliyyat writers of the *qisas* sought Christian, Jewish, and classical writings, both canonical and legendary, to fill some of the gaps the Qur'ān refused to close. They rapidly identified the Musa of the second story with the Midrashic and Christian Moses and identified the unnamed "servant of god" with the legendary prophet, al-Khidr, whom God had gifted with knowledge other than he gave Moses.[11] The commentators and isra'iliyyat writers identified the mysterious Dhu'l-qarnayn of the third story with Alexander the Great – particularly the ascetic and pious Alexander available to the seventh-century Arabic world in Syriac Christian versions of Pseudo-Callisthenes. However, if Dhu'l-qarnayn of the third story is identified with Alexander the Great, a strange inconsistency emerges, because the second story also traces its roots back not only to the Midrashic Moses, but to versions of the Alexander romance where Alexander comes upon the water of life, and does not realize it, while his cook observes the fish's resurrection, and gains immortality.[12] In these, Alexander, far from being God's instrument, is ignorant of God's plans for the world and is there precisely to lose the chance at immortality. In fact, knowledge of the Alexander romance places the reader in a dilemma of her own fashioning. What kind of authority are we to attribute to Alexander the Great? Are we to take as definitive the last story, where he is God's empowered instrument, or should we qualify it by our knowledge of the analogues of the second story where he serves as an exemplar of human ignorance; it amounts to making a choice between pagan and Islamic traditions. Have we gone too far even by making the identification of Dhu'l-qarnayn with Alexander? How much can we know about the elusive figure of Dhu'l-qarnayn and where can we search for that knowledge without straying from received knowledge to futile speculation?

This essential tension seen here in this small example – between the need to know as much as possible, precisely in order to interpret God's revelation and the sura's injunction to wait for God's guidance – runs through the entire history of Islamic epistemology and helps constitute its major movements. It is precisely through such epistemological dilemmas that Islam continually reconstitutes itself as a religion at issue, a dynamic tradition. Looking at any Islamic topic today confirms its ferociously contested nature. And this conflict plays out over time; Islamic intellectual history comes to comprise a series of expansions and contractions; explosions of ecumenical translation and learning such as that which occurred in Baghdad under the Abbasids, or in al-Andalus, as well as in a multitude of localized expansions wherever scholars from different traditions could find patronage and protection and draw upon the resources of the many cultures under Islamic rule to fill gaps and drive their paradigms forward. Conversely, periods of intellectual syncretism could be succeeded by periods of contraction and internal regime building, as Islamic scholars established their own, often competing literary, judicial, theological, and popular traditions, and declared Islam's independence from the traditions of the other cultures and religions that had previously informed it. At other times, contraction was brought on by political changes or successful fundamentalist movements, as when the Almoravids, Almohads, or scholars such as Ibn Taymiyya attempted to draw the Muslim *umma* (the nation) back to the essentials of Qur'ān, hadith, and sunna, the three most respected sources of religious authority – themselves continually interpreted, contested, and recombined, working out through various distinct traditions of jurisprudential interpretation (*fiqh*). At such times, Muslim scholars, writers, and rulers worked to purge Islam of "non-Islamic" elements, calling for a return to the desert stringencies of exclusively Islamic origins, which themselves underwent continual reinvention in the process. This "combined and uneven development" of intellectual syncretism and retraction continues to produce both the conflicts between different Islamic traditions that we see at work in the world today and the staying power of Islam as a complex of evolving traditions.

In the area of Islamic non-fictional literature, this rhythm of syncretism and contraction has fascinating implications for a figure like Alexander or Dhu'l-qarnayn, whose story circulated in so many forms: pagan, Christianized, Judaized, and authoritatively Islamized in the Qur'ān. In the first centuries of Islam, many Muslim scholars worked in an analogous way to the Christian typologists who recast the Jewish scriptures into Old Testament prefigurations of their own new gospel. Early Muslim writers combed through ancient, classical, Jewish, and Christian traditions to construct teleologies prefiguring the inevitable truth of Islam. The line of major biblical prophets, including Jesus and culminating with Muhammad, had already been assembled. But these isra'iliyyat writers also appropriated exemplary figures from many pre-Islamic cultures, and made them into minor prophets avant la lettre sent by God as a mercy to the diverse peoples of the world, so that no people should be wholly without knowledge. Scholars such as Ka 'ab al-Ahbar, Wahb ibn Munabbih, and, later, al-Tabarī, 'Umara, and al-Tha'labi rewrote the lives of pre-Islamic figures – including Alexander – and gathered them together into collections: *Qiṣaṣ al-anbiyā'* (Stories of the Prophets).[13] It is in these *qisas* collections that Alexander becomes a Muslim prophet, along with legendary figures such as Hud, Jirjis (St George) and the Sleepers of the Cave. Together, the *qisas* collections negotiate the belatedness of Islam in reference to the previous monotheisms by showing how Islam was always present in the world and its truths were available to many nations from the very beginning. Later, once Islam had established its independence and strength, many Muslim scholars abandoned and expunged these extra-Islamic sources as unreliable, castigating the early isra'iliyyat writers, and those commentators who transmitted them. They reduced the authoritative canon to the Qur'ān, the hadith, and the sunna, effectively Arabizing an Islam that had been previously been more ecumenical.

Within this contested territory, it becomes particularly difficult to deal with the figure of Dhu'l-qarnayn, who has one foot in the Qur'ān, and the other in virtually every monotheism and polytheism to stray across the globe. The interpretative uneasiness created by the Sura of the Cave – especially about the character of Dhu'l-qarnayn and his relationship to God's providential history – cast a long shadow across subsequent representations of Dhu'l-qarnayn within Islamic homiletic and romance literature. While some commentators read the Qur'ān as authorizing Dhu'l-qarnayn as Alexander the Great by his very inclusion, the most authoritative Sunni commentator and collector of hadith, al-Bukhari (d. 869), is significantly reticent about him, reiterating only that God empowered Dhu'l-qarnayn to do what he had to do, without trying to identify him with Alexander. Z. David Zuwiyya, the editor of the *Qissat Dhulqarnayn*, includes a tremendously learned, extensive, and persuasive survey of Arabic and Aljamiado versions of the Alexander romance.[14] Zuwiyya argues that the uneasiness with Alexander intensified as Islamic knowledge of classical culture grew. Muslim writers, hitherto familiar only with the idealized, monotheistic Alexander of Christian Syriac recensions, came to discover the full range of classical writing on Alexander, where Alexander often figured worldly ambition, luxury, and superbia, a promoter of Greek pagan culture rather than monotheism. As a result, Muslim writers became uncomfortable with the traditional identification of the Qur'ānic Dhu'l-qarnayn with Alexander of Macedon. Some proposed other identifications, lighting instead upon Cyrus of Persia, a biblical conquering saviour. Others gave Dhu'l-qarnayn a 1,600-year lifespan with a conversion in the middle of it: the rash world conqueror learning the limits of his ambition and turning to asceticism in his old age. Some writers, such as 'Umara and al-Tabarī (d. 923 AD) separated him into two figures: first came Dhu'l-qarnayn the miracle-working servant of God, to be followed centuries later by Dhu'l-qarnayn, the pagan world-conqueror of Pseudo-Callisthenes.[15]

However, Zuwiyya shows that as Muslim historiographical learning expanded, it became clear that the pious Alexander of the Syriac traditions had actually derived from the historical Alexander of the Greek tradition, and the two Alexanders came together again in the eleventh-century *Ara'is al-majalis fi Qisas al-anbiya'* of al-Tha'labi: who reconciles them by telling a tale of a conqueror who had a midlife revelation and became a devout servant of God, or prophet. Al-Tha'labi's version laid important groundwork for later versions of the Arabic Alexander. In al-Tha'labi, Dhu'l-qarnayn is still an instrument of God, a prophet before Muhammad – but a second-class one. Unlike the great Islamic prophets, he is not sent into the world with a crucial mission, but rather given his mission within the world. He is instructed not by the angel Gabriel, but by a lower angel in the Muslim hierarchy, Raphael. He is divinely empowered but fallible, and subsequent Arabic versions of his story, including the *Qissat Dhulqarnayn*, often show how his quest for more knowledge leads him to presume against God's mysteries.

Ultimately, the abiding uneasiness about Dhu'l-qarnayn led to his expulsion from the higher echelons of Islamic religious and literary culture. Instead, versions of Alexander's story circulated at the frontiers of the Islamic literary world in *qisas* collections, *sirah* cycles, popular romances, and oral tales, some of which made their way into the ever expanding story collection of *Alf Layla wa Layla* ("The Thousand and One Nights"), whose earliest extant manuscript dates from the fourteenth century. Many of the extant Islamic Alexander romances originate from the ex-centric regimes of al-Andalus, or Persia, including the *Shāh-nāma* of Firdausī, and the *Iskandar-nāma* of Niẓāmī. Among these, the *Qissat Dhulqarnayn* is remarkable both for its subtle management of the cultural dilemma presented by its hero and its return to the original Qur'ānic lesson of the Cave.

## III *The Qissat Dhulqarnayn*: A World in God's Hand

The *Qissat Dhulqarnayn* anchors itself back to the roots of Islam at every opportunity. It begins by recounting the *asbab al-nuzul* of the Sura of the Cave, the story of Muhammad and the three questions. It prefaces each narrative episode with an *isnad*, a chain of authoritative transmitters leading back to one of Muhammad's companions. In fact it pointedly refuses to smooth over disagreements between transmitters at several points – for instance, the nations of Gog and Magog are actually enclosed twice at different points in its narration. It thus displays respect for hadith writers by refusing to judge, collate, or select between authoritative sources in service of a unified narrative. However, for all this show of respect, as Zuwiyya points out, the *Qissat Dhulqarnayn* does not cite the most trustworthy transmitters. It is not, therefore, intended to fool scholars intimately familiar with the weak links in its *isnads:* it neither aims at nor achieves religious authority. Nonetheless, I would argue that it engages in a species of what we might call literary theology. It systematically works through the disjunction between the Qur'ānic focus on human ignorance and the Islamic need to seek more knowledge – the Muslim duty of Talab al-'ilm – and it uses an Islamized Alexander figure to do it.

It prefaces itself with the story of the Muhammad and the three questions precisely, I would argue, because it is about to tell an analogous story: of empowerment, presumption, and rebuke. Accordingly, the first part of the *Qissat Dhulqarnayn* empowers Dhu'l-qarnayn's quest for knowledge and his efforts to bring Islam to the world and discover as much as he can of the wonders of God's creation. However, the second part of the narrative rebukes this ambition and instructs Dhu'l-qarnayn about his human limitations. Lest the comparison between a pagan conqueror and Muhammad, the enormously respected "Seal of the Prophets," seem presumptuous, it is important to note that it was never claimed of Muhammad that he was infallible – the Sura of the Cave itself poignantly demonstrates this.

Furthermore, the narrative itself forges likenesses between the two figures. While it never settles the question of whether Dhu'l-qarnayn is a prophet, it does make gestures. Dhu'l-qarnayn is a "Friend of God" if not his messenger. Moreover, after Dhu'l-qarnayn builds Alexandria (in Arabic, Iskendariyya), the narrative pauses to tell us that: "His name in Greek was Alexander (in Arabic, Iskandar) and in Arabic it was Ahmad b. Asas."[16] The identification of Dhu'l-qarnayn with Alexander is necessary here to explain the name of the city. But at this risky moment when the narrative most explicitly invokes the perplexed literary heritage of the pagan world-conqueror, it swiftly refamiliarizes its hero with an illustrious and unassailably Muslim name. Ahmad is derived from the same Arabic root as Muhammad, and they both mean "praiseworthy." (In fact Ahmad is the comparative form, meaning "more praiseworthy.") Other analogies between conqueror and prophet follow. After studying with Aristotle and gaining a reputation for wisdom and right rule, Dhu'l-qarnayn, like Muhammad, receives visits from the angel Zayaqil (probably a corruption of Rafa'il, who is several steps below Gabriel in the Muslim order of angels).

Even more suggestively, like Muhammad, Dhu'l-qarnayn begins the active world-changing part of his campaign with a visionary flight to the heavens.

> God had ordered Zayaqil [the angel Raphael] to be a good friend to Dhu'l-qarnayn ... He came to him one day when he was sitting on his marble throne looking at the lighthouse he had built [in the Alexandrian harbor]. The angel greeted him and he returned the greeting with great happiness. The angel Zayaqil tucked him under his wing and flew with him into the air for an hour according to earthly time. Then he [Zayaqil] pulled his [Dhu'l-qarnayn's] head out from beneath the wing and said, "Look at the earth. What do you see?" Dhu'l-qarnayn said, "I see my city and the cities around it." ... Again Zayaqil flew for as long as God willed and then stopped and said, "Look at the earth and tell me what you see." He said, "I see my city alone with nothing around it but the seas." It was surrounded by the waters and looked like an island in the depths of a deep green sea. The angel said, "O Dhu'l-qarnayn, what you see is not your city but the entire earth. It is surrounded by the sea. Know, Dhu'l-qarnayn, that the earth is an island in the middle of the sea. You could compare it to a boat sailing on the high seas. The sea [bears up] the island just as it [bears up] a boat. The force behind this lifting is the power of God. O Dhu'l-qarnayn, verily, you should be amazed at the power of your Lord and Creator." Dhu'l-qarnayn replied, "Dear Zayaqil, certainly what I see with my own eyes amazes me. Indeed, after such a vision I testify that there is no [god but God] and that He is One without companion." (*Islamic Legends*, 11–12/72–3)[17]

However, there are fascinating differences between Muhammad's visionary flight and Dhu'l-qarnayn's. In Muhammad's vision, Gabriel escorts him to each of the seven heavens and formally introduces him to his prophetic forebears – he actually comes face to face with the glorious alterity that is God (astonishing Moses, who thought he was the only one ever to have that experience). During Muhammad's flight to heaven, he was given a pre-eminent place in the line of prophets, and works out with God (and some canny bargaining advice from Moses) a new, more merciful dispensation as to how monotheism should be practised. By contrast, Dhu'l-qarnayn is told repeatedly to look down, back to the world, which he misrecognizes (prophetically, it turns out) as his own city. Dhu'l-qarnayn is kept tucked under Zayaqil's wing, only poking out his head from time to time, and is held up by the angel with the same power and tenderness with which God bears up the land in the midst of the sea. The earth is given to him, in the act of seeing it, but it is given in the recognition that both he and it are tiny fragile things, kept from destruction by God's power alone.

That power is not to be underestimated, however. God keeps his word. The miracles begin immediately. Jesus (the prophet who immediately precedes Muhammad in Islamic tradition) walks on water once. Dhu'l-qarnayn spends most of this narrative marching across the surface of the sea from island to island, sinking tent pegs and hobbling horses on the heaving waves (on one memorable morning, "dawn broke and the troops gazed out at the horizon and looked into the depths of the sea [and] were in awe at the power of the Almighty God" [102]). Every day God empowers Dhu'l-qarnayn to cover the distance other men would take a whole year to cross. God never withdraws this support, whatever Dhu'l-qarnayn does.[18] The spectacle of so much empowerment, in fact, virtually short-circuits the need for military display; Dhu'l-qarnayn fights fewer battles in this narrative than in virtually any of the other Alexander stories I've read (though Darius and Porus [here called Labur] turn up to be trounced, almost as interruptions, in the middle of the narrative. Yet while disdaining warfare, the *Qissat Dhulqarnayn* has its own very large task to attend to. It replaces the world's conquest with a fascinated exploration of its sheer immensity and profound history. Thus Dhu'l-qarnayn's inaugural vision of the tiny familiar boat-world borne up by God's power, stretches open to the discovery of an impossibly large, layered, world, filled with races and histories that extend backward even before Eden.[19]

The breadth and depth of this world allows the narrative, I argue, to grapple with the belatedness of Islam. Like many of the other tales of the *qisas* genre, the *Qissat Dhulqarnayn* narrates a conquest of lands in order to perform a conquest of history, in which every figure of wisdom and learning, some strange beyond belief (and their very estrangement helps broaden the narrative's acquisitive reach), comes to witness to the truth, not just of an essential monotheism, but an explicit and eloquent Islam. The narrative resolves the historical anachronism in an episode that also meditates upon the narrative's own appropriative strategies. On the very first island Dhu'l-qarnayn reaches, he finds a magnificent castle of red, white, and green marble (the allegorist in me wants to say that these diverse colours represent the different monotheistic religious traditions – all together in one edifice, but I really have nothing to base this on). The castle, however, has two parts: a bottom section with a door that whirls perpetually around on a spiral and cannot be entered, and an upper part that also starts whirling when it is approached (no elephants – á la Candace's bedchamber – are apparent). Dhu'l-qarnayn asks Zayaqil how he might enter it. The angel tells him:

> Go and build a similar castle, except make yours out of wood. Construct it so that there are boards the length of a man's arm stretched out that protrude from the sides of the castle. Be sure to make your castle taller than the other one. Bring the two castles together and attack. The revolving doors will be jammed by the boards extending out from the sides of your castle, and the castle will become vulnerable. The password to get in is the testimony (shahada): "There is no god but God and Muhammad is the messenger of God." (*Islamic Legends*, 15–76)

Here the narrative both confronts and creatively resolves the problem of Islam's belatedness. As I read it, and forgive me if this reeks of allegoresis, the castle is like the bastion of history itself, a spiralling, impregnable heterogeneity, that excludes all comers both from the intricacies of its mechanisms and the secret it contains. At its centre, it becomes evident, is locked a truth that has been immanent in history from before its inception. Dhu'l-qarnayn is empowered to build his own replica, a sturdy double, that despite a less permanent construction, can overtop, attack, and jam the fortress, halting its turning, and revealing that the truth locked at its centre is the truth of Islam. It is as though the belated, ungainly, protruding prolepsis that constitutes the whole *qisas* genre, is made here, not into a poor copy but a means of self-insertion. And sure enough, in the castle, in a locked chest, on an inscribed tablet, that evokes the ark of the covenant but is far, far older, is a testimony from the pre-Adamic race called the Yanuni, that tells the story of Muhammad, the prophet who, historically, is still 900 years in Dhu'l-qarnayn's future. It is here that Dhu'l-qarnayn becomes not only a friend of God, and a sign to the world of God's miraculous power, but an actual Muslim.

Yet because the narrative is so very interested in showing the eternal immanence of the truth of Islam in the world, there is a sense in which Dhu'l-qarnayn's mission becomes futile. In no way does he pre-empt Muhammad's future work. Rather he circumnavigates a world where the recognition of God's singularity and power is already manifest in a stunning variety of ways. Time and time again, Dhu'l-qarnayn presents the people he encounters with a pious ultimatum: that they must testify to the unity (*tawhid*) of God, effectively declaring the *shahada*, the first pillar of Islam. However, many of the people Dhu'l-qarnayn encounters have no difficulty in making this testament because they already know it. In fact, as he encounters stranger and stranger people – the pre-Adamic race of the Yanuni, the large-eared attenuated people of Tarish, the Bani Mansik whose men have eyes running vertically in their elongated faces – Dhu'l-qarnayn discovers that many of them already believe in the one God. In this way, the image of wonderfully sheltered flight tucked beneath the angel's wings that inaugurates Dhu'l-qarnayn's journey becomes an accurate forecast of it. However far he reaches, he cannot circumvent the angel's embrace; he encounters a world where God's messengers have always been sent out. In response to this, Dhu'l-qarnayn gradually transforms from a conquering monotheist on jihad to the student he used to be. Dhu'l-qarnayn's work, the only work not entirely claimed and, so to speak, post-empted by his more illustrious future namesake, is the work of coming to know the world, and through it, its Creator. Accordingly Dhu'l-qarnayn becomes an incarnation of Talab al-'ilm, eagerly seeking more knowledge about the multitude of ways that incredibly diverse human, pre-human, and superhuman societies bear witness to the singular power of God in the world.[20]

At the same time, however, the discovery of an encrypted Islam at the beginning of Dhu'l-qarnayn's journey creates a more fundamental problem that deepens towards its end. The narrative maintains that God has continually sent prophets to the world, tenderly caring for his creation for longer than the human race has been in existence. In that case, why does he hide the final, most crucial testimony of Islam in a remote castle where only the privileged few can penetrate? Even more troublingly, given the importance of that inaugural discovery, what *else* might he be hiding? We know he is keeping secrets. There is a Land of Darkness on earth, and a Lotus tree of the Ultimate Boundary in heaven.[21] Why, in short, does God withhold revelation when it is so desperately needed? What does he hold in store? Here, it seems, the narrative both responds to the anxieties of its own historical self insertions – and returns us with a vengeance to the uncomfortable epistemological suspensions of the Sura of the Cave.

These questions come to a head in the narrative episode of the Land of Darkness and the figure of al-Khidr who emerges there from among Dhu'l-qarnayn's groping, desperate advisors as the only one to receive God's revelation. This episode dramatizes the contrast between the effortless grace of direct revelation from God, on the one hand, and, on the other, the canniest, trickiest strategies of knowledge-management that Dhu'l-qarnayn can assemble, using all the resources at his disposal – and

Dhu'l-qarnayn's resources are considerable, including an angel, peerless advisors, and a magical instrument of illumination. He knows (and is repeatedly told) that God put the Darkness there to keep people out, but this only galvanizes him. The Land of Darkness rises before him "like a locked house or dungeon" (*Islamic Legends* 129–72) – another fortress of secrets – but Dhu'l-qarnayn prepares to penetrate it with a reconnoitering savvy that puts to shame his feeble (in this narrative) military strategems. First he finds out from Zayaqil the topographical features. Then he doublechecks this information against the independent testimony of his advisor Afshakhir. He has not one but two plans for finding his way out of the darkness. The first is the trick with virgin mares that can be found in virtually all the other versions of the Alexander romance that include this episode. The second concerns the mysterious, all-illuminating bead of the prophets that has come down to him through many hands from Noah.[22] He delegates the power of this bead to al-Khidr whom he orders to lead the column into the Darkness – and in so doing, he separates himself from illumination.[23] In an end-run around Dhu'l-qarnayn and all the apparatus he can muster, God sends Gabriel (not just Zayaqil – this is the real deal) to al-Khidr, to tell him the way to the well of life, where he performs the ritual ablutions and becomes immortal. Since al-Khidr is associated in the *qisas* tales with esoteric knowledge and the keeping of fatal secrets,[24] his gaining of immortality here amounts to his personal transformation into the last earthly fortress for God's hidden knowledge. The scene is remarkable for the brilliant counterplay between al-Khidr's detached and steadfast illumination and the panic of Dhu'l-qarnayn and his men, abandoned in the darkness.

> al-Khidr walked and stopped at the well. He did the ritual ablutions and drank from it, beneath the light of the bead. Meanwhile the people peered into the darkness, hoping the bead would reappear, as time passed slowly ... He put the bead back on the tip of his lance, rode, and left the bank of the river. Soon the bead appeared to the people and they followed it ... So they marched quickly in pursuit until they came to the riverbed. Word spread among them and they said, "There is no doubt that al-Khidr, when he left us, was at this riverbed. Certainly, Dhu'l-qarnayn, this is the middle of the darkness . . . ." Dhu'l-qarnayn said to his companions, "Hurry, let's get out of this darkness." (*Islamic Legends*, 131–73)

Here in the hands of al-Khidr, the secret of immortality is safe forever, hidden in light and silence rather than darkness, at once illuminated and rendered utterly and permanently impenetrable. Before this final "locked house or dungeon," Dhu'l-qarnayn, who exemplifies the best epistemological expertise that any human being could assemble, is left groping in the dark.

Dhu'l-qarnayn receives the rebuke for his presumption in a castle on the other side of the Darkness, far beyond the last human city and in the shadow of the world-circling Mount Qaf. This castle marks a final uttermost boundary not only in earthly space, but earthly time; it is filled with intimations of Judgment Day. Its lower level contains a terrifying, upside-down bird who figures the anti-Christ and swells almost to bursting though the castle walls when Dhu'l-qarnayn tells him of the sin at work in the world (it shrinks back down again when Dhu'l-qarnayn tells him that Muslims are still faithful throughout the world – so, thank goodness for prolepsis). Its upper level contains the horn-blowing angel who will signal Judgment, with one eye perpetually on the heavens, just waiting for the word.[25] The angel gives Dhu'l-qarnayn a little stone which is both a figure and a lesson for Dhu'l-qarnayn himself. When the stone is set in a scale, it outweighs whatever is put in the balance, no matter how heavy. And yet when al-Khidr puts a handful of earth as a counterweight, the stone rises easily. Al-Khidr tells Dhu'l-qarnayn that the stone figures Dhu'l-qarnayn's insatiable appetite, for land, knowledge, and secrets, primed to swallow the whole world, but itself ultimately to be overcome by mortality. From this episode to the ending of the romance, the *Qissat Dhulqarnayn* dwells upon this lesson, dramatizing Dhu'l-qarnayn's struggle to resist it, and finally his acceptance of it. This acceptance of mortality constitutes, paradoxically, the only comfort that the narrative can offer, both its readers and the searchers after knowledge in the Sura of the Cave, because it takes Dhu'l-qarnayn a further step from seeking knowledge to finding wisdom.

This wisdom emerges most poignantly at the narrative's end, when Dhu'l-qarnayn prepares his mother to accept his death in a scene that expands Pseudo-Callisthenes's mention of Alexander's comforting his mother before he dies, by narrating Dhu'l-qarnayn's beautiful letter to her which treats death as a part of a beneficent natural cycle.[26] More performatively, Alexander instructs his mother to throw a great banquet after his death, but invite no one who has not lost a loved one. We get a rare glimpse into Muslim women's culture, as al-Ghayda, the narrative's Olympias, sends to all of the women of the kingdom, rich and poor, to come to her banquet. But as they pass the threshold, she asks them: "Are you grieving the loss of someone?" And as every one of them answers yes, she has lost a son, a daughter, a father, a brother, al-Ghayda realizes that no one can come to this banquet, but, more importantly, that she is not mourning alone. Here, the *Qissat Dhulqarnayn* at least tenders some small comfort for the dilemma of the Islamic Alexander and the Sura of the Cave. We are all in the same mortal and epistemological quandary, but we are at least all there together. The question is: how will we respond to it?

Ultimately, the narrative's refusal or inability to answer this question allows it to gesture at a final secret, the secrets of our own hearts and the mysteries of our own choices. In view of this, I would like to end with two particularly pregnant little episodes that interrupt al-Kisai's narration of the second story of the Sura of the Cave – the story of Moses and al-Khidr. The first meditates upon the enormity of God's knowledge and our tiny opportunistic access to it, the second questions the uses of knowledge itself. Both incidents speak to the epistemological dilemmas that the *Qissat Dhulqarnayn* negotiates.

The first episode offers a grain of comfort in the face of the enormity of God's knowledge; it is the story of Moses and the sea bird.

> When [Moses and al-Khidr] were walking along the shore, suddenly a bird drew near, plunged its beak into the sea and flew away toward the East. Then it returned and plunged again, but this time flew toward the West. Again it returned and cried out.
>
> "Do you know what this bird is saying?" al-Khidr asked Moses.
>
> "No," he replied.
>
> "He says," continued al-Khidr, "That the knowledge which has been given the children of Adam is analogous to the amount of water he has taken in his beak from the sea." And Moses was astounded. (al-Kisai, *Tales of the Prophets*, 248)

This story, once again, reiterates the Qur'ānic lesson that the ocean of God's knowledge is vast and our capacities for receiving it tiny. However, it also naturalizes the processes by which that knowledge is continually being distributed to the East and the West. The bird's cry is what interests me, in the moment before al-Khidr's translation. Is it a warning, a taunt, or a plea to follow it? It is rewarding to choose to see that cry as a plea to follow the bird to the East and the West; and it is this regathering of God's dispersed knowledge that the *Qissat Dhulqarnayn* ultimately attempts through the ambitious but always God-upheld explorations of its hero. Even when Dhu'l-qarnayn trespasses on God's secrets, his empowerment acknowledges that he is doing God's work.

However, the second incident from al-Kisai is more cautionary:

> Moses then walked along the shore, where he found tablets of gold, on which was written:
>
> "In the name of God the Compassionate the Merciful
> There is no god but God
> Muhammad is the Apostle of God.
> How strange it is that one who believes in fate and destiny could be angry or frivolous.
> How strange it is that one who knows he will die could rejoice.
> How strange it is that one who is certain of the transitoriness of this world
> and sees the vicissitudes amongst its people could be tranquil at heart"
> Moses put down the tablets and returned to the children of Israel.
>
> (al-Kisai, *Tales of the Prophets*, 250)

This episode is mysterious. It seems to meditate on the way that knowledge completely fails to affect human behaviour and emotions in any way – and sometimes that is not a terrible thing. Ultimately it questions pessimistically whether there is any point at all to knowing, since we react to the world not according to but despite our knowledge of its few certainties: destiny, death, and change. The palpable weight of the reminder of mortality and transition on these golden tablets – a valuable but very heavy knowledge that underscores knowledge's limits – sends Moses home away from al-Khidr, ending his search for any knowledge other than the revelations that God has given to him and returning him to his mission to the children of Israel. This incident echoes the similar turn to mortality taken at the end of the *Qissat Dhulqarnayn*, but the *Qissat Dhulqarnayn* makes that turn at once more chillingly intimate – as it is inscribed on Dhu'l-qarnayn's body – and more comforting, not graven on tablets that defamiliarize human emotion in the face of mortality, but rather enacted in the love between Dhu'l-qarnayn and his mother al-Ghayda. Here, I believe, we can investigate the full utility of Dhu'l-qarnayn to a Muslim audience as an almost prophet whose ambiguous ancestry and understandable, even salutary, avidities for the knowledge of what God has hidden can be sympathetically explored. And through Dhu'l-qarnayn, we can see how at least one late medieval Muslim writer assimilated a classical figure to explore an abiding problem in Islamic faith: the need to know God and his world.

NOTES

1 Whether and what kind a prophet he is itself is a matter of debate in these stories: al Tha'labi's version makes this clear: "Scholars have differed about his prophethood. It has been related that the Prophet said, "I do not know whether or not Dhu'l-qarnayn was a prophet." If that tradition is correct, then dealing with this question is hypocritical. But they still differed over it and people said: He was not a prophet but only a pious servant (of God) and a just and righteous ruler). Others said: on the contrary, he was a prophet not sent with a message" (609): *Ara'is al-majalis fi Qisas al-anbiya', or Lives of the Prophets*, trans. William M. Brinner (Leiden: Brill, 2002), 605–21.

2 See Paul E. Walker, "Knowledge," in *Encyclopedia of the Quran*, Vol. 3, ed. Jane Dammen McAuliffe (Leiden: Brill Academic Publishers, 2003), 100–4. Franz Rosenthal shows how knowledge, in addition to being associated with light, revelation, and faith itself in various Sunni, Shi'a, and Sufi traditions, is also widely vaunted for its social utility: *Knowledge Triumphant: The Concept of Knowledge in Medieval Islam*, Brill Classics in Islam, Vol. 2 (Leiden and Boston: Brill, 2007), 318–33.

3 See Michael Cook's magisterial study for how profoundly this responsibility underlies questions both of individual activism and social justice throughout the Islamic cultures, and across different schools of Islamic jurisprudence and interpretation: Michael Cook, *Commanding Right and Forbidding Wrong in Islamic Thought* (Cambridge: Cambridge University Press, 2000).

4 Walker, "Knowledge," (see note 2), 100.

5 All quotations from the Qur'ān are taken from the Oxford edition unless noted otherwise: *The Qur'ān*, trans. Muhammad A.S. Abdel Haleem (Oxford: Oxford University Press, 2004).

6 Walker, "Knowledge," (see note 2); Rosenthal, *Knowledge Triumphant*, (see note 2), 108–29, shows how complex the problem of God's knowledge became to Muslim theologists; he concludes "the general view universally entertained among Muslims certainly was that God's knowledge was something different, and, we may add, something rather oppressive from the human point of view. The idea of the existence of such overpowering

divine knowledge could hardly have been a source of inspiration for feeble human efforts at acquiring knowledge" (128).

7 Bruce Fudge usefully analyses a variety of commentaries on al-Kahf while searching for a unifying theme: "The Men of the Cave: Tafsir, Tragedy and Tawfiq al-Hakim," *Arabica* 54:1 (2007), 67–93. For other useful analyses of the sura's analogues, themes and intertexts, see: Hosna Abdel Samie, "Textual Relations in *Srat al-Kahf*," *Journal of Qur'anic Studies* 9:2 (2007), 189–246; Ian Richard Netton, "Toward a Modern *Tafsr* of *Srat al-Kahf*: Structure and Semiotics," *Journal of Qur'anic Studies* 2:1 (2000), 67–87.

8 This account is derived from Ibn Hisham's epitome of Ibn Ishaq's (d. 721) *Sirat Rasul Allah* ("Life of God's Messenger"), the earliest known biography of Muhammad; see Alfred Guillaume, *The Life of Muchammad: A Translation of Ishaq's "Sirat Rasul Allah"* (Karachi: Oxford University Press, 1955), 136–9; Gordon Darnell Newby, *The Making of the Last Prophet: A Reconstruction of the Earliest Biography of Muhammad* (Columbia: University of South Carolina Press, 1989) and Martin Lings, *Muhammad: His Life Based on the Earliest Sources*, 2nd ed. (Rochester, VT: Inner, 1983, 1991, 2006).

9 Guillaume, *The Life of Muchammad* (see note 8), 136.

10 See al-Tha'labī, *Lives of the Prophets* (see note 1), 361–82.

11 See al-Kisai's version and the account from one of the most important early collectors of *hadith*, Sahih al Bukhari. Comparing them with the Quranic account reveals how many narrative gaps these later writers filled: Muhammad Ibn 'Abd Allah al-Kisai, *Tales of the Prophets*, trans. Wheeler M. Thackston (Chicago: Great Books of the Islamic World, Inc., 1997), 247–50; Sahih al-Bukhari, *The Book of Knowledge*, trans. Muhammad Muhsin Khan (Medina: Islamic University, 1985), 1:63–6.

12 "We came to a place where there was a clear spring, whose water flashed like lightning, and some other springs besides. The air in this place was very fragrant and less dark than before. I [Alexander] was hungry and wanted some bread, so I called the cook Andreas by name and said, "Prepare some food for us." He took a dried fish and waded into the clear water of the spring to wash it. As soon as it was dipped in the water, it came to life and leapt out of the cook's hands. He was frightened, and did not tell me what had happened; instead, he drank some of the water himself, and scooped some up in a silver vessel and kept it. The whole place was abounding in water, and we drank of its various streams. Alas for my misfortune, that it was not fated for me to drink of the spring of immortality, which gives life to what is dead, as my cook was fortunate enough to do." Pseudo-Callisthenes, *The Greek Alexander Romance*, trans. Richard Stoneman (Harmondsworth: Penguin, 1991), 121.

13 The relevance of the isra'iliyyat writers to the *Qissat Dhulqarnayn* is helpfully laid out in Zuwiyya's edition, and this part of my argument draws heavily on his account: Z. David Zuwiyya, *Islamic Legends Concerning Alexander the Great* (Binghamton, NY: Global Publications, 2001), especially 1–42.

14 Zuwiyya covers the Dhulqarnayn traditions deriving from Tales of the Prophets. However other Alexander stories are extant and popular in Arabic oral and written forms. For a useful overview, see *The Alexander Romance in Persia and the East*, ed. Richard Stoneman et al. (Groningen: Barkhuis Publishing and Groningen University Library, 2012); Richard Stoneman, "Alexander the Great and the Arabic Tradition," in *The Ancient Novel and Beyond*, ed. Stelios Panayotakis et al. (Leiden: Brill, 2003), 3–22; as well as the extensive scholarship of Faustina Doufikar-Aerts: *Alexander Magnus Arabicus. A Survey of the Alexander Tradition Through Seven Centuries, from Pseudo-Callisthenes to Suri*, Mediaevalia Groningana n.s. 13 (Louvain: Peeters, 2010); "'Afin que jamais il ne tombe dans l'oubli': influences arabes sur l'historiographie occidentale d'Alexandre," in *L'historiographie médiévale d'Alexandre le Grand*, ed. Catherine Gaullier-Bougassas (Turnhout: Brepols, 2011), 105–14; "*Sirat al-Iskandar*: An Arabic Popular Romance of Alexander," *Oriente Moderno* n.s. 22:2 (2003), 505–20; "The Last Days of Alexander in an Arabic Popular Romance of al-Iskandar," in Panayotakis et al. (see above), 23–35; "Alexander the Flexible Friend: Some Reflections on the Representation of Alexander the Great in the Arabic Alexander Romance," *The Journal of Eastern Christian Studies* 55:3–4 (2003): 195–210.

15 Zuwwiya, *Islamic Legends* (see note 13), 24–34.

16 "Wa kana asmahu bi r-rumiyya Iskandar wa bi l- 'arabiyya ahmad, wa huwa ahmad ibn Assas." Ibid., 10, 70.

17 All quotations from the *Qissat Dhulqarnayn* are from Zuwiyya, *Islamic Legends* (see note 13). In the page number notation following each quote *x*/*y*, *x* denotes the page number of the Arabic text and *y* denotes the English translation. Translations are Zuwiyya's except for what I have placed between square brackets.

18 Even when Dhu'l-qarnayn penetrates into the Land of Darkness where God clearly doesn't want him to go, he goes on covering a year's distance every day. In fact in one of the Christian Ethiopic versions of the Alexander romance that might have contributed indirectly to this tale, he's also simultaneously walking on water, though unaware of it – and God is holding him up even as he trespasses.

19 It is instructive to contrast the composed and well-compassed world in al-Tha'labi's version, with its carefully situated compass points and centres, with the impossible sprawl of the *Qissat Dhulqarnayn*.

20 The relationship between this narrative and al-Andalusian history is very difficult to investigate, thanks to the virtual impossibility of dating the narrative. Its two manuscripts are nineteenth-century copies, and although Zuwiyya ventures an association of its dialect to the mid-thirteenth century, he will not commit himself further (Zuwiyya, *Islamic Legends* [see note 13]). However, Dhu'l-qarnayn seems a fitting hero for an audience of al-Andalus which, under convivienca had been one of the richest entrepots of learning in medieval history.

21 See al-Bukhari's account of the *isra' wa l-mi'raj* where the Lotus tree marks the ultimate boundary where Muhammad is halted and beyond which no one can go, where God alone dwells (al-Bukhari, *Book of Knowledge* [see note 11]).

22 The transmission of this bead from prophet to sage to good king seems to implicate both divine revelation's power and persistence, and its capacity to fall into many different hands – a more contagious model of revelation than the exclusive focus on God's singular and personal gift of it to only specific people at specific times.

23 Why does he not lead them himself – is it fear, or does the episode figure the traditional division of labour between king and 'ulama? This tradition was most often theorized by the 'ulama, so it is no surprise, then that al-Khidr comes off best in this round.

24 See al-Tha'labi, *Lives of the Prophets* (see note 1), 365–82.

25 The Christian imagery of this incident ultimately derives from Syriac and Ethiopic Christian versions of the Alexander romance where there are only four odd centuries of anachronism rather than nine: *The History of Alexander the Great, Being the Syriac Version of Pseudo-Callisthenes*, ed. Ernest A. Wallis Budge (Piscataway, NJ: Gorgias Press, 2003); *The Life and Exploits of Alexander the Great*, ed. Ernest A. Wallis Budge (New York and London: Benjamin Blom, 1968).

26 For a comparative reading of the figure of al-Ghayda/Olympias see Jena al-Fuhaid, "Olympias and Infidelity in the Alexander Romances: A Cross Cultural Study," in *Forum for World Literature Studies* 2:2 (2010), 254–69.

# Diaspora as Empire in the Hebrew *Deeds of Alexander* (*Ma'aseh Alexandros*)

RUTH NISSE

Judging from the three distinct Hebrew versions of the Pseudo-Callisthenes *Alexander Romance* composed in the eleventh and twelfth centuries and preserved in European manuscripts, the Macedonian conqueror was a popular if unlikely hero for medieval Jewish readers.[1] Analogues to certain episodes in the *Alexander Romance* famously appear in rabbinic literature, including the Babylonian and Palestinian Talmuds and *Midrash Genesis Rabbah*; while some portray him as a protector of the Jews, they are by no means all favourable to the emperor.[2] These rabbinic texts, moreover, do not in themselves entirely explain why the Greek fantasy version of a pagan ruler of a long-dissolved empire would secure such an enduring place in the medieval Jewish imagination – especially since the actual Alexander's Seleucid successors, particularly Antiochus IV Epiphanes, who defiled the Temple in 168 BCE, are remembered as among the Jews' worst oppressors.

This essay will suggest that it is Alexander's Far-Eastern empire, much embellished in the romances, that interests western Jewish writers as an historical and ideological alternative to Rome. A clue to this view of empire is found in the ninth-century Palestinian midrashic work *Pirḳe de Rabbi Eliezer*: the text lists the ten kings who rule from the beginning to the end of the world: "the eighth king is Alexander of Macedon, who ruled from one end of the world to the other," "wished to ascend to heaven ... and to descend into the depths," and "attempted to go to the ends of the earth to know what was [there]" before his kingdom was "divided to the four winds." Immediately afterwards, the King Messiah, the ninth king "who, in the future, will rule from one end of the world to the other" takes over.[3] The adventurous, learned, but arrogant Alexander of the Greek *Romance* as well as a few rabbinic analogues is in this text an eschatological figure in a sequence like the *locus classicus* of the four empires of Nebuchadnezzar's dream in Daniel 2, the king between Cyrus and Messiah. The midrash, however, pointedly ignores all of the Roman emperors in this list, even though Rome is typically the last and pre-messianic empire in rabbinic interpretation and the *Pirḳe Rabbi Eliezer* elsewhere alludes to both Roman and Arab rule.[4]

The earliest Hebrew translation of the *Alexander Romance*, the *Ma'aseh Alexandros* (Deeds of Alexander), appears in the mid-eleventh century as an interpolation to the hugely influential and widely circulated *Sefer Yosippon*. *Yosippon* is essentially a Hebrew epitome of the sixth-century Latin translation of Josephus's *Jewish Antiquities* followed by the thoroughly Christianized fourth-century Latin version of the *Jewish War* known as Pseudo-Hegesippus.[5] According to the text's most recent editor, David Flusser, *Yosippon* was written in the mid-tenth century, most likely at Naples by someone with access to the extensive library of Duke John III (928–68).[6] Through the inclusion of additional midrashic and apocryphal texts – including parts of 1 and 2 Maccabees, translated from the Vulgate – *Yosippon* fashions an account of the fall of Jerusalem that wrests it away from its Christian exegetical context as the final moment of Judaism's supersession.[7] At the same time, it reworks its primary patristic source to emphasize the Jews' spiritual as well as military resistance to the Romans. *Yosippon*, an anthology of widely divergent historical and scriptural sources, some of which are no longer extant, is marked by a hybridity of narrative tone.[8] By divine judgment, the Romans under Vespasian and Titus punish the Jews for the extremists' atrocities in Jerusalem; the Jews' series of mass suicides, culminating in the final showdown with the Romans at Masada, however, become spiritually heroic, infused with the vocabulary of early Christian as well as Jewish martyrdom.[9] The text ends with a prayer for messianic redemption, in which God will fulfill prophecies of vengeance on Edom (a term that in rabbinic writings signifies both Rome and Christianity), and gather the Jews together in a rebuilt Jerusalem.[10] Among the prophecies *Yosippon* cites in conclusion is Isaiah 11:12, "He will hold up a signal to the nations / And assemble the banished of Israel / And gather the dispersed of Judah/From the four corners of the earth"[11]

*Yosippon* has a complicated manuscript history and exists in three distinct redactions, each comprising different texts and interpolations. The final one, in which Flusser notes the influence of the *chansons de geste* on its celebration of Joseph's heroism in battle, dates from the mid-twelfth century.[12] The Hebrew Alexander Romances became incorporated into the text in two stages of this evolution. The first interpolator added the *Ma'aseh Alexandros*, translated directly from a version of the Greek Pseudo-Callisthenes in Southern Italy in the eleventh century; a second interpolator then later added a "prequel" dealing with Alexander's early days, derived from the Latin *Historia de preliis*, by the mid-twelfth century.[13] As Flusser suggestively points out, the original *Yosippon*'s connection to the court of John III of Naples places its author in the same milieu of classical culture and textual study as Leo the Archpriest, who, as the duke's envoy to Constantinople, transmitted Pseudo-Callisthenes to Italy and produced the new Latin translation that in turn became the basis for the three versions of the *Historia de preliis*.[14]

Alexander appears in *Yosippon* itself, as he does in both Josephus's *Antiquities*, Book XI and the Babylonian Talmud *Yoma* 69a in the ahistorical narrative of his visit to Jerusalem. The account in the medieval text is ultimately deeply ambivalent. Combining elements from both earlier versions with many additional poetic details, *Yosippon* recounts how Alexander, about to attack Jerusalem for its alliance with the Persian king Darius, has a dream in which a man dressed like the high priest holds a sword over his head and warns the king that God has sent him to conquer kingdoms for Alexander. Alexander proceeds to Jerusalem and falls on the ground before the high priest; when his astonished generals ask why he would bow to a man with no military power, he answers that a likeness of the priest has gone before him to subdue all the nations. The text then expands in curious ways upon its sources to recall how the high priest shows Alexander all around the Temple, including the Holy of Holies; how Alexander offers to erect a gold statue of himself in the Temple, and how the high priest politely declines, suggesting that a better use for the gold would be to support the priests and the poor. As a better alternative, the high priest declares that all the priests "in the land of Jerusalem and the land of Judah" would name their sons "Alexander" that year instead, and that when they worship in the Temple it will be a remembrance (*zikharon*) of the king. The high priest then shows the Book of Daniel to Alexander and reveals the prophecy of the He-Goat who defeats the Ram that signifies the Greek defeat of Persia (Daniel 8:20). Alexander has both the prophecy and the high priest's "interpretation" urging him to attack Darius written down and sent to Macedon *and* to Rome.[15]

Alexander emerges from *Yosippon*'s account not, needless to say, as a convert to Judaism, but as a king who acknowledges and even reveres his own place in Jewish eschatology.[16] He delivers formal blessings at the Temple and accepts as a remembrance the marking of the priestly class with his own name; and above all, he himself transmits the prophecy from Daniel to Greece and Rome, ensuring the fulfillment of the sequence of empires. The entire passage of Alexander's visit ends with an especially ominous version of the king's demise and the division of his empire among his four generals. Returning to Daniel, *Yosippon* emphasizes that what followed Alexander's reign was the four-headed leopard that "devoured the people of Judah," Antiochus IV. Looking ahead to the Maccabean revolt, the text continues: it is only because of "the mercy of God who stood in the breach and roused his priests that the memory (*zekher*) of the people of Judah was not erased from the land."[17] *Yosippon*'s entire account, then, self-reflexively focuses on the necessity of transmissions of Jewish texts and memory between and after empires. The figures of the multiple priestly Alexanders suggest precisely such messengers or preservers of a Jewish history of Alexander the Great that has survived Rome.[18]

At the point in the text where Alexander departs for Persia, the interpolator inserts the *Ma'aseh Alexandros*, which concludes with a Hebrew version of a Byzantine chronicle, based on Eusebius, tracing the history of the Jews under the rulers between Alexander and Augustus Caesar. Like Alexander himself at the end of his visit to the temple in *Yosippon*, the text ends by connecting his empire back to Rome. By fitting this text into the frame of *Yosippon*, the interpolator clearly envisages the *Alexander Romance* translated into Hebrew as being, in its way, as crucial for recovering a specifically Jewish history as Josephus, the books of Maccabees, or the Greek apocrypha of Daniel. Steven Bowman compellingly argues that *Yosippon* is truly a "midrashic" work in that it makes its disparate sources conform to a biblical or mishnaic Hebrew style and then provides commentary on them.[19] The *Ma'aseh Alexandros* is in the same way a commentary on *Yosippon*'s previous Alexander narrative and overall epic historiography.

*Yosippon* and the *Alexandros*-interpolator were naturally well-acquainted with the idea of an eternal Roman–Christian empire in the form of the Byzantine rulers who governed over Southern Italy, including the semi-autonomous city of Naples. By the interpolator's time in the early eleventh century, the Ottonian emperors, asserting a direct inheritance and renovation of Roman authority, had also staked claims to the area of Southern Italy where these works were written and circulated among Jewish communities.[20] Both *Yosippon* and the interpolator were also almost certainly aware of the eschatological implications of the Roman Empire in Eastern and Western Christian texts concerning the end of days. In the *Revelations of Pseudo-Methodius,* the seventh-century Byzantine apocalypse that circulated widely in Greek and Latin, a "Last World Emperor," the "King of the Romans" will defeat all the enemies of Christianity and then move to Jerusalem to relinquish his crown and empire to God.[21] *Yosippon,* simply by being a Hebrew account of Rome that ends with traditional Jewish messianic texts on the end of Edom, is by definition a counter-narrative.

The two translations are, in very different ways, clearly concerned with the place of Jews within the Roman *imperium* both as eschatological concept and current-day reality. However, *Yosippon* and *Alexandros* also testify to a desire for cultural autonomy exemplified by the Hebrew-language revival in Byzantine Europe that began in the ninth century with new academies for Torah study. The texts are later products of the same "renaissance" that inspired *piyutim* (liturgical poems) and midrash influenced by models from North Africa and Palestine, including the works of the poets R. Silano and R. Shefatiah mentioned in the remarkable eleventh-century Southern Italian family chronicle the *Megillat Ahimaaẓ.*[22] In light of this linguistic and cultural moment in Italy, the Hebrew *Alexander Romance* performs two functions within the frame of *Yosippon*'s narrative of the fall of Jerusalem; first, it redirects Alexander away from both Jerusalem and Rome into the far east of India and the "lands of marvels"; second, it counters the defeat of the Jews at the end of *Yosippon* with an eschatology that, like the *Pirḳe de Rabbi Eliezer's,* emphasizes Alexander's empire at the expense of Rome. The most common Jewish formulation of the "Four Empires" appears in commentaries on Daniel 2, which usually identify them as Assyria, Persia, Greece, and finally, Rome. The *Alexandros,* however, expands Alexander's empire in ways that challenge the Roman victory over Jerusalem through the conqueror's encounter with an autonomous diasporic Jewish realm. The reception history of *Yosippon* suggests that it was most often read together with the liturgy of Tisha B'av, as "historical" background to the lamentations for Jerusalem; the Alexander interpolations, however, point to another strand of reading, one that provides the diaspora with a more defiant and open-ended narrative.[23]

In the Pseudo-Callisthenes *Romance,* Alexander, having defeated Darius heads off to fight Porus, the king of India. On his way, he stops in "The Land of the Blessed," which is without sunlight. Two birds with human faces appear and, speaking in Greek, tell Alexander to turn back; he cannot conquer the Land of the Blessed, which is "God's alone," even though he is destined to rule India.[24] In the Hebrew version of this tale, Alexander "desired to enter [the place of darkness] to see the generation called *Maḳari* (derived from Greek: "Blessed Ones"), these are the generations of Yonadav ben Rekhav." The Greek-speaking bird-men deliver this rebuke:

> Alexandros, why are you trespassing in the land of God? You cannot see the House of God and the house of his servants! Return, for you cannot walk among the islands where the holy ones of God (*kedoshei elohim*) dwell! Do not compete to ascend to the height of the heavens![25]

With these additions, the Hebrew translator reworks the romance into a midrash on Jeremiah 35, the only biblical passage that mentions the mysterious Yonadav and his descendants. Evidently, an alternate Second Temple, the "House of God" that Alexander had apparently left behind in Jerusalem, is now in the distant diasporic East.

The biblical Rekhavites are models of obedience whom God invokes to Jeremiah in contrast to all the other "inhabitants of Jerusalem" He intends to punish. As they inform Jeremiah, they do not, because of their ancestor Yonadav's commands, drink wine, build houses, or own vineyards or fields; they live in the city since, "when king Nebuchadnezzar of Babylon invaded the country, we said 'Come, let us go into Jerusalem'" (35:11). The prophet finally reports God's lesson to this family of ascetics: "assuredly, thus said the Lord of Hosts, the God of Israel: there shall never cease to be a man of the line of Yonadav ben Rechav standing before me" (35:19). Ronit Nikolsky has detailed at length how early midrashic traditions interpret the Rekhavites as the descendants of Jethro, Moses's father-in-law, and are thus the ultimate "pious converts" to Judaism. Their ascetic practices are, moreover, connected to future mourning for the Temple's destruction.[26] The Byzantine Christian *History of the Rekhavites* and later Jewish texts, however, situate the Rekhavites in faraway lands and transform them into messianic figures.[27] A homily from the sixth- or seventh-century midrash collection *Pesiḳta de Rav Kahana* claims that the descendants of Yonadav ben Rechav will be the first to announce the redemption of Israel to the Patriarchs and Matriarchs in their graves and to bring offerings to the rebuilt Temple.[28] Another homily for the period after Tisha B'Av in *Pesiḳta Rabbati* (probably redacted in Southern Italy or Greece in the eighth or ninth century) mentions the Rekhavites together with the Ten

Tribes banished to either side of the river Sambatyon (which is impassable for six days but then rests on the sabbath) and to Daphne of Riblah (Antioch).[29] All Jews will be gathered together in Jerusalem in the Messianic time including "the Children of Yonadav" said to live in *Sinim*.[30] As John Reeves explains, by the Middle Ages, the biblical *Sinim* (Isaiah 49:12) can also mean "China" – one of many qualities that makes the Rekhavites appealing candidates for the *Alexandros* translator's fantastic Eastern text.[31]

Steven Bowman has suggested that the *Alexandros* author included the Rekhavites as a parallel to the Greek *Romance*'s Brahmans, the naked philosophers whom Alexander encounters in India. In the Hebrew text, as in the Greek, the Brahmans appear after Alexander has killed King Porus as "sages" *(ḥakhamim)* or "in the language of the Greeks *Gymnosophists*," who criticize the conqueror's power and wealth and force him to admit that he is mortal.[32] While both groups are ascetic and unimpressed by Alexander, the Rekhavites represent a specifically Jewish counter-narrative to the Alexander of the *Yosippon*, the transitory Greek "third emperor" in the sequence from the book of Daniel. After his visit to Jerusalem in *Yosippon*, Alexander sends the prophecy from Daniel to Macedon *and* Rome, an indication of the history to come: the Roman fourth empire and the ultimate destruction of the Temple. In this scheme, the Rekhavites signify the "empire" after Rome in Jewish exegesis of Daniel, the final rule of the King Messiah. Flusser explains that while this "fifth empire" is "the definitive eschatological power" in Daniel, it originates with Persian and other Eastern traditions' hopes for revenge against the West.[33] As they appear in the *Alexandros*, however, in contrast to the earlier midrashic texts the Rekhavites seem settled in outer India, and evidently the Temple is with them in the diaspora rather than in a messianic future. In the context of the *Yosippon*, this is a remarkably subversive idea: no sooner does Alexander claim his place in Jewish eschatology than this interpolation suggests that he has no real place. The Eastern empire of the Jews is beyond his reach, and, in his impurity, he cannot even physically *see* this "House of God and His Servants" much less tour around it with the high priest.

*Yosippon*, a translation from both ancient Jewish and Christian sources, is a work that attempts to reclaim Josephus for Jewish history within Christian Europe. It is framed, therefore, with stories about the origins of Rome from Esau and, in some later versions, with an account of Titus's resettlements of Jews throughout the Mediterranean and Josephus's own subsequent founding of a synagogue in Rome itself.[34] The interpolated *Alexandros* then redirects the idea of the diaspora away from Greek and Latin Europe and into the unmapped Asian lands of European romance, territory its author would have recognized as populated by real Jews at least as far East as Babylon and Persia. Due to its hybrid form, it also removes the diaspora from its usual place in rabbinic messianic narrative. The Rekhavites, based on their warning to Alexander, appear to be already living in a kind of "fifth empire" in Asia even as they inform him that he will defeat India and rule in the East.

The dynamics of the Hebrew *Alexandros* in regard to diaspora, even in the limited form of the episode of the Rekhavites, are similar to other texts produced around the same time in different Jewish cultures – and perhaps influenced by the fictive geography of other Greek or Arabic versions of the Alexander romance. According to the letters exchanged between the community of Kairouan in North Africa and R. Ẓemaḥ Gaon of the Babylonian academy of Sura, the mysterious traveller "Eldad ha-Dani," who arrived in the late ninth century, told his hosts that his tribe of Dan and the tribes of Naftali, Gad, and Asher all live in Ethiopia (Kush), where they have a huge land and are constantly at war with the local kings.[35] Although he was probably from Yemen, as Shlomo Morag has argued based on the Arabic-influenced Hebrew in the texts associated with him, Eldad claimed that he and the four tribes only spoke Hebrew. While they had the entire Bible, they did not read the Scroll of Esther (which recounts events in Persia that happened long after the Danites had left Israel) and the Scroll of Lamentations (which would "break their hearts").[36] Moreover, the *Benei Moshe* – the Levites or "sons of Moses" – lived just across the Sambatyon from the four tribes in a utopia much like the Rekhavites' realm; when the First Temple was destroyed, God transported them in a cloud to live in perfect purity and equality.

Moshe Ha-Darshan of Narbonne, the early eleventh-century author of *Midrash Bereshit Rabbati* recounts a more carefully crafted literary version of Eldad's legend of the Ten Tribes, adding all the biblical passages that explain the narrative. He also accounts for the other six tribes, which all live in Greater Persia and Arabia, speaking the local languages. He explains that the tribe of Issachar is fulfilling the verse from Joshua 1:8 "the book of the Torah will not depart from your mouths"; consequently, no yoke of sovereignty achieves dominance over them except for the yoke of Torah." Of the tribes of Shimon and Menashe, he writes that "they are too numerous to be counted. They receive tribute from twenty-five kingdoms, and some of the Ishmaelites even pay them a tax." The tribe of Ephraim "are ill-tempered and dull minded, skilled horsemen [and] professional warriors; one of them [can prevail] over a thousand [adversaries]." Moshe ends the passage with a bitter reminder that "the tribes of Judah and Benjamin, by contrast, are dispersed among all lands" in exile.[37]

What is unusual in these texts, and especially the extremely popular Eldad ha-Dani legends, is that the diaspora of the Ten Tribes and the Levites has become an imaginary *imperium* of sorts beyond these other groups of Jews' purely messianic-eschatological function. They rule other nations with great military power and are not ruled by anyone else; moreover, they maintain a level of holiness and purity greater than the Jews "scattered" in exile.[38] The Levites, or priests, remain untouched by any outside culture, and, above all, none of the tribes even know about the history of the Second Temple or its destruction – which also includes the immense amount of later rabbinic exegesis and messianic thought. Like the Rekhavites, they are unaware of Rome and all that it signifies.

In a European context, these legends, like the Hebrew *Alexandros*, clearly provide a paradigm for a relationship between Jews and imperial power radically different from Jewish and Christian narratives of the Fall of Jerusalem and the subsequent diaspora, which either emphasize the Jews' misery in exile or their supersession by the Church. By reconfiguring the diaspora as an Eastern territory defined by language, scripture, and autonomy, these texts are able to dismiss Rome and its medieval heirs. Similarly, Alexander, in the Hebrew versions of his visit to Palestine and his adventures in the distant East, himself becomes a figure of contradictions: at once imperial, heroic, and assimilated to a diasporic memory of Jerusalem. This Alexander, in his encounter with two sets of Jews – first in Jerusalem and later in the "islands of God's Holy Ones" – is a construct of the medieval European Jewish desire for an *imperium* to counter Roman–Christian power. Penned in the shadows of Daniel's fragmented "fourth empire," between Byzantium and the German "new Caesars," the Hebrew *Alexandros* looks away from Rome altogether, back to the Greek world and ahead to the next empire. Alexander the Great ushers in neither the Romans nor the rule of Messiah but the Far-Eastern realm of Jews whom even he, despite his conquest of the entire world, never subjected to his yoke.

NOTES

1 Wout van Bekkum, *A Hebrew Alexander Romance According to MS London Jews' College, no. 145* (Louvain: Peeters, 1992), 1–34.

2 Jonathan Goldstein, "Alexander and the Jews," *Proceedings of the American Academy for Jewish Research* 59 (1993), 59–101; For an overview of early Alexander literature that stresses the contrast between the positive view of the emperor in Hellenic Jewish texts and the mostly ambivalent or negative rabbinic traditions, see Jean-Pierre Rothschild, "Alexandre Hébreu, ou Micromégas," in *Alexandre le Grand, figure de l'incompléditude*, ed. François de Polignac, Mélanges de l'Ecole française de Rome, Moyen âge 112 (Rome: L'École française, 2000), 27–42. (Thanks to Julia Rubashkin for this reference.)

3 *Pirke de Rabbi Eliezer*, trans. Gerald Friedlander (London, 1916; reprinted New York: Arno, 1972), 82–3. The entire sequence is God, Nimrod, Joseph, Solomon, Ahab, Nebuchadnezzar, Cyrus, Alexander, Messiah, God. See also *Pirke de-Rabbi Elieser: Nach der Edition Venedig 1544 unter Berücksichtigung der Edition Warschau 1852*, ed. Dagmar Börner-Klein (Berlin: Walter de Gruyter, 2004), 119–21.

4 Ibid., 221–2; Louis H. Feldman, "Rabbinic Insights on the Decline and Forthcoming Fall of the Roman Empire," *Journal for the Study of Judaism* 31 (2000), 275–97.

5 The modern edition of Pseudo-Hegesippus is *Hegisippi Qui Dicitur Historiae Libri V*, ed. Vincenzo Ussani, 2 vols. (Vienna: Hoelder- Pichler-Tempsky, 1932). The patristic Latin translation of Josephus's *Jewish Antiquities* was commissioned by Cassiodorus. For the early Christian reception of Josephus, see Heinz Schreckenberg and Kurt Schubert, *Jewish Historiography and Iconography in Early and Medieval Christianity* (Minneapolis: Fortress Press, 1992), 51–85.

6 *Sefer Yosippon*, 2 vols, ed. David Flusser (Jerusalem: Bialik Insitute, 1980–81), 2: 89, 123–4.

7 Ibid., 2: 132–40.

8 Steven Bowman, "Sefer Yosippon: History and Midrash," in *The Midrashic Imagination*, ed. Michael Fishbane (Albany: SUNY Press, 1993), 280–93.

9 *Yosippon* (see note 6), 2: 108–12; 164–7.

10 Ibid. 2: 167–8. On Edom, see Gershon D. Cohen, "Esau as Symbol in Early Medieval Thought," in *Jewish Medieval and Renaissance Studies*, ed. Alexander Altmann (Cambridge, MA: Harvard University Press, 1967), 19–48.

11 *Yosippon* (see note 6), 1: 431. All citations of the Hebrew Bible are from the JPS Tanakh.

12 Ibid., 2: 3–54, 154–64.

13 Ibid., 2: 216–32; Steven Bowman, "Alexander and the Mysteries of India," *Journal of Indo-Judaic Studies* 2 (1999), 71–111.

14 *Yosippon* (see note 6), 2: 123. See also David J.A. Ross, *Alexander historiatus: A Guide to Medieval Illustrated Alexander Literature* (London: Warburg Institute, 1963), 47–8.

15 *Yosippon* (see note 6), 1: 54–7.

16 On the difference between the original narrative in Josephus and the later versions, see Shaye J.D. Cohen, "Alexander the Great and Jaddus the High Priest According to Josephus," *AJS Review* 7–8 (1983), 41–68.

17 *Yosippon* (see note 6), 1: 60.

18 This aspect of the narrative is related to Yosef Yerushalmi's understanding of *Yosippon* and other medieval texts as "vessels of memory" in *Zakhor: Jewish History and Jewish Memory* (New York: Schocken, 1989), 31–52.

19 Bowman, "Sefer Yosippon: History and Midrash" (see note 8).

20 G.A. Loud, "Southern Italy in the Tenth Century," in *The New Cambridge Medieval History*, Vol. 3, ed. Timothy Reuter (Cambridge: Cambridge University Press, 1999), 624–45; Barbara Kreutz, *Before the Normans: Southern Italy in the Ninth & Tenth Centuries* (Philadelphia: University of Pennsylvania Press, 1991), 94–115; Robert Folz, *The Concept of Empire in Western Europe*, trans. Sheila Ann Oglivie (London: Edward Arnold, 1969), 39–52, 61–74.

21 Bernard McGinn, *Visions of the End: Apocalyptic Traditions in the Middle Ages* (New York: Columbia University Press, 1989), 70–6. *Yosippon* demonstrates knowledge of Pseudo-Methodius in a description of Alexander's enclosing the "peoples of the North" behind iron bars (as opposed to Pseudo-Hegisippus, who uses these terms to describe Alexander's locking away the Alans): see *Yosippon* (see note 6), 1: 60n83. On apocalyptic thought in the context of the Ottonian Roman empire, see Benjamin Arnold, "Eschatological Imagination and the Program of Roman Imperial and Ecclesiastical Renewal at the end of the Tenth Century," in *The Apocalyptic Year 1000*, ed. Richard Landes et al. (Oxford: Oxford University Press, 2003), 271–87.

22 Shlomo Simonsohn, "The Hebrew Revival Among Early Medieval European Jews," in: *Salo Wittmayer Baron Jubilee Volume*, ed. Saul Lieberman (Jerusalem: American Academy for Jewish Research, 1974), 831–58. See also *Megillat Ahimaaz*, ed. Benjamin Klar (Jerusalem: Spitzer, 1974).

23 Steven Bowman, "*Yosippon* and Jewish Nationalism," *PAAJR* 61 (1995), 21–51. Flusser's edition of *Ma'aseh Alexandros,* made from the version in Parma ms de Rossi 1087, is in *Yosippon* (see note 6), 1: 461–91; for

Bowman's translation see his "Alexander and the Mysteries of India" (see note 13).

24 *The Greek Alexander Romance*, ed. and trans. Richard Stoneman (Harmondsworth: Penguin, 1991), 121.

25 Bowman, "Alexander and the Mysteries of India" (see note 13), 82; *Yosippon* (see note 6), 1: 472.

26 Ronit Nikolsky, "The *History of the Rechavites* and the Jeremiah Literature," *Journal for the Study of the Pseudepigrapha* 13 (2002), 185–207.

27 Ibid., 196–200.

28 *Pesiḳta de Rav Kahana*, ed. and trans. William G. Braude and Israel J. Kapstein (Philadelphia: Jewish Publication Society, 1975), 481–2. See also John Reeves, *Trajectories in Near Eastern Apocalyptic* (Atlanta: Society for Biblical Literature, 2005), 204–5.

29 Earlier rabbinic traditions in the Palestinian Talmud, Sanhedrin 10.6, 29c and Lamentations Rabbah 2.9 include the same places of exile: the east side of the River Sambatyon and Daphne of Antioch; a third group are covered by a dense cloud. See Reeves, *Trajectories* (see note 28), 203.

30 Reeves, *Trajectories* (see note 28), 200–8. See also *Pesiḳta Rabbati: Discourses for Feasts, Fasts and Special Sabbaths*, ed. and trans. William G. Braude, 2 vols. (New Haven: Yale University Press, 1968), 2: 617–18.

31 Reeves, *Trajectories* (see note 28), 204n13.

32 Bowman, "Alexander and the Mysteries of India" (see note 13), 83; *Yosippon* (see note 6), 1: 474.

33 David Flusser, "The Four Empires in the Fourth Sybil and in the Book of Daniel," *Israel Oriental Studies* 2 (1972), 148–75.

34 *Yosippon* (see note 6), 1: 432–3.

35 Joseph Dan, *The Hebrew Story in the Middle Ages* (Jerusalem: Keter, 1974), 47–61.

36 Shlomo Morag, "The Question of the Origin of Eldad Ha-Dani," *Tarbiz* 66 (2003), 223–46. The letter to R. Ẓemaḥ Gaon is included with other Eldad texts in Abraham Epstein, *Eldad ha-Dani: Seine Berichte über die X Stämme und deren Ritus in verschiedenen Versionen nach Handschriften und alten Drucken* (Pressburg: Alkalay, 1891), 3–8.

37 Reeves, *Trajectories* (see note 28), 212–16.

38 Dan, *The Hebrew Story* (see note 35), 57–8.

# Hebrew Alexander Romances and Astrological Questions: Alexander, Aristotle, and the Medieval Jewish Audience

SHAMMA BOYARIN

The Alexander romance was a relatively popular text for Hebrew translators in the Middle Ages. There are five versions of the Alexander romance in Hebrew. Four of them clearly represent independent translations of the Alexander romance from other identifiable languages or sources into Hebrew; the origins of the fifth are harder to determine and the cause of much scholarly debate. Two of these – found in New Haven, Beinecke Rare Book and Manuscript Library, Heb. ms Supplement 103, and Paris, Bibliothèque nationale ms Heb. 671.5 – were translated in the mid twelfth century from similar Arabic sources.[1] A third – Parma, ms Cod. Heb. Biblioteca I.B. de Rossi 1087 – was translated from Greek some time during the eleventh or early twelfth century.[2] A fourth – Paris, Bibliothèque nationale ms Heb. 750.3 – was translated from a Latin source in the mid-fourteenth century (another manuscript believed to contain a copy of this version was known to be at a library in Turin in the nineteenth century but was lost to a fire).[3] The unique fifth version is represented by three manuscripts – Modena, Biblioteca Estense ms Modena Liii, Oxford, Bodleian Library, ms Heb.d.11, and a lost codex called ms Damascus in the literature – and there is no scholarly consensus as to its source.[4] No other medieval text was translated into Hebrew from so many different languages so many times. This demonstrable popularity makes the Alexander romance unique in medieval Hebrew letters and suggests that medieval Jews had a special interest in this text.

To be sure, part of the popularity of the Alexander romance, for any translator or audience, is due to the fantastical nature of its narrative and the generally abiding medieval interest in Alexander the Great. But why would medieval Jewish readers in particular show such special interest in Alexander? What importance did the translators of these texts see in this text? In this chapter, I seek answers through a close reading of a colophon appearing at the end of one of the two Hebrew Alexander romances translated from an Arabic source, looking at one of the two cases in which a Hebrew scribe or translator commented on the nature of the text and its translation.[5] Based on this colophon, I argue that the *Alexander Romance* could be viewed as a component of the body of esoteric (pseudo-)scientific knowledge then attributed to Aristotle. Significantly for my argument, these esoteric writings were very frequently presented as wisdom transmitted privately from Aristotle to his student, Alexander the Great.[6] It is based on this connection that the author of the colophon I will discuss wishes to connect the *Alexander Romance* to Aristotelian thought. While it is not my contention that the *Alexander Romance* was always viewed in this light by medieval Jewish readers and translators – indeed, there can be no monolithically "Jewish" approach – this brief postscript by one engaged medieval Jew provides a glimpse into the range of possibilities. And surprisingly, as I will take up in the latter part of this chapter, it allows consideration of how Aristotelian esoteric knowledge and the *Alexander Romance* might be read, coherently and *Jewishly*, together.

It is the Hebrew *Alexander Romance* found in New Haven, Beinecke Rare Book and Manuscript Library, Heb. ms Supplement 103 that ends with the following colophon:

> This book is now complete; it was translated by the wise investigator into the true secrets of existence, Rabbi Samuel the son of Rabbi Judah Ibn Tibbon from Granada Spain. He translated it at the same time as he translated the *Guide*, which cannot be valued in the gold of Ophir. Some people possess this book in the translation of al-Harizi, and it is full of errors, because he translated it from [...] language and the aforementioned perfect translator translated it from the Arabic language into the Hebrew language. May his reward be complete.[7]

Samuel Ibn Tibbon was a famous translator living in Provence during the late twelfth and early thirteenth centuries. His father Judah had moved there from Granada, and had worked hard to educate his son in the same way as the Jews of Muslim Spain. Judah also began to translate works from Arabic into Hebrew for the Jews of Provence, and his son Samuel continued the project. Samuel primarily translated the works of Moses Maimonides, but he was also the first to translate Aristotle's *Meteorologica* and Averroes's *Treatise on the Intellect* from Arabic into Hebrew. For these reasons, the eminent philologist Moritz Steinschneider concluded that this *Alexander Romance* colophon should not be trusted, because all texts known to have been translated by Samuel Ibn Tibbon are philosophical and scientific.[8] According to Steinschneider, the *Alexander Romance* could have been of no interest to Ibn Tibbon, and he would not have taken the time to translate it. This argument is based on the assumption that the *Alexander Romance,* which mixes historical accounts with fantastic and legendary fiction to tell the story of the life and deeds of Alexander the Great, would have been viewed by medieval Jews, like Samuel Ibn Tibbon, as something with no connection to Judeo-Arabic philosophy and science. Steinschneider's doubts about the colophon's authenticity and worth are supported by David Flusser, who believes that the translation could not have been completed any later than 1160 CE and therefore that Ibn Tibbon (born around 1150) could not even have been the translator.[9] The colophon's false attribution has led scholars to dismiss it as mostly useless.[10] But is it really? Following Marc Bloch's observation that to prove a text "is not authentic is to avoid error, but not to acquire knowledge,"[11] we must ask: What lies behind this invention? Why would someone seek to attribute the translation of a literary text to a man whose well-known project was the translation of Greek scientific and philosophical materials from Arabic into Hebrew? More importantly, why might such an attribution have been believable?

Even if this colophon cannot tell us who translated this *Alexander Romance* into Hebrew, or exactly when, it can tell us something about the *Romance*'s role in medieval Hebrew letters. Its author highlights precisely the details that cause Steinschneider to suspect its veracity: when he emphasizes Samuel Ibn Tibbon's interest in translating works influenced by Greek philosophy and science ("the true secrets of existence"), he seemingly and needlessly calls attention to another of Ibn Tibbon's translations, the *Guide*. This *Guide,* of course, can be none other than Moses Maimonides's *Guide for the Perplexed,* a philosophical treatise seeking to provide a rational basis for Jewish theology through Aristotelian philosophy. And not only does the colophon's author call attention to exactly the translation interests that Steinschneider sees as contradictory, he juxtaposes them with the alleged interest in the *Alexander Romance* by claiming that Ibn Tibbon's translation of Maimonides's *Guide* was carried out "at the same time" as the translation of the *Romance*. There is at least one obvious reason for this connection: the colophon places the work of perhaps the most influential Jewish medieval neo-Aristotelian, Maimonides, next to the legendary biography of a man who many considered one of the greatest students of Aristotle: Alexander the Great. Samuel Ibn Tibbon's translation project might be described as the importation of Aristotelian and neo-Aristotelian works into Hebrew, and some, obviously including the colophon's author, might have viewed the *Alexander Romance* as a natural component of such a project – if only because knowing more about Aristotle and Alexander can help to illuminate Aristotle's teachings, some of which were believed to be addressed to Alexander. But this is only the simplest connection. A closer look at these texts will show that the colophon preserves a common literary–scientific orientation among medieval Jewish intellectuals, according to which the world of astrological determinism legitimately informs the scientific and religious philosophies of more rigorous rationalists. But before we can see this, we must address an apparent problem in connecting the *Alexander Romance* to the *Guide for the Perplexed.*

Maimonides probably would have agreed with Steinschneider that any connection of the fantastic *Alexander Romance* to Aristotle or to his own serious works detracts from the latter. In fact, the text attributed to Aristotle that shares the closest affinity to the *Alexander Romance* – the *Sod ha-sodot*, a text containing esoteric knowledge purportedly sent in a letter from Aristotle to Alexander – is the kind of text that Maimonides says cannot be viewed as genuinely authored by the Greek philosopher. In his discussion of the mistaken beliefs of the Sabians, Maimonides provides a list of texts that he believes contain Sabian ideas and says, "To this same class of books we count the book *Istimachis*, attributed to Aristotle, who can by no means have been its author, ... a book on talismans attributed to Aristotle, [and] a book ascribed to Hermes."[12] *Istimachis* is one of a group of texts that Charles Burnett discusses in his important essay "Arabic, Greek and Latin works on Astrological Magic Attributed to Aristotle"; Burnett points to the influence of this *Kitab al-Istimakhis* and "its kin" on the *Sir al-asrrar*, that is, the Arabic source of the *Sod ha-sodot*.[13] Since the *Sod ha-sodot* is derived from the *Istimachis*, contains information on using talismans, and is connected to Hermes, Maimonides's objections to these three books – *Istimachis*, "a book on talismans," and "a book ascribed to Hermes" – would certainly apply to it as well.[14] And this is a key moment in Maimonides's thought, because it brings together several aspects of his intellectual and theological position. Maimonides believed that the Sabian belief system – star worship in particular – was the prevalent religion at the time the Torah was revealed, and that it was a belief system that many of the Torah's laws were sent to uproot.[15] When Maimonides identifies a text as Sabian, he is pointing to those texts that he believes are the antithesis of the Torah, and this dovetails with another important goal Maimonides had in his composition of the *Guide,* namely to show how Aristotelian philosophy and Jewish thought confirm one another. In order to accomplish this, it was of utmost importance for Maimonides to deny that Aristotle could have had a hand in composing any of the texts that he believed it was the "principal object of the Law ... to blot out ... from man's heart" (*Guide,* 320). Given the centrality of this in the thought of Maimonides, it is hard to imagine that any medieval reader (the writer of our colophon, for example) was unaware of his position on such texts.

By mentioning Ibn Tibbon's translation of Maimonides's *Guide,* then, the author of the colophon is drawing attention to the very text that dismisses works like the *Sod ha-sodot* as falsely attributed to Aristotle and as the epitome of what the Torah stands against: star worship. How then are we to see these texts as forming an integrated wisdom? One option is to say that the colophon's author makes the connection between these texts because, to truly appreciate Maimonides's stance in the *Guide,* one must become familiar with the texts that Maimonides presents as opposite to the truth. Maimonides himself claims that he names the books that he believes contain Sabian knowledge so that his reader "may learn all that I know of the religion and the opinions of the Sabians" and "thereby obtain a true knowledge of my theory as regards the purpose of the divine precepts" that were given to negate such erroneous beliefs (*Guide,* 318). Such texts are part of the Maimonidean curriculum not because they agree with the *Guide,* but because they are what the *Guide* has come to nullify. It may be, according to this logic, that the colophon describes Ibn Tibbon as translating the *Alexander Romance* into Hebrew as part of his work on the *Guide* so that the reader may have access to those texts that Maimonides thought necessary to his arguments about the purpose of the Torah. This solution aligns the author of the colophon with Maimonides and the *Guide,* but it is problematic, since Maimonides's position on astrology and pseudo-Aristotelian texts was not adopted even by his staunchest supporters. I would like to explore, therefore, the possibility that the colophon's author believes that the *Alexander Romance* and the *Guide* belong together not because they contradict each other, but because they complement each other.

It is precisely those readers who might accept *Istimachis*, a book on talismans, or the *Sod ha-sodot* as the work of Aristotle who might consider the *Alexander Romance* just as relevant to understanding Aristotle as the works of Maimonides or Samuel Ibn Tibbon's translation of Aristotle's *Meteorologica*. In fact, Ibn Tibbon's own comments on Maimonides's work may have resulted in the fact that Maimonides's judgment of Aristotle's esoteric teachings were ignored. As Aviezer Ravitsky shows, Ibn Tibbon believed that Maimonides had hidden esoteric teachings in his works, teachings that could only be pieced together through very careful attention to the text.[16] Moreover, Ibn Tibbon criticized Judah al-Harizi's translation of the *Guide* exactly because al-Harizi was unaware of the esoteric nature of several of the book's chapters (perhaps explaining the colophon's critique of al-Harizi's translation).[17] According to Ibn Tibbon, truths about the secrets of the Torah were hidden both in Maimonides's works and in the original books of Jewish knowledge comprising the Torah itself because the level of knowledge in the world outside of Judaism meant that people were not ready to accept these truths. As the world's philosophers discover more truths, more of the hidden truth found in Jewish knowledge can and must be revealed. In Ibn Tibbon's opinion, Maimonides began to reveal some of these truths, albeit only so much as the wise might unlock, because of the developments of Islamic philosophers. As Ravitsky puts it, "The enhancement and intensification of philosophical education in the non-Jewish world compelled Maimonides and his disciple, Ibn Tibbon, 'to add more clarity to their hints.'"[18]

The Beinecke ms colophon describes Ibn Tibbon as the "wise searcher into the secrets of creation" because of his inquiry into, and exposition through translation of, Maimonides's esoteric teachings. The colophon's author is simply making an easy connection between Maimonides's (neo-)Aristotelian esoteric writings and another group of esoteric teachings thought by some to be written by Aristotle. The similarity between the way Maimonides addresses the *Guide for the Perplexed* to a favoured student and the way some of Aristotle's esoteric teachings are addressed to his favoured student Alexander the Great may have made these texts seem like links in one chain of hidden philosophical truth. And studying the *Alexander Romance* "at the same time as" the *Guide* makes sense if one views Alexander's relationship to Aristotle, and the knowledge transmitted via that relationship, as part of the "the enhancement and intensification" of the philosophical inquiry that led both to the original writing of, and Ibn Tibbon's deciphering of, the *Guide*.

By now it will be clear that even the incidental information contained in the Beinecke ms colophon is critical to its meaning. This is true, too, of its mention of al-Harizi's translation of the *Guide* and the negative comparison of it to Ibn Tibbon's translation, a critique that is surely off topic in a colophon that is ostensibly related to an *Alexander Romance*. But this little digression must also be part of the colophon's carefully crafted rhetoric, since the person responsible for the translation of the *Sir al-asrrar* into Hebrew, or at least believed to be by many medieval and some modern scholars, was none other than Judah al-Harizi.[19] In mentioning him, the colophon's author manages to allude to at least one person of some prominence and stature (even if his translation of the *Guide* was not as good as Ibn Tibbon's) who can be linked both to the study of the *Guide* and to the pseudo-Aristotelian esoteric materials banned by the *Guide*. The colophon, then, itself becomes a piece of esoteric writing: read carefully, it contains clues to how the *Alexander Romance* should be read, and to what other texts it should be connected. The paradox it presents (acceptance of Maimonides's *Guide* as true wisdom and simultaneous denial or ignorance of Maimonides's position on pseudo-Aristotelian texts) suggests that its writer was among one of two thirteenth- and fourteenth-century Jewish intellectual groups that considered themselves disciples of Maimonides but either ignored his unambiguous prohibitions against astrology and wrote as if he believed in it, or tied the study of neo-Aristotelian philosophy to the rising belief in astrology and saw both as anti-Jewish.[20]

It is in this light that I suggest we believe the colophon. It can and should be understood as a serious example of medieval neo-Aristotelian thought and literature, just as any of the texts translated by Samuel Ibn Tibbon might be. Furthermore, once we allow the connection that it makes between the *Alexander Romance* and medieval pseudo-Aristotelian texts, we can also read the *Romance* differently, for the *Romance*'s treatment of astrology stands out as more than a fantastic element of its fiction in this context. Instead, the astrological elements of the *Romance* now seem to address questions about astrology that were consistently treated by medieval Jewish writers, particularly the problem of the relationship between God's power and the power of the stars,[21] and the *Romance* now seems especially to echo the aforementioned pseudo-Aristotelian *Sod ha-sodot*.

Known in Hebrew as the *Sod ha-sodot,* in Arabic as the *Sir al-asrrar,* and in Latin as the *Secretum secretorum,* this text was, like the *Alexander Romance* contained in Beinecke Heb. ms Supplement 103, translated into Hebrew from Arabic. It is presented as a letter written by Aristotle to his student Alexander, and it begins as a response to Alexander's question about what to do with the wise men of the newly conquered Persia but turns to more general advice necessary to Alexander's success as a ruler. Aristotle admonishes his student:

> If you are able, do not rise, or sit, or eat or drink, or perform any work without consulting the stars, as God did not create a thing that does not have a use ... Do not believe the word of those fools who say that the wisdom of the stars is hidden, and cannot be obtained, or those who say that this wisdom will be false to all those who are warned by it. I say that foreknowledge through this wisdom is desirable. This is because even though a man will not be saved from what has been ordained to happen to him, he can protect himself, just like a man acts to remove the cold from himself ... And there is another thing: for if people know events before they occur, it is possible for them to know God's decree, and this will cause them to petition God before it happens, and repent, and cause others to repent and pray to him to remove the thing that they are afraid of.[22]

This defence of astrology runs parallel to an episode in the *Alexander Romance.* As in the ancient Greek *Romance,* Alexander's father in the Hebrew versions is not the Macedonian king Philip but rather the Egyptian king and astrologer Nectanabus, who uses his arts to escape Egypt and seduce the Macedonian queen. He stays in the court and becomes young Alexander's tutor and the queen's confidant. When Alexander suspects Nectanabus of spying on Philip, he challenges Nectanabus to teach him his technique for discovering Philip's secrets. Nectanabus tells Alexander that such ability "comes to a person from watching the stars" (van Bekkum, *Hebrew Alexander,* 46). Alexander then asks whether astrology has predicted his death, and Nectanabus replies, "My end is near, and my own offspring will kill me" (46). That very night, when the two are alone together, studying astrology at Alexander's request, Alexander pushes his teacher into a ditch, and asks him, "Has your science predicted this?" (46–8). Nectanabus calls from the ditch, "Now my science has come true; you, Alexander, are my son; this is what I saw, that you would kill me" (48). When Alexander goes to his mother, she confirms that Nectanabus was in fact his father.

In this episode, Alexander is willing to kill to test and prove the power of astrology, and he finds not only that he is an astrologer's son but also the potential and limitations of astrology. As in the *Sod ha-sodot*, Alexander has a teacher who must admonish him that astrology is a real science. There are important and obvious differences, of course: in the *Sod ha-sodot* the teacher is the Greek Aristotle, while in the *Alexander Romance* he is the Egyptian Nectanabus; in the *Romance*, it is Alexander himself who doubts the validity of astrology, while in the pseudo-Aristotelian letter it is nameless "others" who try to convince Alexander that astrology is not a real art. But the two texts complement each other in important ways too: where the *Sod ha-sodot* presents the validity of astrology to Alexander and the reader as a statement of fact that must be accepted based on the authority of the teacher, the *Romance* provides a graphic illustration of the problems that astrology presents. It is this complementary relationship between the texts' treatment of astrological questions that lies behind our colophon author's efforts to bring the *Alexander Romance* into the medieval Aristotelian fold.

One of the strongest monotheistic arguments against astrology stems from the problems it raises about God's role in the world: if a man's destiny (Nectanabus's death at the hands of Alexander, for instance) is dictated by the stars, how can God have power in the world? We have already seen an answer to this question in the defence of astrology attributed to Aristotle in the *Sod ha-sodot*: the stars simply reveal God's will, and, through repenting and praying to God, the future can be changed, because God is the ultimate power in the universe. While the *Alexander Romance* raises the question through episodes like the one concerning Nectanabus's death, it also offers a complementary monotheistic answer in an episode illustrating that God's will is behind and above those events predicted by the stars. An episode *not* found in the ancient Greek *Romance* from which all Alexander romances are derived but found in Josephus and interpolated into the Latin *Historia de preliis Alexandri Magni* – from which this Hebrew *Romance* and many western versions of the *Romance* evolve – tells of Alexander's attempted conquest of Jerusalem. After the Jewish high priest refuses Alexander's demand that the Jews pay tribute to him instead of his enemy the Persian king, Alexander's anger leads him to military force. The danger to Jerusalem is averted, however, when Alexander inexplicably bows down before the fully regaled high priest. He tells his astonished followers that, when he was in Macedonia, he had

> seen in a dream that [he] was leading an army like this one, standing in a desert like this one ... and an old man looking exactly like this old man, and his clothing and accessories were like this, accompanied [him] and said, "I am the king that will lead you to victory." And when [he] saw him, [he] knew that God had sent him ... as a messenger of help and aid. (van Bekkum, *Hebrew Alexander*, 64)

When Alexander sees the high priest, the earthly representative of the Jewish God, he instinctively recognizes that it is this God that has aided him in his life and conquests. Read through this dream, all of the first part of the *Romance* – all that Nectanabus accomplished through his knowledge of astrology, all of the predictions about Alexander – has come true because of the will of the Jewish God. And this is, again, an answer to the problem of God's role in a world where man's fate might be controlled by the stars: the stars only reveal what God has planned.[23]

That Alexander's destiny stems from the Jewish God is reaffirmed later in the text, and this particular revelation only strengthens the ties that the *Alexander Romance* has to astrological concerns. When Alexander enters the temple in Jerusalem, the high priest reads to him from the Book of Daniel, telling him how it "mentions the youngest king who will rule the whole Earth" (van Bekkum, *Hebrew Alexander*, 64). This refers to chapters 7 and 8 of the Book of Daniel, in which the angel Gabriel interprets visions that refer to Alexander's conquest of Persia.[24] In showing how Alexander's conquest of the world is the fulfillment of Daniel's prophecy, the *Romance* not only places Alexander's story firmly within the framework of biblical (Jewish) history, it also makes Alexander part of the story of Jewish salvation. As Haggai Ben-Shammai has noted, "In the Middle Ages Daniel was one of the most widely read and studied books of the Hebrew Bible, in both East and West."[25] Ben-Shammai attributes this interest to "the subject matter of the book, the hardships of exile, and the longings for redemption."[26] In other words, Jews turned to the Book of Daniel to find out when their exile would end. Thus, when the *Alexander Romance* emphasizes that part of Daniel's prophecy refers to Alexander, it suggests that this story is part of Jewish redemption. When the high priest shows Alexander that his victory is preordained, he is addressing the medieval Jewish reader, assuring him of the fulfillment of Daniel's prophecy, and perhaps even suggesting that the end of the exile may be at hand.

For the medieval Jewish audience, looking back at Alexander's empire and the past is connected to the future empire of the Messiah-King.

Another medieval Jewish text, the *Pirke Rabbi Eliezer*, lists Alexander's kingdom as the final global empire that precedes the empire of the Messiah:

> Ten Kings ruled from one end of the earth to the other: ... the eighth is Alexander of Macedonia ... the Ninth is the Messiah king who will be king from one end of the earth to the next ... and at the tenth King kingship returns to its rightful owner, who was the first and last king [i.e., God].[27]

These linked empires play a vital role in determining the end of the Jewish exile, which is marked by the return of the Messiah-King. Connections between the *Alexander Romance*, the Book of Daniel, and Jewish redemption provide another strong link between the *Romance* and astrology, then, since Jewish redemption was seen as closely connected to the end of days, the calculation of which often involved astrological means.

Indeed, both the science of astrology and the interpretation of the prophecy contained in the Book of Daniel were considered relevant to the calculation of the days of exile and the end of days, and Alexander's career – particularly the fact that he brought an end to the Persian Empire and marked the ascendancy of the Greeks – was an important part of the equation. The twelfth-century rabbi and scientist Avraham bar Hiyya, for instance, devoted an entire book, the *Megillat ha-megalleh*, to calculating when the end of days might come.[28] While in his fourth chapter, he "explain[ed] the calculation of the end and the time of the resurrection of the dead from the Book of Daniel and the other Holy Writings,"[29] in his fifth chapter he employed astrological means, showing that, either way, one arrives at the same date (bar Hiyya, *Sefer megilat*, 89 and 93–5). He insists that he includes his chapter on astrology in case his "composition reach the hands of those who deal with foreign wisdom ... who may think that the opinion of the wise men of the gentiles refutes our calculations" (111). What bar Hiyya wants to show, in other words, is that a calculation arrived at through foreign wisdom – that is, astrology – is the same as that arrived at through Jewish wisdom, such as the Book of Daniel. In this sense, his aim is somewhat similar to that of Maimonides in the *Guide for the Perplexed*, which sought to show how foreign philosophy did not contradict the Bible. This is also an important clue to understanding the role of the *Alexander Romance* in a Jewish context. The story of Alexander's visit to Jerusalem refigures as Jewish what may have appeared not only foreign but explicitly pagan. After Alexander's visit to Jerusalem, both he and the reader know that his identity was shaped by the Jewish God, the God who visited him in dreams and who set down his destiny in the Book of Daniel. What had been revealed about him through astrology was revealed through the will of God and not through any independent power of the stars.

Considering all of this, we can return to our beginnings and reiterate what Steinschneider and Flusser observed: the value of the colophon in Beinecke Heb. ms Supplement 103 lies not in the factual information it provides. Its contribution to Alexander studies, and to medieval Jewish studies, is not in any factual assessment of its authenticity and worth. It is true that we cannot use it to discover who translated the *Alexander Romance* into Hebrew, nor exactly when, nor does it add much to the reception history of various translations of Maimonides's *Guide for the Perplexed*. It does, however, have its own kind of authenticity. It points to an unexpected context for reading the *Alexander Romance*, one that is engaged with the transmission of scientific and Aristotelian knowledge into medieval Jewish thought and theology. The colophon weaves the *Alexander Romance* into some of the most critical debates of Jewish intellectuals in the Middle Ages – debates over astrology and Greek philosophy – and it suggests that the boundaries between literature and science are more fluid and more dynamic than previous scholars have allowed.

## NOTES

1 Both of these have been edited and published with a facing page English translation by Wout van Bekkum. See *A Hebrew Alexander Romance according to MS London, Jews' College no. 145* [a previous shelfmark], ed. and trans. Wout van Bekkum (Louvain: Peeters, 1992) and *A Hebrew Alexander Romance according to MS Héb. 671.5 Paris, Bibliothèque Nationale* (Groningen: STYX, 1994).

2 An edition of this version was published by David Flusser as part of his appendices to the *Book of Yossipon*, since this *Alexander Romance* was inserted into the *Yossipon*. See *Sefer Yosippon* [Hebrew], ed. David Flusser (Jerusalem: Bialik Institute, 1981), Vol. 1, 461–91. For further discussion of this version, see ibid., Vol. 2, 216–51.

3 Yisrael Levi published a description and transcription of the prologue of the destroyed manuscript in "*Sefer Toldot Alexander*" [Hebrew], *Kovets al*

*Yad vehu Sefer Ha'asif* 2 (1886), xiii–xiv. For an edition of the extant manuscript, with a facing-page English translation, see *The Book of the Gests of Alexander of Macedon / Sefer Toledot Alexandros ha-Makdoni*, ed. and trans. Israel Kazis (Cambridge: Medieval Academy of America, 1962).

4 Although the version of the story found in these manuscripts shares some elements of other Alexander Romances, much is unique. Some scholars have argued that it represents a witness to a distinct oral tradition, and that this tradition influences the development of other Romances in various ways. Others argue that it represents an original composition by a Jewish author and bears very little relationship to the rest of the Alexander legend tradition. Similarly, scholars differ regarding the date of composition, some dating it as early as the sixth or seventh century, others to somewhere between the eleventh and thirteenth centuries. A summary of these positions can be found in the introduction to Kazis, *The Book of the Gests of Alexander* (see note 3), 34. Kazis refers Oxford, Bodleian Library, ms Heb. d.11 by a different Bodleian shelfmark (ms Heb. 2797.10), but he is clearly discussing the same manuscript. For a facing-page Hebrew-English edition of Oxford, Bodleian Library, ms Heb. d.11, see *Tales of Alexander the Macedonian: A Medieval Hebrew Manuscript*, ed. and trans. Rosalie Reich (New York: Ktav, 1972).

5 The other case survives in Levi's transcription of the prologue to the destroyed manuscript related to Paris, Bibliothèque nationale ms Heb. 750.3 (see note 3). This example presents an interesting contrast to the colophon discussed here: "Not because I see myself as wise, nor because of my skill with language, have I decided to translate this book from Latin into Hebrew, for I am most ignorant and unwise. Indeed, I wished to translate it after I saw it written in the book of the Christians and painted with nice figures and different colors, and with silver and gold, because of their great love for it. And most people believe its contents, and I am not one of them (even though everything is possible, and maybe I will find some benefit from them). Its translation and composition are sound" (my translation).

6 The most famous example of these texts is the *Secretum Secretorum*, which will be discussed in more detail below. The conceit will also be familiar to scholars of Old English literature, as an Old English "Letter of Alexander to Aristotle" appears in the *Beowulf* manuscript (London, British Library ms Cotton Vitellius A.xv), wherein the student Alexander reports to his teacher about his adventures and discoveries in the East. On this, see Andy Orchard, *Pride and Prodigies: Studies in the Monsters of the* Beowulf-*Manuscript* (Toronto: University of Toronto Press, 1985), 116–39.

7 All further in-text citations of this Hebrew *Alexander Romance* follow van Bekkum, *A Hebrew Alexander Romance* (see note 1), here 205. I have consulted but emended van Bekkum's translations. The London manuscript that van Bekkum worked from is now in the Beinecke at Yale University. Van Bekkum does not comment extensively on the date or provenance of the manuscript or the colophon's lacuna, nor does he mention the scribe who gives his name at the end of the colophon as "Daniel the son of Rabbi A." (205). He suggests that the lacuna that suppresses the language from which al-Harizi translated may be a deliberate omission and notes a previous editor's emendation, but he does not elaborate (23n79). While he claims that he will show that the codex "existed before 1160" (23), the further discussion he offers relates only to the date of composition and not to the date of the manuscript itself (27–30). My own examination of the manuscript (from microfilm) confirms there is no space or apparent erasure or correction following the word "language"; in other words, the only reason to assume a lacuna is because the sentence is incomplete as written. It is perhaps also of interest that the *Alexander Romance* is seventy pages by modern foliation (35 folios) and is the sole text in this codex, although this may not have always been the case. Certainly, further codicological work and research on the scribe will repay the effort.

8 Moritz Steinschneider, *Die Hebraeischen Uebersetzungen des Mittelalters und die Juden als Dolmetscher* (Berlin: Kommissionsverlag des Bibliographischen Bureaus, 1893), 899.

9 Flusser, *Sefer Yossipon* (see note 2), Vol. 2, 216–26, dates the translation of this *Alexander Romance* based on the interpolation of some material from it into the *Sefer Yossipon*. Flusser is primarily interested in the stages of the development of the *Yossipon*, but he deals extensively with interpolations of the Alexander materials and their dates. He shows that Abraham Ibn Daud's *Sefer ha-Qabalah* includes some references to Alexander as recorded in the *Yossipon*, which includes a Hebrew *Alexander Romance* very similar to the one in the Beinecke ms. According to Flusser, this interpolation, and therefore the translation from Arabic, must have been done by 1160.

10 For example, van Bekkum (see note 1) says in the introduction to his edition, "Only one relevant conclusion can be drawn [from the colophon's false attribution to Ibn Tibbon]: its insertion in the London [now Beinecke] ms confirms to a certain extent the 'western European' character of our *Alexander Romance*" (23), since Ibn Tibbon's influence was strongest in Western Europe.

11 Marc Bloch, *The Historian's Craft* (New York: Knopf, 1953), 93.

12 All citations of Moses Maimonides are from *Guide for the Perplexed*, trans. M. Friedlander (New York: Dover, 1956), here 319. Hereafter cited in text.

13 Burnett's essay appears in his *Magic and Divination in the Middle Ages: Texts and Techniques in the Islamic and Christian Worlds* (Brookfield, VT: Ashgate, 1996), here 88. For a similar discussion of this group of texts, see Dov Schwartz, *Astral Magic in Medieval Jewish Thought* [in Hebrew] (Ramat Gan: Bar Ilan University, 2004), 99–103.

14 The Hebrew version of the *Sod ha-sodot* was translated by Maimonides's much younger contemporaries. It is unlikely that he knew it, though he was probably familiar with the Arabic original.

15 On this point see Joseph Stern, "The Fall and Rise of Myth in Ritual: Maimonides versus Nahmanides on the Huqqim, Astrology, and the War Against Idolatry," *The Journal of Jewish Thought and Philosophy* 6 (1997), 185–263, especially the discussion on 187–8.

16 This is the general point of Ravitsky's essay, "Samuel ibn Tibbon and the Esoteric Character of the Guide of the Perplexed," *Association for Jewish Studies Review* 6 (1981): 87–123.

17 As I will mention below, the colophon's author seems to go out of his way to call attention to al-Harizi's translation, only for the sake of mentioning how bad it is, and with no obvious link to the *Alexander Romance*. On Ibn Tibbon's own opinion on al-Harizi, see ibid., 105.

18 Ibid., 114.

19 This point is made by Moses Gaster, "The Hebrew Version of the 'Secretum Secretorum' with Introduction and English Translation," in his *Studies and Texts in Folklore, Magic, Medieval Romance, Hebrew Apocrypha and Samaritan Archaeology* (London: Maggs, 1925), 748–50. In part, Gaster's understanding rests on a misreading of the Beinecke ms colophon that leads him to list al-Harizi as the translator of a Life of Alexander. Despite this obvious problem, however, his argument stands. It is interesting to note that, in this case, the colophon seems to have succeeded in creating the impression that all of these texts were the product of a certain moment in Hebrew literature that centred around the two translators of the *Guide*, Ibn Tibbon and al-Harizi. More crucial to my thinking, Gaster points to a Jewish manuscript tradition that anthologizes various biographical texts dealing with Alexander and includes the *Sod ha-sodot* (749).

20 Schwartz, *Astral Magic* (see note 13), 118–21 and 233–7.

21 For the purposes of this chapter, it is not important to distinguish between judicial astrology, the branch of astrology that uses the stars to explain events both past and future, and astral magic, the branch that harnesses the power of the stars to affect events.

22 Moses Gaster, "The Hebrew Version of the 'Secretum Secretorum': A Medieval Treatise ascribed to Aristotle," *Journal of the Royal Asiatic Society*

(1907), 879–912, here 903. My translation. A similar defence of astrology already appears in the Arabic version of the *Secretum secretorum*: see 'Abd al-Rahmān al-Badawī, *Al-Ušūl al-Yūnānīyah lil Nažarīyāt al-Siyāsīyah fī al-Islām*, Dirāsāt Islāmīyah (Cairo: Maktabat al-Nahdah al-Misrīyah, 1954), 85–6. This is significant on two levels: for the medieval Jewish reader, it suggests that this text, even in its pre-Hebrew form, contains matter that is in accord with, or of concern to, Jewish belief; for the modern scholar, it suggests that this kind of accord between the *Alexander Romance* and other texts may be at play in the Muslim Arabic traditions as well; for more on the *Sod ha-sodot* see my recent article: "The Contexts of the Hebrew *Secret of Secrets*," in *Trajectoires européennes du 'Secretum secretorum' du Pseudo-Aristote (XIIIe-XVIe siècle)*, ed. Catherine Gaullier-Bougassas et al., Alexander redivivus 6 (Turnhout: Brepols 2015), 451–72.

23 Viewed in this way, the high priest is the Jewish counterpart to Nectanabus, perhaps even signifying a permissible model of magic. Various parts of his regalia, which the *Alexander Romance* is at pains to emphasize were put on especially for his meeting with Alexander, were interpreted this way by many medieval Jews: the high priest's diadem is inscribed with the true name of God, a name frequently associated with conjuring in medieval Jewish literature; and fourteenth-century biblical commentaries (such as the *Mayan ganim*, which relies on information found in "Alexander's book of kingship") assign astral significance to the stones in the high priest's *efod* (shoulder decorations). See Schwartz, *Astral Magic* (see note 13), 249, who mentions several sources for such information associated with Alexander, though he does not mention the *Sod ha-sodot*.

24 Although Alexander is not mentioned by name in these chapters of the Book of Daniel, it is clear that the king of Greece whose kingdom is broken into four parts refers to him.

25 Haggai Ben Shammai, "Saadia's Introduction to Daniel: Prophetic Calculation of End of Days vs. Astrological and Magical Speculation," *Aleph* 4 (2004), 11–87, here 11.

26 Ibid., 12.

27 *Pirke Rabbi Eliezer* [in Hebrew] (Jerusalem: Defus Varsha, 1970–1), 28–9. My translation.

28 Shlomo Sela discusses bar Hiyya's writings on astrology in detail in "Abraham Bar Hiyya's Astrological Work and Thought," *Jewish Studies Quarterly* 12 (2005), 128–58.

29 Citations of Abraham bar Hiyya follow *Sefer megilat ha-megaleh*, ed. Adolf Poznanski and Julius Guttmann (repr., Jerusalem: n.p., 1967), 4. My translation. Hereafter cited in text.

# The *Alexander Romance* in Southeast Asia: Wonder, Islam, and Knowledge of the World

SU FANG NG

When the West considers Alexander the Great's connection to Asia, what is best known are his eastern conquests, stories of which spread particularly vigorously in the Middle Ages in the orientalizing mode of the romance tradition derived from Pseudo-Callisthenes's Greek *Alexander Romance.* Not as well known is that the continuing eastern tradition of Pseudo-Callisthenes's Alexander was reproduced as vigorously as the western one, spawning numerous translations, retellings, and adaptations. The range of languages into which the romance was translated testifies to its global reach and power, going far beyond the Mediterranean. From the Syriac an eastern version found its way to Ethiopia, Mongolia, Persia, and India, and thence to Southeast Asia, where it was translated into the Austronesian language of Malay.[1] Offering stories of wonders, the eastern tradition produced an Alexander who travelled further than we imagined – to the Indian Ocean and all the way to the Indonesian islands in the South China Sea.

Despite its apparent remoteness, in its long history Southeast Asia has been remarkably open to outside influences. In the middle of the oceanic trade routes between China and India, Southeast Asia served as a convenient entrepôt. With merchants also came itinerant preachers and scholars with new religions. Southeast Asian historian Anthony Reid notes that a range of religions, Islam (both Sunni and Shi'a), Catholic and Nestorian Christianity, Confucianism, Judaism, and various Hindu and Buddhist cults had all been represented in Southeast Asia since the first millennium by traders and travellers, with Hinduism and Buddhism heavily influencing court culture, but in the late thirteenth and fourteenth centuries Islam established more substantial commercial communities in the ports of north Sumatra, east Java, Champa, and the east coast of Malaya.[2]

As Islam spread more widely in the region and established itself more firmly between 1400 and 1650, it brought with it texts and stories, including the Alexander legend in the form of the Muslim conqueror Iskandar Zulkarnain ("the two-horned"). The Islamic Alexander became available for the fashioning of Southeast Asian identity in response to change, particularly in the new globalization of the early modern period. I have previously considered some of the larger implications of the appropriation of an Islamic Alexander in Southeast Asia to rethink our understanding of the unprecedented European entry into the Indian Ocean.[3] The existence of an Islamic Alexander means that western Alexanders always already had a rival, and Southeast Asian response to the aggressive tactics of the Portuguese in the Indies could be framed in terms of the Islamic history given in romances and other texts brought from the Middle East or India. Here, I analyse the representation of wonders in the Malay Alexander, *Hikayat Iskandar Zulkarnain*, particularly the imbrication of wonder with the Islamicization of the text.

*Hikayat Iskandar Zulkarnain* is a product of Malay acceptance of Islam and absorption of Islamic learning. While Pseudo-Callisthenes is its ultimate source, more immediate ones are Arabic and Islamic. L.F. Brakel suggests that the *hikayat* genre was introduced to Pasai around the mid-fourteenth century, and the Malay Alexander, *Hikayat Iskandar Zulkarnain*, derived from a "Central-Asian Arabic adaptation of a Persian text."[4] The Dutch editor of extracts from *Hikayat Iskandar Zulkarnain*, P.J. Van Leeuwen, finds influences from Islamic sources such as the Qur'ān, the Persian *Shāh-nāma* (Book of Kings) by Firdausī, Islamic legends, and *hadith*, but believes that the text corresponds largely to the Berlin Arabic *Alexander Romance* of al-Sûri; he notes that both Cambridge manuscripts of the *Hikayat Iskandar Zulkarnain*, Cambridge Add. ms 3770 and Or. ms 834, thus reference their source: "Kata Sûri" (Says Sûri).[5] Comparing the *Hikayat Iskandar Zulkarnain* to the Arabic version, the Berlin MS Wetzstein II 530, Brakel argues that the first part is based on the Persian *Shāh-nāma* but that in its language the text is closer to the Malay *Hikayat Muhammad Hanafiyyah*, itself a translation from the Persian, than to the Berlin Arabic Alexander, and so he concludes that it must also have borrowed from the older Malay text.[6] Sir Richard Winstedt similarly believes that "either the Malay work or its source is a compilation," noting that manuscripts in his possession name two authors – "Say al-Suri and 'Abdu-'llah son of مفنغ whose *hikayat* it is."[7]

In addition to the possibly composite nature of the text, there are two recensions, which Winstedt identifies with Sumatra and the Malayan Peninsula.[8] The Sumatran recension begins with a doxology not found in the Peninsular version, while the Peninsular carries the story further, with the most complete ending with the death of Alexander. Of Winstedt's four manuscripts of the Peninsular recension, the most complete is the last, Winstedt ms IV, copied in 1906 by Ibrahim bin 'Abbas for Wan Besar of Kedah.[9] According to Winstedt, it follows closely the text of the 1808 Cambridge Add. ms 3770, previously thought unique, but Winstedt ms IV goes further, continuing for another thirteen pages to complete the romance.[10] More recently, Siti Soeratno Chamamah compared all seventeen extant manuscripts and found the only complete manuscript to be the ms 21 at the University of Malaya in Kuala Lumpur.[11] Winstedt suggests that the Peninsular recension came about when a copy of the *Alexander Romance* was brought by the princess of Pasai marrying a ruler of Melaka in 1436.[12] Thus, the text was part of the strengthening of ties between Islamic states in the region. Located in the north of Sumatra and one of the first ports encountered by traders from the Indian Ocean and other points west, Pasai was likely the first city-state to convert to Islam in the late thirteenth century. Melaka too converted early, professing Islam by the mid-fifteenth century. The Malay Alexander needs to be considered as part of the legacy of the long history of translation of Greek texts into Arabic. The Southeast Asian case shows how wide the ramifications were of that cultural translation.

The two regions producing the *Hikayat Iskandar Zulkarnain*, northern Sumatra and Melaka, also produced court chronicles that appropriated the Alexander myth for their genealogical fictions. They were far from the only ones, as Anthony Reid notes: "The chronicles and letters of Sumatran and Peninsula kings – Melaka, Minangkabau, Palembang, Aceh, Deli, Johor, and Pahang – all claimed that their dynasties descended from Alexander."[13] The Alexander tradition influenced not just Malay literature but also Javanese and Buginese.[14] A comparison of northern Sumatra and Melaka is instructive of the role of Islam in this period. A significant port in the fifteenth century, Melaka was crucial to trading networks that extended as far as Venice: the Portuguese traveller Tomé Pires claimed that "Whoever is lord of Malacca has his hand on the throat of Venice."[15] Melaka's court chronicle *Sejarah Melayu*

(Malay Annals) was produced, however, not during its heyday but by the court in exile after Portuguese capture of the city in 1511.[16] A nostalgic text celebrating the greatness of Melaka, it also struggles to understand the reasons for Melaka's fall.

In the century following, Portuguese-controlled Melaka became a target of numerous attacks by a number of Malay states, including the Melakan court in exile in Johor, as they struggled to claim the dominant position that Melaka had held in the fifteenth century.[17] One such ambitious state was Aceh in northern Sumatra. Rising into prominence in the sixteenth century, Aceh had its golden age during the reign of Sultan Iskandar Muda (1583?–1636). With a name meaning the "younger Alexander," Iskandar Muda was seen as a skilled military commander. Composed between 1607 and 1636, the *Hikayat Aceh*, a panegyric biography of Iskandar Muda, claims for him a glorious ancestry that stretches back to Alexander the Great. In this period, Aceh established trading and diplomatic relations with the Ottoman Empire, strengthening ties with a major Islamic power at a time of increasing Portuguese incursions into the Indian Ocean. A flourishing pepper trade from Aceh to the Red Sea, documented from around 1526, circumvented the monopoly the Portuguese tried to impose.[18] Out of this trade and a common religion, the Acehnese built military alliances with the Ottomans. The Acehnese Sultan Ala'u'l-Din Ri'ayat Shah al-Qahhar (1537?–71) opened relations with Turkey by sending a mission to Istanbul and in turn the Ottomans sent craftsmen and expert gunmakers to Aceh. This mission was recounted in the seventeenth-century religious scholar Nuru'l-din al-Raniri's *Bustanu's-Salatin* (1638) and in *Hikayat Aceh*, which transposes it to the seventeenth-century reign of Sultan Iskandar Muda. As Aceh strove to challenge Melaka for preeminence, it fashioned an Islamic identity in contradistinction to the Christian Portuguese in Melaka.[19]

While the situations of Melaka and Aceh differ, the reception of *Hikayat Iskandar Zulkarnain* appears to have occurred as part of an intensifying of Islamic identity in reaction to Portuguese belligerence. The Islamic states of Southeast Asia turned to Islamic heroes like Iskandar Zulkarnain to construct their own identities, which structured their response to the Portuguese. The vernacular translation and appropriations of the *Alexander Romance* in Southeast Asia are simultaneously inward- and outward-looking. The consolidation of Malay identity is inward-looking, as any vernacular translation necessarily has a bounded and limited audience compared to the original cosmopolitan language.

At the same time, a vernacular translation, in this case from Arabic to Malay, offers an avenue for participation in a larger, more global culture. *Hikayat Iskandar Zulkarnain* is an example of Sheldon Pollock's argument that vernacularizing projects are in dynamic relation with cosmopolitan culture, taking their materials, even their vocabulary, from cosmopolitan languages.[20]

Pollock makes this argument in regard to Sanskrit in his provocative two-millennia-long macrohistory of language dispersion, literary change, and the politics of culture in South Asia. In the second millennium CE around the Indian Ocean, vernacular literary cultures in the Indian subcontinent and in Southeast Asia (both mainland and archipelago) arose from out of Sanskrit's shadow, but still using and transforming the materials of Sanskrit literary culture. Pollock's astoundingly learned study nonetheless needs to be complicated by some attention as to how in Southeast Asia (as well as in, no doubt, Mughal India) vernacularizing projects contended with Arabic alongside Sanskrit in adapting Islamic texts. The narrative of *Hikayat Iskandar Zulkarnain* offers its Malay audience the opportunity to participate in global history through the world conquests of Iskandar. As the Malay world develops a vernacular canon out of materials of the Arabic master language, it participates in an Islamic cosmopolitan culture.

In the context of vernacular and cosmopolitan cultures in productive tension, otherness has a particularly charged resonance. Otherness emerges in *Hikayat Iskandar Zulkarnain* partly in its genre of wonder literature. In his wide-ranging travels, Iskandar encounters peoples with strange customs as well as strange creatures and objects. The episodes of marvels are a heritage of the *Alexander Romance* tradition as well as of the more immediate Arabic source. Through such episodes, the text offers its vernacular audience ways of conceptualizing relations to the larger world. More than simply ethnocentric characterizations of "others," they express awareness of the multifariousness of the world and suggest Islam's openness to absorbing other elements into its universalist empire.

The Islamicizing of the text means that wonder is viewed through a religious lens. In Iskandar's encounter with worshippers of idols, whether in the form of man-made statues or natural objects like stars, the apparent power of idols is undercut by the revelation that they are caused by demon possession. Idols lose their power when confronted by God's prophet and Iskandar's close companion, Khidir. The people converted are instructed in the truth, such as in one episode when

Prophet Khidir teaches Fatah, one of a tribe of worshippers of Saturn, correcting his mistaken belief that the planet is a god:

> Maka sahut Nabi itu, "Hai laki-laki tiadakah kau ketahui bahawa Zuhal itu, suatu daripada bintang yang tujuh jua kitar-kitar sekalian dengan bumi dan melegangkan segala air sungai dan menurunkan hujan, dan menambahkan segala tumbuh-tumbuhan menerbitkan buah-buahan." Setelah didengar Fatah kata Nabi Khidir itu, "Jikalau demikian, sungguhlah tuan kamu itu maha besar, ajarkanlah bagi hamba sahabat." Maka diajarkan oleh Nabi Khidir syahadat dan dicium oleh Nabi Khidir dahinya.
>
> [Then replied the prophet, "O man, don't you know that Zuhal (Saturn) is one of seven stars (i.e. planets) that together revolve with the earth and empties the waters of the rivers and brings down rain and adds to all plants to produce fruits." After Fatah hears what Prophet Khidir has to say, "If that is so, truly your lord is great, teach me, your friend." Then Prophet Khidir teaches him the *shahadah* (the Islamic creed) and kisses his brow.] [21]

The scientific rationalization at work here ascribes natural causes to wonders, even if the supernatural world of demons is also accepted as true. The bright object in the sky is identified as Saturn, a planet, rather than mystified as a divine being. Significantly, this science lesson is given together with the *shahadah*, thus linking the two.

This does not, however, mean that the *Hikayat Iskandar Zulkarnain* utterly divorces Islam from wonder. At the same time that it offers "scientific" rationalizations, the text also associates wonder and strangeness with Islam. Iskandar and his companion, Prophet Khidir, are able to perform marvellous feats because of the grace of Allah. However, this kind of wonder, coming from the power of Allah, is distinguished from marvels of pagan origin. Thus, episodes of wonder convey an Islamic message, teaching the audience how to respond to strangeness. While non-Muslim strangers are enemies of God when they oppose Iskandar's inexorable march across the world, strangers and strangeness can be found acceptable when the other learns to accept Islam.

The link between wonders and Islam is evident in the first conversion of the text, which involves miracles made possible through the power of Allah. Significantly, the first major convert is Iskandar himself. After a history of his Persian ancestors, Iskandar is born to the Macedonian princess Safiya Arqiya by a Persian king. Although his Persian relatives follow the "Majusi" religion or Zoroastrianism, a fire-worshipping faith, Iskandar's Macedonian family is Muslim. At the age of five, Iskandar is given to "Aristatalis" (Aristotle) to be taught the Qur'ān (Hussain, *Iskandar*, 41–2). However, after his Persian victory, Iskandar grows proud, continuing his willful behaviour despite being chided by Aristatalis. God sends Nabi Khidir, the prophet of Islamic popular tradition *al-Khidr* ("the green one"), to preach to Iskandar. While Khidir later becomes Iskandar's close companion, initially Iskandar refuses to listen to Khidir and imprisons him. Khidir only convinces Iskandar after an involved sequence of events in which he escapes with divine assistance. The protection of Allah makes Khidir a miracle worker, breaking heavy chains, escaping a closely guarded prison, and single-handedly defeating a large troop of calvary. In *Hikayat Iskandar Zulkarnain*, Islam becomes the rational explanation for Iskandar's wonder-making success as a conqueror. After conversion, Iskandar embarks on his conquest of the world in order to convert all peoples to Islam. His Islamicization is both the motivation for conquests and the source of his power. It is telling that Iskandar, though raised Muslim, has to be converted again. Necessitated by pride arising from his Persian conquests, his conversion is perhaps a symbolic cleansing of his non-Islamic Persian heritage. More important is the view that one need not be born a Muslim; being Muslim is an active choice. Iskandar undergoes the process of conversion just like the peoples he will later convert.

*Hikayat Iskandar Zulkarnain* shows a fairly capacious community of Islam. No matter how alien, "others" are incorporated into Islam as long as they are willing to accept Allah as God. As such, marvels are not automatically attributed to wicked intentions or seen as fit to be destroyed by Iskandar's Islamic army. Some episodes involving marvels even function to teach Iskandar proper consideration for non-Islamic others. When Iskandar is in danger of succumbing to material desires, Khidir acts to restrain his cupidity. In one instance, Iskandar's army encounters a horseman with an extraordinary sword. Upon closer view, Khidir finds it to be a marvellous moving automaton made of precious metal. Iskandar is so taken by the sword that he wants to seize it, but Khidir dissuades him, arguing that "tuan hamba berjalan ini bukan mengadakan kejahạtan akan makhluk, hanya menyuruhkan maka menyembah manusia akan Allah dan menyentosakan bumi Allah" (my lord journeys here not to do evil to creatures, only to command humans thus to worship Allah and to bring peace to God's earth; Hussain, *Iskandar*, 112–13). Reminding Iskandar of his peaceful and holy purposes, Khidir teaches him not to do harm. If Iskandar destroys the automaton, a useful road marker, simply to possess a precious object, he will be harming subsequent travellers passing that way. While incredibly powerful, Iskandar is not authorized to use his power at will. He must act in accordance to God's wishes.

Consideration for non-Islamic others is also evident in the treatment of (marvellous) animals in *Hikayat Iskandar Zulkarnain*. When Iskandar's army encounters gigantic ants as big as cows and has trouble going by them since they are so numerous, Prophet Khidir admonishes them, "Jangan kita berbuat jahat akan dia" (Let us not do them evil, Hussain, *Iskandar*, 112). More than simply advocating a humane treatment of animals, the text sometimes blurs the distinction between human and animal. Juxtaposing two episodes of wonder where the boundary between animal and human becomes exceedingly thin, I suggest that one dynamic of the text is a drive to incorporate the "other," no matter how strange, into the sphere of what is known, a sphere that is ultimately Islamic. Interestingly, this occurs through the deployment of some familiar Greco-Roman motifs of the satyr and the monstrous. Significantly, what at first glance seems a simple categorization of the world becomes complicated as the apparently stable taxonomies of human and animal get confused and are ultimately undone.

In the first episode humans resemble animals. When Iskandar and his army arrive at a place smelling of mushrooms with groves of sugarcane, it appears uninhabited by humans. But then they meet an old man with a long beard hanging down to his knees, who runs away. Unable to catch him even on horseback, Iskandar is confounded and left desiring the contents of the land. The inhabitants are compared to animals: the old man running is like "kijang yang dangku [*sic*] orang berburu" (a deer supposing that men are hunting it, Hussain, *Iskandar*, 178). When one is caught, he reacts with panic, "menghempaskan dirinya seperti binatang liar" (flinging himself like a wild animal, Hussain, *Iskandar*, 178) and "meratap-ratap hingga tangisnya itu" (lamenting until he is in tears, Hussain, *Iskandar*, 178–9). The apparent barbarity of these people, underlined by Iskandar's observation that the land is unmarked by human habitation, offers a frightening image of people turned into animals. Even Khidir is initially stymied, even though it is his facility with languages, which the text celebrates, that enables Iskandar's conversion of the world – Khidir's ability to speak all the languages of the peoples they encounter makes their conversion efforts effective. Khidir questions the man they caught in one thousand five hundred languages ("seribu lima ratus bahasa," Hussain, *Iskandar*, 179), but the man understands none of them. When he speaks, his voice sounds like lightning striking ("seperti halilintar membelah," Hussain, *Iskandar*, 179). However, these animal-like humans are not excluded from Islamic kinship. Eventually, they are converted to Islam.

The second episode involves animals that look like humans. Out hunting with the Barbar king, Iskandar encounters strange beasts: "Hatta, maka dilihat Raja Iskandar sepuluh ekor binatang, kakinya seperti kaki kambing, mukanya seperti muka manusia" (Then, King Iskandar sees ten animals, feet like goats, faces like humans, Hussain, *Iskandar*, 220). King Dakhlam, king of Barbars – meaning barbarians, but perhaps also referring to the Berbers – tells Iskandar the story of the origins of the goat-men, reminiscent of Greek satyrs:

> seorang gembala kambing, maka dibuatinya seekor kambing. Maka dengan takdir Allah Taala jadilah anaknya jantan, lakunya seperti rupa ini. Maka kemudian beranak pula ia seekor betina lakunya seperti rupa ini juga. Maka jadilah kedua anak kambing itu hingga anak beranaklah ia menjadi banyak.
>
> [a goatherder coupled with a goat. Then with the decree of God the Most High his son happened to have this appearance. Then he had a female child who also happened to have this appeareance. Then the two kids became such that they greatly reproduced until there were many of them. Hussain, *Iskandar*, 221]

While Dakhlam categorizes them as ordinary animals of the hunt, Iskandar has reservations because of their human likeness. After hearing the story, Iskandar desists from the hunt, releasing the captured animals. The implication is that it is improper to hunt them because of their human origin. Both episodes emphasize the closeness of humans to creatures initially categorized as animals. A common humanity is acknowledged even when the creatures are patently unusual.

Elements of the Greco-Roman satyr remain. The origin of this tribe of human-animal hybrids is bestiality. This sexual perversion is then compounded by incest of the offspring of the goatherd. The extreme fecundity of the line of goat-people speaks to the characteristic most often associated with satyrs: their immense sexual capacity. However, the goat-people of *Hikayat Iskandar Zulkarnain* are not reviled as one might expect from a text so concerned with its hero's religious mission.

These episodes go beyond human-animal encounters to consider the intermixing of the two. In so doing they raise issues of epistemology. Iskandar's careful response suggests that he is not always sure how to categorize what he sees in the world. In the case of the goat-people, he chooses to err on the side of compassion. His example suggests that human observation is ultimately untrustworthy, even if the text has a strong anthropological thread running through it. Rather, knowledge of the world must ultimately come from God. Thus, Iskandar refrains from hunting the goat-people because of the potential for kinship with these creatures. This is perhaps an extreme example of that kinship potential that Iskandar activates, or turns into reality, through conversion in all his encounters.

This narrative turn from strangeness into familiarity is consonant with the text's larger overall converting impulse. As peoples of the world become Islamicized through Iskandar's conquests, they become kin in a common religion. While the text thematizes wonder, it does not stop there. Like the marvellous creatures linked to humankind, the alienness of the peoples are turned into familiarity and closeness as the project of conversion proceeds. Wonder serves to raise moral and ethical questions. This is particularly true with what may be the text's greatest wonder: the water of life. In the episode of Iskandar's journey to the Land of Darkness, the water of life is symbolic of Iskandar's vain ambitions, as in the Greek *Alexander Romance*, but with Islamic elements introduced into the story. Wonder and Islam become thoroughly imbricated, as the "magic" forces of good and evil battle each other for the soul of Iskandar. Moreover, the lesson of restraining pride and cupidity hinted at in earlier episodes is reinforced for a moral conclusion to this capacious romance of wonder. For at the end of the romance Iskandar seems to have forgotten that very lesson. The episode of the water of life replays in part the early episode where Iskandar becomes proud and has to be reconverted by Khidir. Iskandar's search for immortal life suggests a reliance on one's senses rather than God for true knowledge, and is thus a manifestation of pride.

The ambiguous opening of the episode of the water of life subtly implies Iskandar's pride. Encouraging his intention to enter the Land of Darkness to find the water of life, his followers claim there is no one more noble. Iskandar's initially modest response ends up claiming a special status in God's eyes:

> Bahwasanya yang terlebih mulia daripada hamba itu terlalu amat banyak, seperti, nabi Allah Adam, dan Syith, dan Nabi Idris, dan Nabi Nuh, dan

> Nabi Hud, dan nabi Ibrahim, dan Nabi Salih, dan lain daripada itu berapa ratus orang lagi, dan yang ada hadir dengan kita ini, yaitu, Nabi Khidhir. Tetapi sekalian mereka itu telah matilah.
>
> [There are those far nobler than I, such as God's prophet Adam and Seth and prophet Enoch, and prophet Noah and prophet Hud, and prophet Abraham, and prophet Salih, and other than that several hundred others, and even the prophet who is present with us here, that is Prophet Khidir [is nobler]. But all the rest of them are dead. Soeratno, *Iskandar*, 2:1373; 620] [22]

Iskandar's followers further encourage him by suggesting that no one else had been permitted by God to see either the "'Ainul Jam'iyyah" (Arabic phrase, *'ainu 'l-jam'îyat*, "the source of life") or the "tirai Dhulmat" ("the curtain of darkness"; *dhulmat* is Arabic for "darkness," in other words, the land of darkness) to which Iskandar readily agrees (Soeratno, *Iskandar*, 2:1373; 620).[23] When his followers pray to God to protect him, Iskandar arrogantly demands to know whether they are trying to frighten him. Nonetheless, he articulates trust in God who has won him victories. Ashamed, his followers protest that their prayer was not meant to frighten him or, interestingly enough, made out of envy ("dengki") but rather from love (Soeratno, *Iskandar*, 2:1374; 621).

In the Land of Darkness, Iskandar's followers themselves learn a lesson about cupidity. Guided by only a single light from the brilliant jewel carried by Khidir, on the sixth day the army hears a clattering sound from the movement of their horses' feet and wonders about the source of the noise. Khidir replies enigmatically: "Yaitulah benda yang gaib-gaib. Maka barang siapa mengambil niscaya menyesal ia. Dan jikalau mengambil sedikit menyesal juga ia" (That is a mysterious thing. If anyone takes them he will regret it. And if he takes only a little he will also regret it. Soeratno, *Iskandar*, 2:1376–7; 622). Some pick up what is on the ground while many others do not. Coming to a place with light on the tenth day, they take out the objects to discover they have precious jewels. True to Khidir's prediction, both those who took many and those who took only a few end up regretting it. Possession of jewels led to futile desire.

His followers' regrets foreshadow what later befalls Iskandar, who decides to pursue the water of life alone, without even Khidir, his constant companion. Iskandar reasons that if his army comes along they too will drink the water and bathe in it. He wishes to be different from them ("berlainan hamba daripada mereka itu," Soeratno, *Iskandar*, 2:1378; 622). The Cambridge Add. ms 3770, as excerpted by van Leeuwen, makes the point even starker with this sentence, not found in Soeratno's edition: "Maka betapa kiranja kelebihan hamba daripada meréka itoe?" (Thus how else would I be estimated greater than them?).[24] After a long absence, Khidir looks for Iskandar but finds instead the prophets Ilyas (Elijah) and Aram at the source of the water of life. God selects him for the privilege rather than Iskandar: "Bermula akan Tuan hamba Raja Iskandar itu tiada bertemu dengan mata air hayat itu dan sia-sialah perjalanannya itu. Tiadalah diperoleh seperti kehendaknya itu" (From the start my lord King Iskandar did not meet with the water of life and his journey was in vain. He did not gain what he desired. Soeratno, *Iskandar*, 2:1387; 626). The lesson of Iskandar's vain ambitions is given proleptically in Khidir's account, narrowing the possibilities of interpretation to guide or even to force its readers to a moral conclusion.

The text's moral inflection hardens as it drives towards its end. This can be seen again from the blurring of the boundary between animal and human in the concluding episode. While previous episodes, as I have discussed, offer opportunities for Iskandar to curb his aggression and violence, the human-like animals do not have inherent moral worth and they are not themselves signs pointing to something beyond. Moreover, Iskandar's reasons to desist from hunting them are not explicitly articulated. The most explicit moral lesson is the one offered by Khidir that Iskandar must not do evil. In Khidir's solo journey in the Land of Darkness, we get another episode of animal-human conflation but with a moral valence. Before meeting the other prophets, Khidir comes across a strange beast: "Maka bertemulah hamba dengan seekor binatang terlalu amat besar kakinya seperti unta, dan tapaknya seperti kaki gajah. Dan mukanya seperti manusia" (Then I met with an animal with extremely big feet like a camel, and its soles were like the feet of elephants. And its face was like a human face. Soeratno, *Iskandar*, 2:1385; 625). This human-like beast, surprisingly, speaks an Islamic formula: "La ilaha illa 'l-lah wahdahu la syarika lah" (There is no God but Allah alone without partner. Soeratno, *Iskandar*, 2:1386; 625). Upon questioning, the beast responds in "Yunan" (Soeratno, *Iskandar*, 2:1386; 625), in other words speaking Greek.[25] It tells Khidir that God made it as an eschatological sign: "suatu tanda daripada tanda hari kiamat" (a sign of the end days. Soeratno, *Iskandar*, 2:1386; 625).

An eschatological cast is present in Iskandar's final adventures as well. Initially, the arc of his journey seems to replicate Khidir's.

Iskandar meets a talking animal, in his case, a bird in a palace, who also speaks an Islamic formula – "La ilaha illa 'llah Muhammad Rasulu 'l-lah" (There is no God but Allah and Muhammad is his prophet. Soeratno, *Iskandar*, 2:1397–8; 630) – and invites Iskandar to contemplate God's greatness. However, Iskandar's subsequent encounters in his single quest deviate more and more from the structure of Khidir's. Entering the palace, Iskandar meets an archangel, Israfil (Asrafil), who rebukes him: "Hai Raja Iskandar, telah *ghurur*lah engkau dengan kebesaran dunia ini" (O King Alexander, you have been self-deceiving with worldly greatness. Soeratno, *Iskandar*, 2:1400; 631). The archangel's chiding leaves him in tears. Although penitent, Iskandar is not rewarded with the water of life. His striving for immortality is in vain, while Khidir, seeking only to restore the army's leader, serendipitously finds the water of life.

As if tears are insufficient evidence of true penitence, Iskandar undergoes several further trials and fails them most abjectly. In one trial, Iskandar meets an old man who turns out to be the devil. The satanic old man tempts him with an apple ("buah tuhfah," Soeratno, *Iskandar*, 2:1407; 634). His senses aroused by the smell of the fruit, Iskandar succumbs to temptation, even though he has just been given sanctified grapes by the archangel Israfil, grapes so potent that whoever eats them will never feel hunger or thirst again nor will ever fall ill. When Iskandar eats the apple, he immediately feels acute hunger and discovers his grapes missing. When Iskandar, realizing that the old man is the devil, asks what he has done to provoke such enmity, the devil responds:

> Adapun akan bapakmu Adam apa kejahatannya akan daku, melainkan daripa[d]a dengkiku juga maka jadi ia merasai kesakitan di dalam dunia ini daripada tempat yang tinggi daripadanya turunlah ia kepada tempat yang rendah. Dan daripada suka cita menjadi duka cita[nya]. . . . . Dan jikalau kiranya tiada dapat aku menipu engkau, niscaya binasa hatiku hingga datang hari kiamat.
>
> [As for your father Adam, indeed what evil did he do to me? It was only because I envied him that I thus casued him to feel pain in this world. (I caused him) to fall from a high place down to a low place. And thus (his) happiness turned into grief … And if supposing I cannot trick you, surely it would destroy my heart until doomsday arrives. Soeratno, *Iskandar*, 2:1408; 635]

Arising from the sin of envy, the devil's enmity is one *Hikayat Iskandar Zulkarnain* firmly rejects: Khidir serves as a moral compass to rein in Iskandar's cupidity and before Iskandar wages war each of the conquered peoples are persuaded to convert to become part of Iskandar's cosmopolitan Islamic community. In contrast, the devil's envy causes him to make war on humans without any rational basis. In subsequent trials, similar encounters with devils in disguise as old men and women, Iskandar learns his lesson and gets better at recognizing them for what they are.

Iskandar's adventure in the Land of Darkness clearly rewrites *Genesis*, as Iskandar re-experiences the original fall. The text's use of Jewish materials is unsurprising given its adoption of Qur'ānic material and testifies to the heterogeneity of its sources. While the devil is a malevolent force, Iskandar is guilty of abandoning both his moral guide, Khidir, and his duties as king to his people because of his desire for immortality. The sensuality of his desire for the fruit becomes a comment on the ultimate bodily foundation of his desire for immortality. In rewriting *Genesis*, the episode of the Land of Darkness replays the fall and offers hope for a new beginning. Consequently, the trials represent his second reconversion.

While a few more adventures follow the episode of the Land of Darkness, when the romance concludes with Iskandar's death it emphasizes his cupidity. The eulogies at his funeral recall Iskandar's worldly desires and worldly glory only to contrast them with the loneliness of death where he is shorn of all possessions. Even his grieving mother speaks of him as a negative exemplum, telling other kings and ministers to heed the lesson offered by Iskandar's life and death. To do so, she first spreads out the fingers of Iskandar's corpse. This gesture shows how his body returns to the earth empty-handed, as it were. That empty hand becomes an emblem of earthly *vanitas* and is poetically described as a "disappointed hand":

> Telah dilaluinya daripada masyri[k] datang ke padang yang luas-luas dan darat dan bukit yang tinggi-tinggi dengan segala bala tenteranya yang tiada terpermanai, sekarang dibuangkan ia ke dalam bumi dengan tangan hampa, tiadalah berharta. Daripada emas dan perak suatu pun tiada. Maka sangatlah kasihan hatinya.

> [He had crossed from the west to come to wide fields and land and tall hills with all his incalculable army; now he is thrown into the earth with a

> disappointed (or empty) hand, without possessions. From gold and silver not even one bit. Thus is he very pitiful. Soeratno, *Iskandar*, 2:1453; 652]

Iskandar is an object of pity all the more because of his great successes. His worldly achievements stand in stark contrast with the levelling nature of death. In life, Iskandar towers above all other men, but in death he is all too human. In life, he is surrounded with wealth and an army so large as to be innumerable, but in death, stripped of possessions, he returns to the earth alone and naked.

*Hikayat Iskandar Zulkarnain* ends on a sobering note, but the elegiac tone of the ending is not one that dominates the text. Rather, it is, in large part, a tale of adventure and of wonder. Depicting the world as variegated and sometimes strange and wondrous, *Hikayat Iskandar Zulkarnain* nonetheless shows that strangeness can be assimilated. In particular, the world can be – and the *telos* of the work suggests that it must be – assimilated and its dangers neutralized by Islam. As I have argued, the reframing of wonders in Islamic terms associates Islam with that which is more rational or scientific in contrast to the depiction of the unbelievers' false gods as superstitious beliefs. At the same time, the text's epistemological understanding is not that of experimental or observational science. It warns against approaching the world solely through human senses. Iskandar often does not understand what he sees and requires the prophet Khidir's help to explicate God's text contained in the natural world. The reframing of wonder contributes to the work of conversion both in the narrative and in the text's possible reception. In the narrative, Iskandar and Khidir invite potential converts to understand the world from their Islamic point of view. Thus the text itself also suggests to its readers ways of seeking explanations for natural or supernatural occurrences that are consonant with Islamic beliefs.

As a tale of wonder, the *Hikayat Iskandar Zulkarnain* introduces a larger world to a vernacular audience. However, this was not a naive audience – particularly if Winstedt is right about the transmission of the text to fifteenth-century Melaka during its heyday – but an audience with a cosmopolitan outlook. Early modern Southeast Asians living in port cities such as ones where *Hikayat Iskandar Zulkarnain* circulated were no strangers to foreign merchants from far-flung places. *Hikayat Iskandar Zulkarnain* could function in part as a geographical guide of the merchants who traded in such places as Melaka in the fifteenth century or Aceh in the sixteenth and seventeenth, or in other parts of Southeast Asia. In his conquests Iskandar traverses much of the world and readers would find Iskandar's adventures taking them to known places such as Persia, Turkey, and China, as well as to imaginary ones such as the land of *jinns*. Recognition of places known through visiting merchants offered additional enjoyment to such vernacular readers who could pride themselves as cosmopolites.

The popularity of the *Alexander Romance* around the world no doubt has many causes. In Southeast Asia, the major factor was the spread of Islam and *Hikayat Iskandar Zulkarnain* was a key text in the early history of Islam there. The encounter with Islam prompted a new vernacular in Malay in a distinctly Islamic register. This vernacular, cosmopolitan in its outlook – what Sheldon Pollock calls the "*cosmopolitan vernacular*, that synthetic register of an emergent regional literary language that localizes the full spectrum of expressive qualities of the superposed cosmopolitan code"[26] – was readily facilitated by a tale of wonders. The translation of a text like *Hikayat Iskandar Zulkarnain* offered knowledge of the larger world as well as helped to mediate and transform it for local consumption. This is particularly true with a text that itself thematizes the search for worldly knowledge even if worldly things are finally rejected as vain.

In the encounter with Islam, early modern Southeast Asia underwent not only a religious conversion, but also a linguistic conversion as its vernacular interacted with Arabic and was invigorated by it. This is fitting work for a text whose driving theme is conversion. The narrative is obsessed with the conversion of the peoples of the world, including that of its protagonist. Iskandar's own conversion becomes highlighted by its multiplicity: He undergoes two reconversions: the first at the beginning by Khidir, and a second in the eschatological end of the episode of the Land of Darkness. It cannot but be also a text of conversion for its new vernacular readers, who can assure themselves that being converts does not make them any less Muslim when even the great conqueror Iskandar requires reconversion. As Iskandar performs mass conversions in his holy wars, the *Hikayat Iskandar Zulkarnain* arguably performs its own conversion of its vernacular audience.

## NOTES

1 For the Syriac version, see *The History of Alexander the Great, being the Syrian Version of the Pseudo-Callisthenes*, ed. and trans. Ernest A. Wallis Budge (Cambridge: The University Press, 1889).

2 Anthony Reid, *Southeast Asia in the Age of Commerce; Volume Two: Expansion and Crisis* (New Haven and London: Yale University Press), 132–3.

3 Su Fang Ng, "Global Renaissance: Alexander the Great and Early Modern Classicism from the British Isles to the Malay Archipelago," *Comparative Literature* 58.4 (2006), 293–312.

4 Lode Frank Brakel, "The Origins of the Malay Hikayat," *Review of Indonesian and Malayan Affairs* 13.2 (1979), 2–33, 18. In his monumental survey of classical Malay literature, Vladimir Braginsky includes the *Hikayat Iskandar Zulkarnain* under works of the early Islamic period, giving a brief summary; there he misquotes Brakel as saying "an Arab paraphrase of a Persian work composed in Central Asia" (*The Heritage of Traditional Malay Literature. A Historical Survey of Genres, Writings and Literary Views* [Leiden: KITLV Press, 2004], 176). Following Braginsky, I repeated his mistake in my earlier article (see note 3); Brakel is here correctly quoted.

5 Pieter Johannes van Leeuwen, *De Maleische Alexanderroman* (Meppel: Drukkerij en Uitgeverszaak B. Ten Brink, 1937), 14–21, 13–14.

6 Brakel, "Origins" (see note 4), 11–15. For the Arabic Alexander, see Faustina Doufikar-Aerts, *Alexander Magnus Arabicus. A Survey of the Alexander Tradition through Seven Centuries: from Pseudo-Callisthenes to Suri*, Mediaevalia Groningana n.s. 13 (Louvain: Peeters, 2010). Comparing the Arabic al-Sûri with van Leeuwen's Dutch summary, Doufikar-Aerts is struck by the similarity of the narrative plot of *Hikayat Iskandar Zulkarnain*; she bases her observation on the evidence of the arrangement of episodes rather than linguistic echoes (Faustina Doufikar-Aerts, "Sîrat al-Iskandar: An Arabic Popular Romance of Alexander," *Oriente Moderno* n.s. 22 [2003], 505–20, 517–19).

7 Richard O. Winstedt, "The Date, Authorship, Contents and Some New Mss. of the Malay Romance of Alexander the Great," *Journal of the Royal Asiatic Society – Malayan Branch* 16.2 (1938), 1–23, 1.

8 Ibid., 5. Van Leeuwen published excerpted selections from both recensions.

9 Ibid., 9. The four Winstedt manuscripts are now kept in the library of the Royal Asiatic Society, London.

10 Ibid., 10.

11 Siti Chamamah Soeratno, *Hikayat Iskandar Zulkarnain: Analisis Resepsi* (Jakarta: Balai Pustaka, 1991), 38–9.

12 Richard O. Winstedt, *A History of Classical Malay Literature*, rev. and ed. Y.A. Talib (Petaling Jaya: Eagle Trading/ Malaysian Branch of the Royal Asiatic Society, 1991 [first edition 1939]), 59. On the historical marriage, see Oliver

W. Wolters, *The Fall of Srivijaya in Malay History* (Ithaca: Cornell University Press, 1970), 159–63.

13 Reid, *Southeast Asia in the Age of Commerce* (see note 2), 153.

14 For a list of Javanese, Buginese, and Malay works borrowing from the Alexander tradition, see Soeratno, *Hikayat Iskandar Zulkarnain: Analisis Resepsi* (see note 11), 2–4.

15 Tomé Pires, *The Suma Oriental of Tomé Pires*, ed. Armando Cortesão, 2 vols. (London: Hakluyt Society, 1944), 2: 287.

16 *Sejarah Melayu: The Malay Annals*, ed. and trans. Cheah Boon Kheng (Kuala Lumpur: Malaysian Branch of the Royal Asiatic Society, 1998).

17 According to D.K. Bassett, "Attacks of major importance were made on Malacca by Acheh, Johore or Japara in 1513, 1537, 1547, 1551, 1568, 1573, 1574, 1575, 1587" ("European Influence in the Malay Peninsular 1511–1786," *Journal of the Malayan Branch of the Royal Asiatic Society* 33.3 [1960], 9–31, 22n5).

18 Marie Antoinette Petronella Meilink-Roelofsz, *Asian Trade and European Influence in the Indonesian Archipelago between 1500 and about 1630* (The Hague: Nijhoff, 1962), 145; Charles Ralph Boxer, "A Note on Portuguese Reaction to the Revival of the Red Sea Spice Trade and the Rise of Atjeh, 1540–1600," *The Journal of Southeast Asian History* 10.3 (1969), 415–28.

19 For Ottoman relations with Aceh, see Anthony Reid, "Sixteenth Century Turkish Influence in Western Indonesia," *Journal of Southeast Asian History* 10.3 (1969), 395–415.

20 Sheldon Pollock, *The Language of the Gods in the World of Men: Sanskrit, Culture, and Power in Premodern India* (Berkeley: University of California Press, 2006). See Part II, "The Vernacular Millennium," and in particular the discussion of Southeast Asia in chapter 10, "Vernacular Poetries and Polities in Southern Asia."

21 *Hikayat Iskandar Zulkarnain*, ed. Khalid Muhammad Hussain (Kuala Lumpur: Dewan Bahasa dan Pustaka, 1986), 113. Unless indicated otherwise, all references to *Hikayat Iskandar Zulkarnain* will be to this edition and given parenthetically by editor and short title. All translations are mine.

22 Siti Chamamah Soeratno, *Hikayat Iskandar Zulkarnain: Suntingan Teks dan Analisis Resepsi*, 2 vols. (PhD diss., Universitas Gadjah Mada, Yogyakarta, 1988). In my discussion of this episode and the ending, I cite Soeratno's edition, based on Kuala Lumpur ms 21. I cite first the page number from the second volume of her dissertation, and then the page number from Soeratno's published edition in *Hikayat Iskandar Zulkarnain: Suntingan*

*Teks* (Jakarta: Balai Pustaka, 1992). This episode is also excerpted in van Leeuwen's edition, found on pages 208–31, based on the Cambridge University Add. ms 3770, which van Leeuwen calls F. Citations given parenthetically by editor and short title; all translations are mine.

23 See van Leeuwen's footnote on *ᶜainuʾl-jamᶜîyat* (*De Maleische Alexander-roman*, [see note 5], 310). There may be a typographical or a manuscript copying error in Soeratno, which uses ᶜ to represent the Arabic letter ᶜayn.

24 Ibid., 211.

25 *Yunani* comes from the Arabic word for Greek that ultimately derives from the Greek name *Ionia*.

26 Pollock, *Language of the Gods* (see note 20), 322.

# Re-writing the Episode of Alexander and Candace in Medieval Persian Literature: Patterns, Sources, and Motif Transformation

JULIA RUBANOVICH

"Candace – thus I read – was a woman-ruler / Alexander came to her in the guise of an eloquent messenger."[1] The tone of this allusion in a panegyric poem by Afḍal al-Dīn Khāqānī-yi Shirvānī, the twelfth-century Persian court poet, to the tale of Alexander and Candace implies the poet's familiarity with the story. At the same time – at the reception end – the succinctness of the reference suggests that the poet's audience had a general acquaintance with the *matière,* thus attesting to a certain prominence that the tale of Alexander and Candace had acquired in the medieval Persian literary tradition. This chapter scrutinizes the peculiar permutations that the episode underwent in medieval Persian literature, notably in comparison with its European, mostly vernacular, counterparts. I shall examine a range of medieval Persian and, where relevant, Arabic sources, in an attempt to pursue the various functional usages made of the story across different genres in the Islamic cultural domain. Further, I shall touch on the convoluted problem of a possible influence of Jewish sources on some Persian accounts of Alexander's meeting with Candace that bear – fortuitously or not – an esoteric and mystical nature. Apart from the comparative interest, focusing on the multiple treatments of one specific episode of the *Alexander Romance,* in itself a highly flexible work with multiple recensions and versions, might provide useful theoretical insights. An opportunity arises here to better grasp the dynamics of motif transformation as well as the mechanisms by which literary traditions merge, diverge, and transmute, that is, undergo processes that could lead to their "reaccentuation" (*pereakcentuacija*), to use Bakhtin's term,[2] in both meaning and function.

## I The Greek Version of the Alexander-Candace Episode and Its Dissemination

The episode of Alexander's audacious visit to the realm of Queen Candace belongs to what might be defined as the "narrative kernel" of the *Alexander Romance*. The tale figures in all the Greek recensions of Pseudo-Callisthenes's *Alexander Romance*, producing a kind of self-sufficient *petit roman* within the larger narrative.[3] To facilitate the discussion I shall briefly recall the contents of this widely known story, relying on Richard Stoneman's translation of Pseudo-Callisthenes (*The Greek Alexander Romance*, Book III, sections 18–23).[4] Alexander, tempted by accounts of the fabulous country that "was ruled by a woman of remarkable beauty, in her early middle age" (*The Greek Alexander Romance*, III, 18) writes a letter to Candace, an Ethiopian queen of Meroe [Meroë],[5] proposing, or demanding, to bring the temple and image of the God Ammon to her borders. Candace refuses, cautioning Alexander against despising her nation "for the colour of our skin" (ibid.). Then follows the rescue of Candace's daughter-in-law from the clutches of the tyrannical king of Bebryces by Alexander, who assumes for the purpose the persona of a bodyguard, invented ad hoc, one Antigonus. Antigonus is introduced to Queen Candace as Alexander's envoy. Although Alexander's trickery had worked well in the case of King Darius (*The Greek Alexander Romance*, II, 14–15), Candace did not need much effort to recognize the young king. Having heard much about Alexander's astounding conquests, she had secretly sent a Greek painter to make a portrait of him, which she kept hidden. At the right moment she showed the painting to the pretended messenger. Confronted with this proof of his identity, Alexander was abashed and furious. The Queen, "godlike in appearance," relishes her mockingly moralizing response: "Know this then, Alexander, that no matter how clever a man may be, another will be able to outwit him. Now Candace's cunning has outstripped even Alexander's intelligence" (*The Greek Alexander Romance*, III, 22).

However, the noble queen promised to keep Alexander's identity a secret. When he departed, Candace bestowed valuable gifts on him in token of her appreciation of his cleverness.[6] Although the text is mute on this point, one cannot fail to sense the ambiguity of the Queen's munificence towards Alexander. In view of her undeniable superiority over him, is she treating Alexander as a ruler equal to herself or rather as an acquiescent but cherished subject?

The tale of Candace and Alexander in the Greek *Romance* is an evident elaboration on the well-known literary topos of *victor victus* – "victor vanquished." The meaning as well as the ethical lesson of the clash between the two protagonists lies pretty much on the surface: the Queen brings about Alexander's humiliation and thus challenges the exclusivity of sagacity and invulnerability that he claims for himself. The same idea of the need for Alexander to realize his frailty in the face of Destiny runs throughout the Greek *Alexander Romance*, being expressed in episodes such as Alexander's encounter with the Brahmans (III, 5–6), or his visit to the speaking trees of the Sun and the Moon (III, 17). In the Candace episode the idea is intensified by the gender difference – a great king is being reprimanded by a single woman (III, 22).

A key episode of the Pseudo-Callisthenes tradition, the tale of Alexander and Candace appears in later Latin versions of the *Alexander Romance*, in medieval European vernacular accounts, notably Old French, Middle English, and Middle High German, as well as in Slavonic adaptations of the Alexander tale, such as Serbian and Old Russian.[7] It also looms large in the oriental Alexander tradition, including the Islamic.[8] The longevity of the episode and its wide dissemination across a variety of national literary traditions and diverse genres make it particularly suitable to cross-cultural examination. Before considering the episode in such a perspective, it will be useful to make some brief observations on the diffusion of the Greek *Alexander Romance* in the Islamic Perso-Arabic domain.

## II The *Alexander Romance* and the Alexander–Candace Story in the Islamic Tradition: Introductory Observations and the Taxonomy of Sources

How the Hellenistic *Romance* entered Arabic and Persian cultural milieux remains an unresolved issue. According to the widely accepted hypothesis of Theodor Nöldeke, there existed a Pahlavi translation of the Greek *Romance*, presumably from the sixth century, which provided a template for the extant Syriac version (sixth or seventh century); this in turn gave rise to an Arabic version (ninth century), assumed to be lost.[9] The validity of this hypothesis, however, was recently questioned by Claudia A. Ciancaglini, who argued that no Pahlavi rendition ever existed and that the Syriac text was translated directly from Greek.[10] To complicate the matter even further, there are some indications that there was more than one Syriac version as well as several Arabic renderings of the *Romance*.[11] However, whatever the obscurity surrounding the transmission, it was certainly through Arabic intermediacy that the Greek *Alexander Romance* made its way into medieval Persian literature.

Another observation concerns the relationship of the Persian Alexander tradition to the Greek source. While the prevailing view holds that the Persian adaptations derive from the hypothetical recension δ*,[12] the nature of which is difficult to establish with any accuracy, I suggest that a number of Persian versions, first and foremost the poem *Iskandar-nāma* ("The Book of Alexander") of Niẓāmī (ca. 1204) and the final part of the *Dārāb-nāma* ("The Book of Darius") absorbed some themes and motifs from the β recension (ca. fifth century), notably from the L version (eighth to ninth centuries), both of which show an affinity for Jewish sources and Jewish-Christian apocryphal literature.[13] In this context it is worth observing that Niẓāmī, offering a glimpse into the sources of his poem, writes as follows:

> The deeds of that earth-treading king (i.e., Alexander) / I did not see written in one [i.e., in a single] scroll. // Tales [about him] that were hoarded like treasures, / Were scattered in every manuscript; // I took up materials [*māya-hā*] from every manuscript, / I bound on them the ornaments of verse. // Besides new histories [*tārīkh-hā-yi navī*], / Jewish, Christian and Pahlavi [probably meaning Persian] // I selected from every book the finest of it [*naghz-i ū*]; / I took out from every husk [*pūst*, i.e., the book] its brain [*maghz-i ū*, i.e., pith, marrow].[14]

In this way Niẓāmī declares having used Jewish and other sources on Alexander, and I shall comment below on a possible Jewish influence on the tale of Alexander and Candace in the Persian tradition.

To conclude these introductory observations on the diffusion of the Greek *Alexander Romance* in the Islamic Perso-Arabic domain, I should point out that the assimilation of the Greek *Romance*, as of the Alexander figure itself – both possessing conspicuously pagan traits – into the Islamic milieu, became possible due to the interpretative process revolving around the enigmatic character of Dhu'l-qarnayn ("The Two-Horned"), who makes an appearance in the Qur'ān, in the *Sūrat al-kahf* (The Cave), 18:83–100. According to one interpretation, ultimately accepted as authoritative, Dhu'l-qarnayn is none other than Alexander – Iskandar ar-Rūmī – sent by God to subdue the peoples of the World and call them to the monotheistic faith.[15] The status of Dhu'l-qarnayn, however, always remained equivocal: while some exegetes conceded that he was a prophet, albeit sent "without a revelation" (*ghayr mursal*), others restricted his standing to that of "a pious servant of God" (*al-ʿabd al-ṣāliḥ*) and a virtuous ruler.[16] The idiosyncratic merging of the two figures facilitated the wide dissemination of the Alexander tale in Islamic literatures, and at the same time strengthened the fictional and legendary elements in it at the expense of the historical. The process is also clearly visible in Arabic and Persian versions of the Alexander–Candace tale which, considered taxonomically, surfaces in one form or another in roughly three types of works.

First are various versions of the Greek *Alexander Romance* proper, where the tale, as a rule, appears in a coherent and entire manner, as an integral part of a larger Alexander narrative. This first type would be represented by a chapter on the reign of Alexander in the poem *Shāh-nāma* ("Book of the Kings") by Firdausī, dating to the end of the tenth–early eleventh centuries; the poem *Iskandar-nāma* ("Book on Alexander") of Niẓāmī; an anonymous *Iskandar-nāma* ("Book on Alexander"), a popular prose romance from the end of the twelfth–early thirteenth century; and – in Arabic – the Occidental Arabic version of the Greek *Alexander Romance*, *Ḥadīth Dhī al-Qarnayn* ("The Story of Dhu'l-qarnayn") of about the same period.[17] As for the *Dārāb-nāma* mentioned earlier, the text contains a number of indications that it once comprised the episode in question; however, it was somehow omitted, plausibly through the vagaries of transmission.[18]

The second type is the writings of Muslim historians dealing with the legendary history of Alexander, usually in the course of their world chronicles. If included at all, the account of Candace is given, as a rule, in an abridged form and follows in its main features the versions deriving from the *Alexander Romance*.[19]

Finally, the third division includes works of purely religious orientation, at times strongly influenced by folk religiosity. They belong to such kindred genres as commentaries on the Qurʾān (*tafsīr*) and the *Stories of the Prophets* (*Qiṣaṣ al-anbiyāʾ*), but also to Ṣūfī mystical poetry.[20] Structurally, in this kind of writing, the episode of Alexander and Candace is either echoed in the form of an allusion or is inserted as an independent narrative unit, as a sort of parable. It seems to me that it is this third type of text that furnishes the most dense, the most imaginative – and as yet the most poorly explored – re-writing of the original Alexander–Candace tale.

## III "God Knows Better": Muffling the Eroticism of the Alexander–Candace Encounter

As a point of reference for examining a variety of treatments of the Alexander–Candace episode, I shall begin with the European tradition. Even a cursory glance at some of the poetic vernacular versions of the *Alexander Romance* in Middle English and Old French of the twelfth and thirteenth centuries shows strong erotic overtones in the handling of the episode which are certainly absent from the underlying Latin sources.[21] Thus, because of her sensual love for Alexander, the noble, even majestic Candace of the Greek *Romance* either immediately plunges into submission and seeks male domination, or acts as a seducer, a frivolous courtesan, never as her elevated self. Whatever the success of these versions, what seems to be essential for the European vernacular tradition in re-writing the episode of Alexander and Candace is the attempt to fit it into the conventionalized framework of courtly love. This demanded not only a transformation of the characteristics of Alexander, who had never been conceived as a "true lover" in the Hellenistic and Latin sources, but also a mitigation of the Otherness of the Ethiopian queen by dodging her exotic features, first and foremost the blackness of her skin.[22]

While most of the European vernacular tradition reworks the Alexander–Candace encounter in a love affair, accordingly altering the functional value of some of the motifs (that of the portrait, for example)[23] and at times fluctuating uneasily between the heroic and romantic modes, the Islamic versions take the episode into different directions. The difference is even more remarkable in view of the fact that the theme of the sexual union between the two was known in the oriental tradition as well: it is explicitly mentioned in the Ethiopic version and in one of the versions of the Hebrew *Alexander Romance*.[24] However, in the corpus of Perso-Arabic writings on Alexander, the theme seems to be reflected only in the anonymous Persian work *Iskandar-nāma*.[25] Although the compiler of this folk romance in prose follows the traditional outlines of the episode, he significantly muffles the motif of Alexander's encounter with Candace: she is docile and compliant with his request to provide his army with supplies; at night she comes alone to Alexander's chamber dressed as a concubine and after having concluded a kind of matrimonial union and had intercourse, Candace makes Alexander promise that upon his return home to Rūm, that is, Greece, he will send for her and she will come to live with him, leaving her kingdom to her son. Although the medieval redactor of the text distances himself from the motif of sexual intercourse between Alexander and Candace with the comment "this saying is not true, and God knows better,"[26] this rather odd but colourful reworking of the episode tallies well with the romance's generally gross emphasis on Alexander's sexual prowess, and, further, is consistent with a misogynist touch characteristic of the anonymous *Iskandar-nāma*. Alexander's traditional humiliation at the hands of the woman is counteracted by her volunteered submissiveness; with all his shortcomings the male still has the upper hand.

## IV Alexander/Iskandar and Candace/Qayd(h)āfa/Qandāfa in Perso-Arabic Historiography

Moving from the treatment of the episode in the folk romance to its appearance in early historical writings, mainly Arabic, one finds a curious shared indifference towards the narrative as a whole, the single exception known to me being the ninth-century composition *Nihāyat al-arab fī akhbār al-furs wa'l-'arab* ("The Ultimate Aim on the Histories of the Persians and Arabs") by Pseudo-al-Aṣma'ī.[27] Neither al-Ṭabarī (d. 923) in his *Ta'rīkh al-rusul wa 'l-mulūk* ("The History of Prophets and Kings"), nor al-Mas'ūdī (d. 956) in his *Murūj al-dhahab wa ma'ādin al-jawhar* ("Meadows of Gold and Mines of Gems") and *Kitāb al-tanbīh wa'l-ishrāf* ("The Book of Admonition and Recension") has anything to say about the story of Alexander and the Queen. Such historians as al-Dīnawarī (d. between 894 and 903) and al-Tha'ālibī (d. 1038) who based their accounts of Alexander's exploits on *some* Arabic translation/s of *some* Syriac version/s of the Greek *Alexander Romance* do not hesitate to treat in detail the stories of Darius, the Indian campaign of Alexander, his encounter with the Brahmans, and others.[28] As for the Candace episode, al-Dīnawarī, for example, having described in some detail the exchange of letters between Alexander and Candace, brings his account to a sudden halt with the phrase "and there were between them all kinds of stories and events" (*fa kānat lahu wa lahā qiṣaṣ wa anbā'*, al-Dīnawarī, *Al-akhbār al-ṭiwāl*, 37). Al-Tha'ālibī justifies the exclusion of the episode from his narrative by its not being appealing or worthy of note:

> And he [Alexander] urged Qaydhāfa (= Candace), the Queen of the Copts, [to supply] all kinds of riches. Had I described this story in detail and told these tales [*al-qiṣaṣ*] in full, I would have occupied (all) the pages and

would have departed from the custom [*rasm*] of this book, based upon the highlights and aphorisms [*al-luma' wa 'l-nukat*]. (Al-Tha'ālibī, *Ghurar*, 432)

Persian chroniclers, such as the anonymous author of the eleventh-century *Mujmal al-tavārīkh va 'l-qiṣaṣ* ("Compendium of Histories and Tales"), for instance, tend to abridge the story in the extreme or omit it altogether.[29]

To account for these attitudes, it would be necessary to examine the treatment of Alexander material in the above works as a whole, a task far exceeding the limits of the present chapter. However, the aloofness demonstrated by the historians seems far from fortuitous. Were they uncomfortably aware of the erotic tinge of the Alexander–Candace tale and reluctant to confront the objectionable material? Did they perceive this particular episode as too much of a fiction and, since striving for factuality was one of the basics of medieval Arabic historical writing, consider it inappropriate for incorporation into their works? In this regard the terminology used by al-Dīnawarī and al-Tha'ālibī is suggestive: both authors relegate the episode to the domain of *qiṣaṣ* (as opposed, for instance, to *akhbār* or *ḥadīth*), that is, tales for popular consumption presented with little critical attention to the factual versus the fictive.[30] Their approach thus resonates with the apprehensive comment of the learned redactor of the anonymous *Iskandar-nāma* cited above.

Together with the above considerations, which pertain to the constraints of the non-fictional genre, I would like to propose a less formalistic explanation, based on conceptions of Alexander in Arabic and Persian historiography. Whether he is depicted as the Qur'ānic Dhu'l-qarnayn, God's messenger and the peoples' defender against Gog and Magog, or perceived as a "universal sovereign" and a king-philosopher, a faithful pupil of Aristotle,[31] these conceptions go counter to the representation as *victor victus* so prominently expressed in the Candace episode; all the more so that his humiliation is articulated by the gender distinction. The importance of the gender factor for the historians' disinclination to recount the Alexander–Candace story emerges quite clearly when it is considered in comparison with another episode, that of Alexander and the King of China.[32]

The story of Faghfūr's visit to Alexander's camp in the guise of his own messenger, and the example of magnanimity and humility he gives to Alexander, provide a kind of a mirror-episode to the Candace tale. Indeed, in addition to many parallel motifs – disguise, exposure to danger on the part of the messenger, Alexander's good will in Faghfūr's release, and the like – the didactic import of their encounter differs but little from the moral lesson taught to Alexander by the noble Queen:

> [The King of China said to Alexander]: "I wished to show you that I had not succumbed to you because of my weakness or feebleness. I saw that the otherworld [*al-ʿālam al-ʿulwiyy al-athīr*] welcomed you and gave you the power over those who are stronger than you. [Yet], whoever contests the otherworld, is defeated [*fa man ḥaraba al-ʿālam al-ʿulwiyy ghuliba*]." (Al-Thaʿālibī, *Ghurar*, 439)

Or, in Niẓāmī's dramatic wording:

man-u tu zi-khāk-īm-u khāk az zamī / hamān bih ki khākī buvad ādamī
hama sarvarī tā bi-khāk-ast-u bas / kas-ī nīst dar khāk bihtar zi-kas

> [You and I are (created) from dust, and the dust (comes) from the earth. / It is best indeed for a man to be dust-like (i.e., humble). Every supremacy (persists) as far as the dust (i.e., grave) and that's it. / In the dust no one is better than another; Niẓāmī, *Sharaf-nāma*, 396:48–9]

One may suggest that the similarity of the episodes could have been perceived by the historians as narrative redundancy and most of the authors opted for the China episode, in which the moral principles were presented to Alexander by a male figure. In this regard, al-Thaʿālibī's attitude is certainly indicative: while eliminating from his historical compilation the Candace story on the grounds of triteness, as noted above, he devotes an extensive account to Alexander's adventure with the King of China (*al-Ṣīn*),[33] no less trite and popular a story than that of Candace. Later Persian historiographers followed their authoritative predecessors and included in their writings the China episode alone, being neglectful or unaware of its narrative counterpart with a woman as a protagonist.[34]

Thus, the male-focused world view of Islamic historiography appears to have been impervious to the character of the self-possessed Queen, entirely superior to Alexander in moral standing. The harshness of her lesson might be alleviated by submitting her either to Alexander's masculinity – the option followed by Persian popular tradition – or to his divine mission as a disseminator of the monotheistic message. The latter alternative is suggested by the treatment of the episode in the *Nihāyat al-arab fī akhbār al-furs waʾl-ʿarab*, where, significantly, the tale is related in full. Pseudo-al-Aṣma'ī makes Alexander/Iskandar repeatedly demand that Candace/Qandāfa smash the idols that she and her people worship, and adopt belief in one God.[35] The emphasis on Alexander/Iskandar's religious election thus mitigates the original intensity of the gender conflict. In this way, with all their seeming indifference, Arabic and Persian historians did have a say in re-writing the Alexander–Candace story: unable to absorb its "feminist" flavour they applied the principle of selectivity towards their source material to make it conform to their vision of the hero.

## V Poetical Versions by Firdausī and Niẓāmī

In contrast to the historical writings, the episode of Alexander and Candace in the versions of Firdausī and Niẓāmī[36] appears as a full-fledged and carefully structured narrative of a preponderantly didactic nature. It lacks any religious-missionary touch, but concentrates on the essence of royal power, its obligations and restrictions. In both poems the encounter with the Queen acts as the turning point in Alexander/Iskandar's education, as she leads him, literally – by means of his portrait – and figuratively, to self-recognition.[37]

Although Firdausī follows very closely, motif after motif, the episode as it appears in the extant Syriac recension, his emphasis is on his concept of ideal ruler and ideal kingship, pivotal for the *Shāh-nāma* as a whole. For Firdausī, Qaydāfa/Candace exemplifies the ideal sovereign, her gender affiliation being of no significance here: she is just, noble, generous, restrained in her emotional reactions, and above all, she possesses the *khirad*, an inborn wisdom. It is her lucid distinction between virtue and sin that places her above Iskandar with his insatiable desire for conquests and riches. In her admonition to Iskandar, Qaydāfa unfolds the didactic tenets that embody the model of an ideal ruler: success is not attained by the personal prowess of a ruler, but is determined by the Guidance of God and Destiny; he who sheds the blood of kings deserves punishment in the Fire of Hell; good deeds and generosity will earn a good name for a ruler in generations to come. This is in fact a kind of "Mirror for Princes" in miniature, reflecting the ethic-moralistic standpoint of Firdausī in his monumental work.

Unlike Firdausī, who is rather faithful to his source(s), traceable, as already noted, to the Syriac recension, Niẓāmī stretches the limits of the familiar material. Furthermore, he introduces materials that remained unknown to Firdausī.[38] In his approach, Niẓāmī appears to have been guided not so much by the considerations of the traditional poetic competition, aiming to outdo Firdausī,[39] as by his desire to put together a full account of Iskandar's story: "I shall amass in this single manuscript / all the deeds of the world-treading King" (*hama karda-yi shāh-i gītī-kharām / dar-īn yak varaq qāghaz āram tamām*; Niẓāmī, *Sharaf-nāma*, 107:27).

Niẓāmī's most essential modifications involve the heroine herself. The poet renames the Queen, giving her a telling name – Nūshāba, "The Water of Life" – that proves especially meaningful in the context of Iskandar's futile search for immortality. He places her domain in the historical locality of Bardaʿ (= Bardaʿa in Perso-Arabic geographical literature), situated not far from his native town of Ganja in present-day Azerbaijan, disregarding therefore Firdausī's locating of the kingdom of Qaydāfa in the Andalus region. In addition, Niẓāmī fuses the Nūshāba tale with that of the Amazons, thus, in contrast to Firdausī, strengthening the feminine element in the story: the Queen is a virgin, a wise, pure, God-knowing soul surrounded by chaste damsels and "in no need to see men" (Niẓāmī, *Sharaf-nāma*, 292:29/2). Furthermore, he inserts into the story the lengthy episode of Nūshāba's abduction by the Rūs and her rescue by Iskandar.[40]

Niẓāmī punctuates his version with an account of a feast in honour of Iskandar, intended to communicate Nūshāba's ethical message to the king in the most tangible way possible. Two cloths are laid in the banqueting hall, one for Nūshāba and her damsels, the other for Iskandar. That of Nūshāba carries food "beyond limit" (*zi-ghāyat burūn*) – lamb and ox, spiced birds stuffed with almonds and pistachio-nuts, various kinds of bread, sweetmeats, fragrant wine – food to everyone's heart's content. Iskandar's is a cloth of gold, and on it is a tray bearing four cups of pure crystal (*bulūr-i nāb*; Niẓāmī, *Sharaf-nāma*, 306:254/2): "One full of gold, and the other of ruby; / the third full of cornelian, and the fourth of pearl" (Niẓāmī, *Sharaf-nāma*, 306:254). Once Nūshāba starts partaking of the meal at her own table, she addresses Iskandar: "Extend your hand; eat of these victuals that are before you" (Niẓāmī, *Sharaf-nāma*, 307:257). Iskandar, however, still not suspecting Nūshāba's intention, replies:

> O simple hearted! [*ay sāda-dil*] / Do not play out of tune [*navā kazh mazan*] in order not to disgrace yourself. // In this my dish of cornelian and tray of gold, / all is stone; how may I eat stone? // How devours a man stone? / How can nature [*ṭabiʿat*] tolerate that? // Bring a kind of food which one can eat, / to which one can extend his hand with delight. (Niẓāmī, *Sharaf-nāma*, 307:259–61)

Hearing this, Nūshāba laughs in the king's face, explaining to him the true meaning of her actions: Why should one boast of things that can't be turned into food? Why do we stretch out our hands so basely (*sufligāna*) to obtain these mean stones? Why heap jewel upon jewel on this path of life that ends with the stone (i.e., grave)? Iskandar acquiesces in Nūshāba's admonition: "A thousand praises on this woman with a sound judgment / who guides us (i.e., me) towards uprightness" (*hazār āfarīn bar zan-i khūb-rāy / ki mā-rā bi-mardī shavad rahnumāy*; Niẓāmī, *Sharaf-nāma*, 308:278). Then the real feast starts.

Even this partial survey of the narrative motifs introduced by Niẓāmī into his account of the Alexander–Candace tale displays his originality in handling the episode, in comparison with other treatments in the Perso-Arabic tradition, discussed above. It also evokes a range of issues regarding the possible historical connections of the narrative. Does the detailed description of Rūs's assault on Bardaʿ echo the sporadic incursions and forays of the Scandinavian-Slavic Rūs in the course of the tenth century, which eventually led to the decline of that flourishing area?[41] Does Iskandar's rescue of Nūshāba from Rūs's captivity and his further arrangement of a marriage between her and the King of Abkhāz reflect a real historical event?[42] Could it have been Niẓāmī's intention to depict Iskandar as a local hero, a saviour, who restores justice? Inquiry into these questions would demand a detailed examination of the historical residue in Niẓāmī's epic on Iskandar as a whole and would lie beyond the scope of the present study.

I shall, however, expand on the curious motif of the feast of precious stones, as well as on the peculiar merging of the Candace episode with that of the Amazons. These motifs call for more attention regarding their origin and patterns of dissemination, for the inquiry would have a bearing on the third kind of writings where the Alexander–Candace tale appears and which I defined above as works of religious orientation, influenced by folk religiosity. I shall attempt to trace the origins of the two motifs, indicating a possible – so far overlooked – Jewish influence on the tale of Alexander and Candace in the Persian literary tradition.

## VI "The Bread of Gold": the Deployment of the Motif in Persian Mystical Literature and the Jewish Connection

I shall look at three versions of the story, each belonging to a different genre in Persian religious literature: *Qiṣaṣ al-anbiyāʾ* ("Stories of the

Prophets") by al-Naysābūrī (eleventh century); a voluminous mystical commentary on the Qur'ān (*tafsīr*) entitled *Kashf al-asrār va 'uddat al-abrār* ("The Unveiling of Secrets and the Instruction of the Pious") by Maybudī (twelfth century); and a Ṣūfī mystical poem, the *Muṣībat-nāma* ("Book of Predicaments") by 'Aṭṭār (d. 1221).[43]

Maybudī makes use of the tale in commenting on verses 15 and 16 of the Qur'ānic *sūra* 11 (*Sūrat al-Hūd*). The verses are as follows:

> 15. Whoso desireth the life of the world and its pomp, We shall repay them their deeds herein, and therein they will not be wronged.
> 16. Those are they for whom is naught in the Hereafter save the Fire. (All) that they contrive here is vain and (all) that they are wont to do is fruitless.[44]

In Maybudī's version an unnamed queen of a country in the West (*bilād al-maghrib*) invites Dhu'l-qarnayn to a feast, serving him pearls and precious gems in golden bowls. The Queen reproaches him, saying: "Since your portion in this world [*dunyā*] is nothing but bread, what are you intending to do with your rule over the Universe? Your share in this world is two loaves of bread; all the rest is futile and vain." (Maybudī, *Kashf al-asrār*, 4:371). Maybudī works the tale into the third, last, level (*naubat*) of his commentary, which deals explicitly with Qur'ānic exegesis in a mystical spirit in accordance with the "hints of the initiated and the allusions of the Ṣūfīs" (*rumūz-i 'ārifān va ishārāt-i ṣūfiyān*; Maybudī, *Kashf al-asrār*, 1:1). (The first two levels involve, respectively, the literal translation of the Qur'ānic verses into Persian and the traditional explanation according to the established authorities.) The story of Dhu'l-qarnayn's encounter with the Queen is followed by Maybudī's reference to the interpretation of the above Qur'ānic passage by Abū Bakr al-Warrāq (d. 893), a Ṣūfī sheikh who was active in Balkh: ... *har ki dunyā dūst dārad az khudā khabar nadārad* ... ("Whoever cares for *this* [my emphasis, J.R.] world, is unaware of God"; Maybudī, *Kashf al-asrār*, 4:371). This purely mystic maxim is the crux of the Queen's message to Dhu'l-qarnayn as well.

Al-Naysābūrī sets his account on an island that Iskandar Dhu'l-qarnayn reaches on his way from the West (*maghrib*) to the East (*mashriq*). There dwell the sages (*ḥakīmān*) who feed on the dried and foul-smelling bodies of the dead. They offer Dhu'l-qarnayn a gold and a silver basin full of pearls and rubies to satisfy his hunger. In response to his question, who is able to eat them, the sages reply: "This is what you are looking for, aren't you? ... But these pearls won't appease your hunger, and our food won't suit you in any way. So what do you want from us?" (al-Naysābūrī, *Qiṣaṣ al-anbiyā*, 326). Having heard this, Dhu'l-qarnayn directs his steps away and leaves the Island of the Sages.

In ʿAṭṭār's poetic version, Iskandar is received by the Faghfūr of Chīn, the Chinese Emperor whose abode is the farthest East. The Emperor serves him jewels and pearls for dinner. Iskandar says that one cannot eat such things. The Faghfūr, apparently astonished, asks whether he, while in Rūm, doesn't eat jewels. Iskandar answers that he, like everybody else, eats two loaves of bread (*garda-yi du nān*) a day and that this is enough for him. The Emperor then wonders whether these two loaves of bread are not to be found in Rūm, so that Iskandar had to go off, conquer so many countries and take the lives of so many people. Iskandar is ashamed, starts on his return journey that very moment, and says that he's had enough of conquests.[45]

In comparison with Niẓāmī's version, the account of the precious stones in the above texts displays a number of permutations. The most essential one affects the identity of Iskandar's host, and seems to result from a process of contamination. The bizarre sages of al-Naysābūrī are probably to be identified with the Gymnosophists, the naked philosophers of India; the Chinese Emperor of Aṭṭār echoes the episode of Iskandar's visit to China (al-Ṣīn), which in turn mirrors the tale of Qaydāfa, as pointed out in the reference to Perso-Arabic historiography above. At the same time, Maybudī's anonymous Queen of the West is undoubtedly none other than Qaydāfa herself. Contrary to the Arab historians, the gender identity of Iskandar Dhu'l-qarnayn's counterpart appears to be of little or no significance for our mystical authors. Rather, the episode is to be grasped as demonstrating the relationship between a mystic with his/her ascetic discipline, his/her denial of excessiveness of any sort, his/her renouncement of *this* world (*dunyā*), and the uninitiated, so prominently symbolized by Iskandar with his cupidity and insatiable appetite for material wealth and forbidden knowledge, futile in revealing the true path to God.

Another noteworthy feature is the inconsistent geographical location of the tale. The original scene in the Greek *Romance* is the Ethiopian kingdom of Meroë; in the Persian sources the episode is variously shifted to the West; to the Island somewhere between the West and the East; to China; to the kingdom of Bardaʿ in the Caucasus. To this one may add the fortified town of Samūra (or Samīra) of the Arab historians, as well as al-Andalus of Firdausī and of the anonymous *Iskandar-nāma*.

Although a similar instability in the localization of Candace's realm is already characteristic of the Greek recensions,[46] in the Perso-Arabic tradition the seemingly disparate geography is underlain by the invariant signifying the extremities of *terra firma*. Indeed, according to Islamic geographers, Samūra is situated on the coast of the Ocean (the Atlantic) and is the most northwestern point of al-Andalus; al-Andalus is perceived as the farthest region of the West, while Qayravān is taken as its beginning.[47] The West (*maghrib*) and the East (*mashriq* = China) represent the limits of the civilized world. As for Barda', the geographers locate it in the sixth clime in the northern part of the world, that bordering on the seventh clime, populated by the unruly Turkic and Slavic peoples; beyond it is the Land of Darkness (= the North Pole).[48] In this manner, the abode of Iskandar's host/hostess is always located at the extremes of the world.

The symbolic motif of the precious stones is not unknown in the Islamic Alexander tradition.[49] However, it does not seem to have an innate relation to the motif of the precious stones repast which is peculiar to certain Ṣūfī mystical texts as well as to the work of Niẓāmī.[50] A careful source study leads me to suggest that the latter might have originated in talmudic and rabbinical literature unfavourable towards Alexander, notably in the Legend of Alexander and King Kaẓia. With few modifications, the legend appears in the Palestinian Talmud (Talmud Yerushalmi), *Baba Meẓia* (2:5, 8:3); in an early Midrash *Genesis Rabba* (33:1), in *Pesiqta de-Rab Kahana* (9:24), and some later compilations.[51]

According to the account in *Genesis Rabba* (fifth century), Alexander reaches the Kingdom of Kaẓia, located behind the Mountains of Darkness. He is greeted with a loaf made of gold placed on a golden tray. "Do I then need your gold?" asks Alexander and gets a pungent answer: "Had you then nothing to eat in your own country that you have come here?"[52] Alexander explains to the King that the only purpose of his coming is to acquaint himself with the judging procedures of the Kingdom. He then witnesses a strange legal case, where both the plaintiff and the defendant are ready to renounce a treasure found in a field in favour of the other. Amazed by King Kaẓia's suggestion that the children of both sides should marry and thus keep the treasure, Alexander observes that in his country both men would have been executed and the find sent to the ruler's treasury.

The version of the Palestinian Talmud (codified about the second half of the fourth century) includes the repast motif as well:

> [King Kaẓia] prepared a meal for him [Alexander], setting before him meat made of gold and chickens made of gold. He [Alexander] said: "Do I eat gold?" King Kaẓia, (thinking in his heart) "A curse upon the man's soul!" said: "If you do not eat gold, then why do you love gold so much?"[53]

In all the versions the account concludes with somewhat enigmatic questions which King Kaẓia poses to Alexander concerning the existence of "small cattle" (*ba ʿīr daqīq*) in his country. According to L. Wallach's interpretation, this designation refers metaphorically to the presence of Israelites in the Empire of Alexander.[54]

The provenance of the King Kaẓia legend in the Jewish sources is debatable: it is argued to be either a product of purely Jewish imagination, or, to derive from a Greek source reflecting the apologetic influence of Hellenistic Jewish literature.[55] Be this as it may, regarding the reception of the account on Islamic soil, three main observations are in order. First, in the Perso-Arabic literary tradition the account became split into two coherent fragments: whereas the tale of the precious stones repast maintained a steady affiliation with the figure of Alexander/Iskandar, the arbitration episode lost any connection with the original protagonists and grew into a self-sufficient narrative, not to be discussed here.[56]

Second, in the Midrashic sources the name Kaẓia is interpreted as derived from the Hebrew *keẓ* (קץ "end," "limit"). According to a gloss in a commentary on *Genesis Rabba*: "He is named King Kaẓia, for he dwells at the end of the world."[57] Indeed, in some of the Midrashic compilations his Kingdom is placed behind the "Mountains of Darkness" and/or in Africa, the latter symbolizing the boundaries of the known world.[58]

Third, in the *Pesiqta de-Rab Kahana* (circa sixth–seventh centuries) and in the compilations dependent on it, such as *Vayiqra Rabba* and *Tanḥuma* (circa eighth–ninth centuries), the Alexander–King Kaẓia account is preceded by the episode of Alexander's encounter with the Amazons, as it appears in most of the Greek *Alexander Romance* versions.[59] The fixed sequence of these episodes points to a firm link between the two tales in the Jewish sources.[60] According to I. Lévi, in this matter the compiler of the *Pesiqta* could have been affected by the Babylonian Talmud, *Tamid* 32b, where the two initially separate episodes form a single narrative unit.[61] It says as follows:

> He [Alexander] came to a place where there were only women. He wanted to make war with them but they said to him: "If you slay us, people will

say: he killed women; and if we slay you, they will call you: the king who was killed by women." [Here ends the Greek *Alexander Romance* version.] He said to them: "Bring me bread." They brought him bread made of gold on a table made of gold. Whereupon he said to them: "Do people here eat bread made of gold?" To which they replied: "If you wanted bread, had you no bread in your own place to eat that you have journeyed here?" When he left the place, he wrote on the gate of the city: "I, Alexander of Macedon, was a fool until I came to the city of women in Africa and I learned sound counsel from women."[62]

In an early-seventeenth-century compilation, *Ḥibbur ma'asiyyot*, the King Kaẓia account is completely amalgamated with the legend of the Amazons: the arbitration is held before the women and not before the King, who entirely disappears from the scene.[63]

There are thus close parallels between the "bread of gold" motif in talmudic and midrashic literature and the motif of the precious stones' repast in the Persian versions discussed earlier: the location of the territory at the edge of the world; the fluctuating identity of Alexander's adversary, including his/her gender instability; Maybudī's and 'Aṭṭār's versions specifically mention loaves of bread as Iskandar's staple-food; Iskandar's expression of gratitude to the wise Nūshāba corresponds to Alexander's appreciation of the counsel he receives from the Amazons. The resemblance in wording between the versions of 'Aṭṭār and of *Tamid* is noteworthy.

Together with the similarities on the micro-level, the mystical–esoteric accounts of the precious stones episode linger within the basic conceptual frame of the Jewish story, whatever the variants. All of them present a world order structured differently from that of Alexander/Iskandar: the judging system of the Kingdom of Kaẓia;[64] the eating habits, if you will, of the Sages; a society comprising women alone and ruled by a woman. All of them share the moral lesson taught to Alexander/Iskandar, to wit, that the greed for riches (and, by extension, for power) is senseless, causing destruction and bloodshed. Alexander/Iskandar is an intruder into an alien milieu, not initiated into it and not conversant with its set of ethical imperatives and spiritual tenets.

The above comparison puts Niẓāmī's re-writing of the Qaydāfa episode in a clearer light. The "remake" appears due to the poet's familiarity with the Jewish tale of the Amazons and the "bread of gold," transposed to the traditional Firdausī's version, ultimately originating in the Greek *Alexander Romance*. This conclusion accords with Niẓāmī's own statement regarding his reliance, among others, on Jewish materials, as pointed out earlier.[65] Not at all undermining the poet's creative force, it thus becomes clear that his treatment of the Qaydāfa/Nūshāba episode is firmly anchored in his sources. Niẓāmī is likewise careful to gloss the town of Bardaʿ as the ancient Harūm[66] – the realm of the Amazons in Firdausī – while his locating of the Women's Kingdom in the northwest apparently follows the tradition that places the Amazons in the Caucasus.[67]

Although as yet unrecognized, the Jewish impact on certain strata of the medieval Persian Alexander tradition should hardly cause surprise. As George Cary has noted, certain episodes and passages derived from Jewish sources possess considerable importance in the history of the medieval conception of Alexander.[68] Jewish esoteric, apocalyptic, and midrashic traditions interpenetrated Islamic exegetical literature, serving as a narrative pool of themes and motifs for *qiṣaṣ al-anbiyāʾ* and *tafsīr* works.[69] Thus, judging from the Alexander material included in the *Qiṣaṣ al-anbiyāʾ* of al-Naysābūrī, a set of narrative units might have circulated that echoed a set of four Alexander episodes in *Tamid,* 31b–32a, namely Alexander at the Gate of Paradise, Alexander and the Amazons, Alexander and the Elders of the South, Alexander's Journey to the Darkness.[70] In addition, in Jewish mystical circles the Alexander figure seems to have encouraged mystical interpretation and was employed to convey messages relevant for the ascetic milieu.[71] The persistence of the motif of the precious stones repast in the Persian exegetical and mystical texts is therefore comprehensible enough.

At the same time, the identification of concrete sources of borrowing can barely be attained. The specific motif – the repast – discussed here is lacking in all the Hebrew recensions of the Greek *Alexander Romance,* as well as in the Arabic and Persian derivatives, and therefore it is unlikely that it penetrated into our texts through a version of the Greek *Alexander Romance.* Supposedly, the main channel of transmission could have been Arabic (Christian?) works,[72] probably of an exegetical and hagiographical nature, which contained isolated Jewish motifs. In this connection I shall draw attention to a work titled *Ibtilāʾ al-akhyār* ("The Predicaments of the Elected Ones"), cited in the Arabic zoological dictionary *Ḥayāt al-ḥayawān* ("The Life of the Animals") by al-Damīrī as a source of various traditions about Iskandar Dhu'l-qarnayn.[73] Among others, in his entry on the elephant (*al-fīl*) al-Damīrī relates in minute detail the story of Iskandar and the Queen of "the most distant part of China" (*malikat al-Ṣīn al-aqṣa*; al-Damīrī, *Ḥayāt al-ḥayawān*, 572–3). Curiously, the learned author has no interest whatsoever in the story proper – in his case we cannot talk about re-writing; he inserts the reference by association with an earlier tale about Faghfūr of Chīn, who, to demonstrate his might, appeared before Iskandar riding on an elephant.

For our purpose, however, the story proves highly instructive. Among the presents the Queen bestows on Iskandar on his departure are "many heads of cattle" (*qaddama lahu … min al-mawāshī shay'an kathīran*; al-Damīrī, *Ḥayāt al-ḥayawān*, 573). Could this quite odd and unexpected detail echo, in a misunderstood way, the question about the "small cattle" that King Kaẓia had asked Alexander?[74] Judging by the title, *Ibtilā' al-akhyār*, unknown outside al-Damīrī, must have been a compilation of the *Stories of the Prophets* genre.[75] The presumed character of this work thus tallies well with a type of composition that, as I've attempted to demonstrate, retained vestiges of the Jewish tales about Alexander.

Not less significantly, in the reported version of the *Ibtilā' al-akhyār* the motif of the precious stones repast gets a stronger mystical emphasis.[76] Before teaching him a lesson, the Queen of China orders Iskandar to be confined in an underground cellar, with no light penetrating into it. There he stays for three days without food or drink. When his strength has nearly left him, the Queen spreads before Iskandar a table with vessels of gold, silver, and crystal-glass, filled with pearls, emeralds, rubies, and sapphires:

> She then ordered to be placed at the bottom of the table a dish containing cakes of wheaten bread and a cup of water, which was accordingly done. She next ordered Alexander to be brought out, and made him sit at the head of the table. He looked at it, and it caused him to be out of breath from astonishment; those gems attracted his sight, but he saw nothing on it for eating. He then looked about and found at the distant end of the table a vessel containing food; he therefore got up from his place and walking to it sat near it, pronounced the name of God, and ate. When he had finished eating it, he drank out of the water as much as he required, then thanked God, and got up and sat in his first place. (Al-Damīrī, *Ḥayāt al-ḥayawān*, 573)

Interpreted in mystical terms, Iskandar's confinement in the dark symbolizes his ignorance as an uninitiated; the trial by hunger on which the Queen imposes him tangibly reflects the means of opening Iskandar's heart to the mystical Truth, while the meagre food he satisfies himself with expresses the ascetic aspiration to moderation and self-control.

The Persian literary tradition thus cast the Alexander and Candace episode in diverse moulds, reaching the most extreme degree of re-writing in some of Ṣūfī works. As this study shows, the figure of Candace, already rich and complex in the Greek *Alexander Romance*, has steadily aroused the literary imaginations of poets, writers and, it appears, Islamic exegetes, through historical periods and cultures, giving rise to various, at times opposite representations.

NOTES

1 *Dīvān-i Khāqānī-yi Shirvānī*, ed. Ḍiyāʾ al-Dīn Sajjādī (Tehran: Zuvvār, 1338/1959), 177. All translations, unless stated otherwise, are mine.
2 See, e.g., Mikhail M. Bakhtin, "Slovo v romane," *Voprosy literatury i estetiki: issledovanija raznykh let* (Moscow: Khudozhestvennaja literatura, 1975), especially 253.
3 See Corinne Jouanno, *Naissance et métamorphoses du Roman d'Alexandre. Domaine grec* (Paris: CNRS, 2002), 88–90, 152, and notes on 123–5 and 181 respectively.
4 *The Greek Alexander Romance*, trans. Richard Stoneman, Penguin Classics (London: Penguin Books, 1991).
5 The information concerning the ethnic identity of Candace and the localization of her realm displays a high degree of instability and confusion already in the Greek recensions and the early versions of the *Romance*, such as the Latin and the Syriac. Meroë, an historical Ethiopian kingdom on the Upper Nile, is conflated with the domains of the legendary Queen Semiramis, with Egypt, with the farthest eastern lands, probably India, with the extreme North and so on. Without trying to account here for this peculiarity, which appears to have originated in certain cosmographic notions of the ancient Greeks (see Jouanno, *Naissance* [see note 3], 211 and 312), I would like to observe that a similar wide fluctuation is characteristic of the Islamic Alexander tradition, and will prove significant for our further discussion.
6 For variations in this episode in some other recensions of the *Alexander Romance*, see *The History of Alexander's Battles (Historia de preliis – the J*[1] *Version)*, trans. Roger Telfryn Pritchard, Mediaeval Sources in Translation 34 (Toronto: Pontifical Institute of Mediaeval Studies, 1992), 170–3, notes 107–9. See also recently Richard Stoneman, *Alexander the Great: A Life in Legend* (New Haven and London: Yale University Press, 2008), 134–6.
7 See still George Cary, *The Medieval Alexander*, ed. David J.A. Ross (Cambridge: Cambridge University Press, 1956), 24–61. See also *The History of*

*Alexander's Battles* (see note 6), 105–11; Alexandre de Paris, *The Medieval French Roman d'Alexandre*, ed. Edward C. Armstrong et al., Elliott Monographs in the Romance Languages and Literatures 37 (Princeton, 1937; repr. New York: Kraus, 1965), 242–52, laisses 246–71; Thomas of Kent, *Le Roman d'Alexandre ou le Roman de toute chevalerie*, ed. Brian Foster and Ian Short, trans. Catherine Gaullier-Bougassas and Laurence Harf-Lancner, Série Moyen Âge 5 (Paris: Champion, 2003), 542–9, laisses 450–5; 596–623, laisses 505–28 ; Pfaffe Lamprecht, *Alexander*, ed. Heinrich Weismann, 2 vols. (Frankfurt a.M., 1850; repr. Hildesheim and New York: Georg Olms Verlag, 1970), Vol. 1, vv. 5360–6243; *Aleksandrija. Zhizneopisanie Aleksandra Makedonskogo*, ed. N.J. Bolotina et al., Biblioteka istorii i kul'tury (Moscow: Ayris Press, Ayris-Didaktika, 2005), 397–439.

8 For the episode of Alexander and Candace in the Syriac recension, see Ernest A. Wallis Budge, *The History of Alexander the Great, Being the Syriac Version of the Pseudo-Callisthenes* (Cambridge: Cambridge University Press, 1889), 118–26; in the Ethiopic version, see Ernest A. Wallis Budge, *The Life and Exploits of Alexander the Great Being a Series of Translations of the Ethiopic Histories of Alexander by the Pseudo-Callisthenes and Other Writers* (London: Clay, 1896; repr. Elibron Classics, 2005), 187–212; for Hebrew versions of the episode, see: *A Hebrew Alexander Romance According to MS London, Jews' College no. 145*, ed. and trans. Wout van Bekkum, Orientalia Lovaniensia Analecta 47 (Louvain: Peeters, 1992), 170–83; *A Hebrew Alexander Romance according to MS Héb. 671.5 Paris, Bibliothèque Nationale*, ed. Wout van Bekkum, Hebrew Language and Literature Series 1 (Groningen: STYX Publications, 1994), 124–37 (fols. 272a–5a); Immanuel ben Jacob Bonfils, *The Book of the Gests of Alexander of Macedon. Sefer Toledot Alexandros ha-Mak*doni. A Mediaeval Hebrew Version of the Alexander Romance*, ed. Israel J. Kazis (Cambridge, MA: The Medieval Academy of America, 1962), fols. 107–9, 110 (Hebrew text), 143–7 (translation). For Arabic and Persian versions of the story see below, notes 17, 19, 20.

9 Theodor Nöldeke, "Beiträge zur Geschichte der Alexanderromans," *Denkschriften der Kaiserlichen Akademie der Wissenschaften in Wien. Philosophisch-historische Classe* (Vienna: Kaiserlich-königliche Hof- und Staatsdruckerei, 1890), Vol. 38, no. 5, in particular 11–24; the gist of Nöldeke's arguments is recapitulated in Rudolph Macuch, "Pseudo-Callisthenes Orientalis and the Problem of *Du l-qarnain*," *Graeco-Arabica* 4 (1991), 232–6, and recently in Faustina Doufikar-Aerts, *Alexander Magnus Arabicus. A Survey of the Alexander Tradition through Seven Centuries: from Pseudo-Callisthenes to Ṣūrī*. Mediaevalia Groningana New Series 13 (Paris, Leuven, Walpole, MA: Peeters, 2010), 3–4. For the arguments in favour of an earlier date of

transmission of the Syriac Alexander material into Arabic, i.e., between the second half of the eight and the end of the ninth centuries, see idem 78–9.

10 Claudia A. Ciancaglini, "Gli antecedenti del *Romanzo* siriaco di Alessandro," in *La diffusione dell'eredità classica nell'età tardoantica e medievale. Il Romanzo di Alessandro e altri scritti. Atti del Seminario internazionale di studio (Roma-Napoli, 25–27 settembre 1997)*, ed. Rosa Bianca Finazzi et al., L'eredità classica nel mondo orientale 2 (Alessandria: Edizioni dell'Orso, 1998), 55–93. Cf. a suggestion by R. Frye that an extant Syriac version was based on an earlier Syriac rendition of the Greek *Romance* without a Pahlavi intermediary (Richard N. Frye, "Two Iranian Notes," *Papers in Honour of Professor Mary Boyce* [=*Acta Iranica* 24 (1985)], 185–8.

11 On this see Karl F. Weymann, *Die aethiopische und arabische Übersetzung des Pseudocallisthenes. Ein literarkritische Untersuchung* (Kirchhain: Max Schmersow vorm. Zahn & Baendel, 1901), 70–1, 83; Faustina Doufikar-Aerts, "'Les derniers jours d'Alexandre' dans un roman populaire arabe: un miroir du roman syriaque du Pseudo-Callisthène," in *Alexandre le Grand dans les littératures occidentales et proche-orientales. Actes du Colloque de Paris, 27–29 novembre 1997*, ed. Laurence Harf-Lancner et al. (Nanterre: Université Paris X, Centre des Sciences de la Littérature, 1999), 61–75, esp. 72; and recently Doufikar-Aerts, *Alexander Magnus Arabicus* (see note 9), 13–91, especially 88–9; also Frye, "Two Iranian Notes" (see note 10). In a Persian context, the possibility that there was more than one Syriac version of the *Pseudo-Callisthenes* and, consequently, several Arabic renditions, is corroborated by the findings which followed from my examination of the sources of a Persian *Alexander Romance* in prose, the *Dārāb-nāma* ascribed to Ṭarsūsī (written down presumably at the end of the twelfth–early thirteenth century). While at first sight the *Dārāb-nāma* appears to have nothing to do with the *Pseudo-Callisthenes* and seems rather to represent some very curious, apparently purely Iranian, branch of the Alexander story, I was able to identify significant traces of the Greek *Romance* in the final part of the text, which have quite probably come down from a by now extinct early redaction of the Syriac recension. See Julia Rubanovich, *Beyond the Literary Canon: Medieval Persian Alexander-Romances in Prose*, PhD dissertation (in Hebrew; The Hebrew University, Jerusalem, 2004), 202–9 (in preparation for publication).

12 Nöldeke, "Beiträge" (see note 9), 34–56; Cary, *The Medieval Alexander* (see note 7), 11; *Iskandarnamah. A Persian Medieval Alexander Romance*, trans. Minoo S. Southgate, Persian Heritage Series 31 (New York: Columbia University Press, 1978), appendix I, 167–85.

13 See Rubanovich, *Beyond the Literary Canon* (see note 11), 180–209; a comprehensive description of the L version and its particularities is given in Jouanno, *Naissance* (see note 3), 271–80.

14 Niẓāmī-yi Ganjayī, *Sharaf-nāma*, ed. Bihrūz Tharvatiyān (Tehran: Ṭūs, 1368/1989), 107:17–21.

15 See Christine Chism in this volume, 51–75; Sayyid Ḥasan Ṣafavī, *Iskandar va adabiyāt-i Īrān va shakhṣiyyat-i madhhabī-yi Iskandar* (Tehran: Mu'assasa-yi intishārāt-i Amīr Kabīr, 1364/1985), 269–305; Armand Abel, "Ḏū'l Qarnayn, Prophète de l'Universalité," *Annuaire de l'Institut de philologie et d'histoire orientales et slaves* 11 (1951), 5–18; William Montgomery Watt, "al-Iskandar," *EI*[2] 4 (1978), 127 and more recently Brannon M. Wheeler, "Moses or Alexander? Early Islamic Exegesis of Qur'ān 18:60–5," *Journal of Near Eastern Studies* 57/3 (1998), 191–215, and Doufikar-Aerts, *Alexander Magnus Arabicus* (see note 9), 135–8, 145–55.

16 For this controversy, see, e.g., Abū Ja'far Muḥammad b. Jarīr al-Ṭabarī, *Jāmi' al-bayān 'an ta'wīl āy al-Qur'ān*, 15 vols. in 30 parts (Beirut: Dār al-Fikr, 1408/1988), part 16: 17–18; Abū Isḥāq Aḥmad b. Muḥammad Ibrāhīm al-Tha'labī, *Qiṣaṣ al-anbiyā' al-musammā bi-'l-'Arā'is al-majālis* (Cairo, 1340/1921–2), 252–3; *ad-Damîrî's Ḥayât al-Ḥayawân (A Zoological Lexicon)*, trans. Atmaram S.G. Jayakar, 2 vols. (London and Bombay, 1906–8), 2:51; Abū al-Faḍl Rashīd al-Dīn al-Maybudī, *Kashf al-asrār va 'uddat al-abrār*, ed. 'Alī Aṣghar Ḥikmat, 8 vols. (Tehran: Intishārāt-i dānishgāh-i Tihrān, 1331–9/1953–60), 5: 735.

17 Abu'l-Qasem Ferdowsi, *The Shāhnāmeh (The Book of Kings)*, ed. Djalal Khaleghi-Motlagh and Mahmoud Omidsalar, Persian Text Series, New Series 1, Vol. 6 (New York and Costa Mesa: Bibliotheca Persica and Mazda Publishers, 1384/2005), 51–74 lines 671–1055; Niẓāmī, *Sharaf-nāma* (see note 14), 290–320; Anonymous, *Iskandar-nāma*, ed. Īraj Afshār (Tehran: Bungāh-i tarjuma va nashr-i kitāb, 1343/1964), 192–8; *Texto árabe occidental de la Leyenda de Alejandro*, ed. and trans. Emilio García Gómez (Madrid: Istituto de Valencia de Don Juan, 1929), 57–67. For lack of access, I was unable to examine the episode in the Arabic *Sīrat al-malik Iskandar Dhu'l-qarnayn*, the so-called Quzmān ms (see Faustina C.W. Doufikar-Aerts, "Alexander the Flexible Friend. Some Reflections on the Representation of Alexander the Great in the Arabic Alexander Romance," *The Journal of Eastern Christian Studies* 55/3–4 [2003], 195–210; Doufikar-Aerts, *Alexander Magnus Arabicus* [see note 9], 58–73) and *Sīrat al-Iskandar* ascribed to al-Ṣūrī (see Israel Friedländer, *Die Chadhirlegende und der Alexanderroman. Eine sagengeschichtliche und literarhistorische Untersuchung* [Leipzig: Teubner, 1913], 179–91; Faustina Doufikar-Aerts, "*Sīrat al-Iskandar*: An Arabic

Popular Romance of Alexander," *Oriente Moderno* n.s 22 [2003], 505–20, 512; Doufikar-Aerts, *Alexander Magnus Arabicus* [see note 9], 196–277). However, judging by the content summary of the latter (see Doufikar-Aerts, *Alexander Magnus Arabicus* [see note 9], 283–367) the episode has only a vague relationship to the Pseudo-Callisthenes tradition.

18 See Rubanovich, *Beyond the Literary Canon* (see note 11), 190–1.

19 Abū Ḥanīfa Aḥmad b. Dāvud al-Dīnawarī, *Kitāb al-akhbār al-ṭiwāl*, ed. Vladimir Guirgass (Leiden: Brill, 1888), 37; *Nihāyat al-arab fī akhbār al-furs wa-'l-'arab*, ed. Muḥammad Taqī Dānish-pazhūh (Tehran: Anjuman-i āthār va mafākhir-i farhangī, 1375/1996), 127–36; Abū al-Manṣūr al-Tha'ālibī, *Ghurar akhbār mulūk al-furs wa siyarihim (Histoire des Rois des Perses)*, ed. and trans. Hermann Zotenberg (Paris, 1900; repr. Tehran: Maktabat al-Asadī, 1963), 432; Anonymous, *Mujmal al-tavārīkh va-'l-qiṣaṣ*, ms HS or 2371 Staatsbibliothek zu Berlin, facsimile, prepared Mahmoud Omidsalar and Iraj Afshar, Persian Manuscripts in Facsimile 1 (Tehran: Ṭalāya, 1379/2001), fol. 22r.

20 Abū Isḥāq al-Naysābūrī, *Qiṣaṣ al-anbiyā*, ed. Ḥabīb Yaghmā'ī (Tehran: Bungāh-i tarjuma va nashr-i kitāb, 1340/1961), 325–6; Maybudī, *Kashf al-asrār* (see note 16), 5:371; Farīd al-Dīn 'Aṭṭār, *Muṣībat-nāma*, ed. Nūrānī Vaṣṣāl (Tehran: Zuvvār, 1338/1959), 232.

21 See Cary, *The Medieval Alexander* (see note 7), 218–20; Catherine Gaullier-Bougassas, "Alexandre et Candace dans le *Roman d'Alexandre d'Alexandre de Paris* et *le Roman de Toute Chevalerie* de Thomas de Kent," *Romania* 112 (1991), 18–44; Gaullier-Bougassas, *Les Romans d'Alexandre. Aux frontières de l'épique et du romanesque* (Paris: Champion, 1998), 405–13; Martin Camargo, "The Metamorphosis of Candace and the Earliest English Love Epistle," in *Court and Poet. Selected Proceedings of the Third Congress of the International Courtly Literature Society (Liverpool 1980)*, ed. Glyn S. Burgess, ARCA: Classical and Medieval Texts and Monographs 5 (Liverpool: Francis Cairns, 1981), 101–11; Martin Gosman, *La Légende d'Alexandre le Grand dans la littérature française du 12e siècle: une réécriture permanente*, Faux titre 133 (Amsterdam: Rodopi, 1997), 253–8; Jacqueline de Weever, "Candace in the Alexander Romances: Variations on the Portrait Theme," *Romance Philology* 43 (1989–90), 529–46.

22 See de Weever, "Candace in the Alexander Romances" (see note 21), 533–44; Gaullier-Bougassas, "Alexandre et Candace" (see note 21), 24–7.

23 Gaullier-Bougassas, "Alexandre et Candace" (see note 21), 27, 36.

24 Budge, *The Life and Exploits* (see note 8), 205; Bonfils, *The Book of the Gests* (see note 8), 145, 147 (Hebrew text fols. 109, 110). In Candace's Dido-like reaction to Alexander's departure, the Hebrew thirteenth-century version

quite probably follows the traditions of the medieval French *Alexander Romance*.

25 See note 17. Niẓāmī too seems to have been aware of the motif, but preferred to play it down (Niẓāmī, *Sharaf-nāma* [see note 14], 319:65); cf. the somewhat suggestive English translation by Clarke (Abu Muhammad bin Yusuf bin Muʾayyid-i-Nizamu-ʾd-Din, *The Sikandar Nama, e Bara*, trans. Wilberforce H. Clarke (Delhi: Low Price Publications, repr. 1995), 499 and n63. Compare also with the strong eroticism of the episode of Alexander's meeting with the Queen of Amazons in a highly curious version of the Hebrew *Alexander Romance* (MS. Bodleian Heb. d.11). See *Tales of Alexander the Macedonian*, ed. Rosalie Reich (New York: Ktav Publishing House, 1972), 54–61 (Hebrew text and English translation).

26 Anonymous, *Iskandar-nāma* (see note 17), 195:15. For the multilayered composition of this work, see Julia Rubanovich, "The Reconstruction of a Storytelling Event in Medieval Persian Prose Romance: The Case of the *Iskandarnāma*," *Edebiyât* 9 (1998), 235–7.

27 See note 19 and also below.

28 For a concise overview of the episodes from the Pseudo-Callisthenes tradition found in Arabic historical and historical-geographical works, see Doufikar-Aerts, *Alexander Magnus Arabicus* (see note 9), 21–34.

29 Cf., e.g., Anonymous, *Mujmal al-tavārīkh* (see note 19), fol. 22r: ... *va sū-yi Qaydhāfa shud va bā vay ākhar-i kār ṣulḥ uftād*; "He went to Qaydhāfa, and eventually peace was reached (between them)."

30 While in the Qurʾān the root *q-ṣ-ṣ* is equivalent in usage to the other two words, from the ninth century onwards the term *qiṣṣa* seems to have undergone a semantic transformation. Together with the meaning of "religious tale," it took on a mildly pejorative meaning and came to denote a "story full of marvels and somewhat unbelievable" (Charles Pellat, "*Ḳiṣṣa*. i. The semantic range of *ḳiṣṣa* in Arabic," in *EI*[2] 5 [1986], 186; see also Ján Pauliny, "Zur Rolle der quṣṣās bei der Entstehung und Überlieferung der populären Prophetlegenden," *Asian and African Studies* 10 [1974], 125–41).

31 For the religious aspects of Iskandar's figure, see the studies mentioned above (see note 15); for his representation in Perso-Arabic Wisdom literature, see François de Polignac, "Cosmocrator: l'Islam et la légende antique du souverain universel," in *The Problematics of Power. Eastern and Western Representations of Alexander the Great*, ed. Margaret Bridges and J. Christoph Bürgel, Schweizer asiatische Studien 22 (Bern and New York: Peter Lang, 1996), 149–64; Mario Grignaschi, "La figure d'Alexandre chez les Arabes et sa genèse," *Arabic Sciences and Philosophy* 3 (1993), 205–13; Cary, *The*

*Medieval Alexander* (see note 7), 22–3; Doufikar-Aerts, *Alexander Magnus Arabicus* (see note 9), 93–133.

32 Although absent from the Pseudo-Callisthenes, the episode of Alexander's visit to China and his encounter with the King (Faghfūr, Khāqān) is related, with plot variations, in the Syriac and Ethiopic recensions, as well as in a host of Arabic and Persian versions of the *Alexander Romance*. See Budge, *Syriac Version* (see note 8), 109–13; idem, *The Life and Exploits* (see note 8), 172–80; al-Dīnawarī, *al-Akhbār al-ṭiwāl* (see note 19), 38–9; *Nihāyat al-arab* (see note 19), 144–6; Firdawsī, *Shāhnāmeh*(see note 17), 6:106–11, lines 1551–1635; al-Thaʿālibī, *Ghurar* (see note 19), 436–40; Niẓāmī, *Sharaf-nāma* (see note 14), 378–412; *Texto árabe occidental* (see note 17), 20–3. Theodor Nöldeke suggests that the China episode must have originated in some Greek text (Nöldeke, "Beiträge" [see note 9], 22).

33 Al-Thaʿālibī, *Ghurar* (see note 19), 436–40.

34 Taken at random, instructive examples in this regard are the tenth century *Kitāb al-kharāj* ("The Book of Taxes") by Qudāma b. Jaʿfar, see Ibn Khurdādhbih, *Al-Masālik wa-ʾl-mamālik. Nabdh min Kitāb al-kharāj wa ṣanʿat al-kitāba li-Abī al-Faraj Qudāma b. Jaʿfar al-kātib al-Baghdādī*, ed. M.J. de Goeje, Bibliotheca Geographorum Arabicorum 6 (Leiden, 1889), 263–5 (French translation 205–6) and the thirteenth century *Al-Muʿjam fī āthār mulūk al-ʿajam* ("The Compendium concerning the Deeds of the Persian Kings") by Ḥusaynī-yi Qazvīnī, see Sharaf al-Dīn Faḍl-Allāh Ḥusaynī-yi Qazvīnī, *Al-Muʿjam fī āthār mulūk al-ʿajam*, ed. Aḥmad Futūḥī-nasab, Anjuman-i āthār va mafākhir-i farhangī 319 (Tehran: Dānishgāh-i Tihrān, 1383/2005), 241–2.

35 Cf. also al-Dīnawarī, *al-Akhbār al-ṭiwāl* (see note 19), 37. It is noteworthy that neither work makes such a requirement of the King of China.

36 See respectively notes 17 and 14.

37 See Claude-Claire Kappler, "Alexandre dans le *Shāh Nāma* de Firdousi: De la conquête du monde à la découverte de soi," in *The Problematics of Power. Eastern and Western Representations of Alexander the Great* (see note 31), 165–90, esp. 173–82; Kappler, "Le roi 'au coeur eveille.' Images du désir et de la mort dans la littérature persane classique," *Mélanges de l'école française de Rome. Moyen Âge* 112/1 (2000), 85–95; Kappler, "Alexandre et les merveilles dans *Le Livre des Rois* de Firdousi," in *Et c'est la fin pour quoy sommes ensemble. Hommage à Jean Dufournet. Littérature, histoire et langue du Moyen Age*. 2 vols., ed. Jean-Claude Aubailly et al., Nouvelle bibliothèque du Moyen Age 25 (Paris: Champion, 1993), 2:759–73.

38 For Niẓāmī's testimony about his sources see above, p. 126 and the discussion below, pp. 139–49.

39 Niẓāmī's attitude towards his predecessor in terms of poetic competition is discussed in E.E. Bertel's, "Nizami," in his *Izbrannye trudy. Nizami i Fuzuli* (Moscow: Izdatel'stvo vostochnoj literatury, 1962), 360–93.

40 Niẓāmī, *Sharaf-nāma* (see note 14), 430–5, 442–95.

41 For the historical events, see Clifford E. Bosworth, "Barḏaʿa," *Encyclopaedia Iranica* 3 (1989), 779–80; for the treatment of the same events by Niẓāmī, see Ṣafavī, *Iskandar* (see note 15), 200–2. In his meta-narrative comment, Niẓāmī is very explicit about the grievous and desolate conditions prevailing in contemporary Bardaʿ, in comparison with the state of prosperity when Iskandar visited it (Niẓāmī, *Sharaf-nāma* [see note 14], 290–1: 3–18).

42 Ibid, 494:70–6.

43 For the bibliographical references see above, notes 16 and 20.

44 Cited according to *The Meaning of the Holy Quran*. An explanatory translation by Mohammed Marmaduke Pickthall (New Delhi: UBSPD, repr. 1997).

45 ʿAṭṭār, *Muṣībat-nāma* (see note 20), 232.

46 See note 5.

47 Qudāma b. Jaʿfar, *Kitāb al-kharāj* (see note 34), 265–6 (French translation 207–8). It has been suggested that the idiosyncratic choice of al-Andalus by Firdausī was somehow influenced by the name of Candace's son Kandaules (see Davoud Monchi-zadeh, *Topographisch-historische Studien zum Iranischen Nationalepos*, Abhandlungen für die Kunde des Morgenlandes XLI, 2 [Wiesbaden: Franz Steiner, 1975], 172n2). However, this suggestion seems to be rather far-fetched in view of the fact that Firdausī would have inherited the name of Kandaules in the form of Qaydarūsh, i.e., as it must have appeared in an Arabic translation of the Syriac version(s).

48 Muḥammad b. Maḥmūd-i Hamadānī, *ʿAjāʾib-nāma*, ed. Jaʿfar Mudarris Ṣādiqī, Bāzkhᵛānī-yi mutūn 6 (Tehran: Nashr-i markaz, 1375/1996), 62–3.

49 The following are some of its usages: in the light the pebbles under the feet of Iskandar's soldiers wandering in the Land of Darkness turn out to be jewels: those who did not pick up anything from the ground, regretted that they got nothing, those who did gather some stones, regretted that they had not gathered more (see, for instance, al-Thaʿlabī, *Qiṣaṣ al-anbiyāʾ* [see note 16], 259; Anonymous, *Iskandar-nāma* [see note 17], 209–10; Firdawsī, *Shāhnāmeh* [see note 17], 6:96, ll. 1406–19; Niẓāmī, *Sharaf-nāma* [see note 14], 521, ll. 81–3; 524, ll. 14–17; *Texto árabe occidental* [see note 17], 15–6, 36 [Arabic text]). In the same journey to the Land of Darkness, Khiḍr is led to the Source of the Water of Life by a magic gem that starts shining on his approach to the spring (see, for example, al-Thaʿlabī, *Qiṣaṣ al-anbiyāʾ* [see note 16], 257–8; *Nihāyat al-arab* [see note 19], 142; al-Naysābūrī, *Qiṣaṣ*

*al-anbiyā'* [see note 20], 331; Firdawsī, *Shāhnāmeh* [see note 17], 6:93, ll. 1362–4; Niẓāmī, *Sharaf-nāma* [see note 14], 517–18, ll. 3–38; *Texto árabe occidental* [see note 17], 33–4 [Arabic text]). In another episode Iskandar reaches a mountain house made of topaz and lavishly decorated with precious stones; the mummy of a dead king reclines inside on a gold couch (see, for example, *Nihāyat al-arab* [see note 19], 149; Firdawsī, *Shāhnāmeh* [see note 17], 6:100–2, ll. 1477–92; *Texto árabe occidental* [see note 17], 65–7 [Arabic text]). Finally, in the description of Candace's palace the emphasis in all the versions is laid on the abundant ornamentation with all kinds of rare minerals and gems.

50 It is worth noting that in a highly unusual account of the Candace episode in recension λ, Alexander is invited to a banquet where all the food and drink is served in dishes made of various precious stones (see Jouanno, *Naissance* [see note 3], 320).

51 For the full list of sources which contain the legend, as well as for thematic variations, see Bonfils, *The Book of the Gests* (see note 8), 20–2 and especially Admiel Kosman, "A Fresh Look at the Aggadic Tale of Alexander of Macedon's Travels to *Katsia*," *Sidra: A Journal for the Study of Rabbinic Literature* 18 (2003), 73–102 (in Hebrew). I am grateful to Dr Reuven Kiperwasser for drawing my attention to this article. An appraisal of talmudic and rabbinic attitudes towards Alexander is given by Jean-Pierre Rothschild, "Alexandre hébreu, ou micromégas," *MEFRM* 112/1 (2000), 27–42. See also Richard Stoneman, "Jewish Traditions on Alexander the Great," *The Studia Philonica Annual* 6 (1994), 37–53.

52 *Midrash Rabbah: Genesis*, trans. H. Freedman and M. Simon (London and Bournemouth: Soncino Press, 1951), 1: 258.

53 Cited according to Bonfils, *The Book of the Gests* (see note 8), 21. The same motif is also found in *Yalqut Shim'oni*, a Midrashic compilation of about the thirteenth century (ibid., 22).

54 Luitpold Wallach, "Alexander the Great and the Indian Gymnosophists in Hebrew Tradition," *American Academy for Jewish Research* 11 (1941), 71–4. For a discussion of this and other interpretations, see Kosman, "A Fresh Look" (see note 51), 78–82.

55 The first suggestion is brought up by Lévi, the other one by Wallach. See respectively Israel Lévi, "La légende d'Alexandre dans le Talmud et le Midrasch," *Revue des Études juives* 7 (1883), 83, 84–5; Wallach, "Alexander the Great" (see note 54), 64–75.

56 See Muḥammad ibn 'Alī Rāvandī, *The Ráḥat-us-sudúr wa áyat-us-surúr*, ed. Muḥammad Iqbāl (Leiden and London, 1921), 74–6; René Basset, *Mille et Un Contes, Récits & Légendes Arabes*, 3 vols. (Paris, 1924–7), Vol. 2, 121,

no. 52; cf. Muḥammad Niẓámu'd-dín, *Introduction to the Jawámi'u'l-Ḥikáyát wa Lawámi'u'r-Riwáyát of Sadídu'd-dín Muḥammad al-'Awfí*, E.J.W. Gibb Memorial New Series 8 (London, 1929), 246, no. 1953.

57 Cited according to Lévi, "La légende d'Alexandre" (see note 55), 86n4. For additional explanations, see Kosman, "A Fresh Look" (see note 51), 75n9; 82n49.

58 Lévi, "La légende d'Alexandre" (see note 55), 85–7. Wallach's repudiation of the Midrashic etymology as "untenable and of no scholarly value whatsoever" (Wallach, "Alexander the Great" [see note 54], 75) is irrelevant for our argument, since we are interested in the "emic" interpretation of the name by medieval sources.

59 See, for instance, *The Greek Alexander Romance* (see note 4), book III, sections 25–6; Budge, *Syriac Version* (see note 8), 127–31; *Nihāyat al-arab* (see note 19), 140–1; Firdawsī, *Shāhnāmeh* (see note 17), 85–9, ll. 1233–1304.

60 Cf. Eli Yassif, "Ha-mesorot ha-'ivriyot 'al Aleksandr Moqdon: tavniyot sipuriyot ve-mashma'utan ba-tarbut ha-yehudit shel yamei ha-beynayim," *Tarbiẓ* 21/3–4 (2006), 98–101.

61 Lévi, "La légende d'Alexandre" (see note 55), 88–9.

62 Cited according to Bonfils, *The Book of the Gests* (see note 8), 16. Cf. a Hebrew *Alexander Romance* (ms Bodleian Heb. d.11), in which the episode of a legal case presented before Alexander is significantly overshadowed by the tale of his encounter with the Queen of the Amazons, the motifs of her opulence and independence looming especially large there. See *Tales of Alexander the Macedonian* (see note 25), 52–61 (Hebrew text and English translation).

63 See Lévi, "La légende d'Alexandre" (see note 55), 90; Bonfils, *The Book of the Gests* (see note 8), 184n56; Rothschild, "Alexandre hébreu" (see note 51), 38n29.

64 Highly instructive in this respect is Kosman's enlightening interpretation of the arbitration episode in the Hebrew sources as an encounter between two types of society, i.e., "the real world" represented by Alexander and "the utopian world" embodied in the Kingdom of Kaẓia (see Kosman, "A Fresh Look" [see note 51], 82–94).

65 See p. 126 above.

66 *Harūm-ash laqab būd az āghāz-i kār / kunūn Barda'-sh khᵛānad āmūz'gār* ("In the beginning it was called Harūm / now the knowledgeable man calls it Barda'"; Niẓāmī, *Sharaf-nāma* [see note 14], 291, line 19). The name "Harūm" is peculiar to Firdausī and not easily explicable. For attempts to elucidate its origin and etymology, see Monchi-zadeh, *Topographisch-historische Studien* (see note 47), 172–6.

67 See A.Sh. Shahbazi, "Amazons," *Encyclopaedia Iranica* 1 (1985), 929.

68 Cary, *The Medieval Alexander* (see note 7), 18.

69 See Steven M. Wasserstrom, "Jewish Pseudepigrapha in Muslim Literature: a bibliographical and methodological sketch," in *Tracing the Threads: Studies in the Vitality of Jewish Pseudepigrapha*, ed. John C. Reeves, Society of Biblical Literature. Early Judaism and its Literature 06 (Atlanta, GA: Scholars Press, 1994), 87–114.

70 Al-Naysābūrī, *Qiṣaṣ al-anbiyā'* (see note 20), 325–6.

71 See Stephanie Dalley, "The Tale of Bulūqiyā and the Alexander Romance in Jewish and Sufi Mystical Circles," in *Tracing the Threads* (see note 69), 239–69.

72 Cf. Wasserstrom, "Jewish Pseudepigrapha" (note 69), 99.

73 Al-Damīrī, *Ḥayāt al-ḥayawān* (see note 16), Vol. 2, 48, 572.

74 See p. 138 above.

75 Cf. the thirteenth-century hagiographic work entitled *Qiṣaṣ al-akhyār* ("Tales of the Elected") compiled by al-Ḥijrī al-Akhbārī (see Ján Pauliny, "Ein Werk Qiṣaṣ al-Anbiyā von Abū 'Abdallāh Muḥammad ibn Sa'īd al-Ḥiğrī al-Aḫbārī," *Asian and African Studies* 6 [1970], 87–91).

76 Among additional features that suggest a Ṣūfī colouring is the figure of the immortal saint al-Khaḍir/Khiḍr who acts as Iskandar's adviser and is perceived as an initiator and spiritual guide in the Ṣūfī tradition. See Friedländer, *Die Chadirlegende* (see note 17); Dalley, "The Tale of Bulūqiyā" (see note 71), 241–3, 261.

# Coptic Miniature Painting in the Arabic *Alexander Romance*

FAUSTINA DOUFIKAR-AERTS

At the end of the nineteenth century the famous German orientalist Theodor Nöldeke charted the Alexander tradition of the Orient, modestly calling his work "contributions": *Beiträge zur Geschichte des Alexanderromans.*[1] He could never have guessed, however, that for decades his survey would remain the leading study in the field. At the beginning of the twentieth century Karl Friedrich Weymann devoted a study to the Ethiopic and Arabic translations of Pseudo-Callisthenes, *Die aethiopische und arabische Übersetzung des Pseudocallisthenes,*[2] in which he tried to reconstruct the Arabic *Alexander Romance* that had served as an intermediary text between the Ethiopic version and the Syriac template. Nöldeke and Weymann both assumed that the Arabic version did not survive, a theory that has not been seriously refuted ever since.

However, a few years ago I traced a manuscript in the Paris collection of oriental manuscripts that bore a considerable resemblance to the supposedly lost Arabic *Alexander Romance,* following the reconstruction of this text made by Weymann. I regard the newly discovered text as a representative of a ninth-century archetype, i.e., an Arabic translation based on the early seventh-century Syriac version of Pseudo-Callisthenes's *Alexander Romance.*

The text, which is entitled *Sīrat al-Malik Iskandar* (Biography of King Alexander), is anonymous but copied by the seventeenth-century Coptic scribe, Joseph the son of ʿAṭīya, known as Quzmān.[3] The manuscript is dated to the year 1104 of the Muslim era and 1409 of the Coptic era, which is equivalent to the year 1693 CE. Shortly after my discovery of the Quzmān manuscript, I traced a second copy of this text in the Berlin collection of oriental manuscripts, and subsequently a third – only partly preserved – copy in a Paris miscellany. More recently, a fourth complete text in a Cairo collection of manuscripts has come to light.[4] The four manuscripts essentially contain the same text, representing a tradition which, for reasons of convenience, will henceforth be referred to as the Quzmān tradition, named after the above-mentioned scribe. The discovery of these manuscripts permits us, at last, to examine the Arabic *Alexander Romance* in its original form and classify it within the framework of an adapted stemma.

The oriental branch of the Pseudo-Callisthenes tradition depends on the δ* recension of the *Alexander Romance*. The Greek archetype of this recension (δ*) is now lost, but it is represented on the one side in the Syriac, Arabic, Ethiopic, and Persian versions, and on the other in the Latin *Historia de preliis* and its derivatives.[5] I situate the Quzmān tradition in the stemma as an offshoot of one of two ninth-century Arabic translations of the Syriac *Romance*. It is a precursor of the Persian tradition, as apparent in the eleventh-century *Shāh-nāma* by the poet Firdausī, and the template for the Ethiopic translation, which can be dated at the earliest to the fourteenth century. The Ethiopian *Romance*, which has been edited and translated by Wallis Budge,[6] underwent substantial changes in comparison to the Syriac *Romance*. These were explained as adaptations made by the Christian Ethiopic translator. However, this hypothesis must be abandoned now, because the adaptations appear to have already existed in the Arabic template. The most obvious changes are as follows:

The Quzmān tradition lacks considerable portions of Book I and some sections from Book II of Pseudo-Callisthenes, a trait that is characteristic for the Arabic and for the Ethiopic tradition as well.[7] Conversely, interpolations can be found in it that derive from Syriac apocalyptic texts, namely the *Christian Syriac Alexander Legend*, dated around 629; Pseudo-Jacob of Sarug's *Alexander Poem*, dated around 636; and Pseudo-Methodius's *Apocalypse*, which is currently dated around 692.[8] There are also additions from the *Dhu'l-qarnayn* tradition,[9] from wisdom literature,[10] and from other sources yet to be identified more precisely. Furthermore, the polytheistic character of the Syriac *Romance* has been modified for a monotheistic context, sometimes of a Christian, sometimes of an Islamic nature. Also remarkable is the interpolation of Alexander's visit to Jerusalem, an episode that in turn reveals a Jewish background.[11]

The scribe of the Quzmān manuscript was a Copt, and is known to have copied other manuscripts.[12] The three other manuscripts containing the *Biography of King Alexander* are undated, anonymous, and

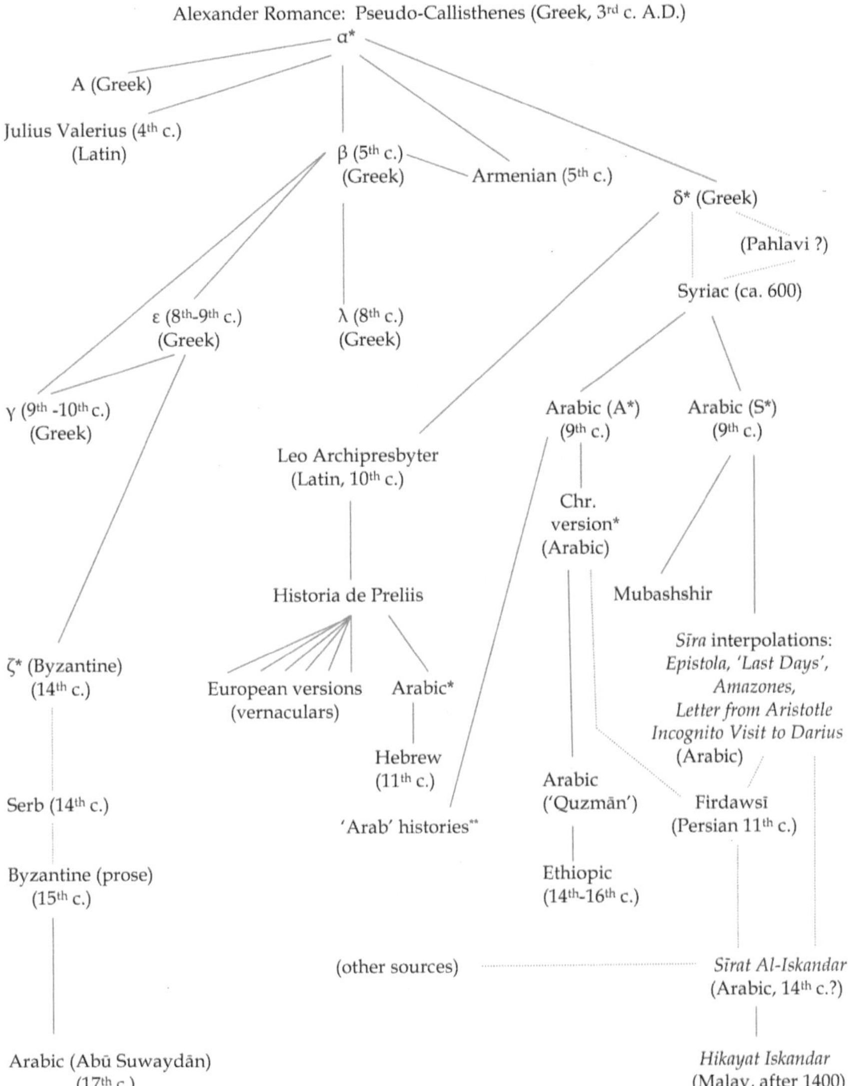


Stemma of the Ps.-Callisthenes traditions of the *Alexander Romance* (adapted from Faustina Doufikar-Aerts, *Alexander Magnus Arabicus. A Survey of the Alexander Tradition through Seven Centuries: from Pseudo-Callisthenes to Ṣūrī*, Medievalia Groningana n.s. 13 (Louvain: Peeters, 2010), 91.

without a scribe's name. The Berlin manuscript is of particular interest and will be the primary focus of attention here, for several reasons.

First of all, of the four manuscripts, its contents correspond most closely to the text of the Ethiopic *Alexander Romance*, which according to widely accepted theories was based on an Arabic template. Second, it contains a series of miniatures. We must realize that illuminated manuscripts, portraying human beings, are comparatively rare in the medieval Islamic world, especially in Arabic manuscripts. This circumstance makes the illuminated Arabic *Alexander Romance* a unique artefact. A disadvantage of the Berlin manuscript, however, is that the text is in a state of disorder; the sequence of the pages, as they were bound in the volume, is completely disrupted. However, the Berlin manuscript has preserved most of the text, apart from a few *lacunae*; this can be established, thanks to the collation of the separate pages with the other manuscripts.[13]

The title on the flower-adorned title page suggests that the manuscript volume originally contained more than one story. From what can be deciphered from the almost illegible remains, it says: "Book of Alexander, and Kalīla and Dimna,[14] and the Son of King (?) [illegible]." The medallion in the middle of the page has the *basmalah* formula, which says: "In the name of God the Merciful, the Compassionate." In the frame on the lower part of the page the words "City of Brass" and "Story of Sindibād" can be discerned. Since the manuscript only contains the *Alexander Romance* this text may have been extracted from a volume that originally consisted of a selection of several legendary stories, as the title seems to imply. This part has probably been sold, separately, and the pages bound anew, out of sequence. Moreover, damaged pages have been restored in such a manner that some words and phrases have become unreadable. Nevertheless, the text as a whole is quite accessible, written in an orderly hand. The manuscript and textual tradition of this work will be treated extensively in the commentary to my critical edition of this text which is to appear as part of my research project.[15] In advance, I will investigate the miniatures in this chapter, since this pictorial material provides additional information on the Quzmān tradition. I will treat the miniatures in accordance with the progression of the story, following the reconstructed sequence of the pages.

The first miniature concerns Nectanabus.[16] It is told that the last Egyptian Pharaoh, Nectanabus, fled from his country to Macedonia, where he settled in the temple as a priest, or rather as a magician. He seduced King Philip's wife, the Queen,[17] when she visited the temple, by appearing in the guise of the god Ammon. After fulfilling his desire, the magician left the temple to bathe in an adjacent pool. The caption for the miniature says: "Image of Nectanabus (*Baqṭānīs*), the magician, bathing in the water of the pond and the mare drinking from its water." What we see in the miniature is a mare drinking from the water of the basin. The left part of the miniature has unfortunately been destroyed, denying us a view of the bathing Nectanabus. Concerning the mare we are told that she became with foal as soon as she drank from the water. The foal was born on the same day as Alexander, whose mother, the Queen, conceived that night from Nectanabus, whom she believed to be the god Ammon. It is this same foal that appears later on in the story as Alexander's horse Bucephalus.[18] The horse's bizarre birth occurs uniquely in this *Romance* and has no equivalent in other romances, except for the Ethiopic, which was based on the Arabic. The Persian poet Firdausī[19] is the only author to mention briefly that Alexander and his horse were born on the same day, a detail that has remained unexplained. In view of the above it is plausible that it derives from the archetype of the Quzmān *Romance*.

The second miniature[20] (Figure 8.1) depicts King Philip of Macedon. Its caption says: "Image of the king with a bird on his head that drops two eggs, one on his head and the other in his lap. A monstrous snake creeps out from the egg reaching for the other egg. With him are the philosophers." In the text we are told that Nectanabus sends a vision to King Philip in a dream, causing him to believe that he returned home from his campaign that same night, to have intercourse with his wife, the Queen. The next day, when he sits outside, a bird drops two eggs from above that fall on Philip's head and on his lap. A giant snake emerges from one of the eggs and disappears into the groves, leading Philip's augurs to foretell the birth of a giant-like son and the birth of a horse that will safeguard his son from danger.[21]

This episode has an equivalent in Pseudo-Callisthenes I, 11 and it is one of the limited number of episodes from Book I that survived in the oriental tradition.[22] However, its details differ on several points from both the Syriac (δ*-recension) and the original Greek (α-recension).The story of Nectanabus and Alexander's alleged descent from this Pharaoh first occurred in the original Greek Pseudo-Callisthenes, which reflected the (Ptolemaic) Egyptian nationalist beliefs in the return to Memphis of the last Pharaoh, Nectanabus II, who fled to Ethiopia when his country was overpowered by the Persian King Artaxerxes III in 342 BC. The Nectanabus episode must be viewed against the background

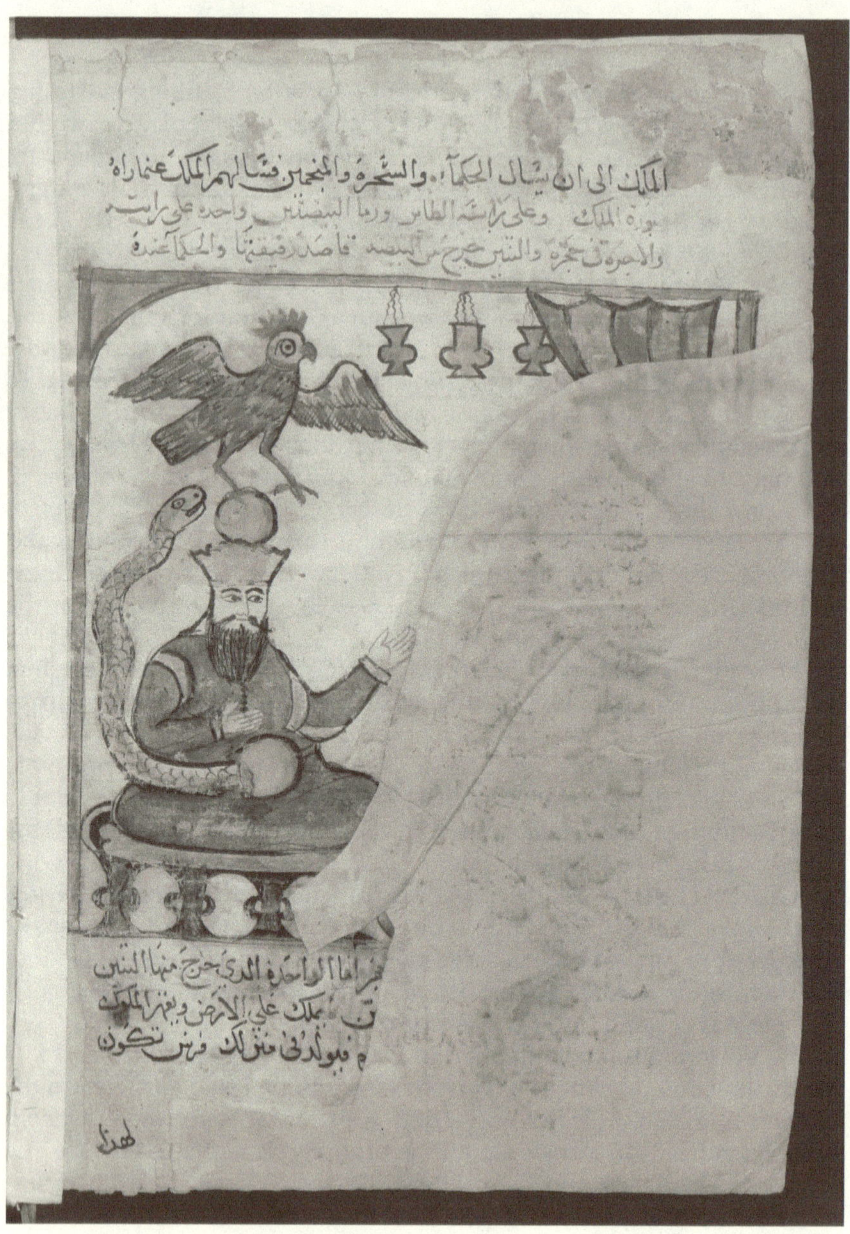

Figure 8.1. "Image of the king with a bird on his head that drops two eggs, one on his head and the other in his lap. A monstrous snake creeps out from the egg reaching for the other egg. With him are the philosophers." Arabic *Alexander Romance* (*Sīrat al-Malik Iskandar*). Berlin, Staatsbibliothek Preussischer Kulturbesitz, ms or fol. 2195, 3v.

of this *Romance*'s provenance, third to fourth-century (Roman) Alexandria. It seems to be meant as an assertion of the legitimacy of Hellenistic cultural dominance and (former) Ptolemaic rule. Nectanabus's parentage of Alexander made the Macedonian conqueror a legitimate heir to the Pharaonic throne and liberator of Egypt from Persian dominion. Nectanabus's seemingly objectionable role as an adulterous trickster actually has to be taken as an act of theogamy (because the Pharaoh is the incarnation of the god Ammon), and therefore as an acceptable, or rather inevitable, measure to restore the Egyptian royal lineage. This could not be relevant to anyone but an Alexandrian seeking to reconcile the Pharaonic past – and Egyptian supremacy – with the Ptolemaic rule and dominant Hellenistic culture, which he experiences as indigenous rather than as foreign. It is difficult, however, to define the author's exact rationale for dwelling on Alexander's Egyptian ancestry, as he himself was living in a period of Roman dominion. Could it be a sign of nationalist propaganda against "foreign" rule?[23] Or does it point to the existence of a conservative movement eager to restore ancient rituals and beliefs in a fundamentally changing (Christianizing?) society?[24] The unfathomable composition of the *Romance* tempts us to consider it not just a piece of *Unterhaltungsliteratur*, but rather as an historical document touching on socio-political issues, which, by a twist of fate, became one of the world's most famous romances, in spite of its mediocre literary quality. Much as these questions merit attention, they need a cultural–historical analysis of the author's motives relative to Roman Alexandria – an approach that this chapter cannot provide.[25]

What we have to deal with here is the Nectanabus story retold in an Arabian context together with the fact that its occurrence is unique within the oriental tradition. One of the few authors to refer briefly to the role of Nectanabus is the anonymous twelfth-century Persian author of the *Modjmel al-Tewarikh*. It is plausible that the book he cites as his source, an *Iskender Nāmeh* (Alexander book), is to be identified as an exemplar of the Quzmān type.[26] In other cases, the oriental tradition gives several descent stories, for reasons that I have explained elsewhere.[27] Quite well known is the variant that presents Alexander as the son of Darius, born from a short marriage of the latter with Philip of Macedon's daughter, frequently called Nāhīd.

The subsequent miniature in the Berlin manuscript shows us Philip's wife, Alexander's mother, surrounded by women and seated on a birth-stool (Figure 8.2).[28]

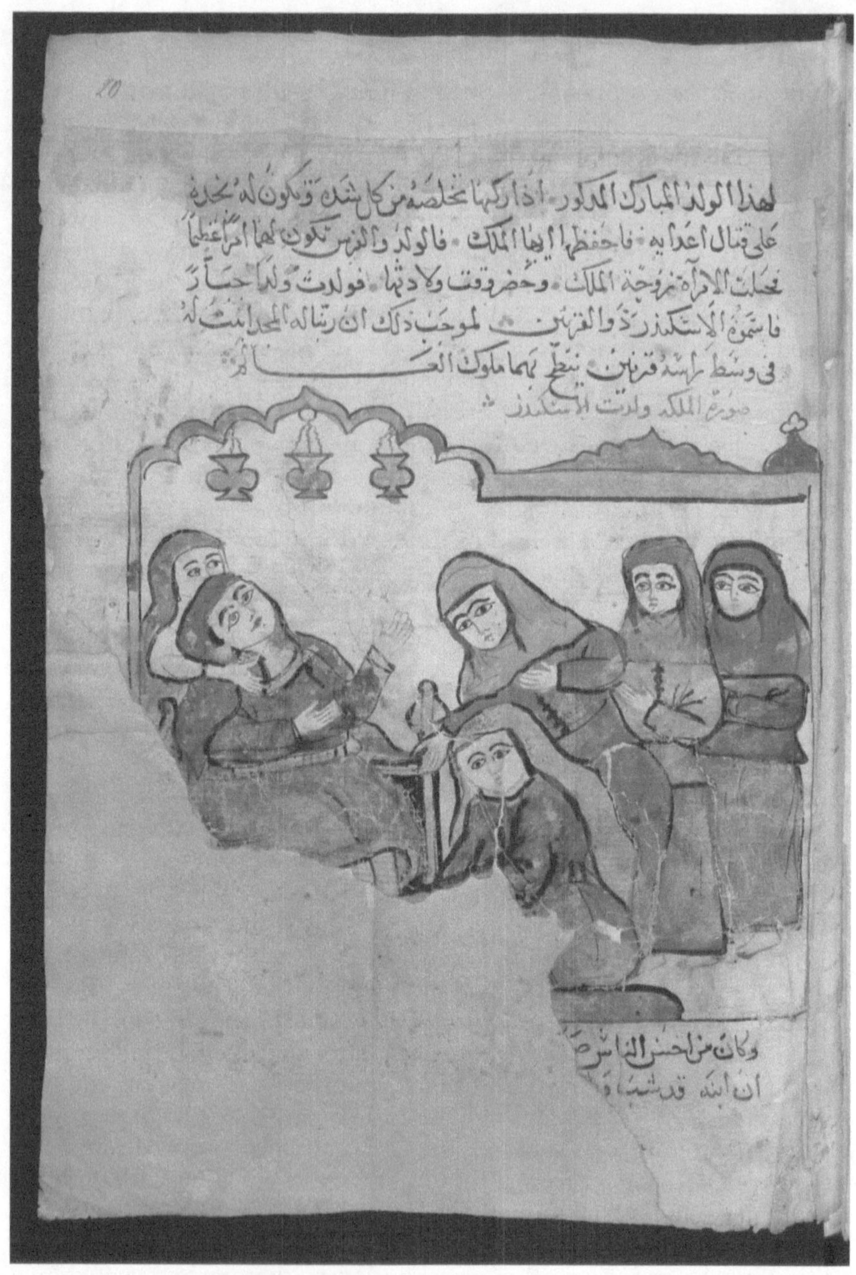

Figure 8.2. "Image of the Queen giving birth to Alexander (al-Iskandar)." Arabic *Alexander Romance* (*Sīrat al-Malik Iskandar*), Berlin, Staatsbibliothek Preussischer Kulturbesitz, ms or fol. 2195, 20r

Its caption says: "Image of the Queen giving birth to Alexander (*al-Iskandar*)." This miniature is unfortunately partly damaged, yet it would appear that the midwife has the child in her hands. The text says: "When the time had come for the Queen to give birth she bore a son, and a giant at that, and they called him *al-Iskandar, Dhu'l-qarnayn* [the two-horned], for the reason that our Lord, glory be to Him, let grow on the middle of his head two horns, that he might thrust therewith the kings of the earth." The text does not reproduce the passage concerning Alexander's birth characteristic from Book I, 12 of Pseudo-Callisthenes, where it is told that Nectanabus urged the Queen to postpone giving birth until the moment of a favourable constellation of the stars. What we read here are nearly the exact words used in the *Christian Syriac Alexander Legend*, which are interpreted as referring to the passage in the Book of Daniel (8:3–8 and 8:20–1). This passage is believed to reference Alexander the Great, i.e., the unicorn goat symbolizing the King of Greece.[29] It is very important to observe that the phrase in the *Christian Syriac Alexander Legend* was reproduced here to explain why Alexander was called "the two-horned." This accords perfectly with the hypothesis first launched by Nöldeke, for which it would ostensibly have provided substantiation;[30] however, this "evidence" remained hidden within a text that Nöldeke was never to set eyes on himself, and that has no parallel in other writings.[31]

Following this, we see a miniature in the Berlin manuscript, captioned as follows: "Image of Dhu'l-qarnayn on top of a mountain and his teacher, Nectanabus, the magician; whilst he is talking to him he all of a sudden throws him [the magician] down from the mountain and he perishes."[32] The miniature itself shows young Alexander. According to the text he throws Nectanabus down from a mountain, because the latter roused his pupil's anger by confiding to him that he himself is Alexander's natural father, and that King Philip is not his real progenitor. This typifies the Quzmān tradition, which, contrary to the underlying passage in Book I, 14, no longer attributes to Nectanabus the role of saviour of the dynasty. In Pseudo-Callisthenes it was not out of anger that Alexander pushed Nectanabus into a pit, but rather in order to try him, being annoyed with his teachings about the stars. Only when Nectanabus's fall appears to be fatal does he reveal to Alexander the truth about his parentage. Alexander then regrets being the cause of his "father's" death, which is apparently no longer the case in the Quzmān *Romance*. Here again the miniature, which is on the verso-side of the folio with the birth-scene, is half-damaged, so that we are missing the image of Nectanabus. Since there is no other representation of Nectanabus in this book his appearance will forever remain concealed from us.

Another miniature in the Berlin manuscript shows us the young Alexander on his mount. Its caption explains: "Image of Alexander mounting the horse that was born with him. He is determined to go to battle as a knight, courageously and vigorously, without any fear."[33] Seated upon his connascent horse, which the text informs us is a man-eater, Alexander is portrayed in the miniature in the same way as many Christian saints and dragon-slayers on horseback. It is also noticeable that Alexander is depicted here, as in other miniatures, with protrusions on his head. Although they sometimes more closely resemble donkey's ears, they are nevertheless meant to be horns, referring to Alexander's Arabic epithet Dhu'l-qarnayn ("the two-horned") as demonstrated by the passage about his birth, where his name is explained.[34]

In the next miniature, which has no caption, we witness a coronation, a motif common to both the oriental tradition and to Quzmān.[35] Alexander is crowned king in the presence of his subjects, whom he addresses in a sermon. They reply to his summons to convert to monotheism, expressing their obedience, and they proceed to place the crown on his head. The scene has no equivalent in Pseudo-Callisthenes, although Book I, 25–6 implicitly possesses this information.

In the following miniature, we witness Alexander's encounter with the Persian envoys. The caption explains: "Image of Alexander and the envoys of Darius (Dārah [*sic*])."[36] Alexander ties up and threatens the envoys of the Persian king, Darius, who had come to collect tribute from him. When they complain that they, being ambassadors, should be treated with respect, he replies: "Don't blame me, but blame your king, who sent you to me with a message unworthy of a king! Thus, I will treat you like robbers as your king called me one!" At the end he releases the envoys and shows them his generosity. The passage is a representation, in a revised form, of the scene in Book I, 37, which can likewise be found in the Ethiopian *Romance*.[37]

The next two miniatures appear to be mislabelled: the caption presented for the first miniature actually describes the scene depicted in the following miniature. In the first miniature, we see Alexander, mounted on his horse and addressing a group of young men. Their clothing and headgear is quite different from the men's clothing in the other paintings. It faintly recalls the knights' uniform of the Burjī Mamluks (1382–1517) consisting of the *malūṭa* cloak and the *zamṭ*, a special cap.[38] Although it is certain that the image is out of place in this part of the text, it remains to be investigated what it really represents and to which episode it relates.

The following miniature is the one to which the previous miniature's caption truly belongs, where it reads: "Image of Alexander entering Jerusalem, and the Jews presenting to him the Torah and the Books of the Prophets."[39] This miniature indeed shows the scene of the Jews raising the Torah and a banner bearing the image of the Prophet Daniel. Alexander's entrance into Jerusalem is uncommon in the earlier redactions of Pseudo-Callisthenes. However, it is part of the later recensions ε and γ, currently dated to the late ninth and tenth–eleventh centuries respectively.[40] An especially elaborated version can be found in the early thirteenth-century *Byzantine Alexander Poem*, which is based on Georgios Monachos.[41] The origin of the Jerusalem episode is much older. It seems to have originated with Flavius Josephus and was later transmitted by the above-mentioned Joseph ben Gorion, the historian Abū l-Fatḥ al-Sāmirī and the author of the Samaritan book of Joshua.[42] The episode in this text is a revision of Flavius Josephus's story, but differs from that presented by Joseph ben Gorion. The closest version seems to be the one in the *Historia de preliis*, which complicates the question of the latter's origin in relation to the Quzmān tradition. This raises an intriguing issue, i.e., whether this episode came to form part of the δ* recension, beyond the one translated into Syriac, or whether it was interpolated into both texts, independently, from a common source.

On the next miniature, we see the death scene of King Darius, which is captioned as follows: "Image of the slain Darius (Dārā); Alexander lifts him to his breast to say farewell."[43] According to the text the Persian king is assassinated by two of his confidants, called Ḥashīsh and Arsās, and is dying in the arms of Alexander. Two groups of soldiers are portrayed, probably Greeks and Persians. The cavaliers are standing next to their horses and lifting flags with a crescent on top. Darius's death, well-known from Book II, 20 (Syriac II, 12), is one of the most dramatic episodes in the *Romance*, a trait no less true for this particular text. The names of the assassins, Ḥashīsh and Arsās, are corruptions from the Greek names, Bessos and Ariobarzanes, possibly via the Syriac intermediary variants Bāgīz and Ānābdēh. Darius's death scene is a much portrayed theme in Persian miniature painting.[44]

The subsequent miniature depicts a scene at the Indian King Porus's court. Its caption says: "Image of Porus (*Fūr*), the king of India (*al-Hind*) who has a letter written to Alexander, Dhu'l-qarnayn."[45] In this painting we see King Porus, seated on his throne with his scribe next to him, to whom he dictates the letter in response to the one sent to him by Alexander. Unlike Book III, 2, the oriental tradition claims that Alexander first wrote a letter (of conversion) to Porus. The letter is rendered thus:

> In the name of God, the Merciful, the Compassionate. From God's servant Dhu'l-qarnayn the son of Philip the Greek, King of the kings of the world, to Porus, King of the Indians. Now then, verily, God raised me and put you down. He granted me victory and laid wisdom and knowledge in my heart. He let me understand His magnitude and power and His elevated position. No obscurity on earth is hidden from Him. He is aware of our secrets and our ignorance, the Creator of all creation. There is no Creator but Him and no God but Him.[46]

This expression cannot be overlooked, as it is highly reminiscent of the Muslim creed.[47] It is clear that the whole letter and its intent are a subsidiary interpolation.

The next miniature is missing a caption.[48] The surrounding text indicates that it concerns a meeting between Alexander and his advisors. It says: "In the seventh year of his reign, Alexander puts on his royal crown and apparel, and summons the chiefs of his armies and governors." These words mark the beginning of an extensive interpolation in the text, based on the *Christian Syriac Alexander Legend*. This scene is an adaptation of Alexander's Voyage to the Foetid Sea, that is, the foul-smelling and dangerous Ocean that surrounds the world. [49]

The following miniature,[50] which has also been left without a caption, gives us a view of the Foetid Sea, with regard to which Alexander's advisors claim that "neither ships sail thereon, and no bird is able to fly over it, for if a bird should attempt to fly over it, it is caught and falls and is suffocated therein. Its waters are like pus; and if men swim therein, they die at once."[51] Despite the warning of his advisors, Alexander is still determined to explore the impassable parts of the earth, even though he is advised not to sail on the Foetid Sea. Therefore, he questions the local governor before leaving:

> "Are there any men here sentenced to death?," "We have 37 men in bonds who are sentenced to death."[52] And the king said to the governor: "Bring hither these evildoers." (...) Now Alexander thought within himself, "If it be true as they say, that everyone who comes near the Foetid Sea dies, it is better that these who are sentenced to death should die," and when they went and arrived at the shore of the sea, they died instantly.[53]

The painting depicts ships with sailors upon a sea with big fish and a faced sun.

The next miniature shows a scene from Alexander's Journey in the Land of Darkness. Its caption says: "Image of the bird in the castle talking to Alexander."[54] According to the text Alexander meets a bird, who questions him about life on earth. With every answer the bird inflates himself to even larger proportions, and then returns to his former condition. The questions concern religious and moral behaviour. One example is: "Are false testimonies often given on earth?" The episode is also known from other texts, with variant questions. It is piquant that Islamic religious laws are quoted in this (Christian-oriented) text: "Do people think it is forbidden to drink wine and eat pork?" Dhu'l-qarnayn's answer is: "No, but they soon will!"[55] This episode is not based on Pseudo-Callisthenes. However, a reminiscent, although revised version, can be recognized in Firdausī's episode of Sekandar with the Talking Birds.[56] The motif of the Talking Bird is widespread in Arabic and Islamic sources. It even occurs in the remaining fragment of a Mongolian story about Sulqarnai (= Dhu'l-qarnayn).[57]

The last miniature depicts Alexander's funeral (Figure 8.3).

The caption to the painting explains: "Image of the deceased Alexander, wrapped in a shroud for burial. He is laid in a golden coffin, and the philosophers are bewailing him."[58] The final part of the *Alexander Romance*, Book III, 27–35, consists of several episodes describing Alexander's "last days," including his death and burial.[59] In the oriental tradition we find a variety of episodes, some of which, in their afterlife, became part of the *Historia de preliis* J[3]. The most prominent of these are the Funeral Sentences and the Letters of Consolation. The traditional Last Days according to Pseudo-Callisthenes are not characteristic for most known oriental texts, although it recently came to light that a translation of this episode into Arabic existed and had survived in some mss of the *Sīrat al-Iskandar*, a romance of the semi-oral popular genre.[60] In our four manuscripts representing the Quzmān tradition we find a tradition that diverges sharply from most other known Last Days' episodes. Moreover, it contains a Testament (*waṣīya*) from Alexander to Raḥamūn (Philemon?), the chief secretary.[61] It also gives a Letter of Consolation from Aristotle to Alexander's mother and an address by Alexander to his disciples, full of biblical references.[62] The Ethiopic *Romance* follows this recension, but unlike the Quzmān tradition, it ends with the traditional Last Days' episodes. These, however, are based on a different Arabic template than the one mentioned above.[63]

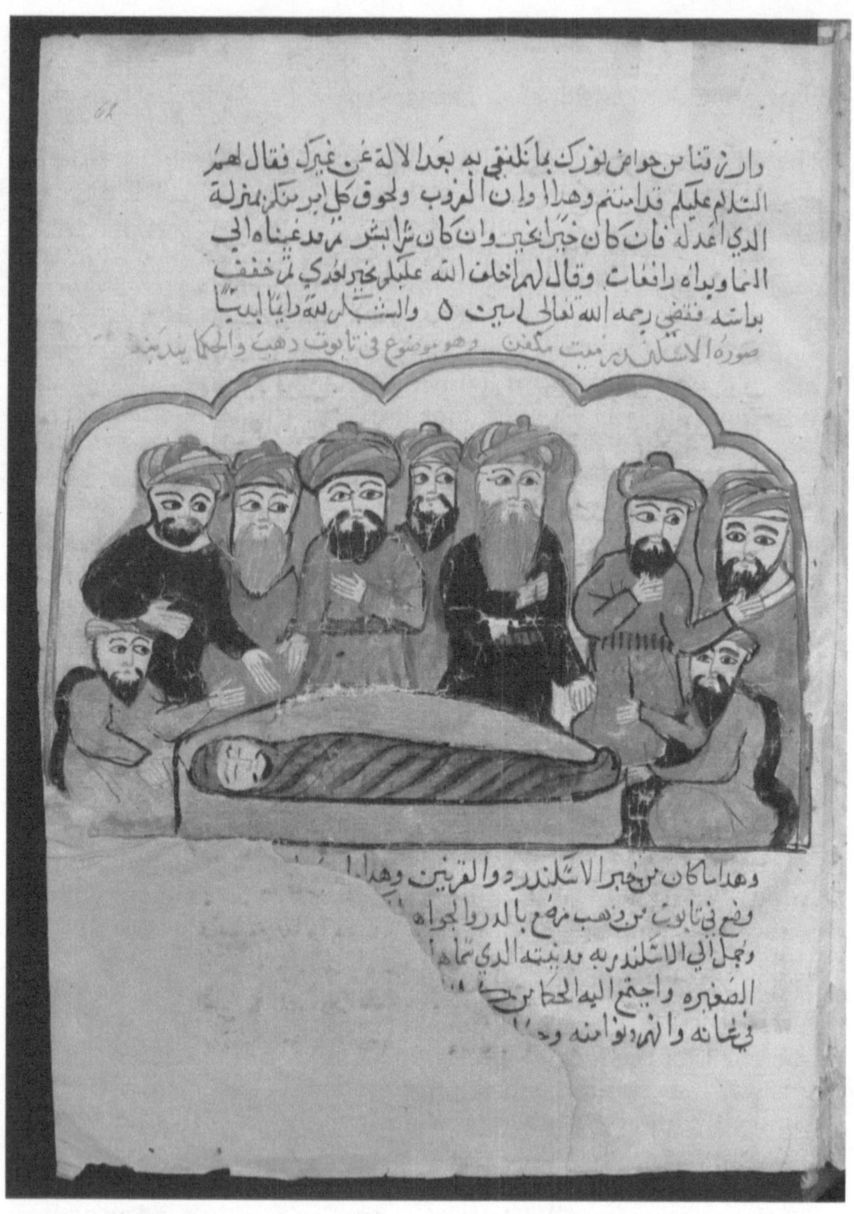

Figure 8.3. "Image of the deceased Alexander, wrapped in a shroud for burial. He is laid in a golden coffin, and the philosophers are bewailing him." Arabic *Alexander Romance* (*Sīrat al-Malik Iskandar*), Berlin, Staatsbibliothek Preussischer Kulturbesitz, ms or fol. 2195, 62r

Some general observations can be made concerning the miniatures. Examination of the paintings reveals a number of peculiar features: Alexander is mostly portrayed with a very strange upwards gazing left eye and a downward looking right eye. It would appear that this depiction was intentional: on the last page we find a description, attributed to Yūsuf Ibn Kariyūn (Joseph Ben Gorion),[64] which states that Alexander's right eye was black and looked down, while his left had the colour of an eagle's eye and looked up in the air. Apparently, the painter made an effort to match the features of this description. This characteristic seems to refer to Alexander's (actual) *heterochromia iridum*, but at the same time it symbolizes the duality of the hero: as a man connected to the world as well as to the heavens.

Another peculiarity is the portrayal of the horned Alexander, as mentioned above. The painter presents him in the appearance of a boy or young man. He never has a beard, until he is lying on his deathbed. Also beardless are the supposed Janissary (?) foot soldiers, which may also be a sign of their youth. All the other male adults, such as the sages, chiefs, and kings have beards. They are all dressed alike, except for their headgear. Persian turbans differ from the Jewish hats and the Burjī Mamaluk or Janissary outfit are readily distinguishable. Olympias (the Queen) and other women are depicted and dressed like the oriental Virgin Mary, as portrayed, for instance, in a hand-written Coptic Bible.[65] The range of colours used is fairly limited and the settings are very stereotyped, featuring red- and green-striped draperies, red- and green-blocked walls, persistently similar couches, and oriental lamps.

We can observe that these miniature paintings exemplify a popular type of art, in a style that developed in the Coptic *scriptoria* of Egypt from the second half of the seventeenth century onwards. This material is quite rare, but it can be found in illuminated manuscripts of the period, mainly in those with religious content, such as bibles, as well as hagiographies and liturgical books, as in this example. The style was also practised for icons. The art historian Zuzana Skalova coined this iconographic style as the "Beylik-Mamluke icon" tradition.[66]

Returning to the prevailing questions: Can we determine that the miniatures are the work of a Coptic painter? And can we find evidence that these illuminations belong to the Coptic iconographic tradition, as I have suggested? The first clue is the fact that the contribution of Muslim artists to miniature painting, image portrayal, is quite modest in Arabic manuscripts, apart from certain categories of writings, such as medical and veterinarian treatises as well as collections of *mirabilia*, fables, and the famous *Maqāmat*.[67] One could well imagine that the *Alexander Romance* might be considered a work belonging to one of these last categories. However, as far as I am aware no other Arabic illuminated Alexander romances are reported to have been made, and none survive.[68] This makes it more complicated to make comparisons.

The second clue is, of course, the fact that the copyist of at least one of the manuscripts, Yūsuf Ibn ʿAṭīya, was a Copt, and that the text incorporated considerable parts of the *Christian Syriac Alexander Legend*.

Conclusive arguments can be sought by comparing illustrations found in other manuscripts probably belonging to the same artistic style. In the Chester Beatty Library we can find an illuminated manuscript, dated around 1670, which contains the *Book of the Seven Climates*,[69] a work on alchemy. According to D. James, the miniatures in this manuscript reveal influences from many sources, including European woodcuts, used to create volume and shading. "Although Islamic influence predominates, there is no doubt that the painter was a Coptic Christian, for the same man also illustrated a Gospel and a copy of the Apocalypse." [70] These remarks on the Coptic iconographic tradition are certainly worth noticing, especially since the Coptic tradition of the seventeenth century is as yet poorly described. Most of the illustrations I could lay my hands on, printed in books, are samples of religious painting, mostly from the Coptic Museum in Cairo.[71] Then, there are a few more texts adorned with miniatures that apparently represent the same style, i.e., the Berlin ms or.fol. 2564, a fable collection integrated in a frame story, which was probably copied by a Copt. Two other texts are Munich ms Code Arab. 615, and the McGill Collection, RBD A1, both containing a copy of *Kalīla wa Dimna*, the last one dated 1645.

When we examine certain details of the Berlin manuscript miniature paintings in the *Alexander Romance*, like the composition of the scenes, the manner of depicting trees, draperies, and couches, the portrayal of physical characteristics of the individuals, and the use of colours, they decidedly correspond to the Coptic iconography of this period.

Therefore, I ponder the idea that the painter of the Berlin manuscripts was a Copt, participating in a school of miniature painting particularly known from the later decades of the seventeenth century.

While the manuscript is highly interesting from an artistic point of view, its contents are worth no less attention. This Arabic text provides us with an *Alexander Romance* that reveals a mixture of Islamic, Christian, and Jewish features. It is based on the Syriac Pseudo-Callisthenes, several Syriac apocalyptic texts, Josephus's *Antiquities*, and on materials from the Islamic tradition, such as Qur'ān Commentaries and Lives of the Prophets. The textual features and the contents of the story are ambiguous as far as the (monotheistic) religious character is concerned. First of all, we have to consider the fact that Alexander is called, occasionally, but throughout the text, by his Islamic epithet *Dhu'l-qarnayn*, "the two-horned," the name that first occurred in the Qur'ān 18:83. As we take, for example, the letter of conversion written by Alexander to King Porus of India we have to bear in mind that no such letter exists in previous Alexander romances, that its purport is obviously Islamic, and that phrases in it are highly reminiscent of the Muslim creed. This letter is clearly an interpolation from a Muslim source, and in my view most of the letters in this text are of Muslim extraction.

On the other hand, we also find in this text passages that can be identified as derivations from the Christian Syriac apocalyptic tradition. This is clearly demonstrated in the sentences dedicated to Alexander's birth and naming, as referred to above. Furthermore, there is a section that is based entirely on the *Christian Syriac Alexander Legend*. Here, we find Alexander praying to the Lord: "You have let grow on my head two horns, that I might thrust therewith the kings of the earth," the same phrase that associates Alexander, simultaneously, with the horns and the Book of Daniel. This link with the Book of Daniel from the Old Testament is precisely the key to the incorporation of Alexander into the Christian apocalyptic tradition and also to the story of Alexander's visit to Jerusalem, which was first told by Flavius Josephus and later by Joseph ben Gorion. The latter, as we have seen, is also mentioned by name in the Berlin manuscript as one of the sources. It is in this connection that the miniature shows the high priest with the Torah and the portrait of the prophet Daniel on the banner.

At the same time, it is the same passage that links the Christian apocalyptic tradition to the Islamic tradition of the two-horned one, provided that we accept the principle of Nöldeke's theories, modified in harmony with the new insights about the dating of these apocalypses. On these grounds, this miscellaneous text must be qualified as a fusion of traditions.

As to the artistic background of the miniatures in the Berlin ms or fol. 2195, the manuscript is a fine example of the material culture of the Middle East and the interchange of artistic conventions between religious and profane texts. What remains to be studied is the milieu in which the composition originated and what may have motivated the revival of interest in Alexander's life and exploits in seventeenth-century Egypt.

## NOTES

1 Theodor Nöldeke, *Beiträge zur Geschichte des Alexanderromans*, Denkschriften der Kaiserlichen Akademie der Wissenschaften. Philosophisch-historische Classe 38, Abhandlung V (Vienna: kaiserlich-königlichen Hof- und Staatsdruckerei, 1890).

2 Karl Friedrich Weymann, *Die aethiopische und arabische Übersetzung des Pseudocallisthenes. Eine literarkritische Untersuchung* (Kirchhain: Max Schmersow vorm. Zahn & Baendel, 1901).

3 Paris, Bibliothèque nationale, ms arabe 3687.

4 Berlin, Staatsbibliothek Preussischer Kulturbesitz, ms or fol. 2195, and Paris, Bibliothèque Nationale, ms arabe 212,[16] which comprises only the beginning of the text. For the fourth manuscript, from Cairo, I am obliged to Adel Sidurus, who kindly brought this text to my attention.

5 The *Historia de preliis*, originally entitled *Nativitas et Victoria Alexandri Magni*, is the Latin translation by Archpriest Leo, made between 950 and 970 on the basis of a Greek manuscript from Constantinople, now lost. See *The History of Alexander's Battles (Historia de Preliis - the J1 version)*, trans. R. Telfryn Pritchard, Mediaeval Sources in Translation 34 (Toronto: Pontifical Institute of Mediaeval Studies, 1992).

6 Ernest A. Wallis Budge, *The Life and Exploits of Alexander the Great, being a Series of Ethiopic Histories of Alexander by the Pseudo-Callisthenes and other Writers*, 2 vols (London: Clay, 1896).

7 See Faustina Doufikar-Aerts, *Alexander Magnus Arabicus. A Survey of the Alexander Tradition through Seven Centuries: from Pseudo-Callisthenes to Ṣūrī*, Mediaevalia Groningana n.s. 13 (Louvain: Peeters, 2010), 1.8.4.

8 *Das Syrische Alexanderlied*, trans. Gerrit J. Reinink, Corpus Scriptorum Christianorum Orientalium, Scriptores Syri 196 (Louvain: Peeters, 1983); idem, *Die Syrische Apokalypse des Pseudo-Methodius*, ed. idem, Corpus Scriptorum Christianorum Orientalium 540, Scriptores Syri 220 (Louvain: Peeters, 1993), trans. idem, Corpus Scriptorum Christianorum Orientalium 541, Scriptores Syri 221 (Louvain: Peeters, 1993); and idem, "Heraclius, the New Alexander: Apocalyptic Prophecies during the Reign of Heraclius," in *The Reign of Heraclius (610–41): Crisis and Confrontation*, ed. idem and Bernard H. Stolte, Groningen Studies in Cultural Change 2 (Louvain: Peeters, 2002) 81–94; idem, "Alexander the Great in Seventh-Century Syriac "Apocalyptic" Texts," *Byzantinorossica* 2 (2003), 150–78.

9 The *Dhu'l-qarnayn* tradition was coined and described in Doufikar-Aerts, *Alexander Magnus Arabicus* (see note 7), chapter 3.

10 In particular the so-called Funeral Sentences. See ibid., 2.3.4.

11 This episode is related to the story in Flavius Josephus (1st c.) *Antiquities of the Jews*, XI:5–6, which also has been revised and transmitted by Joseph ben Gorion (tenth c.), also known as Gorionides and Josippus, and in the *Kitāb at-Tārīkh* (Book of History) by Abū l-Fatḥ al-Sāmirī. See Julius Wellhausen, *Der arabische Josippus* (Berlin: Weidmannsche Buchhandlung, 1897), 9–10, and Eduardus Vilmar, *Abulfathi Annales Samaritani* (Gotha: Perthes, 1865), 84–5, respectively. A short version also occurs in the Samaritan Book of Joshua, written in Arabic, see *Chronicon Samaritanum, arabice conscriptum Liber Josuae*, ed. Theodoor Willem Jan Juynboll (Leiden: S&J. Luchtmans, 1848), 46–8.

12 Paris, Bibliothèque nationale, ms arabe $275^{15}$, a miscellany, and ms arabe 299, containing *Historia Compendiosa Dynastiarum* by Gregorius Abū l-Faraj Ibn al-ʿIbrī. See Gérard Troupeau, *Catalogue de manuscrits arabes*, Vol. 1 (Paris: Bibliothèque nationale, 1972).

13 I have made a reconstruction of the order of pages, which is available now for the users of the Berlin Library.

14 A book of Fables, translated from Pahlavi into Arabic in the 8th century by Ibn al-Muqaffaʿ († 757). My thanks go to Dr H. Kurio, who took interest in examining with me the title page of the manuscript in Berlin, and whose suggestions sustained my readings.

15 *Alexander the Great: a Muslim in disguise. An approach to unravel the process of socio-cultural changes and intercultural interactions as reflected in the recently discovered Arabic Alexander Romance.* This was a project of the Netherlands Organisation for Scientific Research (NWO) in cooperation with Leiden University (2004–8). Edition with translation is in progress.

16 Ms or fol. 2195, 3r. In Greek: ὁ Νεκτανεβώς or ὁ Νεκτανεβής and ὁ Νεκτανεβίς.

17 This refers to Olympias, but her name is never mentioned.

18 The name as such does not occur. Further, we should not make a point of the biological incongruity of the duration of these pregnancies.

19 Dick Davis, *Shāhnāmeh. The Persian Book of Kings, Abolqasem Ferdowsi* (New York: Penguin, 2007), 455. See also Faustina Doufikar-Aerts, "King Midas' Ears on Alexander's Head. In Search of the Afro-Asiatic Alexander Cycle," *The Alexander Romance in Persia and the East*, ed. Richard Stoneman et al., Ancient Narrative Suppl. 15 (Groningen: Barkhuis & Groningen University Library, 2012), 61–79, 66–7.

20 Ms or fol. 2195, 3v.

21 See Doufikar-Aerts, "King Midas' Ears" (note 19), 61–79, 66.

22 See above, p. 154 and note 7. The recensions relevant for comparison are the Syriac *Alexander Romance,* the template for the translations into Arabic and the original Greek α-recension.

23 In I, 32 an omen concerning the future city of Alexandria is explained thus: "the city you have ordered to be built, O king, will feed the whole inhabited world, and those who are born in it will reach all parts of the world; just as the birds fly over the whole earth" in the translation by Richard Stoneman, *The Greek Alexander Romance* (Hammondsworth: Penguin, 1991), 65. Perhaps the phrase stating that "the city will feed the whole inhabited world" refers to the fact that Alexandria was of great importance for the grain supply of Rome and other regions in the Middle East.

24 In the episode concerning the foundation of Alexandria, the Serapis cult has a prominent place. This cult, which was actually founded by Ptolemy I, still flourished in the third century CE. It may have come under pressure soon after; during the last decades of the fourth century the Serapeum in Alexandria was permanently destroyed by order of the Christian Emperor Theodosius.

25 Merkelbach and Pfister omitted the issue in their philological analyses of the sources of the *Alexander Romance.* See Reinhold Merkelbach, *Die Quellen des griechischen Alexanderromans,* Zetemata 9 (Munich: Beck 1954, repr. 1977), especially 1.3, and Friedrich Pfister, *Kleine Schriften zum Alexanderroman* (Meisenheim am Glan: Hain, 1976) and Pfister, *Der Alexanderroman mit einer Auswahl aus den verwandten Texten übersetzt von Friedrich Pfister* (Meisenheim am Glan: Hain, 1978).

26 See M. Jules Mohl "Extraits du Modjmel al-Tewarikh," *Journal Asiatique* 3me serie (1841) 11:136–361 and 12:497–536, here 11:137–8. Mohl identifies the author of the *Iskender Nāmeh* as "Abou-Thaher de Tartessus": he was probably referring to Abu Ṭāher Ṭarsūsī, the author of *Dārab Nāmeh* – in this case he was mistaken, because there is no such story in Ṭarsūsī's book. See Marina Gaillard, *Alexandre le Grand en Iran. Le Dārāb Nāmeh d'Abou Tāher Tarsusi* (Paris: De Boccard, 2005).

27 See Doufikar-Aerts, *Alexander Magnus Arabicus* (see note 7), "Motifs," 1.8.4.

28 Ms or fol. 2195, 20r.

29 See Ernest A. Wallis Budge, *The History of Alexander the Great, being the Syriac Version. Edited from Five Manuscripts of the Pseudo-Callisthenes, with an English Translation, Accompanied by a Historical Introduction on the Origins and the Various Oriental and European Versions of the Fabulous History of Alexander, with Notes, Glossary, Appendixes, Variant Readings, and Indexes*

(London: Cambridge University Press, 1889; reprint, Amsterdam: APA-Philo Press, 1976), 146.

30 The essence of his theory is that parallels can be found in the Qur'ānic verses on Dhu'l-qarnayn (18:82–9) and the *Christian Syriac Alexander Legend*. The hypothesis requires a revision, because Nöldeke's dating of Jacob of Sarug's *Homily* and the *Christian Syriac Alexander Legend* is no longer valid; therefore, it does not need to be rejected, but it has to be viewed from another perspective. See my exposé in *Alexander Magnus Arabicus* (see note 7), chapter 3.3 and note 57. Nöldeke, *Beiträge zur Geschichte des Alexanderromans* (see note 1), 32–3.

31 The Ethiopic *Romance* does not transmit this passage.

32 Ms or fol. 2195, 20v.

33 Ms or fol. 2195, 14v.

34 See above, p. 161.

35 About this motif see Doufikar-Aerts, *Alexander Magnus Arabicus* (see note 7), 1.8.4 and n. 241.

36 Ms or fol. 2195, 11v.

37 In the Arabic versions of the Darius episode a confusion crept in. About the disorder and the interpolation of a letter also known to Eutychius, see Doufikar-Aerts *Alexander Magnus Arabicus* (see note 7), 1.6.4c and 1.8.4.

38 Ms or fol. 2195, 35r.The resemblance of the headgear to the *zamṭ* cap was kindly suggested to me by Robert Irwin. Another idea derives from the art historian Robert Hillenbrand who supposed that the representation might point to the outfit of the Janissaries, the elite troops of the Ottoman rulers. This view is shared by Dr Gillian Vogelsang-Eastwood, the director of the Textiles Research Centre in Leiden, who was so kind as to examine the miniature for me.

39 Ms or fol. 2195, 12v.

40 On this dating see Willem J. Aerts, "Gog, Magog, Dogheads and Other Monsters in the Byzantine World," in *Gog and Magog. The Clans of Chaos in World Literature*, ed. Ali Asghar Seyed-Gohrab et al. (Amsterdam and West Lafayette, IN: Rozenberg Publishers and Purdue University Press, 2007), 23–35, 29.

41 See W.J. Aerts, *The Byzantine Alexander Poem*, Byzantinisches Archiv, Vol. 26 (Boston and Berlin: Walter de Gruyter, 2014), 2 vols. I, Text, see verses 1607–1740, 85–9 and II, Commentary, see 342–8.

42 See above note 11. The story is also known from Talmud and Midrash versions. See also Wout van Bekkum, "Alexander the Great in Medieval Hebrew Literature," *Journal of the Warburg and Courtauld Institutes* 49 (1986), 218–26.

43 Ms or fol. 2195, 30r.

44 See for instance the frontispiece in J. Christoph Bürgel, *Nizami. Das Alexanderbuch Iskandarname* (Zürich: Manesse Verlag, 1991), representing fol. 242b of Halet Efendi 376 preserved in the Süleymaniye Library in Istanbul.
45 Ms or fol. 2195, 26r.
46 Ms B.N. ar. 3687, 31r, my translation. Also see Faustina Doufikar-Aerts, "Alexander the Flexible Friend. Some Reflections on the Representation of Alexander the Great in the Arabic Alexander Romance," *Journal of Eastern Christian Studies*, 55, 3–4 (2003), 195–210.
47 In other cases we find features of the Christianization of the text. See ibid.
48 Ms or fol. 2195, 41r.
49 See Wallis Budge, *History* (see note 29), 144.
50 Ms or fol. 2195, 50v.
51 According to *CSAL* (145), and similarly in ms B.N. arabe 3687, 86v. The Berlin ms. has a lacuna in this episode.
52 See ms B.N. arabe 3687, 70v. See also the *Christian Syriac Alexander Legend*, Wallis Budge, *History* (see note 29). The Ethiopic text has here "guides" instead of "men guilty of death." See Wallis Budge, *Life and Exploits* (see note 6), 224. On the confusion originating from the underlying Arabic terms *adhillā'* (evildoers) and *adillā'* (guides), see Doufikar-Aerts, *Alexander Magnus Arabicus* (see note 7), 1.6.4b.
53 Wallis Budge, *History* (see note 29), 147–8.
54 Ms or fol. 2195, 47r.
55 See Doufikar-Aerts, *Alexander Magnus Arabicus* (see note 7), 3.7.2, especially n. 191. The most extensive questionnaire is transmitted in the *Qiṣṣat Dhī-l-Qarnayn* (Tale of the Two-Horned), as published on the basis of two Madrilene mss., recently edited and translated by Z. David Zuwiyya, *Islamic Legends Concerning Alexander the Great* (Binghamton, NY: Global Publications, 2001), 132–3. A similar text with the same title in the Rabat collection of manuscripts D 1427, which I described in *Alexander Magnus Arabicus*, 1.6.3a, is less complete.
56 See Davis, *Shāhnāmeh* (see note 19), 517.
57 Doufikar-Aerts, "King Midas' Ears" (see note 19), 61–79, 73–4.
58 Ms or fol. 2195, 62r.
59 *Alexander the Great in the Middle Ages. Ten Studies on the Last Days of Alexander in Literary and Historical Writing*, ed. Willem J. Aerts et al. (Nijmegen: Alfa, 1978).
60 See Faustina Doufikar-Aerts, "'Les derniers jours d'Alexandre' dans un roman populaire arabe: miroir du roman syriaque de Pseudo-Callisthène" in *Alexandre le Grand dans les littératures occidentales et proche-orientales. Actes*

*du colloque de Paris 27–29 novembre 1997*, ed. Laurence Harf-Lancner et al. (Paris: Centre des Sciences de la Littérature, 1999), 61–75, and Doufikar-Aerts, "*The Last Days of Alexander* in an Arabic Popular Romance of Alexander," in *The Ancient Novel and Beyond*, ed. Stelios Panayotakis et al. (Leiden and Boston: Brill, 2003), 23–35.

61 Joseph ben Gorion and the tenth-century historian Eutychius mention Philemon as Alexander's *wazir* (minister). See Wellhausen, *Der Arabische Josippus* (see note 11), 11, and Louis Cheikho, *Eutychii Patriarchae Alexandrini Annales*, Corpus Scriptorum Christianorum Orientalium, Scriptores Arabici, 6/7 (Beirut: 1906), 82. Ibn al-Rahīb Abū Shākir calls him "captain of his host." See Wallis Budge, *Life and Exploits* (see note 6), 397.

62 Aristotle's Letter of Consolation, here, is not the one given in Ḥunayn's *Nawādir al-Falāsifa*. An exposé about the Letters of Consolation and the Funeral Sentences can be found in Doufikar-Aerts, *Alexander Magnus Arabicus* (see note 7), 2.3.3 and 2.3.4.

63 See ibid., 1.6.4b and 1.7.

64 See Wellhausen, *Der Arabische Josippus* (see note 11), 9. According to Wellhausen (*Der Arabische Josippus*, 42), the Paris manuscript arabe 1906, containing Josippus' *Tārīkh* (*History*), was copied by a Copt. It is dated 24 Mesori A. 1057 and 24 Rabi I A. 743 H. = Thursday, 27th of August 1342 CE (ibid., 3n2). The text indeed gives these details, although the left eye is said to look like a cat's eye!

65 See for instance "The Annunciation," in Bibl. No 99 (ser. No 28), ed. Nabil Selim Atalla, *Coptic Manuscripts* (Cairo: Lehnert and Landrock, 2000), 120.

66 Zuzana Skalova and Gawdat Gabra, *Icons of the Nile Valley*, 2nd ed. (Cairo: Egyptian International Publishing, 2006), 130–6.

67 Dietrich Brandenburg, *Islamic Miniature Painting in Medical Manuscripts*, 2nd ed. (Basle: Editiones Roche, 1984). Anna Contadini, *Arab Painting: Text and Image in Illustrated Arabic Manuscripts* (Leiden and Boston: Brill, 2010).

68 Zuwiyya, *Islamic Legends* (see note 55), 40, recalls that the ms of the Aljamiado *Rrekontamiento del rrey Alisandre* has preserved the captions of 32 miniatures, which were never produced, but which are likely to have existed in the Arabic original for the *Rrekontamiento*, a text similar to *Qiṣṣat Dhī l-Qarnayn* by Abū ʿAbd al-Malik. See also Doufikar-Aerts, *Alexander Magnus Arabicus* (see note 7), 1.6.3–1.6.3b.

69 "The Death of the King" in *Kitāb al-Aqālim al-Sabʿa*. Egypt, c. 1080/1670. Chester Beatty Library and Gallery of Oriental Art, Dublin, ms 5433, fol. 19.

70 David James and Richard Ettinghausen, *Arab Painting* (Edinburgh: Skilton, 1978), 48.

71 I highly appreciate the materials brought to my attention by my colleagues Gertrud van Loon, Jacque van Vliet, and Mat van Immerzeel. Also see Atalla, *Coptic Mansucripts* (see note 65), and Maria Cramer, *Koptische Buchmalerei* (Recklinghausen: Verlag Aurel Bongers, 1964).

# Poet, Protagonist, and the Epic Alexander in Walter of Châtillon's *Alexandreis*

SYLVIA A. PARSONS

The interest of Walter of Châtillon's late-twelfth-century *Alexandreis* for students of the medieval Alexander lies less in what elements of the Alexander traditions Walter knew and employed than in the way he uses his material to question not only the meaning of Alexander's career but the parameters of the epic form in which he has chosen to treat it. Walter was an erudite and versatile poet. His birth in Lille is usually dated around 1135; he studied at Paris and Bologna, taught at Châtillon, and was a master of satirical lyric as well as epic. The *Alexandreis* is dedicated to William of the White Hands, Walter's patron, a politically powerful bishop who graduated from the see of Sens to that of Rheims, and who was uncle to Philip Augustus. The poem was probably composed in the late 1170s and very early 1180s.[1] Walter uses Quintus Curtius's *Historia Alexandri Magni*[2] as the basis of its historical account and draws on classical Latin epic for its form and style. In the course of the poem, exegesis and Christian historiography, exempla, and even elements of the romance tradition derived from Pseudo-Callisthenes contribute to Walter's portrait of his protagonist.[3] Walter's Alexander is at once the historical overachiever, the explorer who encounters the assessing gazes of the culturally other, the Janus-faced exemplum, and the figure of biblical prophecy whose career fits into a larger and more significant narrative that he himself is unable to access. This mixture of elements suggests, certainly, the completeness of Walter's research and the depth of his awareness of the cultural and historical gaps between his own understanding of the world and those of his historical subject and his literary models. But it also suggests Walter's lively interest in literary experimentation, in the possibilities inherent in his complex authorial position vis à vis epic form. In the *Alexandreis* he multiplies these fertile complications by allowing Alexander a complex relationship to his own role as protagonist.

My focus in the following discussion will be on the use that Walter makes of the self-conscious Alexander, Alexander the image-maker, as both a model for and a challenge to his own poetic self-consciousness. I will be looking in detail at two points early in Alexander's career and Walter's poem: Alexander's first appearance as a twelve-year-old eager for battles he is not yet ready to undertake, and his illness in Cilicia, where the king is threatened with an early death sadly different from the live-heroic-die-young model of Achilles. In both these instances Alexander's body is insufficient for the heroic action he desires; in both, epic fantasies compensate for corporeal limitations; and in both, Walter's authorial voice, in privileged communication with the reader through textual channels of simile or allusion, simultaneously limits his protagonist's epic aspirations and tests the limits of epic. But before I move on to examine these two passages in detail, it is worth glancing at how Walter presents Alexander as the commissioner as well as the star of the *Alexandreis*.

During his visit to Troy, which Walter places at the end of Book One of the *Alexandreis*, Alexander stands at the grave of Achilles, the quintessential epic hero. The grave is modest by comparison with the tombs on which twelfth-century epic and romance lavished detailed ekphrases, though it does feature an epitaph briefly encapsulating Achilles's heroic career. Alexander, however, is not concerned either with the adequacy of the material monument accorded Achilles or with any doubt of his own capacity for equal deeds. Rather, he fears that when he is dead he may lack a poet to give him the fame he desires: "O utinam nostros resoluto corpore tantis/Laudibus attollat non invida fama triumphos" (O that unenvious fame may extol my triumphs with such great praises when my body is undone! [Walter, *Alexandreis* 1.484–5]). For the reader of Walter's poem the programmatic import of this moment is hard to miss: by including Alexander's desire for epic commemoration in the *Alexandreis*, Walter allows his protagonist to commission his poem. In so doing he cedes to Alexander some of the work's generic intentionality, while at the same time he claims as his narrative matter not only Alexander's deeds but Alexander's own representations of his identity.

The combination of an absent body marked by a material monument contrasted with the explicitly epic task of preserving the fame of the heroic dead makes a suitable setting for a programmatic authorial statement in an epic poem. Alexander's self-conscious intervention in the arrangement of these elements, however, alters the force of the passage. My present concern is not how the artistry of poetic representation comes together with the inorganic replacement of the body at the site of the tomb. Instead, I here address Alexander's claims to control the process of poetic representation from within Walter's poem, working through, against, and beyond historically bounded and somatically grounded identity. The vital role of Alexander's body in the poem is not so much that of an acting instrument through which Alexander achieves a heroic identity for the poem to commemorate, nor yet that of an absent signified on which the signifiers of that identity are built. Rather, it is a central arena of the contest Walter stages between his own poetic control and the usurping ambitions he allows his hero towards the authorial sphere of representation.

The beginnings of this contest lie in the opening scenes of the narrative. The first entrance of the boy Alexander onto the stage of the *Alexandreis* offers a preview and overview of the basic lines of contention. The interplay of Alexander's assertions of self-imaging and the controlling authorial voice in that opening passage establishes a pattern: the protagonist's struggles for self-assertion will be fought over his body, and they will evoke from the poet clusters of allusion to the Latin epic tradition, in particular Vergil, that enable the authorial voice to communicate with the reader over the protagonist's head. I turn next to the second book of the *Alexandreis* and to the crisis of heroic identity that Alexander's illness after his plunge into a river in Cilicia precipitates, a crisis shaped by the potential of the king's body to thwart or support his heroic claims. Here, too, Alexander's body is at issue, and the presence of earlier epic – not the Homeric template Alexander can perceive, but a Vergilian base text shared by author and readers – invests Alexander's self-image with overtones that he is not permitted to intend.

## I *Alexandreis* 1.27–202: The Lion King

Alexander enters the *Alexandreis* as a boy of twelve. His first speech is a complaint at being withheld by his age from military action, and the first epic simile of the poem figures that frustration in the vividly somatic image of a lion cub whose thirst for blood has outpaced his physical maturity. These paired imaginings of the body, through Alexander's own voice and then through the controlling and generically marked authorial voice of the simile, establish a dynamic that will operate throughout the poem. By itself, the passage supplies one of the poem's most complex meditations on the body seen through the conventions of epic language.

A few words on the sources of this passage: while the second passage I will be discussing here is a straightforward adaptation of Curtius, in which we can trace Walter's artistic decisions in his alterations and embellishments of his source, Alexander's boyhood is missing from Curtius as his work came down to Walter. The fact that the passage contains one of the *Alexandreis*'s scarce allusions to the *Alexander Romance* tradition, which made the Egyptian sorcerer Nectanabus Alexander's father, led Colker to point to Julius Valerius as Walter's source, and, indeed, the physical descriptions of Alexander available in the Latin sources based on Pseudo-Callisthenes[4] probably contribute to the succession of lions that I will be examining in Walter's account. But it is the sources for the literary set-up of this scene that have most to do with what Walter the poet accomplishes in the passage.

It remained for Otto Zwierlein to identify Claudian[5] as the most important source for the boy Alexander's complaints. Claudian's panegyrics on the third and fourth consulates of Honorius, especially the latter poem, shape Walter's account of Alexander's situation, and supply elements of the poet's phrasing. What Zwierlein could not have observed is that Claudian's strong presence at this point in the poem may owe something to a medieval supplement to Curtius, whose editor offers convincing evidence that Walter may have been among the text's users.[6] The Claudian passage refers to Alexander; the Curtius supplement uses the Claudian reference as a source on the subject of Alexander's boyhood; Walter, in turn, goes back to Claudian and makes a more extended and literary use, not of the part that specifically cites Alexander, but of the situation that prompted the mention of the Macedonian, the complaints of the ten-year-old Honorius to his father Theodosius at not being permitted an active military role in his campaign. The presence of Alexander as an example in Claudian lends to Walter's use of Claudian a kind of allusive irony that is typical of the play of authorial self-consciousness over heroic self-fashioning in this passage: in aspiring to be a martial hero the boy Alexander is made by his author to mimic a boy who is told that he can aspire to be like Alexander.

Within epic codes, Alexander's first appearance is at once displaced and recognizable. He is the boy too young for battle, not only because he as yet lacks the physical strength required for fighting but also because he has not yet achieved the fully defined gender identity of the mature male:

> Nondum prodierat naturae plana tenellis
> Infruticans lanugo pilis, matrique parabat
> Dissimiles proferre genas, cum pectore toto
> Arma puer sitiens ...

> [Not yet had down appeared causing nature's plains to sprout with tender hairs, and he was getting ready to show cheeks unlike his mother's, when the boy thirsting with his whole heart for arms ... (Walter, *Alexandreis* 1.27–30)]

The beard that has not yet begun to appear on Alexander's cheeks[7] will define his difference from his mother, both establishing him as male and detaching him from the defining sphere of the nuclear family to place him in the public realm. The boy at the stage of puberty marked by the first appearance of facial hair makes several cameos in classical epic.[8] Here in Walter, however, the point of the reference is not to mark out an anomalous zone of pathos and eroticism in the ordinary back and forth of the epic battlefield. At this point in the poem the sphere of epic action exists only in the aspirations and self-imaging of the young Alexander.

Walter's own voice marks both the presence and the absence of the proper sphere of epic. We find at the beginning of line thirty not the *arma virumque* which are the objects of the poet's epic song but *arma puer ... sitiens*, the boy thirsting to associate himself with the epic attributes with which the poet has not yet paired him. The allusion to *Georgics* 4.562 that follows[9] implicitly compares Alexander hearing of the victories of Darius to Vergil looking ahead from his pastoral/didactic authorial position to the exploits of Caesar, the potential demands of epic on his future. The allusion assimilates Alexander to an authorial voice. It is not the poet but the hero who here aspires towards epic, and does so from a point that is within epic but still debarred from participation in epic action. This sequence of allusions to Vergilian programmatics will culminate in the first lines of Aristotle's speech: "Indue mente *virum*, Macedo *puer*, *arma* capesce" (assume the man in your mind, Macedonian boy, seize weapons [Walter, *Alexandreis* 1. 82]), in which the boy Alexander is sandwiched between *virum* and *arma*.

It is against this background of allusion to and exclusion from the epic world of arms and men that we should read the peculiar relationship between the boy Alexander and the notes of epic status that informs Alexander's first speech as well as the lion simile with which

Walter caps it. Perhaps the most notable feature of Alexander's complaint is the protagonist's own awareness that in imagining himself on the battlefield he is projecting an element of fantasy even into his fantasy, imagining himself playing the part of a man. The speech is worth quoting in full:

> "Heu, quam longa quies pueris! numquamne licebit
> Inter funereas acies mucrone chorusco
> Persarum dampnare iugum, profugique tyranni
> Cornipedem lentum celeri prevertere cursu,
> Confusos turbare duces, puerumque leonis
> Vexillo insignem galeato vertice saltim
> In bello simulare virum? verumne dracones
> Alcydem puerum compressis faucibus olim
> In cunis domuisse duos? ergo nisi magni
> Nomen Aristotilis pueriles terreat annos,
> Haut dubitem similes ordiri fortiter actus.
> Adde quod etati duodenni corpore parvo
> Maior inesse solet virtus viridisque iuventae
> Ardua vis supplere moras. semperne putabor
> Nectanabi proles? ut degener arguar absit!"
>
> [Alas, how long inaction goes on for boys! will I never be allowed among the deadly battle columns with flashing sword to reject the Persian yoke and to outrun the sluggish steed of the fleeing king with my swift charge, to throw into confusion the disordered commanders, and as a boy marked with the standard of a lion with helmeted head at least to play the man in battle? is it true that Alcides as a boy overcame two serpents in his cradle, crushing their throats? Then I would not hesitate, if great Aristotle's name did not overawe my boyish years, stoutly to undertake like deeds. Take into account, too, that at the age of twelve a greater courage/manliness usually inheres in the small body, and that lofty force makes good the impediments of green youth. Will I always be supposed the offspring of Nectanabus? Far be it that I be proved base-born." (Walter, *Alexandreis* 1.33–46)]

The trappings of Alexander's daydream of the exploits from which he is withheld, *funereas acies, mucrone chorusco*, epic cornipeds, are the stock footage of epic. The picture that follows, "puerumque leonis/ Vexillo insignem galeato vertice saltim/In bello simulare virum" (and as a boy marked with the standard of a lion with helmeted head at least to play the man in battle? [Walter, *Alexandreis* 1.37–9]), acknowledges these trappings as props for the simulation rather than the enactment of heroic identity. Alexander associates the charade of a boy playing the man on a battlefield with the paraphernalia of armour and insignia. The helmeted head and the standard depicting a lion dress up the fantasy while hiding the reality of the physically immature body under the armour. Walter's narrating voice will pick up on the image of the lion in the simile that follows Alexander's speech, further confusing the layers of fiction and identity operative in this passage.

Alexander next adduces the example of the infant Hercules, who strangled serpents in the cradle.[10] Only the name of Aristotle deters his boyish years from similar exploits. As though Aristotle's name has summoned up the sententious style the philosopher will adopt in the long discourse that will occupy most of Book One, Alexander's next thought phrases itself as a general truth, marked by *solet*: "Adde quod etati duodenni corpore parvo/Maior inesse solet virtus viridisque iuventae/Ardua vis supplere moras" (Take into account, too, that at the age of twelve a greater courage/manliness usually inheres in the small body [Walter, *Alexandreis* 1.44–6]). The disjunction between Alexander's physical limits and his ambitions that reappears in various forms throughout the epic appears elsewhere in the voice of impersonal truisms, notably in the episode of Talestris in Book Eight.[11] Here Alexander appropriates this discourse, as he has the repertoire of epic vocabulary, for his own purposes. The specificity of the *duodenni etati*, however, tends to undermine the generality of the qualities of *virtus* possible in the small body of a boy. Finally, Alexander's doubts about his legitimacy (cast in the realm of reputation rather than fact) shed a new light on the comparison to Hercules. The possibility of illegitimacy on the one hand or divine descent on the other highlight the precarious space that Alexander inhabits, a space conceived in terms of rumour and fantasy even while it expresses itself in bodily action and family identity.

In his speech, then, Alexander has marshalled epic diction, the enhancing panoply of military accoutrements, the mythological example of the infant Hercules, and the sententious style that claims for a piece of special pleading the status of a generally acknowledged truth. This flourish of self-imaging, like the elaborately defiant fantasy the king will produce on his deathbed (a passage to which I will come in due course), is directly prompted by the limitations imposed by Alexander's body. His defiance, however, does not issue in an actual trial of what an out-of-sync twelve-year-old body can do on the battlefield. Rather, Alexander's weapons are essentially rhetorical, his speech reaching ahead to represent himself heroically with the tools of the poet. Alexander's most fundamental drive is not for heroic action but for heroic representation. In his depiction of this ambition Walter allows his hero to engage in a struggle for control with the narrative voice of the epic; the contest, here as often later in the poem, is fought over the king's body.

A case in point is the simile following Alexander's first speech, in which the narrator picks up on elements of Alexander's speech to subtly reassert control over the representation of the young Alexander's body:

Qualiter Hyrcanis si forte leunculus arvis
Cornibus elatos videt ire ad pabula cervos,
Cui nondum totos descendit robur in armos
Nec pede firmus adhuc nec dentibus asper aduncis
Palpitat, et vacuum ferit improba lingua palatum,
Effunditque prius animo quam dente cruorem,
Pigriciamque pedum redimit matura voluntas:
Sic puer effrenus totus bachatur in arma,
Invalidusque manu gerit alto corde leonem,
Et preceps teneros audacia prevenit annos.

[Just as in the Hyrcanian fields a lion cub, whose strength has not yet penetrated into all its limbs, nor is it steady on its feet as yet, nor is it sharp with curved teeth, if by chance it sees deer lofty with antlers go towards their pasture, it quivers, and its greedy tongue strikes its empty palate, and it spills blood in imagination before it does so with its teeth, and a full-grown will makes good the laziness of its feet: in this way the unrestrained boy is altogether mad for arms, and impotent in hand he wears a lion in his high heart, and headlong audacity gets ahead of his tender years. (Walter, *Alexandreis* 1.49–58)]

The simile comparing the hero to a predatory animal picks up on the epic trappings of Alexander's fantasy of his potential exploits; the lion has strayed from Alexander's speech within the text to the text's presentation of Alexander.[12] Like the *vexillo leonis* of Alexander's imagination, the lion simile of the poet should be a prop that will aid the boy's masquerade as a mature hero (*vir*). The animal simile is after all a textual marker of epic narration, just as arms and standards are the distinctive signs of military identity. Walter, however, subverts the simile. His beast of comparison is a lion cub, *leunculus*, rather than a lion, and the simile reflects not the ferocity of the imagined action but the impotence of the boy's imagining. The vivid physical indwelling of the lines that follow makes Alexander's experience of his immature body more vividly present within the simile than it is in the lines that describe the boy directly. The alliteration reinforces the parallel of *palpitat* and *palatum* and makes the reader feel in the vocal apparatus an analogue of the lion cub's exploring tongue. The cub who spills blood in the imagination before doing so in reality, "effunditque prius animo quam dente cruorem" (Walter, *Alexandreis* 1.54), is in imaginative competition with the expected fierce predator of the epic simile in the reader's mind just as Alexander's corporeal reality is in competition with his own self-image.

Walter sums up the effects of speech and simile with the three lines that glance once again at the conjunction of arms and the boy, and introduce a last, metaphorical lion:

> Sic puer effrenus totus bachatur in arma,
> Invalidusque manu gerit alto corde leonem,
> Et preceps teneros audacia prevenit annos.

> [In this way the unrestrained boy is altogether mad for arms, and impotent in hand he wears a lion in his high heart, and headlong audacity gets ahead of his tender years. (Walter, *Alexandreis* 1.56–8)]

For the reader processing Walter's text, however, it is hard for this lion to remain uninflected by the modifying lion cub that has preceded it. The lion that Alexander bears in his heart is not, after Walter's simile, strictly in contrast to the boy of tender years not yet strong in deed. The simile, a generic marker of the mode of representation to which Alexander aspires, has sidestepped what Alexander aspires to be to depict instead the process of aspiration. Walter thus reminds the reader that the authorial voice exercises control even over Alexander's ambitions to control the authorial voice.

Before I turn to Alexander's illness in Book Two of the *Alexandreis*, let me return for a moment to Walter's sources for Alexander's boyhood, this time in search of the origins of Alexander the lion king. The leonine associations of the young Alexander appear in descriptions of Alexander as an adolescent in various Latin sources derived from Pseudo-Callisthenes. The *Historia de preliis*, for instance, describes the young Alexander thus: "figura illius neque patri neque matri assimilabatur, sed propriam figuram suam habebat. Coma capitis eius erat sicut coma leonis ... impetus illius fervidus sicut leonis" (His appearance was like neither his father nor his mother, but he had his own appearance. The hair of his head was like a lion's hair ... his vehemence was fiery like a lion's [*Historia de preliis* (J2) I.13]).[13] Such accounts usually compare his hair to a lion's mane,[14] and Julius Valerius, too (though not the epitome), attaches the lion's nature explicitly to temperament as well as appearance (*Res Gestae Alexandri* 1.13).[15] It is notable that Walter's succession of lions neatly alienates Alexander's lion attributes from this unproblematic continuity between temperament and body. The battle standard, the simile that reinforces the author's control of genre markers, the lion in the heart that contradicts rather than complementing the actual body of the young Alexander, combine to depict a protagonist whose corporeal identity is analysed rather than ratified by the epic vehicle.

### II *Alexandreis* 2.153–256: *nudus sine laude*

Appropriately enough, the second passage I will be examining also takes place under the sign of the lion: the scene is set in July and the sun stands in Leo. The incident Walter is here adapting from Curtius is not exactly an example of stirring military action. Alexander, dusty and overheated, bathes in the temptingly cold river, and suffers immediate symptoms of shock that approximate death, followed by a partial recovery into feverish illness. The army and the king alike are dismayed by the risks this breakdown in Alexander's health poses in their delicate military situation and by the unheroic circumstances of the danger. Alexander wants a quick fix, regardless of medical opinion, so that he can return to battle, but a further complication arises when the physician who offers a suitable cure is rumoured to have been suborned by Darius. Alexander nonetheless shows his confidence in the man by simultaneously downing the potion and offering the physician the chance to read the letter that accuses him. His faith is vindicated: he recovers and displays himself, restored, before his army; there is great rejoicing.

Walter's adaptation highlights the fragile connections between Alexander's identity, his body, and the image of himself that he constructs in collaboration with the reactions and projections of his army. Taking over and elaborating the medical details of Curtius's account, Walter's narrative features the body itself as protagonist of a clinical case. The displacement of the inhabiting subjectivity of the protagonist by an independently functioning (or malfunctioning) body generates a compensatory foray into epic projections from Alexander. The anxieties of king and army, the contrast between the kinds of bodily danger that threaten the image of Alexander in his own and other people's imagination and the crisis that has actually befallen him, reinforce the generic presence of epic within the consciousness of the poem's characters as well as that of its narrating voice. And Walter here repeats the technique he used in Book One, bringing a Vergilian subtext into play to both emphasize and question Alexander's self-representations.

Walter's first notable addition to Curtius's narrative[16] is the elaboration of the details of Alexander's physical response to the shock:

Estus erat medius cum sole tenente Leonem
Iulius arderet, medioque sub axe diei
Arida Cyliciae findit vapor igneus arva.
Perfusus Macedo sudore et pulvere membra,
Temperie fluvii captus specieque liquoris,
Corpore adhuc calido subiectis insilit undis.
Horruit extemplo gelido perfusa liquore
Tota viri moles ubi non invenit apertas
Spiritus arterias corpusque reliquit inane.
Frigore vitalis calor interclusus aquarum
Fluctuat, afflictus rex exanimisque suorum
Extrahitur manibus.

[It was the middle of summer, when July burns with the sun in Leo, and under the center of the vault of day the fiery heat cracked the dry plains of Cilicia. The Macedonian, his limbs caked with sweat and dust, drawn by the coolness of the river and the loveliness of the water, leapt into the waves below with his body still heated. Immediately the whole bulk of the man stiffened, bathed in the cold liquid, as the breath did not find open passages and left the body empty. The vital warmth faltered, cut off by the chill of the water, and the king, stricken and inanimate, was dragged out by the hands of his men. (Walter, *Alexandreis* 2.160–71)]

The increased density of medical information contributes a sense of the body as a scene of action in its own right, another layer or level in the action of the poem, between the sphere of the characters' agency and the level of poetic effects acting purely within the text. The detail Walter chooses to omit, Alexander's pallor, is the most outward and observable sign among the symptoms provided by Curtius; the technical clause "ubi non invenit apertas/Spiritus arterias" (as the breath did not find open passages [Walter, *Alexandreis* 2.167–8]), which Walter adds, takes the reader's attention from visible effects perceptible to observing characters to a plane of action that is purely internal, carried out by physiological elements rather than human agents. *Moles viri* and *corpus inane,* also supplied by Walter, further separate the king's body from the king. The process of curing Alexander, and of displaying his restored health to the army, will be as much about re-establishing that connection as about changing bodily ill health into bodily good health.

Walter enhances the dramatic importance of the army's response both by elaborating it and by changing it from indirect to direct discourse. Three aspects of the speech as Walter reports it are relevant to my concerns. First, Alexander's youth and the untimely nature of the catastrophe are conventionally poeticized in the vocative *flos iuvenum* that begins the speech (Walter, *Alexandreis* 2.173) and in the later reference (Walter, *Alexandreis* 2.178) to the king's *florentes annos*. Combined with the image of reaping (*metis*; the subject is *fortuna*), they add a touch of the conventional lyric pathos that often accompanies the death of the young in epic. Second, there is the reproach to Alexander's rashness, *impetus,* and to his dying not, as Curtius has Alexander's men reflect, prosaically by bathing, but rather naked, *nudum*. From Curtius's straightforward statement that Alexander's death by bathing is an even worse disaster than his death in combat would have been, Walter arrives at a formulation that is at once more unflatteringly literal (Alexander is endangered as a result of his own rashness and is at risk of dying literally in the nude) and yet subtly reconfigures the incident in military terms as a kind of ambush (*impetus* often has the sense of an attack; *nudus* can mean not only nakedness but specifically the lack of armour). I will return to this when I deal with Alexander's own complaint at his misfortune.

The last intriguing addition to material derived from Curtius in this passage is the army's rhetorical apostrophe to Fortuna. Many aspects of Fortuna's role in the *Alexandreis* lie outside the scope of my study,[17] but the soldier's familial reading of the relationship between Fortuna and Alexander (Fortuna goes from acting as a mother to playing the stepmother) ties into the complex contextualization of Alexander in imagined alternate family structures that will reappear in Alexander's deathbed fantasy at the end of Book Ten. Alexander's claim to have Jupiter as his father is part of his constant attempt to project himself into a heroic and superhuman role, defying both his corporeal limitations and the imaginative prerogatives of the poet. That Fortune should be his mother both ratifies and undermines this imaginative structure, proposing a supernatural parentage that ultimately reasserts instead of negating the mortal circumstances to which he is subject.

Like the boy Alexander's speech in Book One, Alexander's remarks here, altered by Walter from the Curtian base text,[18] are concerned with the disjunction between the situation determined by his body and the role in which he imagines himself. Curtius gives Alexander's first reflection on his situation in *oratio obliqua* and turns to direct discourse only for Alexander's immediate address to those attending him. Walter's version of the speech cuts out all second person address; although the second half (representing Curtius's direct discourse) retains its jussive elements, the effect of the whole is to some extent assimilated to the ruminative mode of the first half. In that first half, moreover, for all that it is direct speech, the first person is as absent as the second. Alexander ostentatiously speaks of himself in the third person, as *Alexander* and then *rex inglorius exul*, as though to emphasize the fact that he is not so much speaking *as* the character who is the hero of the *Alexandreis* as *of* him.

Nor are the king's concerns identical in Curtius's version and in Walter's. Curtius disposes of Alexander's musings in a sentence. "Vinctum ergo se tradi et tantam victoriam eripi sibi ex manibus obscuraque et ignobili morte in tabernaculo extingui se querebatur" (He was complaining that he was being handed over bound and that so great a victory was snatched from him from out of his hands and that he was snuffed out by an obscure and ignoble death in his tent [Curtius, *Historia Alexandri Magni,* 3.5.10]). For this flat statement Walter's Alexander substitutes a series of three vivid pictures, underlining the temporal urgency taken from Curtius:

> "Ergo" ait "in castris victum sine Marte cruentus
> Victor Alexandrum rapiet? Nam proximus hostis
> Non medicos segnes, non cretica tempora morbi
> Expectare sinit. spoliis ululabit ademptis
> Hostica barbaries, at rex inglorius exul
> Nudus in hostili sine laude iacebit harena ..."

> [Will the blood-stained victor, then," he said, "drag away Alexander conquered in his camp without a battle? For the enemy close at hand does not allow [me] to wait for slothful doctors or the crisis of the disease. For the hostile barbarians will howl over the captured spoils, but the king, an inglorious exile, will lie stripped, without praise, on the enemy sand. (Walter, *Alexandreis* 2.205–10)]

The most interesting image is the last, but the other two have already altered the nature of Alexander's complaint. The *vinctum,* bound, which in Curtius effectively expressed the indignity of the fate Alexander anticipates for himself, is transmuted to *victum* and matched with *victor. Victum* is bracketed by *in castris* and *sine Marte,* as the very fact that there has been no battle makes Alexander the loser of the battle that does not take place. The adjective *cruentus* almost contradicts the adverbial *in castris* and *sine Marte* which expands Alexander's modifier, *victum. Cruentus,* despite its general sense of "cruel," carries strong associations of literal blood: once again, as in the provision of a *victor* and a *victum,* Alexander is projecting the nature of military defeat onto the defeat of being set apart from the category of the military. The spoils the Persians will then claim are presumably general, the appurtenances of the Macedonian army, yet, combined with the image of the stripped king lying dead in the *hostili harena,* the image also suggests the stripping of armour from a defeated combatant in the kind of duel that Alexander sees himself being denied. The term indeed takes us back to the army's lament a few lines earlier, where *nudus* stood in both for the actual circumstance of bathing and for the significance of being ambushed by fortune unarmed, away from the arena in which Alexander might more appropriately have met his death.

The destiny Alexander sees awaiting his corpse is complicated by the Vergilian associations of the line "nudus in hostili sine laude iacebit harena" (2.210). The clearest reference, noted by Colker,[19] is to Aeneas's lament over the fate of Palinurus, "nudus in ignota, Palinure, iacebis harena" (you will lie naked, Palinurus, on an unknown shore [Vergil, *Aeneid* 5.871]). Two other Vergilian *loci,* however, are associatively connected to that one. One is Dido's curse/prophecy on the fate that awaits the absconding Aeneas: "cadat ante diem mediaque inhumatus harena" (let him fall before his time and without burial in the midst of the sand [Vergil, *Aeneid* 4.620]). The other possible link is Aeneas's account of the fate of Priam's body in Book Two: "iacet ingens litore truncus,/avulsum umeris caput et sine nomine corpus" (the huge trunk lies on the shore, the head struck from the shoulders and the body nameless [Vergil, *Aeneid* 2.557–8]). This cluster of associations might also suggest to Walter the baroque meditations on fame and burial in Lucan's lengthy account of the death of Pompey and its aftermath, with its setting on the hostile and liminal shore of Egypt and the frequent recurrence of forms of *harena* (Lucan, *Bellum Civile* 8.692–872).

The essential point of this constellation of associations is that Alexander is conflating an inglorious death with the apparently necessary consequence of an improper burial. This has no parallel in Curtius. *Sine laude* glosses *nudus*; a similar idea appears in the *Alexandreis* in Book Nine when one young warrior declares to another that if they die on their expedition fame will clothe them when they are stripped of their body, *nudatos corpore* (Walter, *Alexandreis* 9.99). There is a powerful and fundamental set of equivalences at work between bodies, reputation, burial, and the verbal commemoration of fame and therefore, implicitly, epic. As Walter allows Alexander's speech to allude to other epics he once again underlines the juxtaposition of Alexander's own self-fashioning aspirations to epic fame and the poetic construction of Walter's epic that contains them.

Walter continues the foregrounding of Alexander's epic self-imaging in the second half of the king's speech:

> Si tamen in medicis est ut reparare salutem
> Arte queant medica, faveat medicina sciantque
> Me non tam vitae spacium quam querere belli.
> Nam licet eger adhuc, si saltim stare meorum
> Ante aciem potero, cursu fugitiva rapaci
> Terga dabunt Persae, Danai sequentur ovantes.

> [If, however, it is in doctors to be able by medical skill to restore my health, let medicine be well-disposed and let them know that I seek a span not so much of life as of war. For although still ailing, if I can at least stand before the battle line of my men the Persians will turn their backs in eager flight, the triumphant Greeks will pursue them. (*Alexandreis* 2.215–17)]

His triple harping on the possibility of medical aid (*medicis, arte ... medica, medicina*) leads up to the line "[sciant] me non tam vitae spacium quam querere belli" (let them know that I seek a span not so much of life as of war), adapted from Curtius's "sciant me non tam mortis quam belli remedium quaerere" (let them know that I seek relief not from death but for war). Walter's parallel of *spacium vitae* and *belli* succinctly expresses the equation that defines one type of epic, the Iliadic model of Alexander's ideal. Walter's biographical model, however many suitable exploits it records, is violating the terms that model in this very scene. Yet Walter's Alexander insists on his identity as hero even in his role as patient. He calls on the powers of medicine to repair not his health but his identity.

Walter emphasizes this point by moving up material from later in Curtius's narrative to occupy the last three lines of Alexander's speech. The lines in which Alexander pictures himself pursuing the fleeing Persians are imported and adapted from Curtius's account of Alexander's impatience with the three day delay imposed on him by the physician Philip: "arma et acies in oculis erant et victoriam in eo positam esse arbitrabatur, si tantum ante signa stare potuisset" (arms and battle columns were before his eyes, and he judged that victory was dependent on him, if only he had been able to stand in front of the standards [Curtius, *Historia Alexandri Magni* 3.6.3]). Walter dwells on and dramatizes Alexander's act of imagination in projecting himself onto the battlefield, a pattern we have already seen in Book One. By expanding Curtius's *victoriam* into the picture of the fleeing Persians and pursuing Greeks, Walter has Alexander not so much considering the consequences of his illness as defying the corporeal limitations of sickness, as he defied those of boyhood, with epic daydreams.

Alexander's recovery (following the incident of the suspected physician, Philip, which need not detain us) emphasizes the king's appearance, the factor Walter chose to omit in his account of the onset of the king's illness. Curtius's account[20] is a continuation of the story of the suspect doctor. The drastic effect of the medication at first confirms the fears raised by Parmenion's letter, but Philip's assiduous medical attentions eventually dissipate the disease. Walter's version is not the story of the physician but a drama in which medicine and symptoms are the sole protagonists, displacing Philip's role:

Inde ubi transmissum medicamen ad intima venas
Imbuit, emeriti perierunt semina morbi.
Exhilarat vultum color et pallore perempto
Emergit facies niveo liquefacta rubore.
Mens redit, et virtus rediviva renascitur intus.

[And then when the medicine, sent through into his inmost parts, imbued his veins, the seeds of the completed disease perished. Colour gladdened his countenance and his face with its pallor gone came clear dewy with snowy rosiness. His mind returned, and his revived vigour was reborn within. (Walter, *Alexandreis* 2.245–8)]

Despite his concentration on the medical arena, however, Walter is also in these lines creating a bridge between the internal medical action and the parade of restored health with which Alexander will reaffirm his position with his army, between the drama of the king's body and the drama of the king's persona:[21]

Rex, cum sol rutilo radiaret crastinus axe,
Insigni prevectus equo per castra videndum
Se dedit et pavidis excussit mentibus omnem
Segniciem vultuque suos ac voce refecit.

[The king, when the sun was shining on the next day from its glowing chariot, mounted on an conspicuous horse gave himself to be seen through the camp and drove all weakness from their frightened minds and restored his men with his face and voice. (Walter, *Alexandreis* 2.253–6)]

The *niveo rubore* of line 248, the mark of health phrased in terms descriptive of beauty, restores Alexander to the category marked in the army's earlier lament by *flos iuvenum* and *florentes annos*. The reappearance of light and colour in his countenance is a private rehearsal of the royal display that will ratify his recovery in the eyes of his army. The king's countenance becomes the source of restoration for the watching army, as well as being symptomatic of his own recovery. The display reminds the reader that Alexander's body operates as a focus of projection for other characters within the poem as well as a site for Alexander's own imaginative self-assertion and Walter's poetic control. Yet Walter's innovative treatment of the clinical action in this episode, his narrative of the body's internal history, independent of the subject who occupies it, imposes a new lack on the heroic subject. The break in the imaginary identification of the subject with the body is not initiated by a Lacanian subject, entering into language and the realm of the symbolic, but by the body itself. Walter makes poetic space for the body's discontinuity. Poet and protagonist both negotiate with the body's unassimilable agenda.

Alexander, of course, recovers from his illness and from the crisis of identity it provokes, but the *Alexandreis*'s pattern of conflict between its protagonist's aspirations to control his own representation and the limits imposed by the poet persists to the very end. On his deathbed in Book Ten Alexander will interpret his death as a summons from Jupiter; the giants are back to besieging Olympus, and the superannuated Jove needs Alexander's help to drive them back (Walter, *Alexandreis* 10.405–17). But Alexander's reading of his death as a promotion to gigantomachy, epic on a divine scale, is a misinterpretation of an event that itself comes about through hermeneutic error: Alexander's death has actually been engineered by Satan, in the mistaken fear that Alexander might turn out to be the rumoured new man who will conquer hell. Walter's own epitaph on his protagonist (Walter, *Alexandreis* 10.448–54) is a mixture of deflation and preservation: Alexander's claim to the world shrinks to his occupation of a few feet of earth, but his reinterment at Alexandria ensures that a man-made monument to his fame and identity endures. Walter's own monument to Alexander may not be quite the poem that Alexander commissioned at Achilles's tomb, but however it may frustrate its protagonist's aspirations to self-representation it also preserves them, dramatically giving Alexander himself a chance to contribute to the undertaking of interpreting his legacy.

## III Conclusion

In making Alexander the hero of a classicizing epic, Walter seems to fulfill Alexander's desire for self-representation, the impulse to commission as well as star in his own *Iliad*. Walter's incorporation of Alexander's capacity for image-making fantasy into the workings of his own authorial representations, however, does more than provide a particular instance of the general complexities of the author's attitude to his protagonist. Certainly the poet uses the medium of epic to problematize as well as immortalize Alexander's career, but he also uses Alexander's epic image-making to problematize as well as perpetuate the workings of epic. The nexus of limited, destructible bodies and immortal names is the binding contract of the Achillean style of epic that Alexander favours. Walter, it turns out, is interested in the subtler gaps he finds within the composite of corporeality, identity, and heroic role-playing. In a world in which these subtler disjunctions are endemic and inescapable, epic's formalized bridging of the acknowledged gap between mortality and permanence loses its monumental authority. There is surely authorial irony in Walter's portrayal of Alexander's epic daydreams in boyhood, in sickness, and on his deathbed, where he responds to the ultimate corporeal limitation of death by elevating himself in imagination from the ordinary epic plane of human heroism to the Olympian ultra-epic of gigantomachy. But irony is means, not end. Alexander's spectacular but ultimately incomplete impersonation of an epic hero in the *Alexandreis* points to the inadequacy of epic's compensatory bargain, not because *kleos* fails to make up for bodily destruction, but because the simple equation of the heroic lack for which *kleos* is the compensation with mortality turns out, in Walter's subtle explorations of corporeality, identity, and genre, to have been a gross oversimplification.

## NOTES

1 Maura Lafferty lays out the evidence for the dating of the *Alexandreis* in an appendix to her study of the *Alexandreis*, *Walter of Châtillon's Alexandreis: Epic and the Problem of Historical Understanding* (Turnhout: Brepols, 1998), 183–9. Her introduction summarizes what we know of Walter's life, 2–13. See also Melvin Colker, introduction to Walter of Châtillon, *Alexandreis*, ed. Colker (Padua: Antenore, 1978), xi–xviii, which prints some of the medieval *vitae* attached to manuscripts of the poem.

2 Citations in this chapter will be from Quintus Curtius Rufus, *Historiarum Alexandri Magni Macedonis*, ed. and trans. J.C. Rolfe, 2 vols (Cambridge, MA: Harvard University Press, 1962). Citations of Walter are from Colker's edition (see note 1). Translations of both Walter and Curtius are my own.

3 On Walter's sources (more in the historical than the literary aspect of his work), Heinrich Christensen, *Das Alexanderlied Walters von Châtillon* (Halle: Verlag der Buchhandlung des Waisenhauses, 1905; repr. Hildesheim, 1969) remains useful.

4 The most convenient summary of the ramifications of the various branches of the Alexander tradition in the Latin West is in David J.A. Ross, *Alexander historiatus: a Guide to Medieval Illustrated Alexander Literature*, 2nd ed., Beiträge zur Klassischen Philologie 186 (Frankfurt am Main: Athenäum, 1988).

5 Otto Zwierlein, *Der prägende Einfluß des antiken Epos auf Walters "Alexandreis"* (Mainz and Stuttgart: Akademie der Wissenschaften und der Literatur, 1987), 20–5.

6 Edmé R. Smits, "A Medieval Supplement to the Beginning of Curtius Rufus's *Historia Alexandri*: an Edition with Introduction," *Viator* 18 (1987), 89–124, 97–8.

7 This detail, too, appears in Claudian (Zwierlein, *Einfluß* [see note 5], 25n30). However, Claudian himself is drawing on a long tradition of liminal adolescents, and Walter would certainly have known the epic precedents for the boy on the verge of manhood directly as well as through Claudian.

8 Likely suspects include, but are not limited to Euryalus in the *Aeneid*, "ora puer prima signans intonsa iuventa"(a boy marking his unshaved face with the first beard, *Aeneid* 9.181); the boy Clytius, "flaventem prima lanugine malas" (cheeks golden with the first down) pursued by Cydon in *Aeneid* Ten (*Aeneid* 10.324); Iolaus in Book Nine (*Metamorphoses* 9.398) and Acis in Book Thirteen (*Metamorphoses* 13.754) of Ovid's *Metamorphoses;* Achilles, somewhat younger, in Statius's *Achilleid* "niveo natat ignis in ore/purpureus ... necdum prima nova lanugine vertitur aetas" (a purple flame swam on his snowy countenance nor had his first period of life turned as yet with the new down, *Achilleid* 1.161–3); Parthenopaeus (likewise a little younger) in the *Thebaid*, "nondum mutatae rosea lanugine malae" (cheeks not yet changed by rosy down, *Thebaid* 9.703).

9 Colker, *Alexandreis* (see note 1), ad loc.

10 Zwierlein, *Einfluß* (see note 5), traces the Hercules allusion to Ovid, addressing the young Gaius Caesar in *Ars Amatoria* 1, 181–91.

11 In this passage that showcases clashing principles in the relation between physical impressiveness and greatness, Talestris holds that greatness goes with a striking appearance. Her maxims (Walter, *Alexandreis* [see note 1], 8.28–32) are all dependent on verbs of thought and judgment (*veneratur, estimat, putat*), and are attributed to *barbara simplicitas*. The alternative view is phrased as impersonal truth in the voice of the narrator: "Sed modico prestat interdum corpore maior/ Magnipotens animus, transgressaque corporis artus/ Regnat in obscuris preclara potentia membris" (But in some instances a spirit capable of great things stands out the more in an undistinguished body, and brilliant capacity overstepping the body's limbs reigns in obscure members. Walter, *Alexandreis* 8.33–5). On the Talestris episode see David Townsend, "Sex and the Single Amazon," *University of Toronto Quarterly* 64 (1995), 255–73.

12 Fritz Peter Knapp, *Similitudo: Stil- und Erzählfunktion von Vergleich und Exempel in der lateinischen, französischen und deutschen Großepik des Hochmittelalters*, Philologia Germanica 2 (Vienna and Stuttgart: Wilhelm Braumüller, 1975), 232–3, traces the image to Claudian, *de III cons. Hon.* 77–80, and to Silius Italicus, *Punica* 4.333–6. The first involves a lion cub who is in fact making the physiological transition to full maturity, the second a mature tiger imagining the kill; neither, therefore, presents the same relationship

of corporeality to imagination as Walter's simile, though the Claudian reference, which Zwierlein also notes (*Einfluß* [see note 5], 22) certainly reinforces the situational allusion of the whole passage.

13 *Historia Alexandri Magni (Historia de Preliis) Rezension J*[2] *(Orosius –Rezension)*, ed. Alfons Hilka, Vol. 1 (Meisenheim am Glan: Hain, 1976).

14 The Curtius supplement does not include this detail, but its allusion to Claudian could have sparked a connection in Walter's mind and generated his simile.

15 Julius Valerius, *Res Gestae Alexandri Macedonis Translatae ex Aesopo Graeco*, ed. Michaela Rosellini (Stuttgart and Leipzig: Teubner, 1993).

16 Curtius's account of the incident begins "Mediam Cydnus amnis, de quo paulo ante dictum est, interfluit, et tunc aestas erat, cuius calor non aliam magis quam Ciliciae oram vapore solis accendit, et diei fervidissimum tempus esse coeperat. Pulvere simul ac sudore perfusum regem invitavit liquor fluminis, ut calidum adhuc corpus ablueret. Itaque veste deposita in conspectu agminis – decorum quoque futurum ratus, si ostendisset suis levi et parabili cultu corporis se esse contentum – descendit in flumen. Vixque ingressi subito horrore artus rigere coeperunt, pallor deinde suffusus est et totum propemodum corpus vitalis calor liquit. Expiranti similem ministri manu excipiunt nec satis compotem mentis in tabernaculum deferunt" (The river Cydnus, about which I was just speaking, flows through the midst, and it was then summer, whose heat burns no region more than that of Cilicia with the sun's warmth, and it had begun to be the hottest time of day. The water of the river enticed the king, caked at once with dust and sweat, to bathe his still heated body. And so with his clothing put off in sight of the army – he thought it would be fitting if he were to show his men that he was content with body maintenance that was untroublesome and ready to hand – he went down into the river. His limbs had scarcely gone in before they began to grow rigid with a sudden stiffness, pallor next overspread him and the vital warmth left virtually his whole body. His attendants received him in their hands like a dying man and carried him off to his tent not altogether in possession of his faculties. Curtius, *Historia Alexandri Magni* [see note 2], 3.5.1–4).

17 For an extensive discussion of the role of Fortuna in the *Alexandreis*, see Dennis Kratz, *Mocking Epic: Waltharius, Alexandreis, and the Problem of Christian Heroism* (Madrid: J.P. Turanzas, 1980).

18 "Vinctum ergo se tradi et tantam victoriam eripi sibi ex manibus obscuraque et ignobili morte in tabernaculo extingui se querebatur. Admissisque amicis pariter ac medicis: "In quo me," inquit, "articulo rerum

mearum Fortuna deprehenderit, cernitis. Strepitum hostilium armorum exaudire mihi videor, et qui ultro intuli bellum iam provocor. Darius ergo cum tam superbas litteras scriberet, fortunam meam in consilio habuit, sed nequiquam, si mihi arbitrio meo curari licet. Lenta remedia et segnes medicos non expectant tempora mea; vel mori strenue quam tarde convalescere mihi melius est. Proinde, si quid opis, si quid artis in medicis est, sciant me non tam mortis quam belli remedium quaerere" (He was complaining that he was being handed over bound and that so great a victory was snatched from him from out of his hands and that he was snuffed out by an obscure and ignoble death in his tent. When his friends and likewise the doctors were let in "You see," he said, "in what a tight place of my affairs Fortune has pounced on me. I seem to myself to hear the noise of enemy weapons, and I who made war of my own free will am now called out. For Darius, when he was writing such contemptuous letters, had my luck in mind, but in vain, if I am permitted to be treated by my own judgment. My occasions do not wait for slow remedies and inactive doctors; for me it is better even to die dashingly than to convalesce tardily. Wherefore, if there is any help, if there is any skill in doctors, let them know that I seek relief not from death but for war." Curtius, *Historia Alexandri Magni* [see note 2], 3.5.10–13).

19 Colker, *Alexandreis* (see note 1), ad loc.

20 "Ceterum tanta vis medicamenti fuit, ut, quae secuta sunt, criminationem Parmenionis adiuverint; interclusus spiritus arte meabat. Nec Philippus quicquam inexpertum omisit; ille fomenta corpori admovit, ille torpentem nunc cibi, nunc vini odore excitavit. Atque ut primum mentis compotem esse sensit, modo matris sororumque, modo tantae victoriae appropinquantis admonere non destitit. Ut vero medicamentum se diffudit in venas et sensim toto corpore salubritas percipi potuit, primum animus vigorem suum deinde corpus quoque expectatione maturius recuperavit" (So great was the strength of the medicine, however, that what followed supported the charges of Parmenion; his breath, stifled, went in and out with difficulty. Philip did not leave anything untried; he applied fomentations to his body, he stirred him up when torpid with the scent now of food, now of wine. And when he first perceived that he was in possession of his faculties he did not cease to remind him now of his mother and sisters, now of so great a victory close at hand. But as the medicine infused itself into his veins and its wholesomeness could gradually be perceived in his whole body, first his mind and then his body also recovered its strength more rapidly than was expected. Curtius, *Historia Alexandri Magni* [see note 2], 3.6.13–16).

21 In Curtius: "quippe post tertium diem quam in hoc statu fuerat in conspectum militum venit" (indeed he came into the sight of the soldiers after the third day for which he had been in that state. Ibid. 3.6.16). Curtius goes on to recount the enthusiastic reception of the doctor Philip (also in Walter, *Alexandreis* [see note 1], 2.250–3, but placed before Alexander's parade in front of the army) and closes with some general reflections on Alexander's appeal to his army (Curtius, *Historia Alexandri Magni* [see note 2], 3.6.17–20).

# *Instrumentum Dei, Exemplum vanitatis, Speculum principis*. Interpretations of Alexander in Medieval German Literature: A Survey

KLAUS GRUBMÜLLER

Subjects and motifs are polyvalent. The history of literature is replete with examples of how they can be made to serve diverse intentions, even to the point of contradictory interpretations. They submit – effortlessly, though also under compulsion if necessary – to the creative wills of their authors, they adapt to the possibilities of specific literary situations. The variability of treatments of Alexander in the German Middle Ages offers an illustration of this. It shows the diversification of German literary production into very different types and areas of use.

From its beginnings until the middle of the twelfth century, German literature was marked by the endeavour to explain the tenets of Christian faith to a laity without any knowledge of Latin. Such projects were carried out on many different paths and with very different degrees of sophistication. This clerical-paraenetic orientation, which is much less in the foreground of French and even less so in Provençal literature, marked the first phases of courtly narrative literature that established itself in German under the influence of French courtly culture in the second half of the twelfth century. It is only in the thirteenth century, in which it becomes a dominant genre, that courtly narrative largely departs from this clerical agenda and becomes a medium for the demonstration and reflection of the ideals of chivalry. In the following centuries these strands become axiomatic, but a certain tendency towards didactic functionalization always reappears, above all in the rapidly proliferating tract publications such as devotionals (as negative paraenesis: a warning against the sin of superbia) or, for the secular realm, in the deportment guides of the *Fürstenspiegel* (*speculum principis*), which presented an ideal model of the wise ruler. The Alexander material lends itself to nearly all of these functions and illustrates them with examples.

# I

Alexander the Great has figured in German literature since almost the very beginning of its history.[1] As early as around 860 in the Alsatian abbey of Weißenburg, the monk Otfrid called upon Alexander to legitimate his attempt to translate the Gospels into a Frankish peasant and warrior language that was entirely unprimed for it. To justify this ambitious project, he stressed, in addition to the Franks' temerity, spiritual gifts, and abundant resources, their genealogy as well: "they are by ancestry and rank related to Alexander, / who struck fear in the heart of the whole world, subdued it with the sword, and subjected it to the heavy chains of his rule" (... sie in sibbu joh in ahtu sin alexandres slahtu, / Ther worolti so githrewita, mit suertu sia al gistrewita / untar sinun hanton mit filu herten banton [I 1, v. 88–90]).[2]

From here on, every century – with the sole exception of the tenth – would conceive its own image of Alexander. The images were usually multifaceted and put to the service of the most diverse interests: in the eleventh century Alexander is mentioned in the *Annolied*,[3] but it is only in the twelfth century that the first Alexander epic in German emerges, a work adapted from the French by Pfaffe Lamprecht, of which two widely diverging versions have been transmitted (*Vorauer Alexander*, *Straßburger Alexander*).[4] From the thirteenth century we have two political propaganda works: the epics of Rudolf von Ems (possibly for Conrad IV of Hohenstaufen, around 1250)[5] and of Ulrich von Etzenbach (for King Wenceslas of Bohemia, around 1290).[6] There are two epics from the fourteenth century, Seifrit's *Alexander*[7] (1352) and the *Wernigeröder Alexander*,[8] the first German adaptation of Quilichinus of Spoleto. The Alexander story is also included in a devotional book, the Low German prose text *Großer Seelentrost*.[9] In the fifteenth century the first two prose histories on Alexander were created, one by the otherwise unknown Meister Babiloth (probably from the beginning of the fifteenth century)[10] and the other by the Munich court doctor Johannes Hartlieb (before 1454).[11]

This essay sets out to highlight several moments in this rich history of the medieval German Alexander material, in order to demonstrate the German Alexander literature's particular profile. My focus will remain throughout on works of the still under-investigated late medieval period of the fourteenth and fifteenth centuries. None of them have been translated into English or found much attention in English-speaking scholarship. I will therefore aim at providing a general picture of medieval German Alexander literature. Above all, I would like to clarify the shifts in perspective on Alexander towards the later Middle Ages, and his multiple functionality for very different discursive intentions.

## II

The image of Alexander as the ruler of the world and as an insuperable military commander who could, according to Otfrid von Weißenburg,[12] as the founder of a German tribe's lineage bestow rank and honour upon it, can be shown – regardless of the concrete sources evidence – to have a forerunner in the Bible. At the beginning of the first Book of Maccabees (1–8), Alexander is described in the following manner:

> The following occurred. The Macedonian Alexander, son of Philip, who had left Greece, defeated Darius, the king of Persia and of the Medes. He who had previously been king over Greece followed him as king. He waged many wars, conquered many fortresses and killed many kings of the earth. He traveled to the limits of the world (Vulgate: *pertransiit ad fines terrae*). He won spoils from a mass of peoples. But as the world fell quiet before him, he overestimated himself and his heart grew proud (Vulgate: *et exaltatum est et elevatum cor eius*). He gathered a military force of exceeding strength, became lord over lands, peoples, and rulers who payed him tribute. But thereafter he sank upon his sick bed and recognized that he would have to die. He summoned those of his court who were held in high regard and who were the friends of his youth. He divided his empire among them while he still lived ...

This image contains (among others that will not be pursued here) all the components that would determine Alexander's contours in the earliest German literature, in this case that of the eleventh and twelfth centuries: as the conqueror of the Persian empire, Alexander assumes a distinguished role in the divine plan of salvation. The subjugation of the entire world and in particular of Persia under Darius is, according to the prediction of the prophet Daniel (7:1–28), a necessary station along the path taken by world rule from the Babylonians to the Persians and Greeks and on into the Roman Empire, where divine salvation could finally be realized in the birth of Christ. Alexander's greatness is evident in his task: he is an *instrumentum dei*. This is how he is presented in the *Annolied* (around 1080)[13] as well as in the oldest German Alexander epic, the *Vorauer Alexander* (around 1170),[14] which ends with the victory of Alexander over Darius, that is, with the transfer of world rule to the Greeks. In addition, as a frail and merely human being stricken by sickness and death at the height of his power, Alexander serves as a reminder of the evanescence of earthly glory. The more comprehensive version of Pfaffe Lamprecht's early German Alexander epic,[15] the *Straßburger Alexander* (shortly after 1180), presents him as an *exemplum vanitatis*, underscoring the contrast by extending Alexander's drive for conquest to the exploration of the earth, and by following him to the gates of Paradise. Step by step it is revealed to him that the accumulation of earthly goods has its limits, and that happiness and eternal salvation cannot be achieved through them.

To the extent that the state of transmission permits conclusions, this spiritual accentuation of Alexander, on the one hand eschatological, on the other hand moral–didactic, is, in the twelfth century, a particularity of the German literature. Neither the Latin epics (Walter of Châtillon and, later, Quilichinus of Spoleto) nor the French place such an emphasis. Both literatures lack, owing to their learned and clerical foundation in the former instance, and their courtly basis in the latter, all the lay-didactic components that make the German tradition distinct.

In the case of Alberic of Bisinzo (around 1140),[16] for whom both German versions served as sources, it is difficult to deduce an overall plan, but his primary emphasis is on Alexander's warrior virtues. From the decasyllabic version produced around 1150/60,[17] it is primarily the childhood stories that have survived, and here as well little can be discerned of a spiritual orientation. In Alexandre de Paris's *Alexander Romance* (around 1185)[18] the hero can do no wrong; even as the conqueror of the world he enjoys God's protection.[19]

## III

In the German epics of the thirteenth century the spiritual instrumentalisation of the Alexander character and of the Alexander material recede completely. After the chivalric epic in the French fashion is established, the German literature gives up its marginal niche existence to an extent and begins to share features of the Alexander image of the Latin and French compositions: that of the bold warrior, the sovereign ruler, the exemplary knight.

Rudolf von Ems, one of the greatest poets of the second generation of the classical courtly period in Middle High German literature and a great admirer of Gotfrid von Straßburg, depicts Alexander as a flawless hero.[20] Most notably, his dangerous tendency towards *superbia* recedes altogether. As Helmut Brackert writes, "For Rudolf, Alexander is an exemplary prince, who justifiably won *der welte prîs* [the glory and honour of this world] and can be presented to contemporaries as the perfected embodiment of *werdekeit* and *ere* [nobility and honour]."[21]

The ruler's life as described by Rudolf in the *Alexander Romance*, unfolds beneath the star of *saelde* (God-ordained good fortune). The youthful Alexander begins his earthly life as the beneficiary of fortune; all of his undertakings succeed for the best; mishaps are, if they ever arise at all, only temporary setbacks. At the end he always meets with success. Whatever the *saelden rîche* (the one blessed with fortune) takes up leads to a good end. And Rudolf leaves no doubt about it that this privileging by fate lasts up until Alexander's death, which, as the epic breaks off at a point significantly prior to it, is not described. The crisis or the sudden fall by which, for the sake of the *exemplum*, many medieval versions bring the life of the Macedonian king to an end, is apparently not foreseen in Rudolf's version.[22]

To be sure, Rudolf does incorporate one more element of the German tradition: Alexander's great and exemplary nature does not exist merely for itself. God has (according to the epilogue of the third book, vv. 12894–909) connected it to the task of taking vengeance on the pagans for their defiance. The exemplary prince is therefore also a servant of the divine order of salvation.

## IV

The lines plotted in the poems of the twelfth and thirteenth centuries were extended and drawn out in the most diverse ways in the Alexander stories of the German late medieval period. In the epics, the moral-didactic aspect did not play much of a role any more. To some extent, this aspect was shifted to the domain of clerical devotional literature, where it is represented with all the more determinacy.

In the Low German devotional text from the second half of the fourteenth century, the *Großer Seelentrost*,[23] the Alexander story is included as a parable of warning. The key term shaping the story appears early on, in the introduction to the section on Alexander: greed, understood as one of the cardinal Christian sins. The story begins with a warning: one must beware of greed, one may not covet the property of others, one should avoid injustice, because nobody can satisfy the greedy man (*wente dem ghirighen mynschen kan nement genogen*) (258, 8–10). Alexander's deeds are then narrated in light of this preamble. His insatiability drives him ever onward, even to the gates of Paradise, where his messenger is of course advised that admittance can be gained only by humility. To Alexander it must remain shut on account of his *superbia*. In a stark antithesis, his fate of eternal damnation is then pronounced, whereupon the readers should be moved to turn away from a life according to Alexander's example and to recognize the transient, even ruinous nature of earthly glory:

> Also genget eme: De wile, dat he leuede, so was he weldich ouer alle de lude; nu is siner de duuel weldich. Korte wile vor he wol; ewekliken sal he ouele varen. Hir was he rike ene clene tid; nusal he arm wesen ane ende. Hir ne kunde eme numment vullen met gude; nv wert he veruullet met deme helscen vure. Hir hadde he grote wertlike ere; nu heuet he de grote scande. Hir nam sin herscap enen ende; nu ne wert siner pine nummer ende. Hir ne wolde he nicht holden de both vses heren godes; nu mot he horsam wesen den duuelen in der helle. (271, 20–7)]
>
> [Thus he fared: As long as he lived, he ruled over all people; now the devil rules over him. For a short time, he fared well; in eternity, he shall meet with misfortune. Here, he was rich for a short time; now he shall be poor without end. Here, nobody could fulfill his desire for riches; now he will be filled up with the fire of hell. Here, he had great earthly honour; now he has great shame. Here, his reign came to an end; now his pain will never cease. Here, he did not want to keep God's commandment; now he has to obey the devil in hell.]

While Alexander's image is completely negative in the *Großer Seelentrost* – so much so that he would even seem to take up with the devil by submitting to him – Seifrit[24] presents him with the same one-sidedness in his own epic, but as a shining hero. In his epic, precisely dated to St Martin's Day 1352, the otherwise unknown, probably Austrian author, glorifies Alexander as a military commander and world ruler. With the exception of a brief mention of his fiery temper and susceptibility to wine (v. 8974), the dark sides of his character are completely elided. Even the journey to the gate of Paradise (vv. 6229–316) is absolved of its burden of *superbia*. It is not attributed to a decision made by Alexander – rather, it is a random occurence. By following the course of a river, he suddenly arrives unawares before the wall of Paradise.

The archangel Michael sends him back, and the clod of earth that should, according to tradition, remind the emperor of his mortality, now serves merely as proof that he has been to the edge of Paradise. Alexander is even acting in the service of God. In what amounts to a rather willful interpretation of Alexander's traditional role of *virga dei*, the scourge of God, he is sent by God to punish the people for *their* transgressions and vanity – which is itself a willful shifting of the *superbia*-reproach. Alexander is presented as a *chestiger, unparmhercziger richter, der obrist Gottes richter* (vv. 72–80: castigator, a merciless judge, God's highest judge). As God's instrument, Alexander is well-prepared to execute His will in the unfolding of history as well: Seifrit's *Alexander* is the most radical realization of this tendency to incorporate Alexander into the history of salvation that is so characteristic of the early German interpretations. Seifrit develops it in a largely secularized variation, as the lesson of the *translatio imperii* (specifically mentioned vv. 8939–47), which at its political core was to legitimize the German kings as the heirs of the Roman emperors. To this end, he makes use of a suggestive analogy: the divinely ordained transition of world rule from the Persians to the Greeks, which has been achieved through Alexander's victory over Darius, is highlighted by an enthronement ceremony that is meant to evoke associations of the coronations of the German emperors:

Auf einen tran er gesas,<br>
mitten auf dem palas,<br>
der was rot guldein,<br>
Tyrus hiez in machen darin.<br>
do chronat man in schon<br>
mit des reiches chron,<br>
die was achtper und reich.<br>
im swuer allermenigklich<br>
zu dienen seinen hulden,<br>
sy wolten gern dulden<br>
in seinem dienst allew natt<br>
williklich unczt in den tadt. (vv. 3856–67)

[He sat upon a throne in the middle of the palace that was reddish-gold in hue and which Tyrus had had built. Then he was crowned with the Empire's crown, which was impressive and mighty. Everyone swore to pay him homage. To serve him they were glad to suffer every pain willingly until their death.]

After Alexander (who up to this point was never referred to as *kaiser*) has sat down on the throne and been crowned with the imperial crown, he proclaims his new stature:

> Wir chaisser Allexander,
> chunic ob allen chunigen her
> des werden gots Amons sun,
> schreiben und auch chundt tun
> allen fuersten und hern
> paidew nachant und verren,
> allen stetten und leutten
> lassen wir es auch bedeutten,
> wie sy sind genantt
> zu Persya in dem landt,
> unser frewdt und holden muett,
> unser gnad und alles guett. (vv. 3872–83)

> [We, Emperor Alexander, king and lord of all kings, son of the great god Amon, hereby write and announce to all princes and lords of countries near and far, to all cities and peoples, so that they will know the names by which they are known in the land of Persia, our joy and faithful will, our mercifulness and everything good.]

The description of the coronation, the homage of the subjects, and the emperor's letter are flavoured with the political vocabulary of the medieval feudal system (e.g., *dienst* and *huld* [service and favour]), and function with the traditional instruments of rule and the ideological catchwords of the German kings: confirmation of the officials (*richter, haubtman*, or *phleger* [judge, leader, or custodian]), the declaration of freedom for everyone, the validity of one and the same law for everyone, the duty to protect widows and orphans, and the declaration of general peace in the country. After his death, Alexander's corpse is then once more decorated with the imperial crown and, belatedly, with the highly revered insignia of the medieval emperors (the sceptre and the imperial apple) (vv. 8793–6). In light of such unbridled medievalisation, it can come as no surprise that researchers have tried to identify the occasion of this work's composition in the contemporary political situation. They believe they have found it in Charles IV's attempts to consolidate his rule,[25] which was fragile and often contested in its first decade (elected 1346, crowned king 1346, again in 1349, crowned emperor in 1355): "The hypothesis suggests itself that this work was meant to serve the imperial ideology in the days of Charles IV."[26]

## IV

Johannes Hartlieb conceived his *Puech von dem großen Alexander*,[27] composed before 1454,[28] with emphatic clarity and, without having a model of it in his source, as a *speculum principis*. He places at the book's very beginning, even before his own preface, a summary of Seneca's teachings on the good prince: he should read ancient writings (*leggende, coroniken vnd getatt*), *daz sy sich fleyzzen, dem zu volgen, daz guett ist, vnd daz meyden, daz pozz ist* (ll. 19–21; legends, chronicles, and deeds, so that they might strive to follow that which is good and to avoid that which is base). In the preface, which he specifically claims to represent his own creation and as being independent of his source – *die vorred, die doctor Hartlieb haut gemacht* (l. 37 the preface, which Doctor Hartlieb created) – this is reiterated again: it is supposed to be about *wie sich ain fürst halten sol, als dann Seneca geschriben hat* (ll. 37–8; how a prince should behave, according to Seneca's writings). Since this could be learned particularly well from the Alexander story, he had been hired by his own prince, Duke Albrecht III of Bavaria, along with his wife, to translate the *Alexander Romance* into German. For the *Alexander Romance* contained an inexhaustible number of stories and chapters through which a prince *gross adenleich tugentt vnd manhaitt horen, sechen vnd auch erlanngen mag* (ll. 39–41; could hear, see and even achieve great noble virtue and manliness). This is the goal Hartlieb is aiming at with his work. But what exactly are the contents of the ruler ideal that is to be disseminated here? In a description that runs closely parallel to a compilation composed at the Tegernsee monastery, and that can be traced back, over mediate versions, to Julius Valerius and Archpriest Leo, the text recounts Alexander's well-known path, which begins with his doubtful birth and passes from there to his seizure of power in Macedon, to the first conquests leading to his victory over the Persian king Darius, the campaign to India and the subjugation of a number of peoples, the victory over King Porus, the encounter with the abstemious Oxidraces, his imprisonment by Queen Candace, the confrontation with the Amazons; then, Alexander's return to Babylon, his murder at the instigation of Antipater, and the ensuing turmoil in the empire. It also contains a long letter by King Dindimus that includes a comprehensive description of the way of life of the Brahman and their ideal of simplicity (ll. 4555–5336), an equally extensive letter to his teacher Aristotle about the wonders of India, with addenda in a shorter letter to his mother Olympias that include descriptions of his griffin-journey and of his exploration of the depths of the sea. I will extract a few points from the story that are symptomatic of how its meaning is constituted:

First, the early German tradition of instrumentalising Alexander as an agent of the divine plan of salvation no longer plays any role. The source itself makes this difficult: Darius is not killed by Alexander, he is murdered by traitors from his own country. Of course, this would not necessarily prevent the transfer of power to Alexander and thereby to the Greeks from turning out to be a divinely ordained moment, nor does it preclude its celebration as a more-or-less consensual solution, harmoniously underscored by Alexander's marriage to the daughter of Darius. This would not, however, advance Hartlieb's goal of writing a *speculum principis*. The interest in Alexander has shifted and has a new goal. For the role of *exemplum vanitatis*, Alexander's other key use in the earliest German poems, he can likewise no longer be used.

Second, Alexander's questionable birth (his mother's adultery with the deceitful magician Nectanabus, who convinces Olympias he is the god Amon who would conceive a son with her),[29] in Hartlieb's romance is in the very beginning disarmed by an unabashedly mariological tinting of the mother's innocence, and transformed into harmony by Philip's goodness, which he seems to have picked up from Jesus of Nazareth himself. The terrible signs that accompany Alexander's birth instruct him to adopt the child as his son and to raise him, *als ob er von meinem leib geboren wär* (l. 454; as if he were born of my body). The fact that the heavenly signs were in fact the machinations of Nectanabus, intended only to serve the purpose of deceiving Philip and his wife, is not discussed. The evil in Alexander, which he must have inherited from his father, is hereby pushed back in favour of an emphasis on God's guidance and mercy. At the end it can be summarily stated that Alexander had been under God's protection for the whole course of his life: *vnd die gottleich genade was im also bey gestanden* (l. 7009; and God's mercy had therefore remained with him).

Third, for one who is led by God's mercy, even the great temptations Alexander is usually subjected to do not present any real danger. *Curiositas* and *superbia* keep to the margins or else they receive new functions. Of the episode that most vividly captures Alexander's overzealous curiosity, his greed to uncover the mysteries of creation by travelling to the gates of Paradise, there is no trace. His endeavour to touch heaven with the aid of a team of griffins is ultimately prevented by divine power (l. 6860), but the flight is halted only just before its goal. There is no ensuing injury that might be understood as a punishment for illegitimate curiosity. He thus immediately makes plans, without the least hesitation, to fathom out the depths of the sea, and it all goes off without a hitch, as he relates to his mother in a letter. His report of the wonders of India leaves no room for scruples in its unqualified expression of pride in his own desire for knowledge and drive to explore: *sy sein wol der mue werdt, daz man sy beschreib vnd ir nichtt vergess, wann ich hab sy mitt grozzer arbaitt erforen, gesechen vnd durch forschett* (ll. 5384–7; they are by all means worth the trouble it takes to describe and record them for posterity, for I have only by great effort discovered, seen, and explored them), he says in his letter to Aristotle. (The Latin text has only: *vidi per summos labores et pericula.*)[30] The function many of these episodes previously had – of demonstrating to Alexander the limitations of Man, of teaching him humility – has become superfluous, for Alexander has long since learned his lesson. The simple *Oxidraces*, whose request for immortality he could not fulfill, had already shown him his earthly limitations, and he presented himself to them with perfect humility: *Die vrsach meines vmbcziechens ist nichtt anders wann ein schickung vnd einflüss der ewigen weyßhaitt* (the Latin text has: *superna providentia*), *die von oben ist vnd ich pin der selben dienner*[31] (The cause of my peregrination is none other than the will and influence of that eternal wisdom that comes from above and whose servant I am). He is in fact constantly taught that his fate is not in his own hands: Candace, for example, permits him to experience that he, the conqueror of the world, cannot even free himself from the hands of a woman. He nearly collapses from this realization: *Im was czerrunnen aller weyßhaitt vnd synne vnd da er nichtt verrer mochtt* (ll. 4063–4; All wisdom and sense fled him, and from there he could not depart). In another instance, the god Sesonchosis makes it clear in his speech that it is he who rules the world and everything that happens in it. Alexander asks him for his protection: *Herr ich pitt dich, daz du mich nemest in deinen segenn* (ll. 4185–7; Lord, I beg you to put your blessing upon me) and the god agrees to make the whole world subject to him, which is to say he makes Alexander his tool.

At the end of the dialogue with the gods (this is before the encounter with the Amazons and Brahmans, before the wonders of the Orient, before the journeys of extreme height and depth), Hartlieb's narrator goes beyond his source in summing up: *Alexander hett nun wol verstanden, daz aller menschen synne kchlain mugen sein, wann den selben die gottleich hilff nichtt pey bestatt vnd sy laytt vnd kerett zu dem allerpesten* (ll. 4299–301; Alexander had by now grasped that the powers of humans can only be minimal, as long as they are not granted divine help, which leads them and turns them towards the highest good).

In the extremely expanded correspondence with the Brahman King Dindimus this wisdom is developed further. It ends in Alexander's renewed realization of his fallibility: *Ich erkenne auch nun mein armes leben, auch wann ich leb in großen sorgen vnd maniger sorgffelttigkaitt* (ll. 5281–2; I now also recognize the poverty of my life, and that I live in great need and am burdened with many cares).

The *Oxidraces*, the pagan gods, King Dindimus: they all teach Alexander about divine omnipotence and about the abandonment of Man. With Candace, Alexander actually endures his powerlessness; it is otherwise merely explained to him in discussions and letters, where the object of his pleas (which are, compared to the source, significantly expanded and intensified) is to be granted guidance:

> Darumb hab ich gedachtt, dier, Dindime, zuschreiben, daz du mich aygenttleich vnderweysest und mier verkundest, wiee ewr leben sey vnd durch was sach willen ir so gar abgeschayden seytt von allem menschleichem leben. Schreibtt auch mier, ob ir das thuentt von lernung der kchunst phylozophya oder von ander sach wegen, daz woltt ich vast gerenn wißen. Wann thatt ir daz von lernung wegenn, so hett ich daran ain gancz wolgefallen, wann was zu vnderweysung der weyßhaitt gehoret, darczue wellen wier helffen vnd ratten vnd vermainen, vns auch ze geben in die schuel vnd gehorsam der lernung, wann was wier piss her yee gethan haben, so haben wier allweg die weyßhaitt vnd die vernunfft allen dingen vor gesacztt.

> [ll. 4520–30. That is why I thought to write to you, Dindimus, so that you would actually instruct me and tell me what your life is like and for what reason you have so separated yourself from all human life. Please write to me whether you do it for the sake of studying the art of philosophy or for some other reason- I would very much like to know this. For if you do it on account of learning I would certainly be glad, for we want to be of assistance and counsel to whatever belongs to instruction in the ways of wisdom. We too want to become a student and disciple of learning, for in

everything we have done to this day, we have always placed wisdom and reason before all other things.]

The emperor, the great Alexander, writes to Dindimus to ask for wisdom and to beg for instruction in its ways. And Dindimus praises him for this urge to be taught. With the catchword *des begierlichen fragens* (passionate questioning), which was added to the source, he redirects Alexander's worldly greed, his thirst for conquest and domination, his alarming *curiositas*, towards a yearning for wisdom: *Als Alexander begerett zu wißen, was rechtte vnd ware weysshaitt sey, ob du daz nichtt wayst vnd doch darnach begierleich fragest, daz ist gross an dier zu loben* (ll. 4557–9; That Alexander desires to know what proper and true wisdom is, that he does not know and yet passionately asks about it – this deserves great praise). Wisdom is namely the foundation of all rule. One might seize power without wisdom, but no empire could endure for long without it, no ruler could, without a philosophical education, exercise his power with the necessary sovereignty: *Wann weleicher kchayßer oder kunig weyßhaitt vnd der waren phylozophia mangelt vnd daran ist, der mag nichtt gehayssenn ain kunig, sunder ain dienner aller der, die mitt im wonen vnd wanndeln* (ll. 4564–7; If any emperor or king lacks wisdom and true philosophy, he cannot be called a king, but rather a servant of everyone among whom he lives and walks).

Dindimus is propagating the learned, philosophically educated ruler: a ruler ideal that is, at least as an ideal, completely foreign to the High Middle Ages. It has no place, for instance, in the likes of a Rudolf von Ems, where the ruler is buttressed by his genealogy and charisma, his warrior virtues, his courtly ethos, and his knightly perfection. The wise ruler is an ideal that the scholars and thereby the church (in particular the Dominican order) begins to develop from the thirteenth century onward, for instance in the writings of Aegidius Romanus. Johannes Hartlieb's prose romance is apparently adapting this ideal to Alexander, and he easily succeeds in integrating the darker shades that are inscribed in this character; this is a ruler who does not submit to his lust for glory, but rather resists everywhere the temptation of *superbia*, channelling his otherwise ruinous *curiositas* into the perfection of his personality for the good of his subjects.

And so in the end, the critical eye has shut on Alexander: shortly before his death he orders an inscription to be made at all the cities he has founded and to which he has given the name *Alexandria*. It is an inscription by no means lacking in self-confidence: *Die geschrifft an der mawren was also lawttendt: "Der kunig Alexander hatt mich gepawen. Er was von dem geschlächtt Iuppiters vnd alle werltt mochtt im mitt streytt nichtt vberwinden"* (ll. 7360–3; The writing on the wall read: "The king Alexander built me. He was of the race of Jupiter, and not even the whole world could defeat him in battle"). Such arrogance would seem to invite critical reproof; it must certainly appear as an expression of unbridled *superbia*. Yet Johannes Hartlieb lets it stand without comment; it has staked a place for itself in the awe-inspiring portrait of a great man and exemplary wise ruler.

## V

By his conception and birth, Alexander is destined for heroism. In the eyes of his mother he is the son of a god, and in the eyes of nature he is as well: the earth trembles, the sky darkens, lightning flashes, and thunder pounds the skies. And even if Olympias has been deceived, Alexander's real father, Nectanabus the magician, who comes to her in the form of a dragon, is still anything but an everyday human. The (real or supposed) demigod bears all the marks of exorbitant corporeality befitting a mythical hero.

In the German Alexander epics, not much remains of this heroic exorbitance. At best, it can be seen in the spectacular deeds of his youth – his taming of the horse Bucephalus, for example, or his intermittent outbursts of heroic rage. Only in the oldest epic, the *Vorauer Alexander*, is it still central to the text's meaning, as can be seen in the violent gesture by which Alexander personally decapitates Darius. On the whole, the mythic potential is domesticated, either by means of its insertion into the plan of divine salvation, its deployment to moral-didactic or state-philosophical ends, by heavy-handed courtliness, or through its political instrumentalisation. In the ensemble of German literature, the Alexander material therefore remains robustly distinct from the heroic epic. It constitutes, rather, an outstanding example of the taming of myth in the German Middle Ages.

Translated by John Koster.

## NOTES

1 See Trude Ehlert, *Deutschsprachige Alexanderdichtung des Mittelalters. Zum Verhältnis von Literatur und Geschichte* (Frankfurt a.M.: Lang, 1989).

2 Otfrids *Evangelienbuch*, ed. Oskar Erdmann, Altdeutsche Textbibliothek 49, fourth ed. by Ludwig Wolff (Tübingen: Max Niemeyer, 1962). For the traditional background see Gisela Vollmann-Profe, Kommentar zu Otfrids *Evangelienbuch*, part 1: Widmungen, Buch I, 1–11 (Bonn: Rudolf Habelt, 1976), 144–6.

3 Das *Annolied*, ed. and trans. Eberhard Nellmann, Universal-Bibliothek 1416 (Stuttgart: Reclam, 1975).

4 Lamprechts *Alexander*, ed. and comm. Karl Kinzel, Germanistische Handbibliothek 4 (Halle a.S.: Buchhandlung des Waisenhauses, 1884). See also Christoph Mackert, *Die Alexandergeschichte in der Version des "Pfaffen" Lambrecht. Die frühmittelhochdeutsche Bearbeitung der Alexanderdichtung des Alberich von Bisinzo und die Anfänge weltlicher Schriftepik in deutscher Sprache*, Beihefte zur Poetica 23 (Munich: Fink 1999).

5 Rudolf von Ems, *Alexander*. Ein höfischer Versroman des 13. Jahrhunderts, ed. Victor Junk, 2 vols., Bibliothek des Litterarischen Vereins 272/274 (Leipzig: Hiersemann, 1928/1929).

6 Ulrich von Eschenbach, *Alexander*, ed. Wendelin Toischer, Bibliothek des Litterarischen Vereins 182 (Tübingen: Litterarischer Verein, 1888). It is regarded as a mystification exploiting the nimbus of Wolfram von Eschenbach that this edition ascribes the work to one Ulrich von Eschenbach on the basis of some of the evidence in some of the manuscripts. See Hans-Joachim Behr's summarizing entry "Ulrich von Etzenbach," in *Die deutsche Literatur des Mittelalters. Verfasserlexikon*, Vol. 9, ed. Burghart Wachinger et al. (Berlin and New York: Walter de Gruyter, 1995), 1256–64. See also Claudia Medert, *Der "Alexander" Ulrichs von Etzenbach. Studien zur Erzählstruktur und Gattungsproblematik*, Palaestra 287 (Göttingen: Vandenhoeck und Ruprecht, 1989).

7 *Seifrits* Alexander. *Aus der Straßburger Handschrift*, ed. Paul Gereke, Deutsche Texte des Mittelalters 36 (Berlin: Weidmann, 1932).

8 *Der Große Alexander*. Aus der Wernigeröder Handschrift, ed. Gustav Guth, Deutsche Texte des Mittelalters 13 (Berlin: Weidmann 1908).

9 *Der große Seelentrost*. Ein niederdeutsches Erbauungsbuch des 14. Jahrhunderts, ed. Margarete Schmitt (Cologne: Böhlau 1959).

10 *Deux temoins en prose du roman d'Alexandre a la fin du moyen âge en Allemagne: l'Alexandre du "Grosser Seelentrost" et l'Alexandre de Wichbolt*, ed. Peter H. Andersen (Amiens: Presses du Centre d'Etudes médiévales, 2001). See also Hans Hugo Steinhoff, "Meister Babiloth," in *Die deutsche Literatur des Mittelalters. Verfasserlexikon*, Vol. 1, ed. Kurt Ruh et al. (Berlin and New York: Walter de Gruyter, 1978), 577.

11 Johann Hartliebs *Alexander*, ed. Reinhard Pawis, Münchener Texte und Untersuchungen zur deutschen Literatur des Mittelalters 97 (Munich: Artemis, 1991).
12 See note 2.
13 See note 3.
14 The older version of the epic of Pfaffe Lamprecht, see note 4.
15 See also note 4.
16 Ulrich Mölk and Günter Holtus, "Alberichs Alexanderfragment. Neuausgabe und Kommentar," *Zeitschrift für romanische Philologie* 115 (1999), 582–625.
17 *The Medieval French Roman d'Alexandre*, Vol. 3, ed. Alfred Foulet, Elliott Monographs 38 (New York: Kraus 1965), 61–100.
18 *The Medieval French Roman d'Alexandre*, Vol. 2, ed. Edward Armstrong, Elliott Monographs 37 (New York: Kraus 1965).
19 Susanne Friede, "Alexanders Kindheit in der französischen Zehnsilberfassung und im *Roman d'Alexandre*. Fälle, literarischer Nationalisierung' des Alexanderstoffs," in *Alexanderdichtungen im Mittelalter. Kulturelle Selbstbestimmung im Kontext literarischer Beziehungen*, ed. Jan Cölln et al., Literatur und Kulturräume 1 (Göttingen: Wallstein, 2000), 82–136.
20 See note 5.
21 Helmut Brackert, *Rudolf von Ems. Literatur und Geschichte* (Heidelberg: Winter, 1968), 127.
22 Ibid., 128.
23 See note 9.
24 See note 7.
25 Rüdiger Schnell, "Seifrits *Alexander* und die Reichspublizistik des späteren Mittelalters," *Deutsche Vierteljahrsschrift für Literaturwissenschaft und Geistesgeschichte* 48 (1974), 448–77.
26 Kurt Ruh, "Epische Literatur des deutschen Spätmittelalters," in *Neues Handbuch der Literaturwissenschaft, Vol. 8, Europäisches Spätmittelalter*, ed. Willi Erzgräber (Wiesbaden: Athenaion, 1978), 117–88, 149.
27 Hartliebs *Alexander* (see note 11), l. 39. All further quotations from this edition.
28 Frank Fürbeth, *Johannes Hartlieb. Untersuchungen zu Leben und Werk*, Hermaea 64 (Tübingen: Max Niemeyer, 1992), 71–2.
29 See Manuel Braun, "Vom Gott gezeugt: Alexander und Jesus. Zum Fortleben des Mythos in den Alexanderromanen des christlichen Mittelalters," *Zeitschrift für deutsche Philologie* 123 (2004), 40–66. Florian Kragl, "De ortu Alexandri multiplicis Nektanebus ze diute getihtet," *Troianalexandrina* 6 (2006), 35–80.

30 *Liber Alexandri Magni. Die Alexandergeschichte der Handschrift Paris, Bibliothèque Nationale, n.a.l.310*, ed. Rüdiger Schnell, Münchener Texte und Untersuchungen zur deutschen Literatur des Mittelalters 96 (Munich: Artemis 1989), ll. 1557–8.

31 Hartliebs *Alexander* (see note 11), ll. 3710–12, cf. *Liber Alexandri Magni* (see note 30), ll. 1164–5.

# Science and Learning in the Middle Ages: *Le Roman d'Alexandre en prose* – A Study of Ms Stockholm, Royal Library Vu 20[1]

MAUD PÉREZ-SIMON

In Europe, one of the richest and most popular manuscript traditions in the Middle Ages was that of the *Roman d'Alexandre* in both its verse and prose forms. My earlier studies have focused on the sixteen surviving manuscripts of the Old-French version of the latter, among which eleven are illuminated.[2] Both the textual and the iconographic cycles in this *Roman d'Alexandre en prose* tradition remained relatively unchanged throughout the different manuscripts produced from the thirteenth to the fifteenth century.[3] David Ross's work established that, beyond a stable set of illustrations within the manuscript text, most changes were themselves only variations on a predetermined suite of images that he dates back to Late Antiquity. There are between seventy and ninety identical visual motifs to be found in the illustrations of most of the illuminated *Roman d'Alexandre en prose* manuscripts. The degree of similarity within the corpus is striking; images are similar in subject, content, arrangement, rubrics, and place of insertion in the text. Textually, the changes are even fewer as they are most often reduced to mere syntactical variations, and larger alterations are indeed rare.

Beyond the textual and iconographic stability, it is these small but significant changes that ultimately render this *Roman* tradition interesting and comprehensible.[4] This gives us an intriguing insight into the *Roman d'Alexandre en prose* and into the reception it received. For example, a manuscript made in France for the future Queen of England, Marguerite d'Anjou, during the Hundred Years War, and one made for Philip VI, King of France, in the 1330s – two closely related manuscripts as far as text and images are concerned, but very remote in time and iconographic style – illustrate two contexts of reception and therefore two different possible readings offered by a single text. The first (London, BL Royal 15 E. vi) updates Alexander into a champion of the English royal family, carrier of the Lancastrian Red Rose; the second (London, BL Royal 19 D. i), depicts Alexander as a conqueror of the East, integrated into a skillful plea for the king to keep his promise of going on Crusade.[5] Such conclusions can only be drawn from a careful and precise study of text and image in this series of manuscripts. Image and text are interlaced to reinforce a particular reading of the *Roman*. The textual and visual variants allow us to understand both medieval social imaginaries and the imaginings of the text's patrons.

The *Roman d'Alexandre en prose* manuscript from the Royal Library of Stockholm (Vu 20)[6] on which we focus here stands out in this tradition for three reasons: because of its oriental origin, because of the encyclopedic accretions it contains, and because of the drastic reduction of the iconographic program. I would like to show that these three particularities have to be understood in relation to one another and to establish that the images serve to remodel the text in order to offer a particular reading of the *Roman d'Alexandre en prose*.

The manuscript from the Stockholm Royal Library, Vu 20 dates from the middle of the fourteenth century. The Catalan features of the vocabulary and the patent exoticism of its imagery (such as palm trees, exotic architecture, or Aristotle sitting cross-legged with a turban on his head writing pseudo-Arabic characters on a roll) have long confused scholars. After a careful linguistic analysis (noting some vocabulary specific to this part of the Mediterranean), and a comparison with manuscripts of the *Livre du Tresor* illuminated in the Mediterranean area, Fabio Zinelli[7] has suggested that, as far as the *scripta*, the miniatures, and the pen-flourished initials are concerned, it was made by a Catalan scribe working in Cyprus, where many of the Outremer Christians found safety after the fall of Acre in 1291.[8]

This manuscript, made up of eighty-five folios, partakes of the relatively stable textual and illustrative tradition of the *Roman d'Alexandre en prose* witnesses. However, our manuscript is subject to both narrative and visual variations. Not only are there small – yet important – textual modifications but also lengthy insertions and iconographic amendments of various types that accompany the aforementioned passages. Furthermore, it has fewer illuminations than most (twenty-three illustrated folios versus an average of eighty for the other manuscripts), rendering these changes all the more significant. As we will see, the images help both to structure the text and to integrate the insertions within it.

One of the primary novelties of Vu 20 is the appearance of excerpts derived from medieval encyclopedias within the body of the narrative. In total, there are four large textual insertions in the *Roman*.[9] One comes from a French version of the *Secretum secretorum*, two from Brunetto Latini's *Livre du Tresor*, and one, until now unidentified, comes from another encyclopedic compilation: *De septem herbis ad Alexandrum* or its Greek source.[10]

The *Secretum secretorum* was allegedly written by Aristotle for Alexander the Great, but it was most probably composed in Arabic during the tenth century.[11] John of Sevilla made a partial translation into Latin in the first half of the twelfth century, and Philip of Tripoli was responsible for a complete version in the first quarter of the thirteenth century. From the last third of the thirteenth century on it was translated into Old French, both completely and in passages.[12] It was by far the most widely read encyclopedia of the High Middle Ages: no fewer than 600 manuscripts of the Latin version have been found and ten different translations in French.[13] It purports to be the long response Aristotle wrote for Alexander in reply to the latter's announcement of his victory over King Darius. The version chosen for insertion in manuscript Vu 20 is a late one[14] in which Alexander is subsequently said to require Aristotle's presence. The philosopher and tutor to Alexander claims to be too old to undertake the journey to rejoin his pupil and help him with the governance of his new subjects, and thus writes a long missive on governance and justice. The selection of this specific translation is of particular importance as this late version of the *Secretum secretorum* was written specifically to reflect Alexander's participation in the epistolary exchange. The text itself lies at the crossroads of literature, encyclopedic works and didactic *miroir de prince*.[15] It deals with subjects as diverse as morality, hygiene, gastronomy, astrology, physiognomy, science, and nutrition, as well as with the use and implications of power. Beyond Aristotle's assertion in the text that he has gathered in this epistle all the knowledge necessary for Alexander to govern, the narrative itself is a hybrid in both style and content, a mix of philosophy, history, and science.

The origin of the *Livre du Tresor* is less obscure. Written by the Florentine master Brunetto Latini between 1260 and 1265, during his exile in Paris, it is a purely encyclopedic work.[16] The book was intended for one of his friends, who was to become a *podestà*. It was designed as a manual of politics, of *podestà*, and therefore included teachings on many of the sciences. From the prologue on, the tone is established: knowledge must be at the source of politics, of self-mastery, and of public governance. It was originally written in Old French and is a larger work than the *Secret des secrets*, although similar in purpose, which explains their early circulation in the same manuscripts. The *Livre du Tresor* is also one of the first attempts in Old French to catalogue and encompass all known knowledge of its time, covering the history of the world since its creation, providing basic and often simplified information on lands, nations, animals, and the cosmos, as well as digressions on politics, ethics, and hagiography. As its name implies, it claims to contain the treasures of the wisdom of its age. Even if the *Livre du Tresor* has no obvious link to Alexander, it seems to have been associated with the Macedonian by the medieval public, as the manuscripts attest: in one manuscript a miniature of the *Livre du Tresor* refers to the conversation between the conqueror and the wise Brahmans. In another manuscript, the *Livre du Tresor* is copied alongside a *Livre de moralité et gouvernement de Seigneurie par Aristote à Alexandre le Grand*.[17] Given these contexts, it is clear why our compiler did not find it inappropriate to merge two extracts from the *Livre du Tresor* in a *Roman d'Alexandre*.

The *De septem herbis ad Alexandrum* belongs to the hermetic tradition. It is a "planetary collection," a catalogue of the medicinal and magic virtues of seven plants (*affodilus, poligonia, chinosbacos, arnoglossa, pentadactilus, iusquamus, vervena*) linked to seven planets (Saturn, Sun, Moon, Mars, Mercury, Jupiter, Venus), with instructions on how to use them. *De septem herbis* is the name of the Latin translation – attributed to Paschalis Romanus[18] – of a text that existed in Greek in two versions: the first is anonymous and the second attributed to Alexander the Great.[19] The Stockholm manuscript gives a French version of the *De septem herbis*. Up to now, no French version was known to have circulated in either the Orient or in Europe at this time: the earliest inventoried French versions date to the era of printed books.[20] Was our text translated for this manuscript? The fact that the two other accretions in manuscript Vu 20 had already circulated in French versions leads me to think that the compiler chose the texts for the insertions amidst an existing francophone corpus of encyclopedic works linked to Alexander the Great. In our extract, the names of the plants are given in Greek and not in Latin. Should we consider that the French text was translated directly from Greek without any Latin intermediary? It is an option that ought to be considered.[21]

The *Secret des secrets*, the *Livre du Tresor*, and the *De Septem Herbis* in its French version have all been chosen for their link to Alexander and for their didactic and encyclopedic content. The four insertions in the Stockholm manuscript take place in the last two thirds of the narrative.[22] While we do not know who is responsible for their inclusion – it may have been due to a patron's wishes by, or to the work of a compiler – we can study how skillfully the insertions are interwoven into the text: first, thematically, because the passages chosen in the encyclopedic works correspond perfectly to the narration of Alexander's exploits, and second, iconographically, by examining the illustrations.

What do they tell us about the *Roman d'Alexandre en prose*? We will answer these questions through a study of the passages in the order of their appearance.

The first amendment to the text takes place on fol. 35v, shortly after Alexander's wedding to the Persian princess Roxane, itself the consequence of his victory over her father, King Darius. In the *Roman* tradition, Alexander writes one letter to his mother to tell her about his marriage and another to his tutor, Aristotle, to tell him about his conquests. It is a very short passage. The textual addition from the *Secret des secrets* includes their epistolary exchange, in which Aristotle excuses himself for not being physically able to make the journey to see him, and offers advice on how to be a powerful and just ruler. This comes in the form of several treatises on generosity, empathy, abstinence, planning, and forethought (fols. 35v–41v). The beginning of the amended text is blended into the pre-existent narrative quite well by means of a rubric ("Ci dit coment Alixandre manda letres a son maistre Aristote faisant li assavoir coment il avoit conquise la terre de Perse et qu'il le deust mander conseill que il feroit"), but, in the margin, the word *"hic"* followed by a symbol (the letter "I" going through the letter "o") signals to the reader that it is noteworthy.

The image (Figure 11.1) that accompanies this insertion is rather complex and entirely new to the iconographic cycle of the *Roman*.

It appears about two-and-a-half folios *into* the insertion. Therefore, it does not mark the beginning of the insertion itself, but rather the start of Aristotle's answer to Alexander, the didactic portion of the epistolary exchange. It is a single image divided into two levels. In the upper half, the illumination shows Alexander's wedding to Roxane, and the lower half illustrates the epistolary exchange between pupil and tutor. Let us stress the novelty of this image that associates the wedding and the epistolary exchange, the new status of Alexander and the need of advice for good governance. The end of the insertion is marked by a miniature of Alexander leaving Persia followed by his troops (fol. 41v).

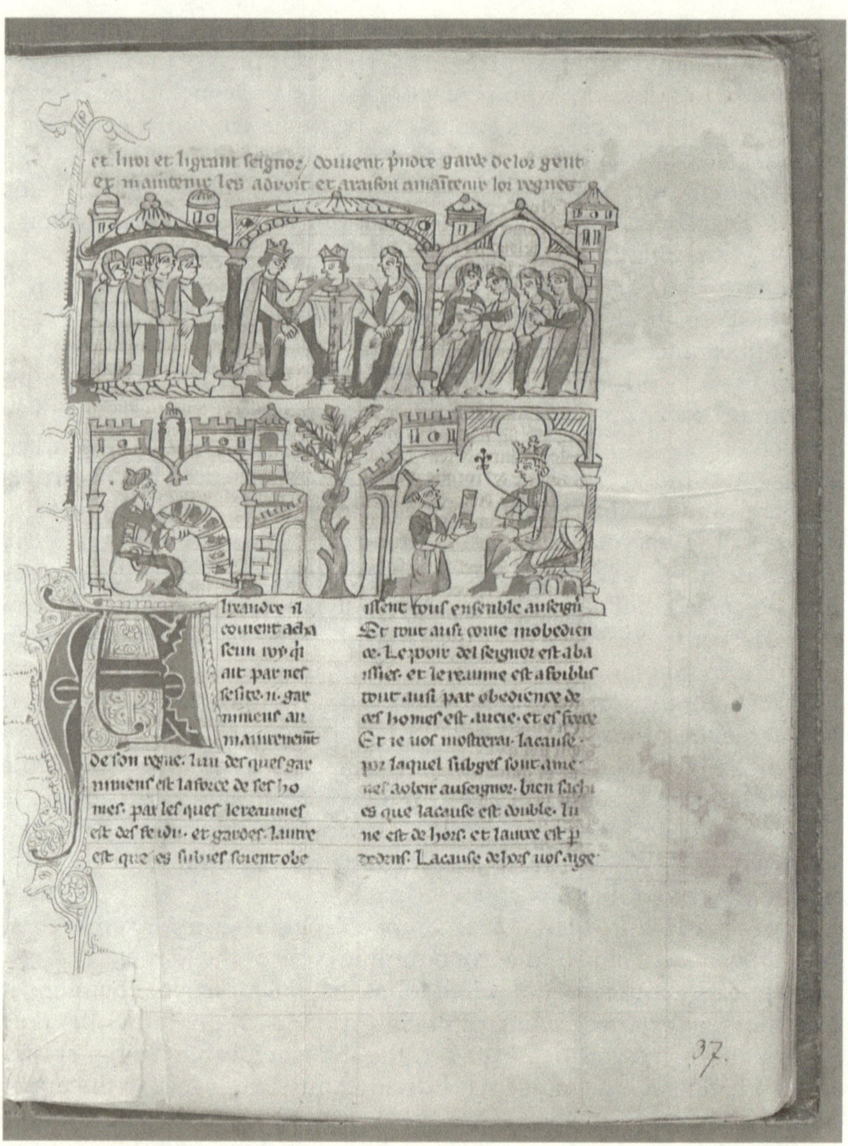

Figure 11.1. In the upper half, the illumination shows Alexander's wedding to Roxane, and the lower half illustrates the epistolary exchange between pupil and tutor. *Roman d'Alexandre en prose*, Stockholm, Kungl. biblioteket, ms Vu 20, 37r. © Kungl. biblioteket – National Library of Sweden.

This new image in the corpus (it is not a passage that is usually illustrated) is a variation on a previous illustration, showing Alexander leaving Macedonia followed by his troops (fol. 8r). This repetition of a previously used pattern calls our attention to the image more as a tool for textual organization than as a means of introducing new information, an implement to smooth the transition and to facilitate the resumption of the narration.

The second textual insertion comes from a French version of the *De septem herbis*. It occurs at the point in the narrative after the siege of Ambria, in which poisoned arrows injure many among the Macedonians. The *Roman* describes a dream in which the god Amon, under the guise of the god Mercurius, offers Alexander a medicinal plant that will cure his men, and how upon his waking the king finds such a plant next to his bed. The Stockholm manuscript expands the dream to explain that Amon in fact offers more than one plant to the Macedonian king, along with an encyclopedic explanation of the provenance and medicinal uses of seven of them (fols. 65–6v). Even if no editing was needed to fuse texts in the case of the first insertion, here a narrative addition (in bold below) is incorporated to better couple the traditional account and the exhaustive botanical description that follows.

> Mais cele nuit senbla Alixandre en avision que li Dieus Amon li venoit devant en senblance de Mercuriuset si mostroit une herbe et li dissoit: "Fis Alixandre done me ceste herbe a ceaus qui sont naffrés et le venins ne leur grevera mais garont. **Et autres herbes y a que sont profitables a moult de choses de lesques herbes je vos en dirai des vii principaus lor nons et lor manieres et lor vertus.**"[23]

It is followed by a rubric that obviously repeats the narration.

> Ci dit des vii herbes principaus que une nuit senbla a Alixandre en avision que li dieus Amon li venoit devant en senblance de Mercurius. Et se li mostroit vii. herbes herbes (*sic*) principaus entre lesqueles herbes en y avoit une. Et disoit "Fis Alixandre done moi ceste herbe a ceaus qui sont [malades] et nul venins ne lor grevera."

To create this new rubric, the compiler has copied part of the preceding text and inserted a modest modification, changing the number of plants from one to seven.

The suture between the two texts is very skillfully done by five means: 1) The first plant to be described is a plant that does indeed cure venom, which is exactly the plant that Amon gives to Alexander in the original passage – but without instructions. It is therefore coherent. 2) The seven plants listed to Alexander are each linked to a planet[24] (Mercurius, [Saturn,] Sun, Moon, Mars, Jupiter and Venus). Where, in the source of the insertion, the list begins with Saturn,[25] the first plant here is explicitly and from the beginning linked to Mercurius ("Ceste herbe est aproprié a Mercurius," fol. 65v), which is the guise under which Amon introduces himself to Alexander. It helps merge the beginning of the insertion into the text. 3) The compiler introduces the innovation of initiating a direct speech addressed to Alexander by the god beginning with the rubric ("Et disoit: 'Fils Alixandre ...'"), making the didactic text an extension of the direct speech and rendering it less artificial. 4) Several rubrics making reference to Alexander are interspersed within the inserted narrative. Each time a new plant is referred to in those rubrics, the name of Alexander is added (in bold below). He is successively mentioned as a mere interlocutor of the angel: "Ci parole d'une bone herbe **a Alixandre** qui a nom Cinabatos qui est moult profitable a mout de choses": "Ci parole encores **a Alixandre** d'une herbe qui a nom Acarome et aucuns la noment Jusquiamus" (fol. 66r). Alexander is also addressed by the angel: "Alixandre, ci parole d'une herbe qui a nom Arnoglofa et est bone a moult de choses," "Alixandre, ceste herbe a a nom Pestereon et Herbe Colonbine" (fol. 66r), "Alixandre, cest herbe est aproprié a Venus" (fol. 66v); and he is given the active role of baptizing a plant: "Ci parole de l'erbe qui a non Pologonie **et Alixandres l'apelle herbe dou solaill**" (fol. 65v). By these means, both repetitive and varied, the didactic text is turned into a narrative text. 5) The supporting illustration (Figure 11.2) is both unique to the *Roman* tradition and accurate in its representation of the entire passage.

The image represents the Macedonian king asleep and the god Amon[26] offering him many plants on a platter. It is placed at the beginning of the textual insertion, immediately after a transitional phrase and subsequent rubric, and has a prefatory role in the narrative: it represents both the traditional and the amended texts, and acts as a connective tool between them.

Thanks to the rubrics and to the image, the didactic accretion is very cleanly integrated to the narration. The contrast between the story and the scientific explanation remains evident nonetheless. Even if the text

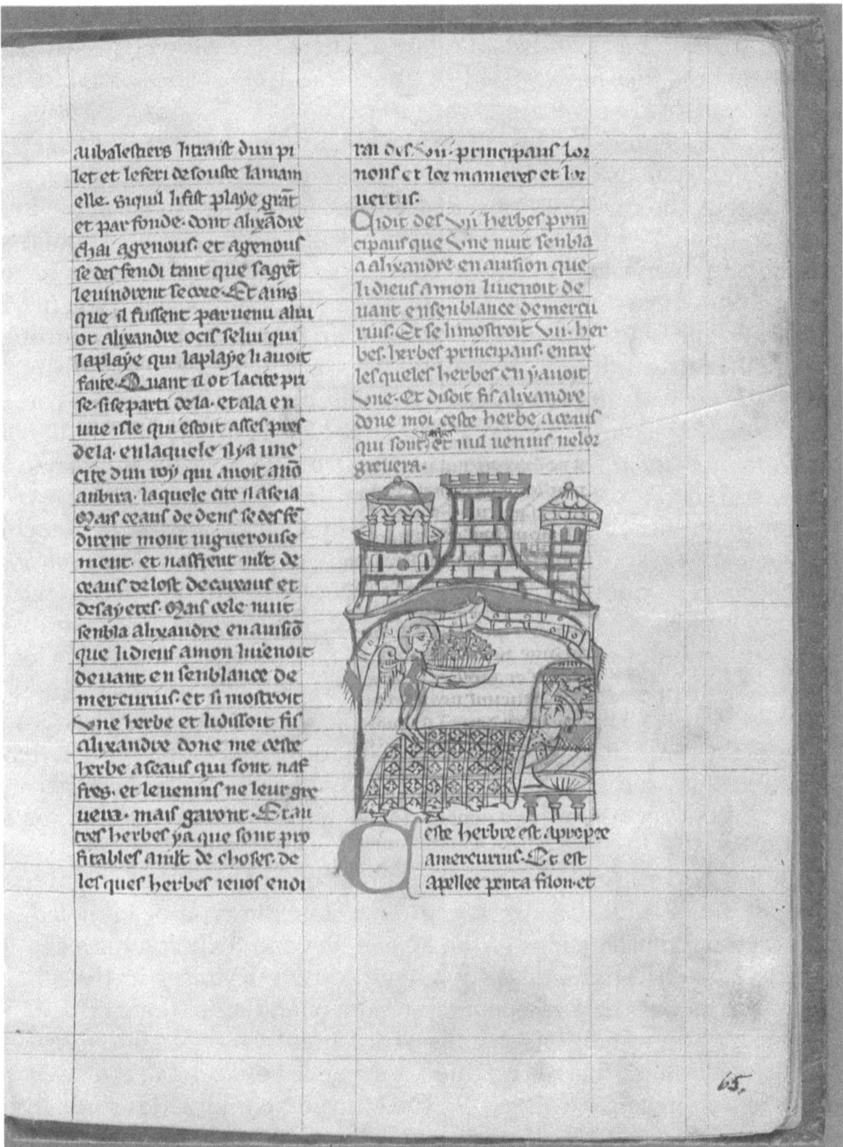

Figure 11.2. The Macedonian king asleep and the god Amon offering him many plants on a platter. *Roman d'Alexandre en prose*, Stockholm, Kungl. biblioteket, ms Vu 20, 65r. © Kungl. biblioteket – National Library of Sweden.

used as a source has a relationship to the Alexander epic, it remains a botanical catalogue. The distant relevance to the storyline in this extract shows that the *Roman* was used as a *pretext* as well as an *opportunity* to convey knowledge of all kinds.

Bernard Ribémont has traced encyclopedic lists of plants and vegetation in literary texts.[27] He states that a list of exotic fruits in *Le Conte du Graal* recalls the medical terms of *Platearius* or of the *Antidotaire Nicolas.* The authors of *Aucassin et Nicolette, Le Roman de Renart,* Thomas's *Tristan* and Marie de France (in her *Lai de Frêne*) also seem to have known, and wished to convey, knowledge of the properties of plants.[28] This can be linked to a desire for summation that spread across Europe during the thirteenth century, named the "century of encyclopedism"[29] by Jacques le Goff. It is in this context that major encyclopedic works such as the *De naturis rerum* of Alexander Neckam (end of twelfth c.), the *De proprietatibus rerum* of the Franciscan Barthelemy the English (ca. 1240), and the *Speculum Majus* of Vincent de Beauvais (ca. 1250) were written. Even closer to our subject are the first encyclopedias in French, a didactic poem written in 1246 by Gossuin de Metz (*Image du monde*), and the aforementioned *Livre du Tresor* (1266). The interconnected relationship between didactic works and literature is further demonstrated by the insertion of excerpts *from* literature *into* encyclopedic texts. Gossuin de Metz refers to a magic spring, *topos* of courtly romances, in his *Image du Monde.*[30] The encyclopedic material serves the literary purpose while at the same time giving it a new authority. Even in a context that promotes this kind of interplay between literature and science, narrative and didactic, our manuscript stands out by virtue of the insertion's length.

The last two additions to the Stockholm manuscript come from the *Livre du Tresor* and also display an encyclopedic type of knowledge unknown in other versions of the *Roman.* Beyond their common provenance, both insertions take advantage of two instances in the story where Alexander seeks to expand his understanding of the world, and the two long enumerations that result are adeptly merged into the narrative even though there is no direct relevance between the two texts.

In the first instance (fols. 68–9), the Macedonian king descends into the depths of the Red Sea by means of a glass barrel to observe the sea life. The experience is briefly described before he returns to the surface, unwilling to further detail the marvellous things he saw for fear that they would not be believed by his men. In Vu 20, however, the original passage is broken off after the description of some whales and their retreat, to allow for the immediate insertion of a passage from chapter CXXX[31] of the *Livre du Tresor*. The selected excerpt begins with another discussion of marine fish and with a discussion of whales, thus making a skillful transition, if a bit repetitive. "Whale" is the key word that facilitates the merger between the two texts, as the word "Mercurius" was in the previous example. This is followed by a series of short, sentence-length extracts from five chapters of the *Livre du Tresor* ("De Cete," "De Coquille," "Dou Delfin," "De Ypotame," "Des Sieraines")[32] that are presented in the same order as they appear in the original text. Further effort was made to include Alexander in this passage by interpolating references to him throughout the text's narrative. References to Pliny or to "the author" in the *Livre du Tresor* are transformed to associate Alexander explicitly with the original text. As in the other insertions, the compiler added references, making Alexander a witness of the sea life: a sentence from the *Livre du Tresor* such as "Poissons sont sans nombre, ja soit ce ke **Plinius en conte**" becomes in the Stockholm manuscript: "Et autres manieres de poisons y a asés que **Alixandre vit**,"[33] and the describer of his own discoveries: "Serene, ce dient **li auctor**" becomes "Des seraines dit **Alixandre** que il en vit .iii.." (fol. 69).[34] At the end of the passage, the compiler has artfully changed the dry transition of Brunetto Latini, "Mais des diversites des poissons ne de lor nature ne dira ore li contes plus ke dit en a, ains dira des autres animaus ki sont en terre" into a topos of the inexpressible stating that the marvels are too numerous to be detailed: "Mais des diversites des poisons que Alixandre vit ne dira ores plus Alixandre. Car trop longue chose feroit a raconter les merveilles et les diversites que Alexandre vit ou fons de la mer" – a rhetorical device that both terminates and extends the description by suggesting many more marvels.[35] The compiler took the opportunity provided by this episode to teach his reader. According to Erich Köhler, this tendency reflects the medieval authors' growing awareness of a mission to teach and transmit knowledge. Knowledge becomes the wisdom that leads to truth.[36]

Placed approximately in the middle of the excerpt, the illumination for this section of the manuscript comprises two images, side by side (Figure 11.3). Only the right-hand illustration corresponds to the text and its rubric: "C'est le devisement et la maniere et la nature des poissons que Alixandre vit en la mer quant il estoit ou parfont de la mer" (fol. 68v). Alexander is shown inside the glass drum, tethered to a boat and surrounded by many fish. The left-hand image represents the king in a tent surrounded by a group of people. In the absence

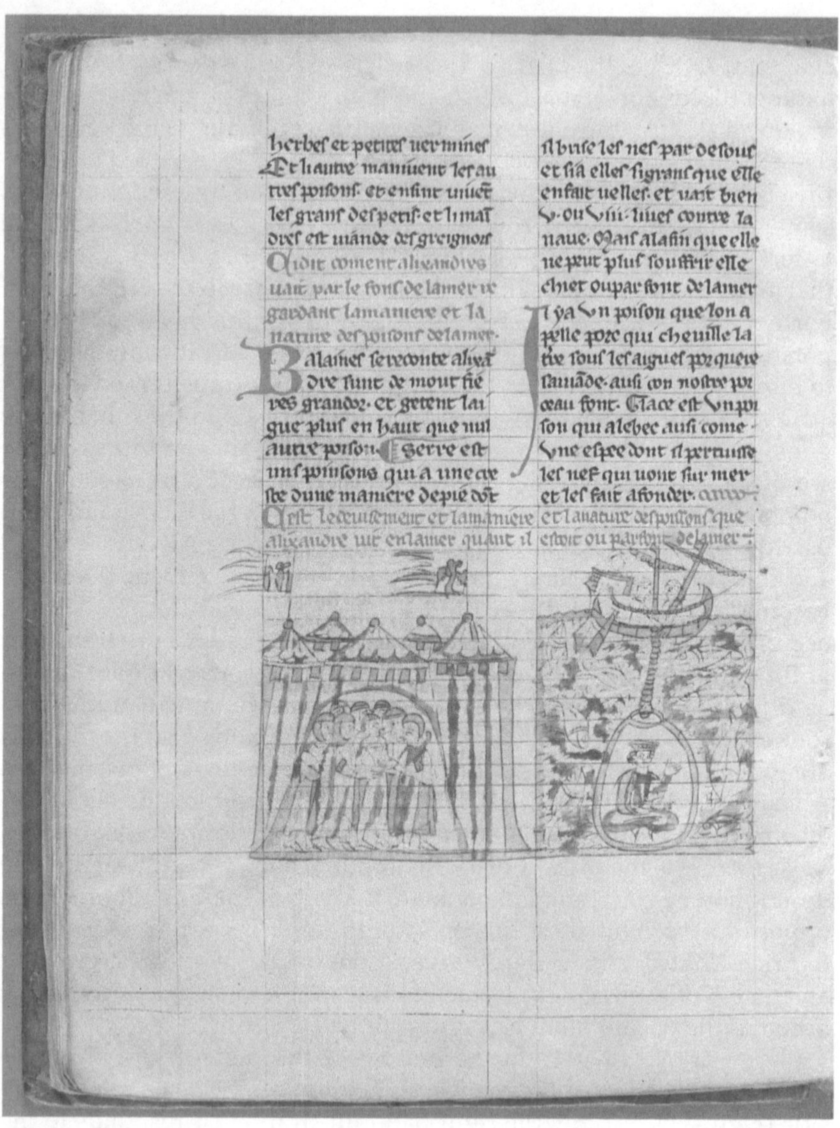

Figure 11.3. Alexander is scolded by his counsellors for having unnecessarily risked death; Alexander explores the Red Sea in a glass barrel. *Roman d'Alexandre en prose*, Stockholm, Kungl. biblioteket, ms Vu 20, 68v. © Kungl. biblioteket – National Library of Sweden.

of any textual clue, this image can be interpreted as representing a passage preceding and following the scene under the ocean, or as a synthesis of both, as they are parallel episodes. They relate how Alexander's counsellors and noblemen surrounded the intrepid ruler after he had returned to solid ground – in the former instance, after Alexander had flown into the heavens by means of a group of griffins, and in the latter after his descent into the ocean's depths. The first time, Alexander is acclaimed by his soldiers for his boldness, the second time he is scolded by his counsellors for having unnecessarily risked death, potentially leaving his entire army helpless in a foreign country. It is most probably this last episode that is illustrated, even if this implies a reverse chronological order in the illustration (assuming the left part of the image should depict an earlier scene than its right part). The left-hand position is probably intended to indicate greater importance and to condition the reader's understanding of the episode. In this important passage, not illustrated elsewhere in the tradition of the *Roman d'Alexandre en prose,* Alexander delivers a highly didactic speech and reproves his counsellors by relating to them all that he learned from his travel in the sea.

> Seignors, li home qui entent a vengier sa honte ou acroistre son los et son pooir se doit souvent abandoner as perils de Fortune ni ne doit mie penser qui soit pareaus com ses henemis qua pareillite n'en gist proesce ne valor a ce je me suis abandonnés en ce perill. Je ai tant gaaigné que je en governerai plus sagement mon ost tos les jors de ma vie. Car je ai esprové que tout soit il grant avantage d'avoir force en soi, nequedent petit vaut fort sans engin car j'ai veu que les petis poisons par engin desconfirent les greignors qui par nulle force n'i peussent avenir. (fol. 69v)

From the observation that small fish are able to fool big fish thanks to their wit, he infers that force is nothing without intelligence and concludes that he will become a better ruler than he ever was. The image therefore conveys the didactic portion of the text. The convergence in this folio of the insertion of a didactic text and of the invention of a new image calls attention to this passage and signals it as particularly significant.

The second extract from the *Livre du Tresor* occurs after the Macedonian king has become ruler of Babylon and thus of the entire world. In the *Roman,* different European peoples come to his court to render homage, present gifts, and to proclaim their allegiance to him, solely because of his accomplishments and not due to force, since the young emperor had never set foot into Europe. Alexander then writes a letter to his mother and another one to his tutor, Aristotle, to tell them about his latest accomplishments and the marvels he has encountered. These letters mirror the ones Alexander wrote after conquering Persia, yet here he is no longer asking for counsel. He has become his own man, and is merely chronicling his conquests. In Vu 20, a passage from the *Livre du Tresor* is inserted at the moment when Alexander's new subjects come to pay their respects, with a sentence of transition. The text of the *Roman d'Alexandre en Prose* reads: "Quant Alixandres conut que tous ceaus del monde li estoient obeïssant comme a signor, si envoia ses lettres a la roïnne Olimpias sa mere et a Aristote son mestre et lor fist asavoir les batailles et les travaus qu'il avoit eües et les manieres de bestes qu'il avoit trovees[...]." In the Stockholm manuscript we have instead: "Quant Alixandre conut que toute la gent dou monde li estoient obeissant come a seignor, **si li vint en volenté et en corage que il voloit savoir l'us et la maniere des terres et regions en lesqueles il non avoit esté,** ne pris a l'espee" (fol. 72).[37]

Once he has conquered the world, the new emperor becomes curious about the lands he has not yet visited and asks their people to tell him of them. A long insertion from the encyclopedia is then added almost word for word, describing Europe in its entirety (fols. 72–4), beginning with Italy – coincidentally, the first European country mentioned in the *Roman* text. Though no modification is made to insert Alexander into the narrative, some noteworthy changes do take place: the manuscript omits what can be best described as anecdotal passages (i.e., the locations of Hercules's columns and of St James's coffin) from the otherwise geographical enumeration of European peoples and territories. Furthermore, our chronicle systematically substitutes the word "city" for "diocese" and "archdiocese," thus neutralizing an anachronistic political referent to Alexander's time. Finally, the insertion is neatly interwoven into the traditional text by means of a slight modification that – as with the previous addition from the *Livre du Tresor* – better contextualizes and justifies the amended section: the letters Alexander writes to Queen Olympia and Aristotle are, in this case, not only to tell them about his adventures but also specifically about the new European peoples and lands under his rule. The image accompanying this insertion (Figure 11.4) is the one from our group of four that most faithfully follows the traditional iconographic cycle.

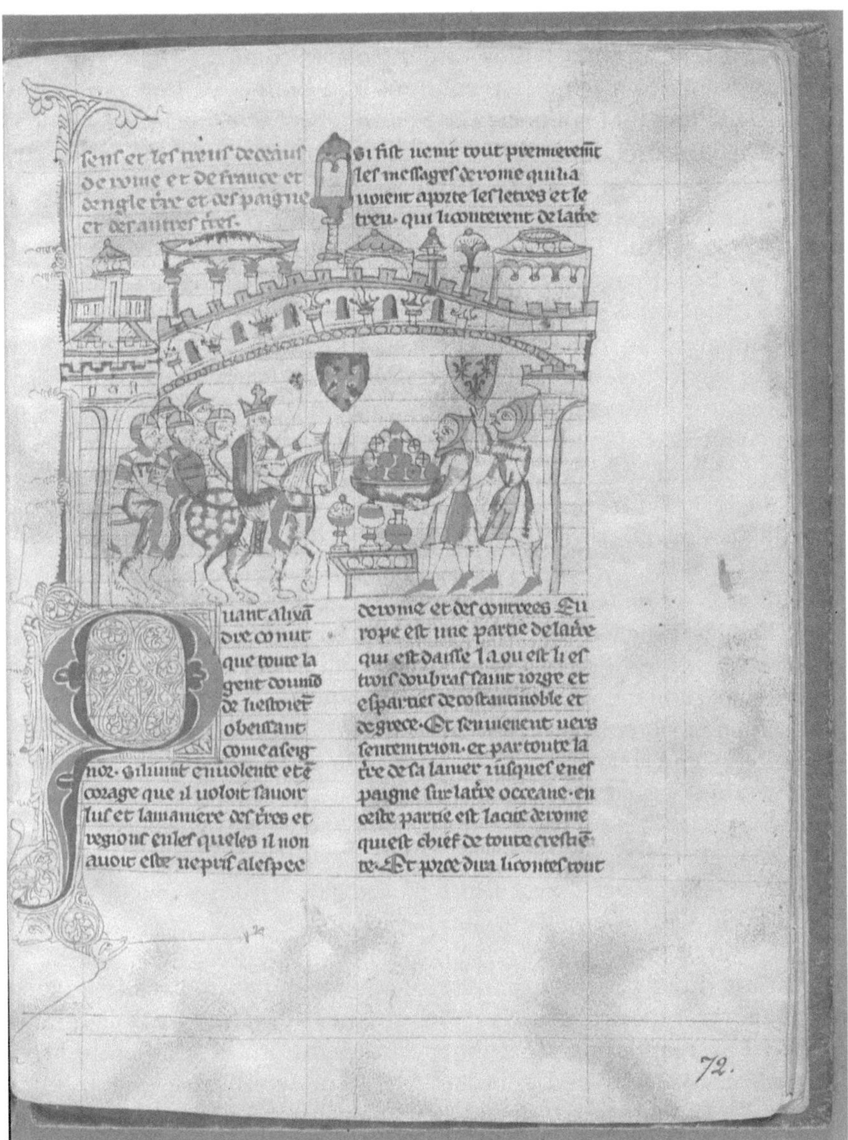

Figure 11.4. Alexander and his army entering his new palace, and two men, representing some nations among many, coming to meet him, carrying presents. *Roman d'Alexandre en prose*, Stockholm, Kungl. biblioteket, ms Vu 20, 72r. © Kungl. biblioteket – National Library of Sweden.

It depicts Alexander and his army entering his new palace and two men, representing some nations among many, coming to meet him, carrying presents. Spanning two columns and literally sitting astride the transitional text that connects the *Roman* with the encyclopedia, it has been placed immediately after the corresponding rubric and shortly before the narrative insertion from the *Livre du Tresor*. This image is a traditional representation of this episode and can be found in other manuscripts of the *Roman d'Alexandre en prose*.[38] The compiler felt no need for a new image; on the contrary, this conventional one helped to integrate the new content into the narration.

I would also like to mention a last insertion, a very long rubric, which seems to be an invention of the compiler rather than an extract from a foreign text. The compiler makes very skillful use of the rubrics to organize his text, as we have seen. It is thanks to the rubrics that he is able to perform the "fonction de régie" described by Genette, organizing the text as if he were a narrator. This long rubric is inserted in the middle of Alexander's long monologue during his death agony.

> Ci dit de la roe de Fortune coment les uns montent et les autres descendent. Les uns sostient et les autres tresbuche. Tes est huy riches que demain sera povres et tels est huy vif que demain sera mors. Et ce poés vos veoir apertement dou roi Alixandre et des autres plussors rois et seignors. Alixandre qui monta si haut qu'il fu seignor et rois sur tos les autres Rois. Et fu coronés en Babiloine a estre empereres de tout le monde. Et quant de tout Fortune l'avoit fait seignor, elle, par lui que elle avoit henoré, vost demostrer a tous ceaus que apres lui vendront example que nul ne se doit fier en la gloire terriene. Alixandre, qui fu sus haut ou soumeron de la roe de Fortune, or est desoz tresbuchies, tout en siut est il de cest monde come vos le véés. (78r)

The rubric describes the exemplarity of Alexander, and his fall, using the allegory of the wheel of Fortune. It takes up half of the folio and is followed by a large miniature that occupies the other half (Figure 11.5).

Two topics are treated simultaneously: one vertical – the wheel of Fortune[39] – and one horizontal – Alexander dictating his will to a scribe. The fact that Alexander is represented in majesty, sitting on his throne, holding his sceptre and pointing his finger at the scribe, shows him as a figure of authority when, according to the narration, he ought to be lying in his bed.[40] The image thus induces the reader to assimilate the dictating Alexander and the enthroned king about to fall from the

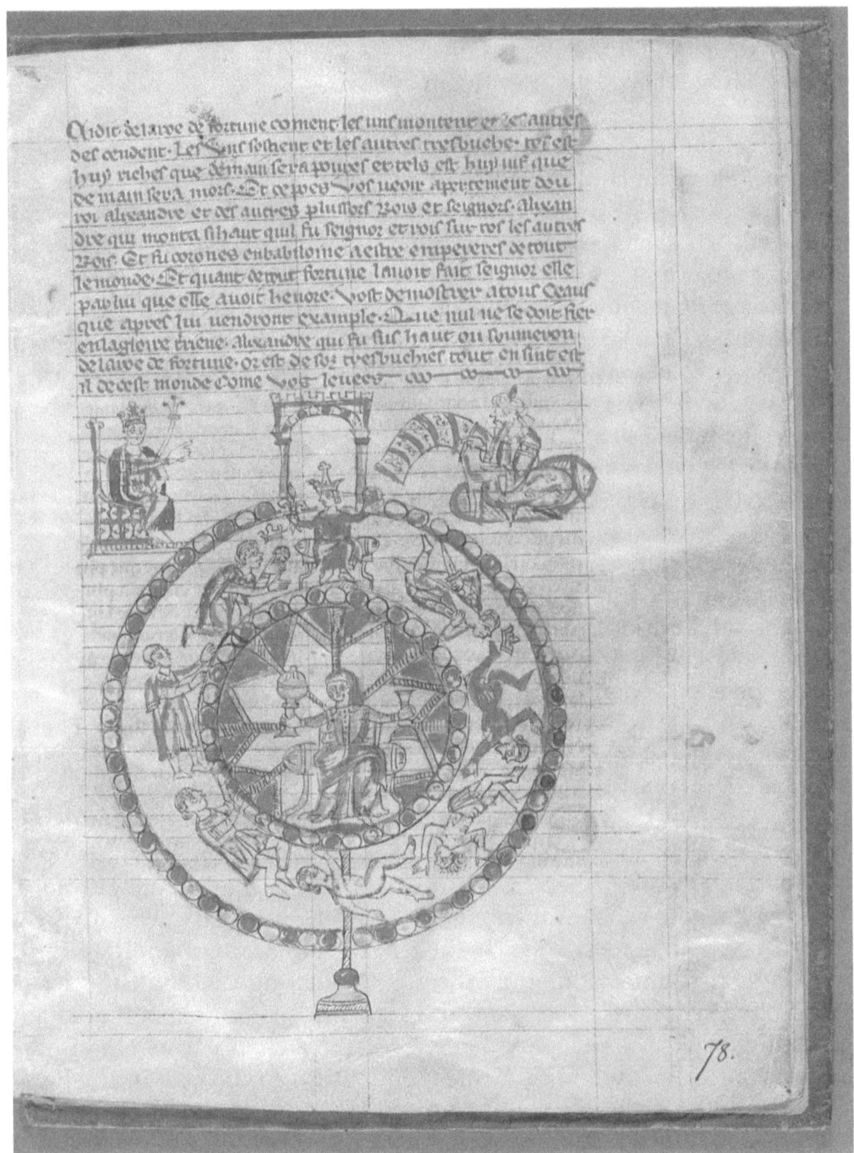

Figure 11.5. Alexander dictating his will to a scribe; the Wheel of Fortune. *Roman d'Alexandre en prose*, Stockholm, Kungl. biblioteket, ms Vu 20, 78r. © Kungl. biblioteket – National Library of Sweden.

top of the turning wheel of Fortune.[41] This insertion is justified by the fact that Alexander mentions Fortune on his deathbed, in the passages immediately before and after the image.

> **Fortune, que jusques a celui bon jour m'avoit assis au souverain siege de sa roe**, plus haut et plus noblement que elle n'eust onques mais a home fait jusques a celui jour, et quant de tout m'avoit fait seignor, et elle par moi que elle avoit henoré vost demostrer par moi a tous ceaus qui apres moi venront essample que nul ne doit fier en la gloire terriene. **Car de tant come hom cuide plus estre au desus en est hom au desous.** Le jour meismement que je me fis coronés de tout le monde et cuidoie estre venus a la fin de mon travail et au comencement de repos, par ceaus meismes que je avoye noris et alevés tant chierement come mes enfants **fui empoissonés de tel poisson** dont je sui certains qu'il me covendra morir, car je ne truis ne pitié ne merci en la mort. Et ce n'est pas chose en quoi il ait mestier, force, ne poeir. (fol. 77v and p. 252)

Alexander explains that he has reached the summit of his glory and that he is now doomed to fall. The image makes this very explicit as we see the king fall and lose his attributes until he is completely naked at the bottom of the wheel. The rubric invites us to *look* carefully at this image ("Et ce poés vos veoir apertement dou roi Alixandre," "vost demostrer a tous ceaus que apres lui vendront example," "tout en siut est il de cest monde come vos le véés") and to *interpret* it. This allegory of Fortune is unusual: the personification, represented in the middle of the wheel, holds a chalice and a flask, offering humanity a sweet and bitter drink, honey and gall. This representation appears very rarely,[42] and never in association with the wheel. This unusual merger of two iconographical types of Fortune calls for interpretation, all the more so as this image is hyperbolic both in its size and in the length of the accompanying rubric.

A look at the previous miniature, representing the last banquet of Alexander, helps us understand the visual device to which it belongs. The king drinks the poisoned beverage from a chalice given to him by his servant (fol. 76v).[43] The chalice is identical to the one in the hand of Fortune, as if she were the true sender of the poison.[44] Therefore, the image gives a moral significance to the death of Alexander, urging the reader to think about the precariousness of wealth, about the vanity of earthly possessions, and of prestigious positions. The rhetoric of the frailty of terrestrial power, Christian in substance, but enriched with some ideas and topoi from pagan Antiquity, is common in the late centuries of the Middle Ages.[45] One can find the wheel of Fortune in some manuscripts of the *Livre du Tresor* (inserted, for example, in a decorated initial in ms BnF fr. 566).[46] The link between Alexander and Fortuna has a long history, beginning with Plutarch[47] and continuing through to Christine de Pizan, who, in her *Livre de Mutacion de Fortune* (1400–2), dedicated to the dukes of Burgundy and Berry, devoted the seventh and last book to Alexander the Great. His exemplary life and his death, caused by Fortune, are given a political and moral meaning.[48] This image and its rubric belong therefore to the didactic thread of this manuscript.

## Conclusion

The four inserted passages in manuscript Vu 20 all come from encyclopedic books. They were chosen for their didactic and moralizing content as well as for the language they were written in (French) and for their obvious link with Alexander the Great. The compiler has completed these accretions with a smaller passage of his own, patently didactic in tone, on the role of Fortune, also linked to didactic material. This revision introduced to the *Roman* what the text itself seemed to require: a continuation and an expansion of the story. This study has shown that the insertion of these texts was often made smoother by a keyword ("Mercurius," "baleine," "Italie," "Fortune"). The compiler added to the accretions a series of rubrics that helped the didactic texts become narrative. Lastly, a series of small textual modifications in the *Roman* and in the additions (additions, repetitions, omissions) helped to complete the suture.

The strategy of illustration is not as uniform and straightforward. The compiler has used images that belong to the long-standing iconographic cycle of the *Roman d'Alexandre en prose* manuscripts, some of them in altered form, but has also inserted new images otherwise foreign to this tradition. The miniatures can appear at the beginning of the insertion or in the middle. This absence of uniformity in the strategy of insertion helps to merge the different texts since there is no one way of distinguishing the insertions visually. Furthermore, we have seen how some images serve the didactic content of the texts, either by their placement (the image illustrating the *Secret des secrets* is placed in the midst of the insertion, indicating thereby the beginning of the *didactic* part), or by their content (the image illustrating Alexander among his warriors stresses the moral significance of his underwater travel in the

Red Sea, the syncretic image of Fortune links the fall of Alexander to the transience of power). The intent appears to have been for the illustrations to serve less as markers of the textual cleavage than to ensure the integration of the encyclopedic passage into the *Roman* narrative. We can infer that both text and image were likewise conceived as interlocking components of the same narrative mechanism.

Can these elements help us draw a conclusion concerning the provenance of this manuscript and the context of its creation? It certainly is the outcome of a century marked by its taste for encyclopedic knowledge and "encyclopedically" shaped books. Bernard Ribémont credits the thirteenth century's interest in encylopedism to three main causes: the rapid development of urban life and culture, alongside the influence of main centres such as Chartres or the princely courts at which the clerics played a major role; that the authors of encyclopedic works, having been raised during the Renaissance of the twelfth century, attached great importance to nature in their conception of God's Creation; and the discovery, beginning around the start of the twelfth century, of Arabic texts and the reception of the whole *corpus aristotelicum* up to 1270, which made it necessary to spread new doctrines, in highly simplified forms, to a larger public.[49] It is to this last cause that we can link our manuscript, as demonstrated by the sources of the various accretions discussed above. The discovery of the fourth insertion's source makes it tempting to link this manuscript to the court of Alfonso X El Sabio, king of Castile and Leon, famous for its literary and scientific activity. This does not necessarily contradict Fabio Zinelli's hypothesis that the manuscript was made in Cyprus. The fact that it was written by a scribe whose language has Catalan features allows us to think that the compiler might perhaps have come from Spain. There, he may have discovered the kind of literature that inspired the idea of an enriched version of the *Roman d'Alexandre en prose*, ultimately having it illuminated in Cyprus where he lived. In the same way, the *Livre du Tresor*, composed in Europe, travelled to the Orient and came back in an enriched version.[50] The book of Sidrach (1268–91), another encyclopedic book, similarly seems to have been written in the Latin Orient by a "Franc" from the Occident, though the prologue mentions a link to Toledo.[51]

Furthermore, the fact that the *Secret des secrets*, the *Livre du Tresor*, and the *De septem herbis* are all linked to *Miroir de Prince* literature leads us to believe that the manuscript might have been compiled for a person of power, or one intended to play a political role. The overall absence of images of the "Marvels of the East" in the Stockholm manuscript, usually numerous in the *Roman d'Alexandre en prose* manuscript tradition (they represent more than 30 per cent of the iconographic corpus)[52] and the absence of interpolation linked to these marvels, when it would have been very easy to include them, seems to confirm this hypothesis of a compilation oriented towards mechanisms of power – from their principles to the risk of a fall.[53]

What does this tell us about the *Roman d'Alexandre en prose*? Unlike the *Roman d'Alexandre en vers*, the prose version is very faithful to its Latin model. There is no narrator to orient our reception of the text. It is my contention that this absence of oriented meaning given to the *Roman* from the beginning is what led to such highly divergent interpretations, ways of reading, from a book of marvels to a *Miroir de Prince*, a Book of Crusade, a courtly tale, a collection of moralistic *exempla*, to a treatise on good and bad governance.[54] From one manuscript to the other, the nature and even the topic of the text changed.[55] The insertion of texts helped to provide a particular meaning and serve a peculiar purpose.

The recounting of the conquest of the world by an inquisitive and overachieving hero such as Alexander the Great provided medieval scholars with an excellent opportunity for encapsulating the vastness of human experience and knowledge, all the more so since the chronicle contained so many narrative ellipses. The *Roman* offers a narrative plot susceptible to textual grafting and, subsequently, to the reorientation of the text's meaning. By borrowing from encyclopedic works and by integrating them into the narrative, Vu 20 seems to respond to the horizon of expectations created by the story of the *Roman d'Alexandre en prose*, while at the same time exploiting the vast potential within the text for channelling the knowledge of its epoch. Furthermore, though the manipulation of the accompanying images seems at first to highlight the textual insertions, in fact they blur the extraneous nature of the amended texts. The complementary illustrations are more than a tool for understanding the message contained in the insertions; they serve primarily to focus the knowledge contained within them. As it happens, the images furnish the necessary context for a smooth fusion of genres and narratives. Ultimately, in the Stockholm manuscript, the interaction between text and image converts the Alexander saga into an inventory of medieval scientific understanding, analogous to the very encyclopedias it has assimilated. As described by the author of the *Livre du Tresor* himself, this manuscript is the harvest of honey made from many flowers:

> Et si ne di je pas que le livre soit estrais de mon povre sens ne de ma nue science; mais il ert ausi comme une bresche de miel coillie de diverses flours, car cist livres est compilés seulement des mervilleus dis des autours ki devant nostre tans ont traité de philosophie, cascuns selonc çou k'il savoit partie.[56]

NOTES

1 I would like to thank Luis Pérez-Simon and Oleg Voskoboinikov for their advice and help to write this article.

2 Maud Pérez-Simon, *Mise en roman et mise en image. Les manuscrits du* Roman d'Alexandre *en prose* (Paris: Champion, 2015).

3 David J.A. Ross, *Alexander historiatus. A Guide to Medieval Illustrated Alexander Literature*, Warburg Institute Surveys 1 (London: Warburg Institute, University of London, 1963 [reprint Athenäums Monografien Altertumswissenschaft 186, Frankfurt am Main: Athenäum, 1988]); Ross, *Illustrated Medieval Alexander Books in Germany and the Netherlands, a Study in Comparative Iconography*, Publications of the Modern Humanities Research Association 3 (Cambridge: The Modern Humanities Research Association, 1971); Ross, "Olympia and the Serpent," *Journal of the Warburg and Courtauld Institutes* 26 (London: Warburg Institute, University of London, 1963), 1–21; Ross, *Alexander and the Faithless Lady: A Submarine Adventure* (London: Birkbeck College, 1967).

4 For a stimulating essay on textual "mouvance," see Bernard Cerquiglini, *Éloge de la variante, Histoire critique de la philologie* (Paris: Seuil, Des Travaux, 1989) and Paul Zumthor, *Essai de poétique médiévale* (Paris: Seuil, 1972). For interesting examples of interpretation of iconographical "mouvance," see Anne D. Hedeman, *Translating the Past, Laurent de Premierfait and Boccacio's* De Casibus (Los Angeles: The J. Paul Getty Museum, 2008) or Chrystèle Blondeau, "Du plaisir des sens à la passion du sens: l'illustration d'un cycle du *Lancelot Graal* et ses remaniements," L'*artiste et le commanditaire*, ed. Fabienne Joubert (Paris: PUPS, Cultures et civilisations médiévales, 2001), 99–114.

5 For a complete study of the manuscripts of the *Roman d'Alexandre en prose* tradition, see Pérez-Simon, *Mise en roman et mise en image* (see note 2), chap. VI. See also Pérez-Simon, "Mise en scène du corps et discours politique dans un manuscrit du *Roman d'Alexandre en prose* du XVe siècle," in *Conter de Troie et d'Alexandre*, ed. Laurence Harf-Lancner et al. (Paris: Sorbonne Nouvelle, 2006), 271–89; Pérez-Simon, "Prose et profondeur temporelle: du Merveilleux à l'Histoire dans le Roman d'Alexandre en prose," in *Dire et penser le temps au Moyen-Âge, Frontières de l'histoire et du roman*, ed. Emmanuèle Baumgartner and Laurence Harf-Lancner (Paris: Presses de la Sorbonne Nouvelle, 2005), 171–91.

6 *Olim* Fr. 51.

7 David Ross suggested that the manuscript was written in Spain (*Alexander historiatus* [see note 3], 55), but Fabio Zinelli reappraised this identification. Fabio Zinelli, "L'atelier des chansonniers *IK* et la tradition du *Trésor*," *Medioevo Romanzo* 31 (2007), 7–69, particularly 65–8.

8 On the *translatio*, in Cyprus, of the Saint-Jean d'Acre workshop, see Jaroslav Folda and Peter W. Edbury, "Two Thirteenth-Century Manuscripts of Crusader Legal Texts from Saint-Jean d'Acre," *Journal of the Warbourg and Courtauld Institutes* 57 (1994), 243–54, and the bibliography in Zinelli, "L'atelier des chansonniers" (see note 7), 50n179. For a very convincing study of the Outremer features in this manuscript, see Maria Jouet, *Le Roman d'Alexandre en prose: le manuscrit Vu 20, Kungliga biblioteket*, Stockholm: édition et étude linguistique (Stockholm: Stockholm University, 2013). She provides a very good study of the Catalan features in the text.

9 For a transcription of these insertions, see Werner Soderhjelm, "Notice et extrait du manuscrit français du manuscrit 51 de la Bibliothèque Royale de Stockholm," *Mémoires de la Société néophilologique de Helsingfors* 6 (1917), 305–33 (first and second insertion) and *Der Altfranzösische Prosa-Alexander Roman*, ed. Alfons Hilka (Halle: M. Niemeyer, 1920), XLV–L (third and fourth insertion). See also Jouet (see note 8).

10 I warmly thank here Isabelle Draelents, Iolanda Ventura and Oleg Voskoboinikov for their contribution in this discovery and for the information they generously gave me on this text and its tradition.

11 It was written under the name *Kitâb Sirr al-'Asrâr*, circa 950–75. See Jacques Monfrin, "La place du secret des Secrets dans la littérature française médiévale," *Pseudo-Aristotle, The Secret of Secrets – Sources and Influences*, ed. W.F. Ryan and Charles B. Schmitt, Warburg Institute Surveys 9 (London: Warburg Institute, University of London, 1982), 73–113.

12 A transcription of a manuscript of *Le secret des secrets* (manuscript Baltimore, Walters Arts Gallery W 308) can be read on line, ed. Denis Lorée, http://www.sites.univ-rennes2.fr/celam/cetm/S2.htm (last accessed 3 March 2012), see end of prologue and first chapters.

13 Yela Schauwecker, "Dimensionen der Wissenvermittlung im *Secré des segrez* von Jofroi de Waterford," in *Transfert des savoirs au Moyen Âge. Wissenstransfer im Mittelalter. Actes de l'Atelier franco-allemand, Heidelberg, 15–18 janvier 2008*, ed. Stephen Dörr and Raymund Wilhelm (Heidelberg: Winter, 2008), 129–38; Steven J. Williams, *The Secret of Secrets: The Scholarly Career of a Pseudo-Aristotelian Text in the Latin Middle Ages* (Ann Arbor: University of Michigan Press, 2003).

14 The *Secretum Secretorum* was translated into Old French more than once. The Stockholm manuscript of the *Roman d'Alexandre en prose* most likely cites a later version (mid-fourteenth century) that both keeps the passage on magic and reinforces the connection of the *Secretum secretorum* with the Alexander legend. This translation remains unpublished. See Jacques Monfrin, "La place du *Secret des Secrets* dans la littérature française médiévale" (see note 11), 84 and 97.

15 Steven J. William, "The Pseudo-Aristotelian *Secret of Secrets* as a Didactic Text," in *What Nature Does Not Teach*, ed. J. Feros Ruys (Turnhout, Brepols, 2008), 41–57.

16 Brunetto Latini, *Li Livres dou Tresor*, ed. Francis J. Carmody (Berkeley: University of California Press, 1948). See also the very good new edition: *Brunetto Latini: Tresor*, ed. Pietro G. Beltrami (Turin: Einaudi, 2007).

17 Oleg Voskoboinikov, *Le texte et les images dans* Li livres dou Tresor *de* Brunet Latin, Mémoire de DEA rédigé sous la direction de Jean-Claude Schmitt, EHESS (Paris, 2000), 43 and 59, unpublished.

18 Paschalis Romanus is also the translator of the *Kyranides*. *Le* liber aggregationis, *un texte à succès attribué à Albert le Grand*, ed. Isabelle Draelants (Firenze: SISMEL, 2007), 61.

19 It is not rare for Alexander to be associated with didactic material. The *Compendium Aureum* links Alexander to Peonia ("*Alexander autem Magnus hac potione usus multa vidit* ***in somniis*** *oracula de iis quae sibi acciderunt et dicitur quod regina Amazonum dederit sibi pro munere pretioso*"; ibid., 61). See also André-Jean Festugière, *L'astrologie et les sciences occultes* (Paris: Belles Lettres, 1981), 137, and Friedrich Pfister, *Pflanzenaberglaube*, Pauly-Wissowa Real-Encyclopädie der classischen Altertumswissenschaft XIX, 1450–1.

20 Draelents (see note 18), chap. 1.

21 Antonella Sannino is preparing an edition of the Latin and Greek texts of the *De Septem Herbis*. She was not aware of the existence of this French version. She has expressed willingness to research it, and it is my hope that it shall help us to understand more of this fascinating tradition.

22 The first is on fol. 37 and the other three are grouped between fols. 72 and 75.

23 Fol. 65, God Amon was coming to him in the shape of Mercurius and he was showing him a plant and he was saying to him: "Son Alexander, give this plant to those who are harmed and poison will not harm them, they will heal. *There are other plants that are useful for many things and I will tell you the name, the use and the properties of seven of them*"; all translations are the author's. I have italicized the addition.

24 The author gives more than one name for each plant. The link to a planet is not mentioned for the second one, most probably because of the inverted order: 1. Pentafilon/ Décline/ Calipontalion (Mercurius), 2. Effodillus (Saturn), 3. Pologonie/ Herbe du solaill/ Cameleonte (Sun), 4. Cinabatos (Moon), 5. Arnoglofa (Mars), 6. Acarome/ Jusquiamus (Jupiter), 7. Pestereon/ Herbe Colonbine/ Cheroboran (Venus).

25 André-Jean Festugière (see note 19), 146. He calls this type the "Saturn-Moon" type. It is the variant specifically associated with Alexander. Mercurius should be the third planet/plant in the list.

26 The god Amon, who appears to Alexander under the guise of Mercurius, as the text states, is here represented as an angel with a halo.

27 Bernard Ribémont, "Littérature, plantes et encyclopédies," in his *Littérature et encyclopédies du Moyen Âge* (Orléans: Paradigme, 2002), 177–86, here 177–8.

28 Ibid.

29 Jacques Le Goff, "Pourquoi le XIIe siècle a-t-il été plus particulièrement un siècle d'encyclopédisme?" *L'enciclopedismo*, ed. Michelangelo Picone (Ravenna, 1991), 23–40.

30 Bernard Ribémont, "Une 'botanique' encyclopédique confrontée à la merveille: l'exemple du *De proprietatibus rerum*," in his *De Natura rerum, Etudes sur les encyclopédies médiévales* (Orléans: Paradigme, 1995) 187–210, here 187.

31 Chap. CXXX's heading is: "Chi dist de la nature des animaus et premierement des poissons" (Here is told about the nature of animals and primarily of fish). *Tresor* (see note 16), 230.

32 Ibid., chaps. CXXXII–CXXXVI, 236–42.

33 For example "Fish are countless according to what **Pliny** recounts" (ibid., 230) becomes "There are many other types of fish as **Alexander** witnessed" (fol. 68b).

34 For example "Mermaid, **according to the author** ..." (ibid., 240) becomes "Of Mermaids, **Alexander says** ..." (fol. 69).

35 "But about the diversity of fish and about their nature the story will say no more than it already has, it will now explain about the animals that live on land ..." (ibid., 242) is replaced by "But about the diversity of fish that Alexander saw, Alexander will say no more. It would indeed be too long to tell of the marvels and diverse things that Alexander saw at the bottom of the sea" (fol. 69v).

36 Erich Köhler, *L'Aventure chevaleresque* (Paris: Gallimard, 1974), 59–60.

37 "When Alexander realised that all the peoples of the world recognized him as their sovereign, he sent letters to Queen Olimpias his mother and

to Aristotle his teacher to let them know the battles and the suffering he had undergone and the different types of animals he had encountered." *Der Altfranzösische Prosa-Alexander Roman* (see note 9), 242. In the Stockholm manuscript we have instead: "When Alexandre realised that all the peoples of the world recognized him as their sovereign, he decided in his mind and heart that he wanted to know about how were the lands and regions he had not visited and not conquered by the sword" (fol. 72).

38 See, for comparison, ms London, BL Royal 19 D. i, fol. 40r; Berlin, Kupferstichkabinett 78 C 1, fol. 71v; Bruxelles, Bibliothèque royale 11040, fol. 76r; London, BL Harley 4979, fol 75r. The same images can be seen, with a slightly different setting in Chantilly, Musée Condé 651, fol. 60r; London, BL Royal 20Av, fol. 76v.

39 The assocation between the Goddess Fortune and the wheel dates back to Boetius. Howard R. Patch, *The Goddess Fortuna in Medieval Literature* (Cambridge, MA: Harvard University Press, 1927), 119, 152, 159. On the iconography of Goddess Fortune, see also Jean Wirth, *L'image à l'époque gothique* (Paris: Cerf, 2008), 329–39.

40 For comparison, in the *Tristan in prose* manuscripts, Tristan is seen in his deathbed, dictating his will to his men, saying farewell to them and forgiving Mark. Ms BNF fr. 760, fol. 123.

41 On his throne, the king at the top is about to fall. In the *Roman d'Alexandre en prose*, the growing interest in Fortune is clear. The translator added four allusions to Fortune that did not exist in Latin (Pérez-Simon, *Mise en roman et mise en image* [see note 2], chap. VI). The compiler of the Stockholm manuscript responded to this insistent presence.

42 For other allusions on this rare iconographical type, see Alanus de Insulis and Henricus Septimellensis (*Trattato*, 1730, 4: 'Mellea felle'), Howard R. Patch, *The Goddess Fortuna* (see note 39), 52 n. 4. See also Emile Mâle, *L'Art religieux du XIIIe siècle en France* (Paris: Le Livre de Poche, 1958), Vol. I, 183–8. In a *Roman de la Rose* manuscript, it is associated with the *topos* of the blindness of Fortune (BnF fr. 380, fol. 46v).

43 For a study of the iconographical relationship between these two images, see Pérez-Simon, *Mise en roman et mise en image* (see note 2), chap. IV, 2c.

44 On the collaboration of Fortune and Death, see Alexandre de Paris, *Le Roman d'Alexandre*, trans. Laurence Harf-Lancner (Paris: Livre de Poche, Lettres gothiques, 1994), v. 7359, 7787–8 and 7817, and Patch, *The Goddess Fortuna* (see note 39), 119. The type "Fortune holding honey and gall" is not usually associated with Death.

45 See *La Fortune: thèmes, représentations, discours*, ed. Yasmina Foehr-Janssens and Emmanuelle Métry (Genève: Droz, 2003).

46 Voskoboinikov, "Le texte" (see note 17), 45.
47 Plutarque, *La Vie d'Alexandre*, trans. Robert Flacelière and Emile Chambry (Paris: Autrement, 1993).
48 Christine de Pisan, *Le Livre de la Mutacion de Fortune*, ed. Suzanne Solente (Paris: A. & J. Picard, Vol. I (v. 1–4272), 1959 and Vol. IV (v. 21249–3636), 1961). See also Catherine Gaullier-Bougassas, "Histoires universelles et variations sur deux figures du pouvoir: Alexandre et César dans l'*Histoire ancienne jusqu'à César, Renart le Contrefait* et le *Livre de Mutacion de Fortune* de Christine de Pisan," *CRM* 14 (2007), 7–28.
49 Bernard Ribémont, *De Natura rerum* (see note 30), 78. The role of the Dominicans in this whole process has to be acknowledged. They collected ideas by traveling and copying excerpts, which Vincent de Beauvais was able to bring together, merge and organize in his *Speculum majus* (ca. 1250). Marie-Christine Duchenne and Monique Paulmier-Foucart, "Vincent de Beauvais à l'Atelier," *Vulgariser la science: les encyclopédies médiévales, CRM* 6 (1999), 50–74.
50 Fabio Zinelli (see note 7), 65–8.
51 Charles-Victor Langlois, *La vie en France au Moyen Âge de la fin du XIIe au milieu du XIVe siècle, d'après les moralistes du temps: La connaissance de la nature et du monde d'après les écrits français à l'usage des laïcs* (Paris, 1927) Vol. 3, 198–275, and Auguste Thomas, "L'ancien français 'pichar' et l'étimologie du français 'cloporte.' Réponse à une question," *Romania* 56 (1930), 161–77.
52 Pérez-Simon, *Mise en roman, mise en image* (see note 2), chap. IV.
53 Oleg Voskoboinikov has demonstrated that the French and Italian manuscripts of the *Livre du Tresor* were not illustrated similarly. French ones were much more highly illustrated than the Italian ones due to a difference of culture and of use. Voskoboinikov, "Le texte" (see note 17), 69, 70, and 73. We need more studies of this kind to understand the reception of encyclopedic material in medieval times.
54 Pérez-Simon, *Mise en roman, mise en image* (see note 2), chap. VI.
55 "C'est, je dirai, le charme profond de l'écriture encyclopédique ; cette éternelle recopie, ce palimpseste absolu qui, au détour de chaque ouvrage, introduit les infimes variations qui, partant de la nature des choses, donne au lecteur la nature d'un texte." Bernard Ribémont, "*Naturae descriptio*: expliquer la nature dans les encyclopédies du Moyen Âge (XIIIe siècle)," in his *De Natura Rerum* (see note 30), 129–49, here 144.
56 *Tresor* (see note 16), 6.

# The Visual Image of Alexander the Great: Transformations from the Middle Ages to the Early Modern Period

THOMAS NOLL

Johannes Aventinus (1477–1534), the Bavarian court historian, bears eloquent witness to the popularity of Alexander the Great on the threshold between the late Middle Ages and the early modern period. In his *Bavarian Chronicle*, completed in 1533, Aventinus writes that Alexander "is more familiar to our population, even the uneducated, than their king and emperor, whose names and descent are unknown to them."[1] As a consequence, he too believed it necessary to polish Alexander up a bit: in his own words, "[ihn] ein wenig herfür [zu] puzen,"[2] in his history. At the beginning of the chronicle, Aventinus reveals his most authoritative sources. Alexander's life and deeds had been well described according to contemporary requirements by Arrian (in the first half of the second century), whose work Emperor Sigismund (who had governed the Holy Roman Empire since 1410 as the Roman king and was crowned emperor in 1433) had ordered translated into Latin by Pier Paolo Vergerio.[3] In Latin there were the ten books of Quintus Curtius,[4] which Erasmus of Rotterdam had published nine years earlier (1518) in Strasbourg.[5] Finally, Aventinus refers to the German *Histori von dem grossen Alexander*, which had been commissioned by the predecessors of the reigning sovereigns, Duke Albrecht III and Duchess Anna of Brunswick, and composed by their personal physician, Johannes Hartlieb, shortly after 1450.[6] Aventinus cautioned that this work was not a good translation, since the doctor had not mastered enough Latin for the task and had inserted a great deal of amusing material that was really only old wives' tales.[7]

Aventinus represents himself here as critical of the sources and basing his own historical narration on reliable authors. Arrian and Quintus Curtius, indeed the authors of two of the most important and most extensive surviving biographies of Alexander, are drawn into the foreground. In contrast, Hartlieb's work, which was not based on historical reports but rather on derivations of the influential third-century *Alexander Romance* of Pseudo-Callisthenes, is firmly dismissed not only from a philological but also from an historical viewpoint. Evidently, a pronounced historical awareness was present at this moment that was capable of and interested in differentiating between actual fact and poetic fiction. Thus it should not surprise us that pictorial representations of the Macedonian king from the period are also indebted to this historical awareness.

Albrecht Altdorfer's *Battle of Alexander at Issus* of 1529 originated as one of (at least) eight pictures by different artists in the framework of a cycle with the deeds of famous commanders and heroes commissioned by Duke Wilhelm IV and his wife Jacobaea for an (as yet not securely identified) room in the Munich Residence (Figure 12.1).[8]

This depiction of the king of the Macedonians, second in fame only to the ancient Alexander mosaic from the Casa del Fauno in Pompeii (of around 100 BC), is on the same level with the descriptions of the Bavarian court historian; in addition, Aventinus was probably the author of the first German epitaph elaborating on the image's contents, written on the originally larger slab on the upper margin of the (originally larger) painting.[9] According to the geographic and historical standards of the early sixteenth century, Altdorfer correctly illustrated the Battle of Issus of the year 333 BC, Alexander's second victory over the Persian king Darius III. From a bird's eye view – although with two different horizons[10] – the artist unfolds an Eastern Mediterranean panorama.[11] From north to south the view reaches from Issus – the city in the middle ground – and the island of Cyprus to the seven-armed delta of the Nile and the three lakes from which its source waters spring. The Red Sea adjoins on the left and even further left we see the Persian Gulf; the ball-shaped rise on the left margin of the image depicts the remains of the tower of Babylon. The geographical details correspond to the historical exactness of the depiction, following to an astounding extent the arrangement and movements of the different Greek-Macedonian and Persian forces as described in the ancient sources (Arrian, Quintus Curtius, Diodorus).[12] Alexander's position here, awaiting his opponent at a narrow pass (in reality between the Ammon mountain range and the sea coast of Issus; Aventinus calls it a bottleneck), also corresponds to actual events.[13] Largely following the details in Hartmann Schedel's *Weltchronik* (1493) and in Aventinus's work, the numbers of the forces

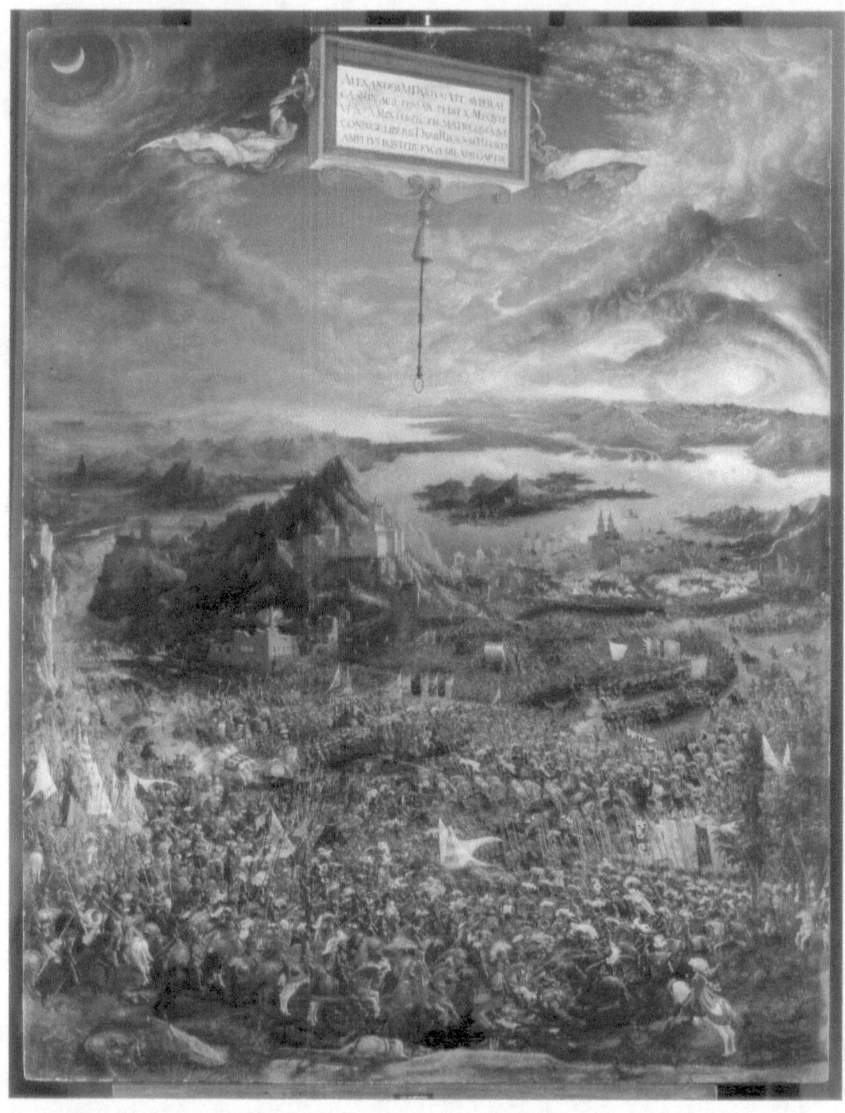

Figure 12.1. Albrecht Altdorfer, *Battle of Alexander at Issus*, 1529, oil on basswood. Alte Pinakothek, Bayerische Staatsgemäldesammlungen, Munich.

of infantry and cavalry and the losses on both sides are noted on the standards of the armies.

Altdorfer, in this picture, provides a very nearly exact reproduction of an historical event, while not excluding contemporary references or updates, probably supported by Aventinus or based on his chronicle.[14] Just as Aventinus explicitly distances himself from the fabled reports of authors like Hartlieb and thus from the *Alexander Romance* tradition, the painter here separates his scene from depictions of an episode in the *Romance* criticized decisively by Aventinus, one that constitutes the main motif of medieval Alexander iconography. This is Alexander's Celestial Journey, his flight to the heavens with the aid of two (or sometimes several) large birds or griffins.[15] The *Alexander Romance* and its manifold derivations, including the different versions of the *Historia de preliis*, describe how the Macedonian king had these animals captured and chained to a basket, how he climbed into the basket and brought the creatures to fly higher and higher with morsels of meat that he held before their beaks on a rod, and finally how he was forced back to earth, either by a winged being in the form of a man or, as in the *Historia de preliis*, by a divine force. This motif, an example of which can be seen in a twelfth-century capital in the ambulatory of the Basle Münster[16] (Figure 12.2), dominates among independent motifs about Alexander in the Middle Ages, that is, those not included in a cycle of illustrations of the Macedonian king's life and deeds.

It was probably most often understood negatively, as an example of the sin of pride. In the late twelfth- or early thirteenth-century pediment of the south portal of S. Maria della Strada in Matrice near Campobasso, however, the flight can definitely be interpreted positively; its axial relationship to the Lamb of God suggests an example of the soul (after death) striving towards heaven and Christ, or, in a Christological sense, a prefiguration of the ascension (Figure 12.3).[17]

Aventinus's rejection of this and other depictions of the *Alexander Romance* as old wives' tales is hardly unexpected when we consider his knowledge of ancient historical sources. It is also scarcely surprising, in light of historical sensibilities sharpened in this way, that no further portrayals of the Celestial Journey are found after the early sixteenth century.[18] Nonetheless, it was not source knowledge in itself that decided the fate of a motif like this one. Arrian's *Anabasis* may only have become widely known after antiquity in Latin Europe during the Renaissance via Vergerio's translation, to which Aventinus refers, probably in the 1430s; and Plutarch's *Life of Alexander* in the *Parallel Lives* only came to

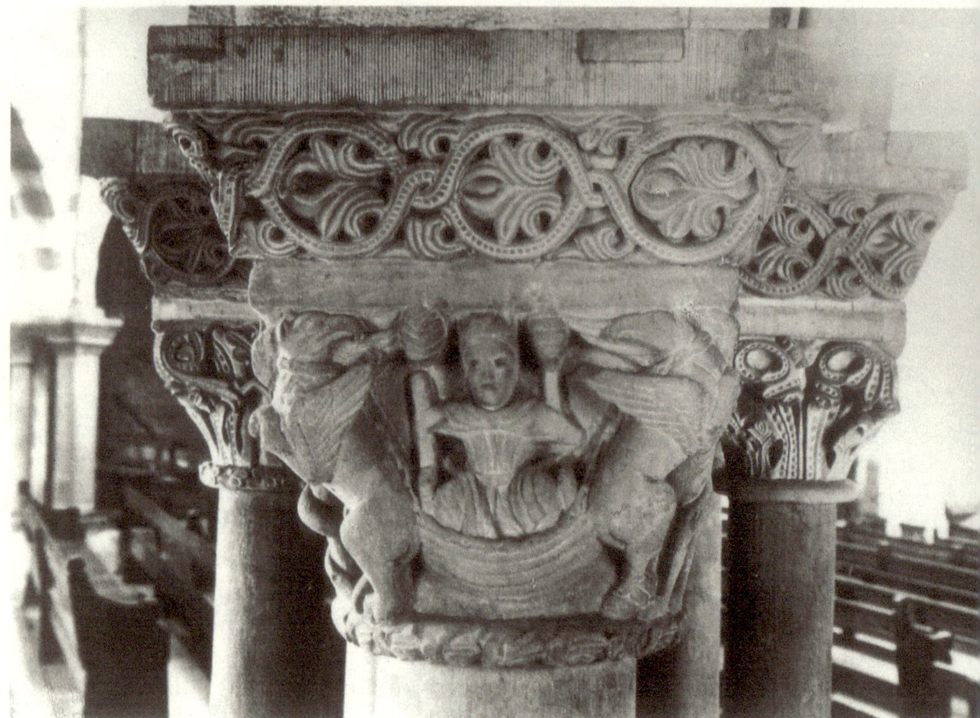

Figure 12.2. *The Celestial Journey of Alexander the Great*, capital, last quarter of the twelfth century, sandstone. North pillar of the ambulatory, Münster, Basle.

light in the West a little earlier. Still, a Catalan version of Plutarch very probably came into existence in the last third of the fourteenth century, before 1377, which found its way to Florence towards the end of the century; shortly afterwards, before 1408, Guarino da Verona prepared the first Latin translation, which appeared in print with the other lives in 1470.[19] Quintus Curtius, however, had been known during the Middle Ages and served as the most important source for the *Alexandreis* (ca. 1180) of Walter of Châtillon.[20] Knowledge of such sources alone would not have been enough to bring motifs like the Celestial Journey to an end; only source criticism of the type to which Aventinus's work testifies could lead to new depictions like that of the *Battle of Alexander at Issus*.

As important as it was, however, even changing historical awareness cannot fully explain transformations in iconographic conventions about

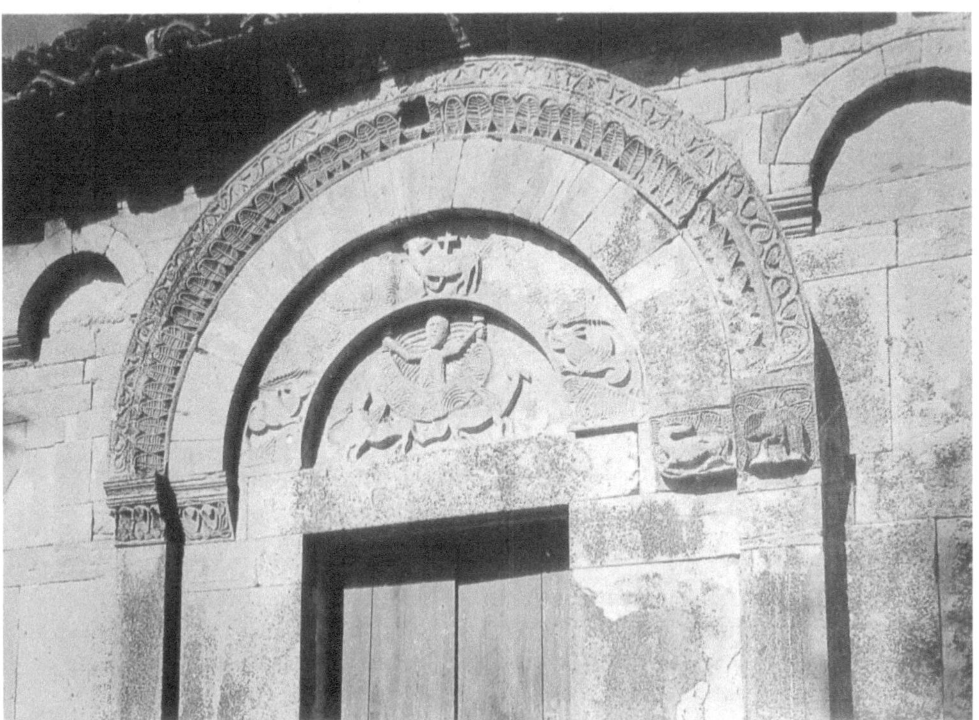

Figure 12.3. *The Celestial Journey of Alexander the Great and the Lamb of God*, late twelfth or early thirteenth century. South portal, S. Maria della Strada, Matrice / Campobasso.

Alexander like the one presented so strikingly with the contrast between the motif of the Celestial Journey and Altdorfer's *Battle of Issus*. A half century before Aventinus, the Portuguese author Vasco da Lucena was no less aware of the questionable historical qualities of the *Alexander Romance*. In 1468 he prepared a French translation of Quintus Curtius for Charles the Bold, the last Duke of Burgundy, filling in the holes in this account with material from other historical sources. In his, in many ways, highly revelatory prologue, however, he explains the reason for omitting certain details from the *Alexander Romance* that his patron was obviously expecting. If certain stories were missing in the book – for example, the tale of Alexander's ascent into the sky or his descent into the sea in a barrel, or his conversation with the prophetic trees of the

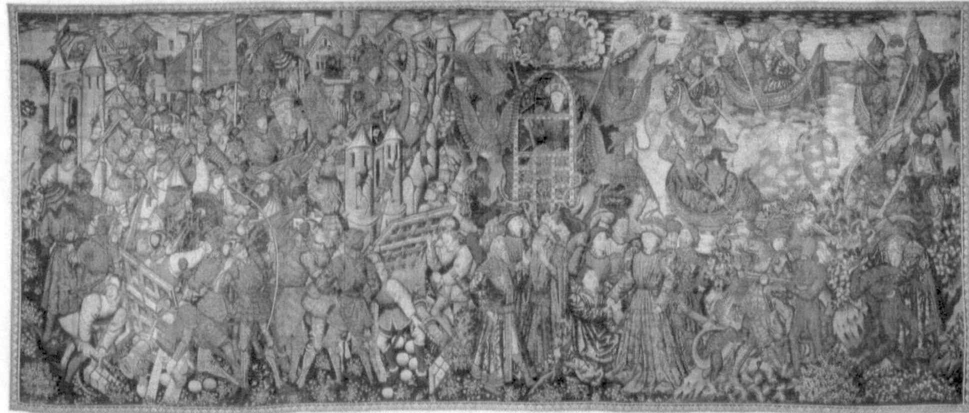

Figure 12.4. *Scenes from the life of Alexander the Great*, Tournai, around 1460, tapestry. Palazzo Doria Pamphili, Rome.

sun and other fairy tales from the tongues of men, who, in ignorance of the nature of things failed to recognize that all of these things were false and impossible – then this occurs intentionally, because the emphasis of the story was on the recognition that Alexander had conquered a geographically plausible Orient. In this account, later princes could be shown how to achieve such accomplishments, even without ascending into the sky, diving into the sea, or possessing the strength of a Raignault de Montaubain, Lancelot, or others like them.[21]

At about the same time as Vasco's translation, probably in Tournai around 1460, a tapestry sequence was completed with scenes from the life of the Macedonian king (*Arazzi Doria*; Palazzo Doria Pamphili, Rome; Figure 12.4).[22]

Whereas the first tapestry shows events from Alexander's youth up to his assumption of the throne, the second recalls some of his later heroic deeds, among them his descent into the depths of the sea and the Celestial Journey. As early as 1913, Aby Warburg remarked of these tapestries that they portrayed the then-Duke of Burgundy, Philip the Good, and his son, Charles the Bold, "similarly to a portrait":

> Courtly romanticism, which flatteringly equated Philip the Burgundian with the Macedonian, nurtured Prince Charles in this ideal world of classic antiquity, which had been reawakened in a northern style. In this way,

> pagan antiquity was reflected in the minds of the Burgundian court in the age of Philip the Good, and wild enthusiasm for the greatness of antiquity spoke even from its shadowy late medieval disguise.[23]

Though the resemblance to a portrait is not absolute, and the person who commissioned the piece and its original location can no longer be identified,[24] still the Alexander scenes must doubtlessly be understood as a presentation of admirable, heroic deeds in which contemporary rulers – Philip the Good or Charles the Bold – might see themselves reflected. It goes without saying that the Celestial Journey takes its place there – notwithstanding its frequent negative connotation as an example of pride – as one of the astounding achievements of the Macedonian king.

While Vasco da Lucena with critical, sharp eyes alerted his Duke in so many words to the impossibility of these activities and the foolishness of the person who reported them, the depiction of this tapestry suggests that the taste for fabulous deeds like this and others included in it persisted; Jean Wauquelin's prose romance, the *Faicts et Conquestes d' Alexandre le Grand* (ca. 1440), which returns repeatedly to Pseudo-Callisthenes's *Alexander Romance*,[25] is hardly swayed from its course by Vasco's translation of Curtius. From this state of affairs we can infer that in mid-fifteenth-century Burgundy, a source-critical historical awareness like that to which Vasco da Lucena testifies was still not so widespread and the process of drawing boundaries between fiction and truth not so sharply developed that they would have been sufficient to ban the Celestial Journey or even the descent into the sea from the canon of Alexander's deeds.

Closely connected with it, albeit with its own weight, was a second matter that determined the image of Alexander the Great in the visual arts and its transformations: the constant need for means to visualize certain themes or concepts, if with varying degrees of emphasis and for different lengths of time. Alexander's journey with the griffins was not portrayed on the Basle capital or the portal of S. Maria della Strada in order to illustrate an episode from his life, but instead to provide an example of the sin of pride and the longing for heaven respectively. The Celestial Journey is taken up as a means of visualizing universal themes that could also be depicted in other fashions. There is similarly little concentration in the Burgundian tapestry on Alexander the Great himself; rather, he serves there as an example from antiquity for bold, heroic deeds. Under these circumstances, Alexander's journey with the griffins had to lose its meaning as soon as it appeared unsuitable as an example of hubris or a longing for heaven or of ancient heroism. It only became unsuitable, however, when the proliferating knowledge of ancient historians and a growing critical awareness jeopardized the stability of the motif's potential for convincing its audiences. Still, the *Alexander Romance* in the version of Johannes Hartlieb was beloved not only in the fifteenth century, but well beyond. At least six editions of the book appeared before 1500, and at least three editions in the sixteenth century, and the book appears to have found publishers in the seventeenth century as well.[26] In Italy, where it was read in the sixteenth and seventeenth centuries, the popularity of the *Alexander Romance* was no different; the *Alessandreida in Rime*, printed for the first time in 1512, enjoyed "great success for exactly two centuries."[27] The incredibility of the Celestial Journey in itself thus may not be the reason that this motif disappears from the visual arts after the early sixteenth century – or at least not that alone – but rather its lacking suitability for universal themes or concepts that it had presented as an example up till then.

The problem can be grasped clearly in the case of another episode from Alexander's life. Several ancient authors report the generosity of spirit with which he treated Darius's family after the Battle of Issus, Quintus Curtius (III, 31–2) among them, and the incident was well-known all through the Middle Ages. Based on the *Alexander Romance*, Alexander's treatment of Darius's mother, wife, and daughter "with great honor"[28] is even praised in a medieval *exempla* collection on the Ten Commandments, the *Seelentrost* (printed in 1478 and again in 1483), which otherwise pictures the Macedonian king, as a cautionary example, as the Devil's prey and eternally damned for his pride (see Klaus Grubmüller's essay in this volume). The scene in which Darius's mother, wife, daughter, and son confront Alexander for the first time, in which Sisigambis, the mother of the Persian king, who at first prostrated herself mistakenly before Alexander's friend Hephaistion, is raised to her feet by Alexander and excused and comforted in the kindest way, is found for the first time as an independent motif (i.e., not included in a cycle) only in the Renaissance. It appears initially in the fifteenth century on *cassoni* or wedding chests;[29] then around 1516 for the first time as a large-format separate depiction in one of the murals created by Giovanni Antonio Bazzi, called Il Sodoma, for the Sienese banker and merchant Agostino Chigi in his *camera* or bedroom in the so-called Villa Farnesina (named after its later owners) in Rome (Figure 12.5).[30]

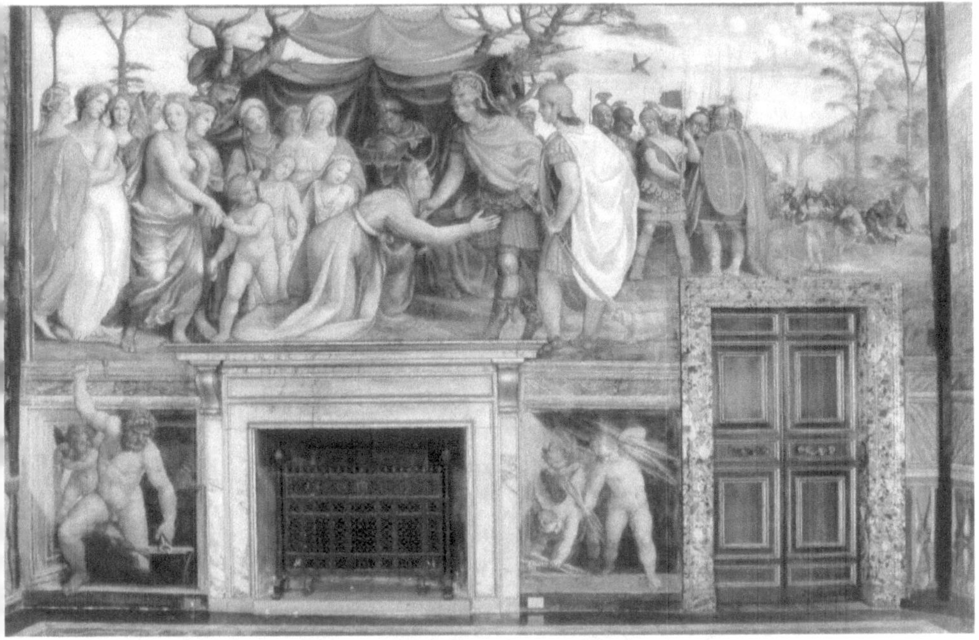

Figure 12.5. Giovanni Antonio Bazzi, called Il Sodoma, *The Family of Darius before Alexander*, around 1516, fresco. Sala delle Nozze, Villa Farnesina, Rome.

Ancient authors apprehended this episode as an *exemplum virtutis*, an example of Alexander's magnanimity and self-control, as did the *Seelentrost*; Sodoma's depiction of the incident in the biographical context of the art's patron should be understood similarly. In the figure of Alexander, particularly in his moderation and reserve in response to the beautiful women at his mercy, Agostino Chigi is reflected. Again, the point is not primarily Alexander the Great, but rather the overarching theme of virtue, for the visualization of which Alexander's encounter with Darius's family is selected. This well-known episode from Alexander's life becomes an important motif of Alexander's iconography in subsequent centuries,[31] because the concept of virtue, which had been distilled from the study of antiquity, demanded a visualization and the biography of the Macedonian king offered a fitting example. (A similarly prominent example is the well-known *Generosity of Scipio*.)

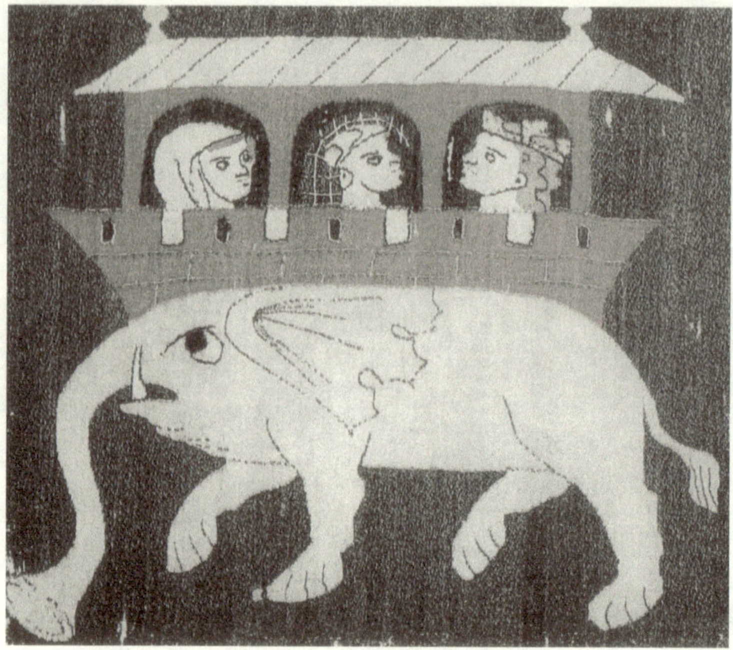

Figure 12.6. *Alexander the Great with Queen Candace and a Servant*, tapestry from the Dominican convent of Adelhausen near Freiburg im Breisgau (Detail), Upper Rhine (Freiburg im Breisgau or Constance?), around 1320, wool and linen, embroidered. Augustinermuseum, Freiburg im Breisgau.

It is not only the appearance of such new themes and concepts, but also their transformation, that is instructive for our discussion. The theme of the *Minnesklaven* or feminine guile played a considerable role in the visual arts and literature of the late Middle Ages; Alexander the Great could serve as an example in this context as well. A heraldic tapestry from the Dominican convent of Adelhausen near Freiburg im Breisgau from around 1320 displays, in addition to a depiction of *Aristotle and Phyllis*, the Macedonian king in the palace of the oriental Queen Candace. In the building – which, according to the description of the *Alexander Romance*, was drawn by elephants, but here is saddled upon an elephant – between the crenellated battlement and the roof, we find the heads of Alexander, Candace, and a servant woman in three round arch windows (Figure 12.6).[32]

Alexander appears in a negative sense – corresponding to the depiction of his teacher Aristotle – as a victim of feminine wiles. Candace had sent a painter to Alexander's camp to make a portrait of him and had it brought to her; when the Macedonian king tried to trick her by presenting himself at her court as a mere messenger, she produced the portrait. Alexander was outwitted and in the Queen's power.

An example for the same overarching theme is the mid-fourteenth century cycle of twelve (and probably originally fifteen) medallions, now destroyed, in a room on the first floor of the house *Zur Kunkel* in Constance, in which *Minnesklaven* from Adam to King Arthur were pictured with the women who had betrayed or outwitted them (Figure 12.7).[33]

As an alternative to the story of Candace, we see Alexander this time during his trip into the depths of the sea, for before this activity the Macedonian king had entrusted the chain to which his diving vehicle was fastened to his favourite among numerous lovers – a story known in German lands only since the thirteenth century.[34] The lover, however, threw the chain into the sea, in order to devote herself to a different man (or let the chain fall into the sea in a moment of weakness), and Alexander barely escaped death. Here again he appears as the victim of feminine guile, and his relationship to women in independent depictions of the late Middle Ages is defined with this theme.

The very different role that Alexander played as lover in Renaissance art is displayed magnificently again in the bedchamber of Agostino Chigi in the Villa Farnesina. The second main image of the room – and the first independent depiction of a subject that would reappear frequently afterwards – is based on a previous drawing by Raphael and portrays *The Marriage of Alexander and Roxane*, the daughter of the king of Bactria and later satrap Oxyartes, of whom ancient sources report (Figure 12.8).[35]

The fact that Sodoma's mural draws upon an ancient *ekphrasis*, the description of a picture with a corresponding motif in Lucian's *Herodotus or Aetion*,[36] can only be mentioned here.[37] Decisive for our context is the completely transformed conception of Alexander's relationship to women, the dismissal of older motifs, and the assumption of a new one. Still, we must continue to emphasize that this depiction is not primarily concerned with the person of the Macedonian king, but rather with an overarching theme that Alexander exemplifies. In the place of the *Minnesklaven* of the later Middle Ages, who served the male observer as a warning about the snares of feminine guile, the gallant lover of early modernity emerges, the representative of a somehow idealized

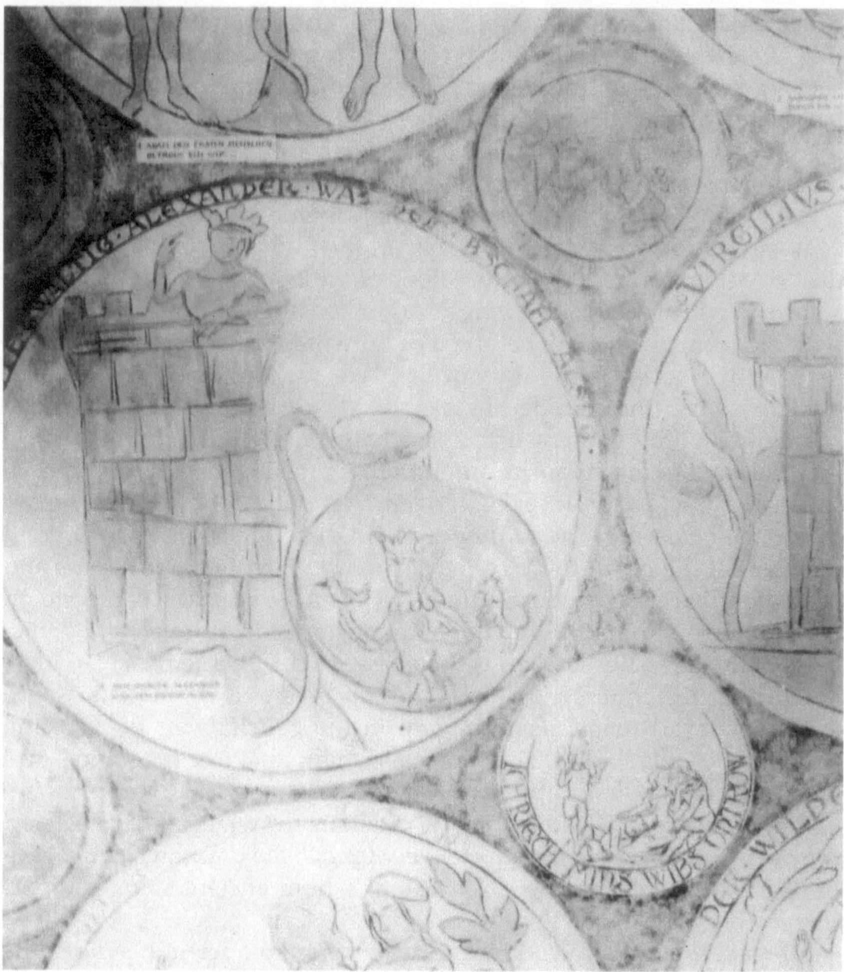


Figure 12.7: *The Diving Journey of Alexander the Great*, sketch of a wall decoration in the house *Zur Kunkel*, Constance, original from the mid-fourteenth century.

understanding of love, as model or reflection, for their own part, of the art's patron or addressee. (In the case of the Farnesina this means Agostino Chigi, who reflected his marriage to Francesca Ordeaschi, the daughter of a Venetian merchant family, in Sodoma's mural.) Following this conception only a few years after the Farnesina frescos, Alexander

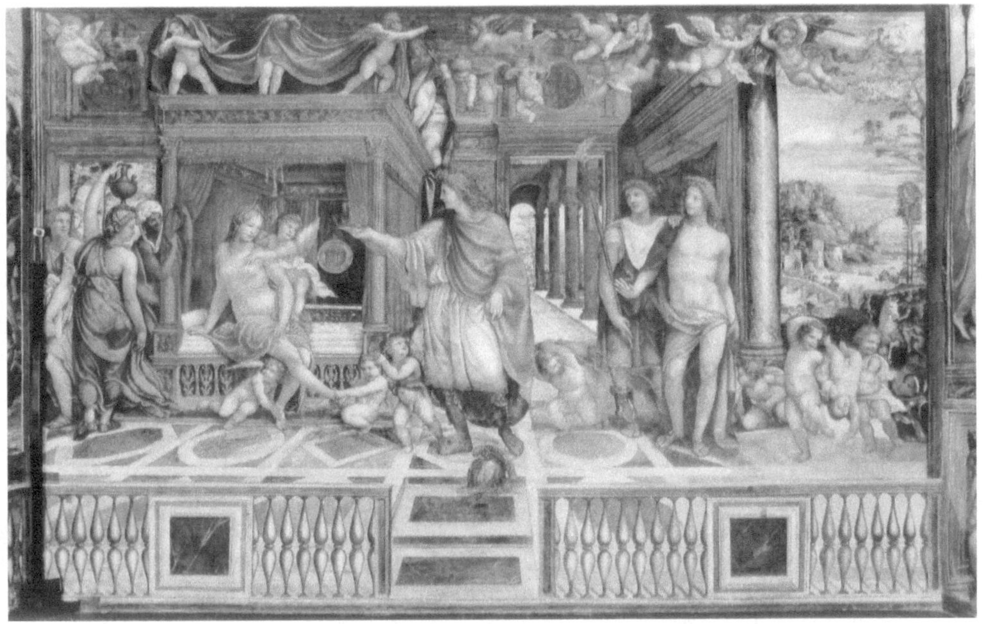

Figure 12.8: Giovanni Antonio Bazzi, called Il Sodoma, *The Marriage of Alexander and Roxane*, around 1516, fresco. Sala delle Nozze, Villa Farnesina, Rome.

the Great also appears above all as a lover in the extensive picture cycle that Francesco Primaticcio executed between 1541 and 1544 in the Palace of Fontainebleau at the behest of François I.[38] Here it is the French king and his self-understanding about which the sequence of scenes informs us, again rather than the life of Alexander the Great.

The profundity of the transformation that the great Macedonian king's image experienced in the transition from the Middle Ages to early modernity notwithstanding, certain continuities can still be observed. The last important theme in the iconography of the Middle Ages that treats Alexander the Great as an example is that of the *Nine Worthies*.[39] Next to the three Old Testament figures Joshua, David, and Judah Maccabee and the three Christians, King Arthur, Charlemagne, and Geoffrey of Bouillon, the conqueror of Jerusalem (1099), Alexander the Great stands with Hector of Troy and Julius Caesar in the third trio, comprising three virtuous pagans. All nine heroes embrace, with the complete number of three times three, the entire history of the world and thus appear as representatives of the stages of salvation *ante legem, sub lege,* and *sub gratia*. This grouping of princes and leaders is used frequently in the later Middle Ages, and Alexander the Great, who with his Celestial Journey can simultaneously figure as an example of pride, embodies here for his part an ideal sovereign.

With this universal theme of the exemplary prince, albeit detached from the circle of the *Nine Worthies,* which does not survive the Middle Ages, Alexander assumes the position he was later to hold in the art of the modern period. The fivefold sequence of the *Triumphs of Alexander,* which Charles Le Brun executed for Louis XIV between 1660–1 and 1672–3 at the latest, may serve as a representative example of countless works that testify to this continuity.[40]

If we review the themes in which Alexander the Great appears in the art of the Middle Ages and early modern period, in the Middle Ages it is at first primarily only the Celestial Journey, as well as depictions in the themes of feminine guile and the *Nine Worthies,* where Alexander, sometimes positively, sometimes negatively, appears before our eyes. In early modernity the spectrum of themes widens, and in particular the independent motifs that visualize his life and deeds multiply rapidly, in sometimes extensive cycles. In general, moreover, a much more advantageous light falls upon the Macedonian king, who can serve as victorious commander and charming lover, as hero of virtue and patron of the arts, as representative of the third world monarchy (the penultimate one before the final, fourth, Roman world monarchy). From time to time, he still appears more or less negatively, as the pagan, immoderate conqueror or as a figure of contrast to the self-sufficient Diogenes in his tub. The positive sides, however, outweigh the darker themes and testify to the increasing need for artistic depictions of themes and concepts in which Alexander the Great was found suitable to play a prominent role – not as an unmistakable individual or singular phenomenon of world history, but rather as *exemplum,* as type, and as figure of identification.

Translated by Susan Boettcher.

NOTES

1 "Der künig Alexander der gros ist unsern leuten, auch den ungelerten, bekanter dan ir künig und kaiser, deron si auch weder näm noch stäm

wissen." Johannes Turmaier, genannt Aventinus, *Sämmtliche Werke*, Vol. 4, bk. 1, *Bayerische Chronik (Buch I/II)*, ed. Matthias Lexer (Munich: Kaiser, 1882), 153, 336–7; on Aventinus see Eberhard Dünninger and Erich Stahleder, *Aventinus zum 450. Todesjahr 1984*, Schriften der Gesellschaft für Altbayerische Geschichte und Kultur der Weltenburger Akademie 2 (Abensberg: Aventinum e.V. Verlag der Weltenburger Akademie, 1986). For the translation of my article I should like to thank cordially Prof. Susan Boettcher, University of Texas.

2 Aventinus, *Bayerische Chronik* (see note 1), 162, 368.

3 David J.A. Ross, *Alexander historiatus. A Guide to Medieval Illustrated Alexander Literature*, 2nd ed., Beiträge zur Klassischen Philologie 186 (Frankfurt am Main: Athenäum, 1988), 80–1; Friedrich Pfister, "Die Entdeckung Alexanders des Großen durch die Humanisten," in *Renaissance und Humanismus in Mittel- und Osteuropa. Eine Sammlung von Materialien*, Vol. 1, ed. Johannes Irmscher, Deutsche Akademie der Wissenschaften zu Berlin. Schriften der Sektion für Altertumskunde 32 (Berlin: Akademie-Verlag, 1962), 57–75, 66.

4 It is uncertain when he lived. For example, Ross, *Alexander historiatus* (see note 3), 67, with 100n337, sees him as a contemporary of the Emperor Claudius; see also the essay by Thomas Hahn in this volume; he was also placed in the early third century rather than in the middle of the first: Jean-Pierre Callu, "Alexandre dans la littérature latine de l'Antiquité Tardive," in *Alexandre le Grand dans les littératures occidentales et proche-orientales. Actes du colloque de Paris 27–29 novembre 1999*, ed. Laurence Harf-Lancner et al., Littérales (Hors Série) (Nanterre: Centre des Sciences de la Littérature, Université Paris X, 1999), 33–50, 38–9.

5 Cf. Ross, *Alexander historiatus* (see note 3), 67–8; Pfister, "Entdeckung Alexanders des Großen" (see note 3), 66. Aventinus is referring to the edition: *Quintus Curtius de rebus gestis Alexandri Magni regis Macedonum*. Cum annotationibus Des. Erasmi Roterodami [...] (Strasbourg: Matthias Schürer, 1518).

6 Cf. Ross, *Alexander historiatus* (see note 3), 49–50; Klaus Grubmüller, "Hartlieb, Johannes," in *Die deutsche Literatur des Mittelalters. Verfasserlexikon*, Vol. 3, 2nd, revised ed., ed. Kurt Ruh et al. (Berlin and New York: Walter de Gruyter, 1981), 480–96, 490–1; on the dating, see Reinhard Pawis, *Johann Hartliebs Alexander*, Münchener Texte und Untersuchungen zur deutschen Literatur des Mittelalters 97 (Munich and Zurich: Artemis-Verlag, 1991), 40–1.

7 See Aventinus, *Bayerische Chronik* (see note 1), 153, 337.

8 Franz Winzinger, *Albrecht Altdorfer. Die Gemälde. Tafelbilder, Miniaturen, Wandbilder, Bildhauerarbeiten, Werkstatt und Umkreis. Gesamtausgabe* (Munich

and Zurich: Hirmer, R. Piper and Co., 1975), No. 50; most recently, see Thomas Noll, *Alexander der Große in der nachantiken bildenden Kunst* (Mainz: von Zabern, 2005), 29–31 and Table 20, with further literature.

9 Gisela Goldberg, "Die ursprüngliche Inschrifttafel der Alexanderschlacht Albrecht Altdorfers," *Münchner Jahrbuch der bildenden Kunst*, Dritte Folge 19 (1968), 121–6.

10 Joseph Harnest, "Zur Perspektive in Albrecht Altdorfers Alexanderschlacht," *Anzeiger des Germanischen Nationalmuseums* (1977), 67–77.

11 On the topography see especially Cord Meckseper, "Zur Ikonographie von Altdorfers Alexanderschlacht," *Zeitschrift des Deutschen Vereins für Kunstwissenschaft* 22 (1968), 178–85.

12 See especially Wolfgang Pfeiffer, "Zur Ikonographie der Alexanderschlacht Albrecht Altdorfers," *Münchner Jahrbuch der bildenden Kunst*, Dritte Folge 44 (1993), 72–98.

13 Aventinus, *Bayerische Chronik* (see note 1), 158, 346–7.

14 See Barbara Eschenburg, "Altdorfers Alexanderschlacht und ihr Verhältnis zum Historienzyklus Wilhelms IV.," *Zeitschrift des Deutschen Vereins für Kunstwissenschaft* 33 (1979), 36–67.

15 See Noll, *Alexander der Große* (see note 8), 10–8, with further literature.

16 Ibid., 12 and Table 1.

17 Ibid., 14 and Table 7.

18 A late manifestation is a woodcut formerly ascribed to Hans Schäufelein. Noll, *Alexander der Große* (see note 8), 17 and Table 10.

19 Ross, *Alexander historiatus* (see note 3), 81–2; Pfister, "Entdeckung Alexanders des Großen" (see note 3), 66; Vito R. Giustiniani, "Sulle traduzioni latine delle Vite di Plutarco nel Quattrocento," *Rinascimento. Rivista dell'Istituto Nazionale di Studi sul Rinascimento*, Seconda serie 1 (1961), 3–62, 3–9 and 34–5.

20 Ross, *Alexander historiatus* (see note 3), 67–8 and 72; Pfister, "Entdeckung Alexanders des Großen" (see note 3), 58; Simon Dosson, *Étude sur Quinte Curce. Sa vie et son oeuvre* (Paris: Hachette, 1886), 360–80. On the *Alexandreis*, see *Alexanderdichtungen im Mittelalter. Kulturelle Selbstbestimmung im Kontext literarischer Beziehungen*, ed. Jan Cölln et al., Literatur und Kulturräume im Mittelalter 1 (Göttingen: Wallstein, 2000), here the contributions by Hartmut Wulfram, Andreas Glock, and Corinna Killermann.

21 "Sy n'y trouverez pas que Alexandre ait vollé en aer a tout quartiers de moutons, ne vagué par dessoubz mer en tonneaux de voirre, ne parlé aux arbres du soleil, ne autres fables faintes par hommes ignorans la nature des choses, non cognoissans tout ce estre faulx et impossible, et mesmes

non entendant que quant Alexandre seroit eslevé en aer ou vagueroit par dessoubz mer, sy ne consuivroit il point la fin de son entente, car lui eslevé en aer ne verroit nes que d'une tour, obstant la fragillité de nostre veue; et dessoubz mer le tonneau romperoit, se le voirre estoit tendre et, se espés estoit, il ne verroit goute. Moult donques est utile ceste histoire qui nous aprent au vray comment Alexandre concquist tout Orient et comment ung autre prince le peut arriere concquester sans voller en aer, sans aller soubz mer, sans enchantemens, sans geans et sans estre sy fort comme Raignault de Montaubain, comme Lancelot, comme Tristan ne comme Raynouart qui tuoit cincquante hommes coup a coup." Robert Bossuat, "Vasque de Lucene, traducteur de Quinte-Curce (1468)," *Bibliothèque d'Humanisme et Renaissance* 8 (1946) (Reprint: Amsterdam: Swets and Zeitlinger, Geneva: Droz, Slatkine, 1974), 197–245, 213; on this see Ross, *Alexander historiatus* (see note 3), 69–71; Pfister, "Entdeckung Alexanders des Großen" (see note 3), 60.

22 Anna Rapp Buri and Monica Stucky-Schürer, *Burgundische Tapisserien* (Munich: Hirmer, 2001), 230–45; Noll, *Alexander der Große* (see note 8), 15–17 and Table 9.

23 Aby M. Warburg, "Luftschiff und Tauchboot in der mittelalterlichen Vorstellungswelt," in idem, *Gesammelte Schriften*, Vol. 1, with assistance from Fritz Rougemont ed. Gertrud Bing (Leipzig and Berlin: Teubner, 1932; repr. Nendeln / Liechtenstein: Kraus, 1969), 241–9, 247–8.

24 Rapp Buri and Stucky-Schürer, *Burgundische Tapisserien* (see note 22), 243.

25 Ross, *Alexander historiatus* (see note 3), 17; Jehan Wauquelin, *Les Faicts et les Conquestes d'Alexandre le Grand*, ed. Sandrine Hériché, Textes Littéraires Français 527 (Geneva: Droz, 2000).

26 Pawis, *Johann Hartliebs Alexander* (see note 6), 73–90 ("Die Drucküberlieferung des Alexander"). Here the conclusion: "(…) seit dem bereits recht frühen Erstdruck des Werks im Jahre 1473 läßt sich eine zwar allmählich abflauende, im Grunde aber über fast zwei Jahrhunderte währende kontinuierliche Nachfrage nach Hartliebs Alexanderübersetzung beobachten" (73).

27 Joachim Storost, *Studien zur Alexandersage in der älteren italienischen Literatur. Untersuchungen und Texte*, Romanistische Arbeiten 23 (Halle a.S.: Niemeyer, 1935), 180; see also Ross, *Alexander historiatus* (see note 3), 63, who speaks of at least fifteen editions between 1512 and 1712. See also Elisabeth Schröter, "Zur Inhaltsdeutung des Alexander-Programms der Sala Paolina in der Engelsburg," *Römische Quartalschrift für christliche Altertumskunde und Kirchengeschichte* 75 (1980), 76–99, 97.

28 *Der Seelentrost (Der sele trost)* (Augsburg: Anton Sorg, 1483), Bl. CLXIIIIr; see Nigel Palmer, "Seelentrost," in *Verfasserlexikon* (see note 6), Vol. 8 (1997), 1030–40.
29 Paul Schubring, *Cassoni. Truhen und Truhenbilder der italienischen Frührenaissance. Ein Beitrag zur Profanmalerei im Quattrocento*, 2 vols., 2nd ed. (Leipzig: Hiersemann, 1923), catalog n. 150, 160 and Table XXX; Noll, *Alexander der Große* (see note 8), 35 and Table 23a.
30 Julian Kliemann and Michael Rohlmann, *Wandmalerei in Italien. Die Zeit der Hochrenaissance und des Manierismus 1510-1600* (Munich: Hirmer, 2004), 199 and Table 77 (Michael Rohlmann), with an exemplary color reproduction; Noll, *Alexander der Große* (see note 8), 32–3 and Table 21b.
31 Bernhard Aikema, "Exemplum Virtutis. The Family of Darius before Alexander in Renaissance and Baroque Art," in *Alexander the Great in European Art*, ed. Nicos Hadjinicolaou (Athens: Pergamos, 1997), 164–70, see also ibid., Nrn. XI.1–13, 171–86.
32 Jutta Eißengarthen, *Mittelalterliche Textilien aus Kloster Adelhausen im Augustinermuseum Freiburg* (Freiburg i.Br., 1985), 11–22; *Bestandskataloge der weltlichen Ortsstiftungen der Stadt Freiburg i.Br.*, ed. Sebastian Bock and Lothar A. Böhler, Vol. 5: *Die Textilien*, prepared by Sebastian Bock with assistance from Anca Berberich and Maria Effinger (Rostock: Hinstorff, 2001), Nr. 16, 141–7, 141–4; Noll, *Alexander der Große* (see note 8), 34–5 and Table 22; see also Trude Ehlert, "Alexander und die Frauen in spätantiken und mittelalterlichen Alexander-Erzählungen," in *Kontinuität und Transformation der Antike im Mittelalter. Veröffentlichung der Kongreßakten zum Freiburger Symposion des Mediävistenverbandes*, ed. Willi Erzgräber (Sigmaringen: Thorbecke, 1989), 81–103.
33 Werner Wunderlich, *Weibsbilder al fresco. Kulturgeschichtlicher Hintergrund und literarische Tradition der Wandbilder im Konstanzer Haus Zur Kunkel* (Constance: Stadler, 1996); *Sangsprüche in Tönen Frauenlobs. Supplement zur Göttinger Frauenlob-Ausgabe*, ed. Jens Haustein and Karl Stackmann, 2 vols., Abhandlungen der Akademie der Wissenschaften in Göttingen, Philolog.-hist. Klasse, Dritte Folge 232 (Göttingen: Vandenhoeck and Ruprecht, 2000), Vol. 1: *Einleitungen, Texte*, 35–9; Noll, *Alexander der Große* (see note 8), 22 and Table 15.
34 David J.A. Ross, *Alexander and the Faithless Lady, a Submarine Adventure* (London: Birkbeck College, 1967); Noll, *Alexander der Große* (see note 8), 22–3.
35 Richard Förster, "Die Hochzeit des Alexander und der Roxane in der Renaissance," *Jahrbuch der Königlich Preußischen Kunstsammlungen* 15 (1894), 182–207, with a list of sources; Achim Gnann, "The Depiction of the

Marriage of Alexander and Roxana," in *Alexander the Great* (see note 31), 214–24; see also ibid., Nrn. XVIII.1–14, 225–44; Kliemann and Rohlmann, *Wandmalerei in Italien* (see note 30), 199 and Table 77–8, with exemplary color reproductions; Noll, *Alexander der Große* (see note 8), 33–6 and Table 21a.

36 Cf. *Lucian in Eight Volumes*, Vol. 6, Herodotus or Aetion, with an English translation by K. Kilburn, 2nd ed. (London: Heinemann and Cambridge, MA: Harvard University Press, 1968), 141–51, 146–9.

37 More details are included in Noll, *Alexander der Große* (see note 8), 33.

38 Ibid., 36–7 and Table 29.

39 See Robert L. Wyss, "Die neun Helden. Eine ikonographische Studie," *Zeitschrift für Schweizerische Archäologie und Kunstgeschichte* 17 (1957), 73–106; Horst Schroeder, *Der Topos der Nine Worthies in Literatur und bildender Kunst* (Göttingen: Vandenhoeck and Ruprecht, 1971); Norbert H. Ott et al., "Neun Gute Helden," in *Lexikon des Mittelalters*, Vol. 6, ed. Norbert Angermann et al. (Munich and Zurich: Artemis und Winkler, 1993), 1104–6.

40 Donald Posner, "Charles LeBrun's Triumphs of Alexander," *The Art Bulletin* 41 (1959), 237–48; Alescha-Thomas Birkenholz, *Die Alexander-Geschichte von Charles Le Brun. Historische und stilistische Untersuchungen der Werkentwicklung* (Frankfurt am Main et al.: Peter Lang, 2001); Noll, *Alexander der Große* (see note 8), 37–8 and Table 25.

# Contributors

**Shamma Boyarin** is an Assistant Teaching Professor of English and Religious Studies at the University of Victoria, BC.

**Christine Chism** is an Associate Professor of English at the University of California, Los Angeles.

**Faustina Doufikar-Aerts** is a Professor of Arabic and Islamic Studies at the University of Amsterdam.

**Klaus Grubmüller** is an Emeritus Professor of Medieval German Literature at the University of Göttingen.

**Thomas Hahn** is a Professor of English at the University of Rochester.

**Su Fang Ng** is an Associate Professor of English at the University of Oklahoma.

**Ruth Nisse** is an Associate Professor of English at Wesleyan University.

**Thomas Noll** is a Professor of Art History at the University of Göttingen.

**Sylvia A. Parsons** holds a PhD in Medieval Studies from the University of Toronto. She is an independent scholar.

**Maud Pérez-Simon** is a Maître de conférences in Medieval Literature at the Université Sorbonne Nouvelle Paris 3.

**Emily Reiner** is a Lecturer of English Literature at Assumption College, Worchester, MA.

**Julia Rubanovich** is a Senior Lecturer in Persian Language and Literature at the Hebrew University of Jerusalem.

**Markus Stock** is an Associate Professor of German and Medieval Studies at the University of Toronto.

# Index of Manuscripts

*Index by Walker Horsfall*

# Index of Names, Places, People, and Works

*Index by Walker Horsfall*

www.ingramcontent.com/pod-product-compliance
Lightning Source LLC
LaVergne TN
LVHW090153080826
844660LV00013B/791/J

* 9 7 8 1 4 4 2 6 4 4 6 6 3 *